KUNG-FU
MONTHLY

THE ARCHIVE SERIES

THE POSTER MAGAZINES
VOLUME ONE

COMPILED AND EDITED BY
CARL FOX

PIT WHEEL PRESS
BARNSLEY

THE KUNG FU CODE!

KUNG FU IS NOT A GAME. KUNG FU IS A HIGHLY SKILLED ART WHICH, IF MISUSED BY THE UNTRAINED, CAN BE DEADLY!

IT TOOK BRUCE LEE MANY YEARS OF BACK-BREAKING TRAINING TO MASTER THE ART OF KUNG FU, AND WHEN HE DIED, HE WAS STILL LEARNING. BRUCE NEVER USED KUNG FU AGAINST ANYONE IN ANGER IN HIS LIFE. HE KNEW ONLY TOO WELL ITS DANGEROUS POWER; THE SAME POWER THAT THE FIGHTING SHAOLIN MONKS SWORE NEVER TO USE TO DELIBERATELY KILL OR INJURE ANY OPPONENT.

SO IF YOU ARE THINKING OF TAKING UP THE MARTIAL ARTS, AND WHO ISN'T AFTER A GLIMPSE OF THE LITTLE DRAGON'S EXPLOITS ON THE SILVER SCREEN, BE PREPARED TO DEVOTE A LARGE PART OF YOUR DAILY LIFE TO ITS STUDY AND PRACTICE. ALSO, MAKE SURE YOU JOIN A REPUTABLE CLUB RUN BY SOMEONE WHO KNOWS WHAT THEY'RE TALKING ABOUT.

AND IF YOU'RE NOT PREPARED TO BECOME A KUNG FU DISCIPLE, THEN LEAVE THE FIGHTING TO THE EXPERTS!

Published by
PIT WHEEL PRESS LIMITED
www.pitwheelpress.com

Copyright © 2022 Carl Fox.
All Right Reserved. No part of this book may be reproduced, scanned or distributed in any printed or electronic form without permission.

KUNG-FU MONTHLY

Copyright © 1974-1984 by H. Bunch Associates Ltd. (except where copyright on certain photographic material already exists). This publication or any parts thereof may not be reproduced in any form whatsoever without permission in writing from the copyright proprietor.

A Pit Wheel Press edition, published by special arrangement with Dennis Publishing, London.

Printed in the United Kingdom
ISBN 978-1-915414-01-4

BRUCE LEE is a trademark of Bruce Lee Enterprises, LLC.

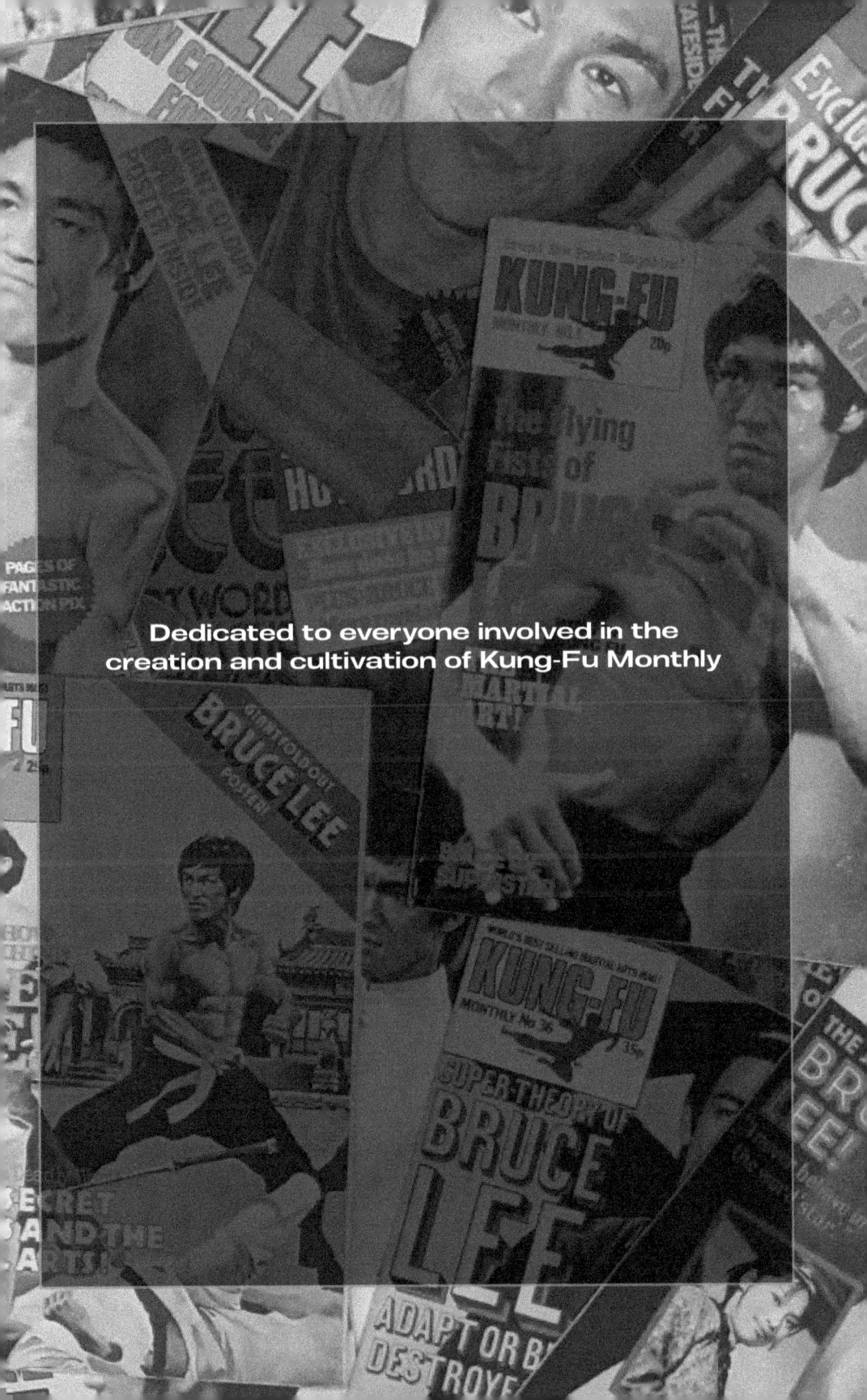

Dedicated to everyone involved in the creation and cultivation of Kung-Fu Monthly

ACKNOWLEDGEMENTS

I would like to thank the following people for their help and participation in the making of this book:

Richard Adams
Don Atyeo
Ricky Baker
James Bishop
Fergus Byrne
Kieran Clarkin
Jeff Cummins
Jonathon Green
Peter Jagger
Colin James
David Jenkins

John Little
Bey Logan
Tony Lundberg
Michael Nesbitt
John Overall
Dick Pountain
Matthew Robins
Bruce Sawford
Carlotta Serantoni
Paul Simmons
Andrew Staton

CREDITS

Original Poster Magazine Staff

Richard Adams, Don Atyeo, Felix Dennis, Jonathon Green
Colin James, Bey Logan, Perry Neville, Dick Pountain
Mikki Rain, Chris Rowley, Bruce Sawford & Paul Simmons

The Kung-Fu Monthly Archive Series

Research, Editing, Layout & Design
Carl Fox

Editorial Assistance
George Fox

Photograph Acknowlegements
**Kung-Fu Monthly, Carl Fox, Richard Adams
& Tony Lundberg**

Kung-Fu Monthly Collage Image
Copyright © 2022 Carl Fox

KUNG-FU MONTHLY

THE ARCHIVE SERIES CONTENTS

ISSUE	01
ISSUE	01
ISSUE	02
ISSUE	03
ISSUE	04
ISSUE	05
ISSUE	06
ISSUE	07
ISSUE	08
ISSUE	09
ISSUE	10
ISSUE	11
ISSUE	12
ISSUE	13
ISSUE	14
ISSUE	15
ISSUE	16
ISSUE	17
ISSUE	18
ISSUE	19
ISSUE	20
ISSUE	21
ISSUE	22
ISSUE	23
ISSUE	24
ISSUE	25
ISSUE	26

063
077
093
107
121
137
151
165
181

211
225
243
257
271
285
299
313
329
343
359
373
387
403
419
435
451

KUNG-FU MONTHLY

THE ARCHIVE SERIES
ABOUT THE SERIES

Kung-Fu Monthly is a name synonymous with Bruce Lee, not only in the United Kingdom but throughout the world. It is a legend in its own right and a brand immediately recognisable by not only the font but also the famous 'flying man' logo.

The popularity of the magazine at the peak of the Kung Fu Craze in the 1970s was unrivalled and its success was almost entirely down to pure luck.

Legend has it that *Kung-Fu Monthly* began life as a gamble by underground comic book publisher Felix Dennis after questioning a queue of kids outside a Soho cinema, waiting to see *Enter the Dragon* in early 1974. On paper, the idea seemed to serve the then-current trend of Bruce Lee and was deemed to have a shelf life of three to six months but a year after its launch, *Kung-Fu Monthly* had become the biggest-selling Bruce Lee magazine in the world.

After the demise of the Official Bruce Lee Fan Club in 1976, *Kung-Fu Monthly* launched their own. The KFM Bruce Lee Society ran for thirty quarterly newsletters from 1976 to 1983 and at the time of closing, had seen over five thousand eager Bruce Lee fans become members throughout its tenure, with the formidable Pam Hadden at the forefront throughout its seven active years.

Kung-Fu Monthly and The Bruce Lee Society were jointly responsible for the UK's first Bruce Lee Convention held on May 19th 1979 and the first Bruce Lee Film Festival held on December 1st 1979.

Kung-Fu Monthly and later *Personal Computer World*, had turned H. Bunch Associates from an underground publisher on the verge of bankruptcy to a publishing powerhouse, eventually becoming Dennis Publishing, named after its founder, Felix Dennis.

That leads us to today.

In February 2021, I approached Dennis Publishing with an idea for a project that I'd considered for many years - scan, convert, edit and compile all seventy-nine issues of the iconic *Kung-Fu Monthly* magazine into book form, in order to present it to a new audience, as well as preserve its place in history.

It was the longest-running dedicated Bruce Lee magazine of its kind anywhere in the world (by frequency and circulation) and I wanted to pay homage to that. Such was its success and popularity that it was licensed throughout the world; in fourteen countries and in eleven languages. That doesn't even take into account the non-official bootlegs which appeared in China and Turkey. Nothing has matched it before or since. It truly has stood the test of time and having done so, has reached legendary status.

Kung-Fu Monthly is a snapshot of a time long gone; a time which the original fans remember with fondness and a time which new fans will hopefully discover.

The *Kung-Fu Monthly Archive Series* is dedicated to Felix Dennis and everyone associated with the magazine; not just the staff but also the fans, who would buy copies of the magazines in their millions over its lifetime and help cement the publication's place in British Pop Culture history.

Special thanks must also go to Carlotta Serantoni at Dennis Publishing for her assistance in allowing this project to go ahead.

Carl Fox
February 2022

KUNG-FU
MONTHLY

THE POSTER MAGAZINES
INTRODUCTION

For me, *Kung-Fu Monthly* is a British institution, just like Fish and Chips, Beans on Toast or the humble Sausage Roll. Even though it was published in other parts of the world, it was in Britain - its home - where it was the most popular and is most fondly remembered. It was one of the first of its kind; its folded poster magazine format being cutting edge for the time.

History has always been important and of great interest to me. Being born halfway through Bruce Lee Mania meant that my introduction and education of it came much later. *Kung-Fu Monthly* is representative of the start of the Kung Fu Craze in 1974, through its peak at the end of the 70s with the release of Lee's final film *Game of Death*, to its demise in 1984, a decade after it all began.

Everyone has a story of how they discovered *Kung-Fu Monthly*. As a six-year-old around 1984, I discovered an older cousin watching *Enter the Dragon* on home video, after which he gave me some of his spare *Kung-Fu Monthly* posters. Like a lot of fans at that time, his interest dwindled, and I copped for his 'hand me down' collection of Bruce Lee memorabilia; not that I complained though. It was also a time when I would go with my late Dad to the local video store - The Chantry above the Chinese restaurant on Peel Parade in Barnsley - and sit on the floor at the top of the stairs looking at the Kung Fu video covers, pestering the poor bugger to rent *The Chinese Boxer, The Dynamite Brothers*, *Dragon Claw*s or whatever else they had. The funny thing is, he did. He'd happily rent whatever X-Rated Kung Fu video for the eight-year-old me; how cool (and irresponsible) was that?! But that was how my love of Kung Fu movies started. Seeing the *Kung-Fu Monthly* font and logo takes me back to that time. I can almost smell the Chinese food that wafted through the open window of the restaurant kitchen as I climbed the stairs of The Chantry or see the dirty grey carpet I'd sit cross-legged on when I got up those stairs.

A few years after that time, at the age of ten, I began training at the Barnsley Shotokan Karate Club with Mick and Lynn Padgett. The club was located above Mick's Zanshin Martial Arts shop located just two doors up from the old Chantry video shop I had frequented several years earlier. As well as being great ambassadors for Shotokan Karate and the Karate Union of Great Britain, Mick and Lynn have become good friends over the years and in 2021 taught the second generation of my family when my son began training under their wonderful and respected tutelage.

A lot of *Kung-Fu Monthly* collectors regard opening the old poster magazines as something of a special treat. Due to the age and the paper they were printed on, repeated opening and closing weakened the folds and risked permanent damage to their beloved collection. Due to that risk, very few collectors and fans bother to read the magazines anymore which is such a shame, as the articles and letters contained within are a rare snapshot of the material that the first generation of Bruce Lee fans enjoyed.

In February 2021, I tentatively approached the copyright owners of *Kung-Fu Monthly*, Dennis Publishing, to enquire about reprinting the material in a volume of books. After holding an internal meeting and to my astonishment, their Head of Licensing informed me that they had given me permission to go ahead with the project with their blessing. With Dennis Publishing's permission, I began the mammoth task of scanning each magazine, converting the images to text with optical character recognition software and correcting each one manually before reassembling it with a new layout.

While working on editing the magazines, I had the opportunity to speak with *Kung-Fu*

Monthly contributors Don Atyeo, Richard Adams, Bruce Sawford, Jonathon Green, Paul Simmons, Dick Pountain, Jeff Cummins and Felix Dennis biographer Fergus Byrne to ask them about their experiences of working on the magazine and/or with Felix Dennis. After completing the first twenty-six issues at over four-hundred pages, it was apparent that the books containing the poster magazines would have to be split into three separate volumes due to concerns that too many pages would put too much strain on the spine. With that in mind, I decided to write a history of *Kung-Fu Monthly*, to be split into two parts; Part One would cover the first half of the publication's life from 1973-1979 and Part Two would cover the second half from 1980-1984.

From reading the articles as I edited them, I found a new love and appreciation for the material of the time. Some of the articles were extremely informative and looking back at them, its amazing how accurate they were at a time when there was no internet. There are first-hand accounts and reactions to key milestones in the Kung Fu Craze such as the anticipation and then disappointment to the release of Lee's final unfinished film *Game of Death* in 1978 and the organisation of the First Official Bruce Lee Convention in 1979. By reading the magazine articles, you really get a feel of what it must have been like for the fans in those early years. Their overwhelming excitement for one last chance to see their idol on screen in *Game of Death*, turned to bitter disappointment at what they actually saw when the time came; a mish-mash of a plot with a whole now-classic fight scene removed by the British Board of Film Censors. You feel their excitement and hope and then their pain and disappointment; every single last bit of it.

The staff at *Kung-Fu Monthly* realised very early on that if they put in the work, the fans would keep coming back for more, which they did. Their investigative journalism at the time was second to none in terms of Kung Fu magazines, which is hardly surprising considering their pedigree.

Other key features in the magazine include interviews with long-forgotten people of the time as well as full write-ups regarding Linda's forgotten ill-fated attempt to make a Bruce Lee biopic in partnership with Jon Peters and Barbra Streisand, a decade-and-a-half before she finally got *Dragon: The Bruce Lee Story* made with Universal Pictures in 1993.

I have tried to reproduce the magazine articles as closely as possible to the originals but I changed certain things if I felt the need to such as rearranging the order of the Kickback letters page to better utilise space or to correct spelling and grammatical errors. Most of the images were left as they were, with slight amendments to remove lines where the paper folds were. I did have the opportunity to replace some of the images with ones of better quality but if I did that, it wouldn't have been *Kung-Fu Monthly* and therefore I decided against doing so.

I have chopped and changed designs so many times in the past twelve months until I finally felt that I stumbled upon something that I felt truly represented the look and feel of *Kung-Fu Monthly* and here is the result of that work. It is something I am immensely proud to be associated with and I hope that you enjoy reading it - it really has been a labour of love for me.

'Til next time...

Carl Fox
February 2022

KUNG-FU
MONTHLY

A HISTORY
THE GENESIS OF AN ICON
1973-1979

Oz was an independent underground magazine published in the 1960s and founded by the late Richard Neville. First published in Sydney, Australia in 1963, a London edition was published from 1967. Though Neville would remain as a central editor on both instances of the magazine, the London publication was co-edited; firstly with Jim Anderson, then later with Felix Dennis and Roger Hutchinson. In 1970, the London magazine was targeted by the Metropolitan Police's Obscene Publications Squad and their offices were raided on several occasions for obscene material, which was the basis of the infamous *Oz* obscenity trial of 1971. Two years of legal wrangling had taken their toll and by the time of the last issue of *Oz* in November 1973, sales of the magazine had fallen sharply and the publishers were in dire straits.

During the *Oz* trial, several of the magazine's staff had started working for *International Times* or *IT*, an 'underground' fortnightly publication by Cardinellar in London. Among them were Don Atyeo, Jonathon Green, Roger Hutchinson and Dick Fontaine - all of whom would later become key figures in the publication of *Kung-Fu Monthly*. Felix Dennis, like Richard Neville and Jim Anderson was banned from editing for several years after the *Oz* trial and therefore did not join *IT* until some time later.

International Times No.160 was published on 11th August 1973, a mere two weeks after Bruce Lee's death and for the first time ever, featured the late Mandarin Superstar on the front cover of a UK publication. The two-page article by David Jenkins - written under the perhaps misjudged pseudonym David Chinkins - featured not only Bruce Lee but also featured other emerging Kung Fu stars such as Sammo Hung and Angela Mao, as well as future film classics such as *The Killer, Hapkido, Sisters, The One-Armed Swordsman* and *King Boxer*. David Jenkins revealed his reason for writing the article, "I was a film editor/critic of *International Times* and I went to any screenings going. I saw some Kung Fu movies, loved them, enthused to the big cheeses/my pals at *IT* about them, took colleagues to see them, had drunken lunches in Chinatown restaurants with other converts - and because of all that, it was decided to do a Kung Fu special with Bruce Lee on the cover." The Editor of *International Times* No.160 was Don Atyeo, future co-writer of *Bruce Lee King of Kung-Fu* with Felix Dennis and who would later to be famously known as Don Won Ton to millions of *Kung-Fu Monthly* readers. Atyeo remembered the issue fondly, "David Jenkins wrote the story. He was the film editor at the time. He and I had both travelled through the Far East on the hippie trails in the early 70s and we'd come across movies, though not Bruce Lee movies, obviously. They were mainly costume dramas, but had all the same components as the Bruce Lee stuff, or Kung Fu, martial arts and people

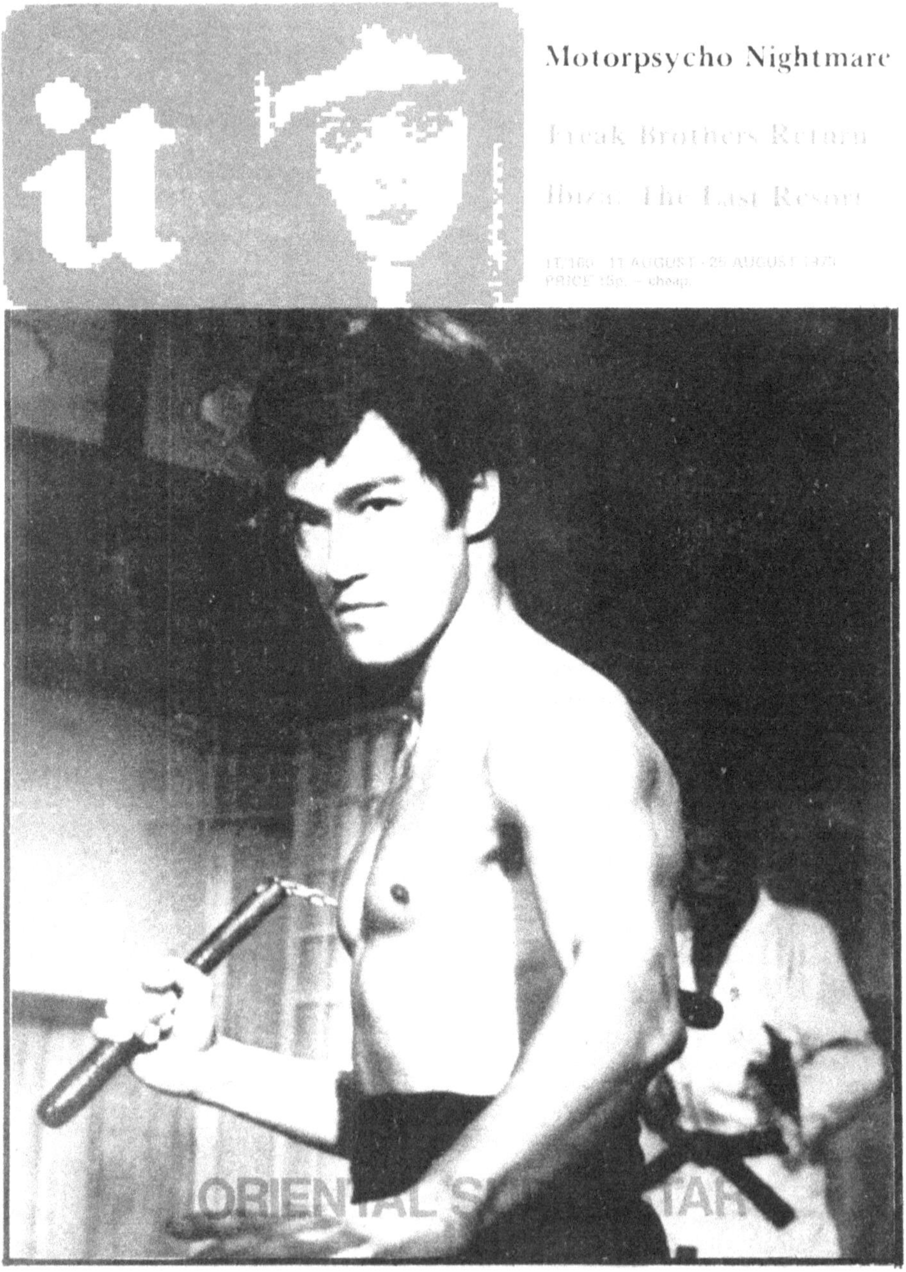
it
Motorpsycho Nightmare
Freak Brothers Return
Ibiza: The Last Resort
ORIENTAL

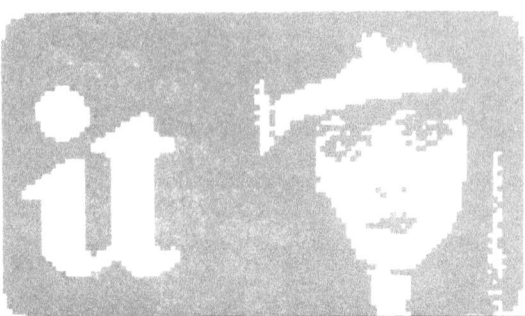

leaping around and jumping off buildings and all that sort of stuff. I remember him coming in and we talked quite a lot about it, because he really liked those movies and he was raving on about Bruce Lee, how he was a sort of a westernised version of that and was going down well in the West. I think that was the reason why we stuck him on the cover, because both of us were pretty much enthused about martial arts movies from the Far East. So that was about it."

The news editor role in that issue was credited as being 'In Hiding,' although Farnworth-born writer Roger Hutchinson claims that it was he who would have held the news editor position on that particular issue stating, "I was on holiday for that issue and Don stood in for me." Roger Hutchinson would later become the editor of *International Times* and on Volume 2 Number 1 in 1974, Bruce Lee appeared on the front cover again, though little Lee content could be found inside the magazine's pages.

A few years prior to working on *International Times* in the early 1970s, Hutchinson had been convinced to relocate from Barnsley to London by Felix Dennis in order to become editor of *Oz* magazine. Born in Farnworth near Bolton, Hutchinson later attended Bretton Hall College near Barnsley to study English. Whilst there, he founded and edited the short-lived publication *Sad Traffic* (later becoming alternative newspaper *STYNG* or *Sad Traffic Yorkshire News & Gossip*) out of a small office in the Yorkshire mining town. Hutchinson would later reminisce about the house he and other students lived in during his time at college. "It was a three-floor terraced house and we rented all three floors of it. It was myself, Richard Keys (who became an artist and was on the arts course at the same time as me) and other friends in the middle floor and on the bottom floor as well."

Hutchinson would leave *Oz* magazine during the obscenity trial in order to serve as editor on *International Times* and *Time Out*, but would later collaborate with old friend Felix Dennis in 1975 on the 'lost' *KFM* book, The *Wisdom of Bruce Lee*.

The financial burden of the obscenity trial had severe implications for *Oz* magazine as one newspaper headline declared, "Hippie Magazine Bankrupt with £20,000 Debts."

There are several stories around regarding the origins of *Kung-Fu Monthly* but they all share common elements. One story goes that one day in early 1974, one of the office workers left H. Bunch Associates' office in London's Goodge Street, to feed his lunch time hunger. Walking back to the office, he noticed a large queue outside one of the cinemas in Leicester Square, where hung a poster for a movie entitled, *Enter the Dragon,* which was attracting huge cinema crowds and the Kung-Fu Craze hadn't even begun. Dick Pountain recalls, "I believe that it was Jim Anderson, one of the three *Oz* editors that was in the trial, who was walking down Wardour Street and he saw a queue of young kids outside the door so he went over and asked them what they were waiting for. They told him it was a Bruce Lee movie, and he came back to the office and told Felix and Don Atyeo that he'd just seen this queue of kids waiting for this movie. So Felix and Don ran down there to see what was going on and that was how Felix got it into his head."

Designer Richard Adams somewhat backs up Pountain's story. He explained, "Felix had a flat in Soho, which was not very far away from Goodge Street and he would walk between home and the office. One evening in the heyday of *Cozmic Comics*, he was walking home through Leicester Square when he saw a cinema queue that ran almost around the entire building. He saw it and noted that it was a Bruce Lee film; *Enter the Dragon*, I think. He went home and had a bath which triggered his eureka moment! He knew nothing about Bruce Lee, but it was the combination of the length of the cinema queue together with the recent success of a unique poster magazine format that the sports journalist and publisher Bob Houston created that clinched it. "

Felix Dennis' recalled in a 1997 interview, "I was just coming across Soho and I saw a bunch of school children one Saturday morning queuing up outside one of the sex cinemas. They said they were there to see a Chinaman who beats people up. I had to see this, so I paid my money, went in and sure enough, I saw a Chinaman beating people up. And I thought, 'Whoa, let's do a book - a biography, a picture book. Let's do anything. Let's do a magazine.' And that's how *Kung-Fu Monthly* was born. Bruce Lee was it, as far as Kung Fu was concerned, so of course, we had him on every single issue. I would have called the magazine *Bruce Lee Monthly* but I thought his Estate and relatives might get a bit upset about that, so we called it *Kung-Fu Monthly*. The interesting thing about our audience was that it consisted of both boys and girls, which was very unusual."

Don Atyeo had a slightly different recollection of how the idea for *Kung-Fu Monthly* came about. "It could well have happened because after we did our *International Times* cover. *Time Out* did a Bruce Lee cover as well in 1974 - the February 15th to 21st issue. *IT* put him on the cover in 73 and then *Time Out* put him on in 74. When I was with Richard Adams and Felix Dennis, we were doing these poster magazines of various people, pop groups and so on, the same format as *Kung-Fu Monthly* but just 'one-shots' - one-offs of people like Bjorn Borg, Sports Stars or whoever was the popular band of the time, like the Bay City Rollers, all that sort of crap. Felix, who was a big buddy of Tony Elliot, the owner of *Time Out* was the publisher. I remember him coming in saying that he just had a meeting with Tony, who was going on about how much that issue of *Time Out* had sold with Bruce Lee on the cover, and he was quite flabbergasted by it. Felix thought that it would be a good idea to do a 'one-shot' on Bruce Lee but why that wasn't it just a one off? I don't know why it became an ongoing magazine but it was the only one we ever did like that. I always thought that we did it was because of Felix talking to Tony Elliot, and him deciding to cash in on the interest that *Time Out* had created."

The image of that February issue of *Time Out* magazine featuring Lee on the cover plus the Atyeo-edited International Times No.160 persuaded Dennis to take a gamble on a poster magazine about the then-unknown 'Deadly Art of Kung-Fu.' Their initial idea was to print the poster magazine and sell it to the kids waiting outside the cinemas.

The poster magazine was to be published through Dennis' publishing company H. Bunch Associates Limited, named after Honey Bunch Kaminski, a character created around 1968 by controversial illustrator Robert Crumb and featured in *Snatch Comics* #1. Crumb was also the creator of the even more controversial character Fritz the Cat, who like Bruce Lee, would give the British Board of Film Censors no end of headaches.

Richard Adams, who had worked as a designer on *Oz* magazine, was brought in to design the new poster magazine and designed it with several factors in mind. Adams recalled, "The attraction of this format - ripped off I might add from Bob Houston, the publisher of Cream magazine - was its simplicity and economy when it came to printing cost, but it required people to write, edit, design and produce each copy at breakneck speed. Bob Houston had a created a production formula for the poster magazine but I can't for the life of me remember who was featured in his magazine, a pop star of the moment I imagine. I must give him credit for taking being ripped off in his stride. From the time that we got final copy from Don, established the running order, created the technical specification and found a printer that could deliver, we actually put the first magazine together in the space of about twelve hours or thereabouts. An all-night session followed by a vicious deadline. There were few, if any, problems where the format and design was concerned. It was a simple and infinitely repeatable formula."

"HONEY BUNCH" KAMINSKI, 13 of L.A.

Inside the poster magazine, Adams would be credited inside as Rik Kemo Sabi - just one of the creative pseudonyms the team would use. Others included Felix Yen (Dennis), Don Won Ton (Atyeo) and Jo Nat Hon (Jonathon Green). Whose idea it was to write under the pseudonyms is up in the air but Jonathon Green had an idea. "I would imagine it would have been Don Atyeo or maybe Richard Adams. I think I made my own name up - it was hardly very clever. Rik Kemo Sabi was presumably a culturally misplaced tip of the hat to the Lone Ranger's Native American buddy Tonto, who addressed his white pal as Kemo Sabe." Richard Adams confirmed the Lone Ranger reference, "I was Rik Kemo Sabi and Kemo Sabe was the Lone Ranger's henchman. In the popular television series he was the Native American Indian who rode on the piebald horse, usually several paces behind the Lone Ranger who, I recall, rode a pure white horse. Rik was just a shortened version of Richard. Don Won Ton was an amalgamation of a popular Chinese dish, Wonton soup, together with the name of the pub across the road in Goodge Street we all used to drink in called The One Tun. This is where we used to spend evenings, getting shit-faced before, or after going back to the studio or the office to work late into the night. On all-nighters, there was an Indian restaurant situated just across the road from the office in Goodge Street which I think was called The Nel Kamal, where we would eat from a classic south Indian menu. It was in a dingy basement where the house wine was Blue Nun - there was nothing smart about this place. After that, we would then go back to the studio for more alcohol, get stoned and work on the magazine." Not everyone was happy with the team using nicknames however. "The magazine distributor apparently told off Felix right at the

start for putting jokey names on the masthead," said Bruce Sawford.

The designing of the magazine was one thing; the process of actually getting it printed was another. Dick Pountain remembered, "In those days, we published comics basically. So to us, publishing meant something with like thirty-two black and white pages and a cover wrapped around it. Somebody decided not to do that. They decided to do this folded poster magazine, which was a totally new format - nobody had ever done it before. The printers were completely boggled by it; they didn't like it at all. So I had to find some people who could print that." Their usual printers which they used for the comics were one step above a local Prontaprint, who were the equivalent of a small local business whose main work came from printing the business cards, note paper and other stationary of other local businesses. "We used a guy called Sid who was a little bit above that. He actually did some smutty magazines and stuff like that," said Dick, "But he had a sheet fed printer - a Heidelberg KORD - which printed single sheets but he could print a sixteen-page section on one sheet as well. We used him for the comics' covers only and the insides of the comics were printed by Web Offset up in Norfolk. We told him we need to do something that's an A1 poster on one side and eight-to-view A4 on the other side which he said he could print for us."

However, as one problem was solved, another presented itself. Though their usual printer was able to print what they wanted, there was one issue - cost. The comics they printed were black and white on news print; what they now wanted was A1 size and full colour and that was going to prove expensive. As well as cost being an issue, another one emerged - the printer couldn't actually fold it correctly anyway. Dick said, "His own paper folder wouldn't fold it in the right way because printers are set up for printing sections of a magazine that are going to be trimmed, wrapped around three edges and then bound together. So another problem was finding someone who could fold it, which we finally did. Anyway, we got one out and it sold like hotcakes. And it just took off like a rocket. We were a tiny outfit at this point and had been on the verge of bankruptcy a year before. Suddenly, for the first time, we got something that was just going completely ape shit."

The title of this book is self explanatory. The graphic, easy to understand illustrations by Paul Simmons and the carefully conceived step by step instructions make this the perfect book for beginners wishing to take up kung-fu. Unlike certain other publications on the market, this book has been carefully planned and meticulously executed. We claim it to be the best book of its kind for kung-fu novices in the world! Chapters include: HISTORY AND ORIGINS, EXERCISES, STRIKES, KICKS, BLOCKS, DEFENSE AND COUNTER ATTACK and STANCES.

Many thousands of KFM readers have already ordered their copy of this exciting book. If you are genuinely interested in taking up kung-fu then our advice to you is to order your copy today! Only an order through KFM can *guarantee* you will obtain a copy. Mail £2.00 by cheque or postal order made out to Kung-Fu Monthly and enclose your carefully printed name and address. All orders to: KUNG-FU BEGINNERS BOOK OFFER, Kung-Fu Monthly, 39 Goodge Street, London W1P 1FD.

Eventually, a 'Trade Dummy' - a low-cost, low-quality mock-up - of the proposed poster magazine was produced to present to the British magazine wholesalers. "It was printed in black and white by hand on a proofing press two months before the first real issue of *KFM* hit the news stands," wrote Dennis. It was almost identical to the final released issue of No.1 apart from the cover, the giant fold-out poster, a couple of small images and the obvious lack of colour. Initially, three copies of the 'Trade Dummy' were printed; one copy

Brand New Poster Magazine!

KUNG-FU
MONTHLY NO. 1   20p
TRADEMARK

GIANT COLOUR POSTER

The Flying Fists of BRUCE LEE
KING OF KUNG FU

THE MARTIAL ART!

BRUCE LEE SUPERSTAR

was held by the publisher and the Editor-in-Chief of the magazine but the third copy went missing around 1975. It was later reprinted in a limited edition run of 500 copies and sold exclusively at *KFM*'s Bruce Lee Convention and then through the *KFM* Marketplace advertisements within the magazine. The proofing press version of the 'Trade Dummy' was not the only one produced. It would have been expensive to print the three copies on the proofing press, so to save money, some more were photocopied. As Dick Pountain recalls, "If we only wanted 10 copies, we would have done them on the Xerox machine." Due to the low budget approach of these copies, not a single one is known to exist today.

Another contributor to *Kung-Fu Monthly* No.1 was artist Paul Simmons, who, as a teen, had moved to Hong Kong, where he studied Judo and Kung Fu at after-school clubs and had a knowledge of Bruce Lee and Kung Fu movies which most westerners wouldn't have had at that point in time. "As a result I knew about Bruce Lee and often used to go past Shaw Studios," said Simmons. "They sometimes used to film on the road outside school." Upon returning to England, he trained at St Martin's School of Art (The London Institute), just half a mile from *Kung-Fu Monthly*'s Goodge Street office. Paul says, "I was lucky really as I was at art school just down the road and had been drawing comics for Felix as well as stuff for the last issue of Oz." Then, one afternoon in early 1974, he got a message from Felix about a top-secret project he was working on. "I got a message from Felix to go in after Art College," recalls Simmons. "It turned out I was the only person he knew, who knew much about Kung Fu at that point. I signed a non-disclosure agreement before he showed me a mock-up of issue one. I did most of the writing on issue one with info that my girlfriend's brother sent me from Hong Kong."

The first issue of *Kung-Fu Monthly* was published on the 9th April 1974. As well as hitting news stands, the team also stuck to their original idea of selling to the kids queuing outside the cinemas, with Don Atyeo recalling, "I know that when we launched the magazine, we did a lot of work ourselves. Instead of just giving it to the distributors - which is what we did with all the other ones and they put them in newsagents - for some reason, we had big piles of these ourselves. We went down - all of us - to make some money directly by selling to the kids in the line outside of the cinema which I think was the Rialto in Leicester Square. We went down there with these big piles of magazines just to see if we could make a few quid. It was quite extraordinary, because as soon as we got near, the queues just broke and they charged towards us. They were thrusting money at us and we couldn't get rid of the magazines fast enough. I remember that after we'd sold everything, they all went back into line and started reading their *Kung-Fu Monthly*s. We went to a pub at the back of the Leicester Square, sat down and began to empty our pockets of all our ill-gotten gains, which was pretty satisfying for people in our position because, quite frankly, we didn't have a pot to piss in at that stage."

Such was the breathtaking success of *Kung-Fu Monthly* No.1, the Goodge Street office started to look like a Royal Mail sorting office. "As a result of this first issue, the new *KFM* office staff were deluged with a staggering 5,000 letters from fans in the first fortnight of publication," wrote Dennis. "Perhaps a degree 'primitive' when compared to succeeding issues - though its charm remains undeniable - still the fans forked-out in their hundreds of thousands to buy it. Within a week, the entire edition had sold out and one of the world's most unexpected publishing success stories had begun."

After putting together *Kung-Fu Monthly* No.1 and observing its runaway success,

Dennis realised how the idea of a monthly poster magazine could now be a viable business opportunity but there were two problems; they had very little information and they had very few photographs. To help tide things over until Atyeo returned with his newly acquired wares in the *KFM* office, Felix turned to Rhona McVay, the then-President of the Bruce Lee Fan Club and formed a mutually beneficial alliance with her and her five-thousand strong fan base. Felix came up with an ingenious, yet slightly dubious plan, as Richard Adams explained, "We discovered the name and the contact details for Rhona McVay, who was the UK president of the Bruce Lee Fan Club and paid her a visit. She lived somewhere in the far reaches of west London, a long way out. Felix and I got a mini cab to take us and I remember this was the first time I'd ever heard him use the expression, 'Born to be driven.' He never learned to drive and had no interest in it whatsoever. Rhona was a very engaging and capable woman, and we came away from the meeting with a bundle of photographs of Bruce Lee. They were film stills for the most part, mainly black and white with some full colour transparencies. There were others but that was where most of the photographs came from to fill the first couple of issues. There was something of a scoop in a black and white photograph of Bruce Lee in his coffin. I'm not sure where that came from, possibly from her but I don't recall exactly, it was 50 years ago. Most of the images for the first few issues came from Rhona."

Thanks to *Kung-Fu Monthly*'s partnership with The Official Bruce Lee Fan Club, another door was opened to them for material, as future editor Bruce Sawford would recall, "A lot of the detail came from a man called Roy Byrne who worked at Golden Harvest in London's Soho Square. He also slipped us many of the images. We

Bruce Lee Fan Club president Rhona McVay being interviewed by editor Don Atyeo for KFM No.9 at the Kung-Fu Monthly office in Goodge Street. *Photograph © Copyright Richard Adams 1974.*

Felix Dennis poses with a black and white photograph of Bruce Lee, possibly obtained at his first meeting with Bruce Lee Fan Club president Rhona McVay in early 1974. *Photograph © Copyright Richard Adams 1974.*

were also sent stuff by the mega fans later on."

The pictures and information they got from Rhona would only last so long; therefore Don Atyeo was booked on the next flight to Hong Kong to bring back as much Bruce Lee information as he could. "There was very little we could do but we did as much as we could," recalled Atyeo. "I wrote for us because I was the only journalist amongst us as I'd worked on newspapers in Australia and done some stuff in England as well when I arrived, such as journalistic stuff for *The Observer* and various people. I tried as much to do an honest job on it with whatever material I could get, but it was really just nothing. It was just his movies and it was very, very little, but that's when Felix said, 'This is a winner.' He got me the cheapest flight you could get to Hong Kong, and sent me off with the idea of doing *Kung-Fu Monthly*. He then came up with the idea that we should do a book on him because there were no books at all on him. We couldn't find anything published about him in the West so off I went and spent some weeks trying to glean as much as I could from various radio stations, *the South China Morning Post*, people who knew him and various other people or contacts that I made over there and came back with." Felix Dennis also remembered, "Don Atyeo interviewed scores of people including medical staff at the Queen Elizabeth Hospital and is why we know that Bruce Lee's death was nothing more than a wretched accident occasioned by an allergic reaction to medication. These interviews of Don's convinced us that his death, while very sad, was an accident. Don also interviewed

Kung-Fu Monthly's Designer and Art Director Richard Adams.
Photograph © Copyright Richard Adams 1974.

many people in the Hong Kong movie business, as well as friends and acquaintances of Bruce Lee. Over the course of Kung Fu Monthly's life, we published nearly all the material we had gathered in Hong Kong from those interviews." There was another reason for sending Don Atyeo to Hong Kong rather than someone else, as Jonathon Green stated, "Don, being an Aussie, had done the hippie trail in reverse. He'd stayed in various places en route, and I think Hong Kong was one of them. I imagine he would have been seen as the 'expert' in the area."

Whilst in Hong Kong, Atyeo spoke to everyone he could; family, producers, co-stars, directors, film extras and anyone else who had a Bruce Lee-related story to tell. He also brought back a reel-to-reel recording of an interview which Lee did with British journalist Ted Thomas for a local Hong Kong radio station. Dennis, ever keen to increase the money coming in, transferred it to cassette tape and sold it through the *KFM* Marketplace pages. "When I was in Hong Kong, I went to RTHK, which was the government radio station," said Don. "I was chatting to a journalist there, who was one of the last people to interview Bruce Lee. I was chatting away and I said, 'Well, you haven't got a copy of that interview have you?' to which he said, 'Yes.' He went to get it, which was a big reel-to-reel tape, and he gave it to me. When I got home, I thought, 'This is good. I'll just transcribe stuff,' which I did but Felix instantly grabbed it and said, 'Great,' and he put it all on cassette. He put it on thousands of cassettes, labelled them up as 'Bruce Lee: The Last Interview,' and charged about five quid or something extortionate. He just couldn't get enough of these tapes; cranking them out day and night."

Don Atyeo went back to Hong Kong a short time later and on that occasion, he met with Betty Ting Pei, the actress whose apartment Lee was found in on the night of his

Bruce Lee Fan Club president Rhona McVay being interviewed by Kung-Fu Monthly editor Don Atyeo for KFM No.9.
Photograph © Copyright Richard Adams 1974.

death. Don said, "I was going to do a book with her. She was keen and I did have discussions with her but in the end, she decided not to do it. I think that she was a bit scared of Bruce Lee's wife in Seattle and the legal side of it and so on. So in the end, she decided not to go ahead with it. She was pursued everywhere and it's no wonder that she packed it in and disappeared."

As Atyeo ran around Hong Kong gathering photos and information, it was left to Felix Dennis, Dick Pountain and Richard Adams back home to hurriedly cobble together *Kung-Fu Monthly* No.2, again roping in their former *International Times* colleague Jonathon Green (credited at Jo Nat Hon) to help out. "Felix got into a tizz about how it had to be done really, really fast," recalled Adams. *Kung-Fu Monthly* No.2 was an instant hit and its first run sold out within days of arriving on news stands, so much so, that Dennis and Co. had to reprint it, with a notable difference. "If your second issue is slightly less glossy than the rest," wrote Dennis, "Then it's one of the reprints; the first editions look normal." The 'Flying Man' design in the magazine's logo was changed from *KFM* No.2 onwards for legal reasons. "I think it had something to do with Raymond Chow," said Dick Pountain. That reason seems plausible as the image was from *The Big Boss*, a film that was owned by Golden Harvest at the time. Rights have since transferred to Fortune Star after their acquisition of the Golden Harvest back catalogue, which was where Bruce Lee's daughter Shannon had to go in order to obtain permission to use the logo for Bruce Lee Enterprises. As much as that may be true, there may be another reason for the change and one suggested by Richard Adams. "I'm pretty sure the logo design was a collaborative effort between Felix, Don, Dick and me. We would have chucked ideas and scribbles around the table which I would go on to develop and refine through to the finished design. We were the core team but Felix had strong opinions about most things, the *KFM* logo notably. The position of the arm a on the first issue is different to the one on the others. I think that the reason for that could be - and I can't be sure about this - but on the logo on the first issue, his left arm is raised and superimposed on the letter F, making it quite hard to read. It could even be an E in that position so KUNG-EU doesn't read well, let alone sound well. Come the second issue, the arm is now downward-pointing, so you can see clearly that this is a letter F and hey presto, KUNG-FU, there's no mistaking it. That's my best shot and all I can offer." From that explanation and from a design point of view, that could well be true. Both reasons appear completely legitimate and the real reason as to why the logo was changed is a combination of both.

Kung-Fu Monthly No.2 was one of the only early UK issues where Bruce Lee shared the magazine with other stars such as David Carradine and Angela Mao. This was possibly down to two reasons; the obvious fact that Bruce Lee became too popular to share the magazine with and, considering the urgency of Don Atyeo's little jaunt to Hong Kong, they lacked Bruce Lee information and more importantly, images, to include in that issue. This theory was backed up by Richard Adams, "There weren't very many of them at all, but the fact that we did a poster magazine lent itself very healthily towards using few pictures, but big."

Once Don Atyeo returned from Hong Kong, *Kung-Fu Monthly* just grew and grew; sackfulls of mail arrived each and every day at the Goodge Street office, full of cash, postal orders and cheques, from ecstatic fans, eager to get whatever merchandise was advertised in the magazine. As the Mail Order Department grew, Bruce Sawford was brought in to

THE KUNG-FU MONTHLY ARCHIVE SERIES

Brand New Poster Magazine!
KUNG-FU
MONTHLY NO. 2   20p

GIANT BRUCE LEE POSTER INSIDE

The Spirit Of
BRUCE LEE
Lives On

HARD FACTS! HOT PICTURES! HIGH ACTION!

Extracts from 'THE BEGINNERS GUIDE TO KUNG FU'

DAVID CARRADINE
The Grasshopper Rebel

keep on top of the stack of envelopes arriving daily, eventually being fondly remembered as the 'Mail Order King.'

With the unexpected success of *Kung-Fu Monthly* No.1 and No.2, they outgrew their printer, as Pountain explained, "It was costing way, way too much money. So then I had to go to look for big heat set web offset colour printer who could print it for us and that was a whole different ball game. Their machines couldn't fold it the right way either. So my involvement for the first six months of *Kung-Fu Monthly* was finding someone who could print it for a sensible price because the circulation was going up and up. I can't even remember what the top circulation was now, but it was hundreds of thousands."

With the success of *Kung-Fu Monthly*, the money coming in was phenomenal but as incomings increased, so did expenses. Pountain testified to this, "It put me in a whole different ball game. I was having to buy paper and was spending millions of pounds a year on printing instead of the few thousand pounds when we were doing the comics. I was having to buy paper from Finland and stuff like that. This was the first time I got involved in proper printing and being treated like a print buyer."

Dennis knew from the very beginning that selling the magazine was only one way to bring in money and included mail order items right from the start and the fans lapped it up. As Jonathon Green remembered, "I was going into the Goodge Street office with some work one day and there was Felix and I think, Wendy Kasabian with a few post office mail sacks. They had done a mail order shot in one of the early editions of *Kung-Fu Monthly* and this was the result. They were emptying the sacks, opening the mail and tossing the notes into one cardboard box, the cheques into another and the postal orders into a third one. It was then I thought, 'You've cracked it, Felix. You've cracked it!'"

Most items sold through *Kung-Fu Monthly* didn't present a problem but Dennis was caught out with one small product advertisement for a Bruce Lee poster in *KFM* No.1. After a copyright claim by Cathay Films, Dennis was forced to issue an apology in *KFM* No.2, though he would run into copyright issues again in 1975, when he was forced to pay out £25,000 after it was discovered that he had used photographs of Bruce Lee in the magazine without the copyright holder's permission.

After Don Atyeo returned from Hong Kong with his suitcases full of Bruce Lee information, Dennis construed a plan to make even more money - one involving books. He contacted the relatively small publishing company Wildwood House and attempted to sell the idea of a Bruce Lee biography to the company's founders Oliver Caldecott and Dieter Pevsner. They agreed and in July of 1974, the Felix Dennis and Don Atyeo-penned biography Bruce Lee King of Kung-Fu was released, where it was snapped up by eager fans. Richard Adams recalled Don returning from Hong Kong. "*Bruce Lee King of Kung Fu*, which we went on to produce for Wildwood House, was published four months after the first issue of *Kung-Fu Monthly*. In those four months we'd produced four issues of the magazine and Don had been to Hong Kong to conduct interviews with key people and gather photographs for the book and magazine. We were ahead of the game at that point and had amassed a considerable amount of material." However, as successful as the book was to be, the printing process was not without its problems. Well-respected Bruce Lee historian Andrew Staton recalls, "My Mum bought a copy for me from a book stall in Leeds Market just after it was released. After excitedly getting it home, I took it out of the bag and began to flick through the pages. I couldn't believe my eyes; the first few pages were printed

fine but the rest were completely blank. I was absolutely gutted. Luckily, the book stall exchanged it for me a few days later." Despite the initial printing problems, the book was a smash-hit and due to its successful UK sales, Dennis published it in America via Straight Arrow Press, where it continued to sell in considerable numbers. Dennis later recalled, "Eventually the book sold hundreds and hundreds of thousands of copies in more than a dozen languages around the world."

After the unbelievable success of *Bruce Lee King of Kung Fu*, the *KFM* team began writing and releasing several more books. They were joined on these projects by people such as illustrator Mikki Rain, and again by artist Paul Simmons, who was back on writing duties. "I wrote several of the specials such as The Power of Bruce Lee, as well as doing all the black and white Kung Fu drawings every month which also appeared in the specials such as *The Book of Kung Fu*," says Paul. He also collaborated with Felix Dennis on *The Beginner's Guide to Kung Fu*, a step-by-step instructional martial arts book, which due to the lack of bonafide Kung Fu clubs around the country, sold by the millions.

One of the most exciting publications released in the midst of the *Kung-Fu Monthly* years, was *The Secret Art of Bruce Lee*, which was to feature for the first time ever, the photographs taken by the late photographer to the stars, Chester Maydole. It was an amazing scoop for the team at *KFM* and one that happened almost by accident. Taken on a variety of locations over four shooting sessions at three separate locations in late 1966 to early 1967; Portuguese Bend, Lee's apartment in West Los Angeles and Palos Verdes, California near *Batman* star Adam West's beach house, Bruce Lee and Dan Inosanto posed for a variety of martial arts action photo-

graphs. Several shots were also taken of Lee, Inosanto and West as they posed on West's beach house veranda. Lee and West had worked together on the *Batman* and *Green Hornet* crossover episodes and Maydole was hired to shoot some publicity photographs for both series and their stars. "I'd done some shots of *Batman*, which was very successful at that time," remembered Maydole in 1975, "and I was asked by the company to take pictures of Bruce and Van Williams."

The reason for the photographs is unclear; some reports state they were taken for Maydole to sell to the martial arts magazines to promote Lee while some state Lee and Adam West were going to release some sort of martial arts training guide. The truth may lie somewhere in between. Unfortunately, Lee and Maydole both found themselves heavily in demand for their skills in the years that followed and their paths never crossed again, with Maydole sadly remarking, "It was just circumstances. Both of us trying to make a living. And, of course, I'm really sorry I didn't do the book."

Pure luck brought the Maydole photographs to the *KFM* office via one of Felix's contacts. "We rely quite a large extent on outside researchers - both for pictures and information," explained Felix at the time of the book's publication. One day, Felix had a phone call from one of these external researches called Fred, who explained to Felix that he had a huge collection of martial arts photographs he may be interested in and could he call by the office the following week, to which Felix duly agreed.

The following week, as Felix and the team were checking through features for *KFM* No.21 and reading the never-ending stream of mail, Fred arrived at the office. Dennis remembered, "He came in, threw a large unopened box on to my desk and suggested we go out for something to eat." After arriving back from lunch and saying their goodbyes, Dennis returned to his office and went to look for the box of photographs but was surprised to find it missing. Realising that the library people were probably booking them in, Felix made a mental note to check on them later. At 3pm, they were still booking them in, so a puzzled Felix went to investigate. "I walked into the library and moved over to the huge, pile of pictures," wrote Felix. "Not knowing exactly what to expect, I idly flipped through the first three or four and the truth took roughly thirty seconds to hit me! Now, that may seem a long time to you, but sometimes it takes a few seconds for the mind to accept the impossible. Then, the truth started to sink in. How could over a thousand pictures of Bruce remain undetected for all these years?" Everyone in the office crowded around, gawping at the unbelievable paper treasure that they had unwittingly stumbled upon. "Hour after hour we flipped through the treasure trove of Bruce Lee photographs, handling each priceless print as though it were something out of Britain's crown jewels," continued Felix. "Obviously their value was beyond measure - not only to the collector, but also to the serious martial arts student. Here finally, was living proof of the Little Dragon's ultimate gift to the fighting world. Move-by-move action sequences of him demonstrating his own unique style of Jeet Kune Do abounded. No one could ever again doubt the efficiency of Bruce Lee's twentieth century fighting formula. Each picture flowed like liquid from the one before - sheer poetry in motion - and the beauty behind his deadly art was enough to take one's breath away. It was the nearest thing I had ever known to personal instruction from the master."

The only downside to this breathtaking find was the lack of written instruction or descriptions about the photographs. Luckily, writer and artist Paul Simmons, with his Kung Fu and Judo knowledge, was on hand to assist. Paul recalls, "One thing not many people know about the Chester Maydole photographs is that Felix gave them to me, asked me to sort them into sequences as best I could and then write all the descriptive captions to fit. This was me doing the best I could with my martial arts knowledge, research into Jeet Kune Do and a large dose of guesswork - I seem to remember these ran across at least two specials." Those two specials were the books, *The Secret Art of Bruce Lee* and *The Unbeatable Bruce Lee.*

Merchandise throughout the *Kung-Fu Monthly* years was another important sideline to the *KFM* business model. Mugs, rings, candles and even pillowcases were adorned with Lee's image. Richard Adams recalled, "The mail order side of the business was hugely successful from the start. The first issue went out, it cleaned up really and we all remember being at the office when the postman struggled up the stairs with two big great big sacks of post, full of postal orders, cash and cheques but there was a huge amount of interest. There were all sorts of really mad stuff that was being sold and it was being bought, just like the Bruce Lee pillowslip, which was printed one colour - red on one side of this really cheap horrible cloth." The candle, dubbed the 'Bruce Lee 24-hour Memorial Candle' didn't last as long as the name suggested as Don Atyeo would later testify, "We did try and burn it once and I think it lasted about two hours. I know; it's shocking."

Kung-Fu Monthly was featured on national television, though in a rather negative light. Millions of viewers watched That's Life presenter Esther Rantzen rip into *Kung-Fu Monthly* on the show, accusing them of being a bunch of con artists. Felix Dennis was concerned about the damaging effect that would have on the business, but he needn't have worried. Don Atyeo recalls, "The problem wasn't a supply issue; it was more because it was such a shitty product. Felix was not very bountiful. It was pretty thin stuff. I forget what they got in there but it wasn't a lot of stuff anyway and that was a reason why Esther Rantzen did a big thing about it. It was because it was such poor value for money and I hesitate to say, a rip-off, but it was sailing in those waters. She sort of laid it out and we thought, 'Oh hell, that's a bit poor.' But the next day, we had more orders for the damn things and they just kept coming. I mean, that's the power of advertising. We had sack loads of mail, just absolute sack loads. We were working out of this tiny little thing in Goodge Street. On the ground floor was a paint shop and there was a corridor between to leading up our rickety stairs to our second floor offices. The mail man opened the door and just held these great sacks full of mail in his hands, all with cash and cheques in them, so Esther Rantzen, thank God, did not harm our business at all. In fact, it was quite the reverse. We had a lot of stuff like that though."

Designer Richard Adams remembered the weird and wonderful merchandise fondly, "We all just sat around and smoked and drank, and thought up this God-awful crap. But the Bruce Lee pillow-slip was a winner. Sacks of mail started to arrive. Sometimes you could hardly get through the door because of the sacks of mail."

Another nailed-on seller for *Kung-Fu Monthly* was posters, despite the magazine containing one in the fold-out. In 1975, a budding twenty-one year old artist and Bruce Lee

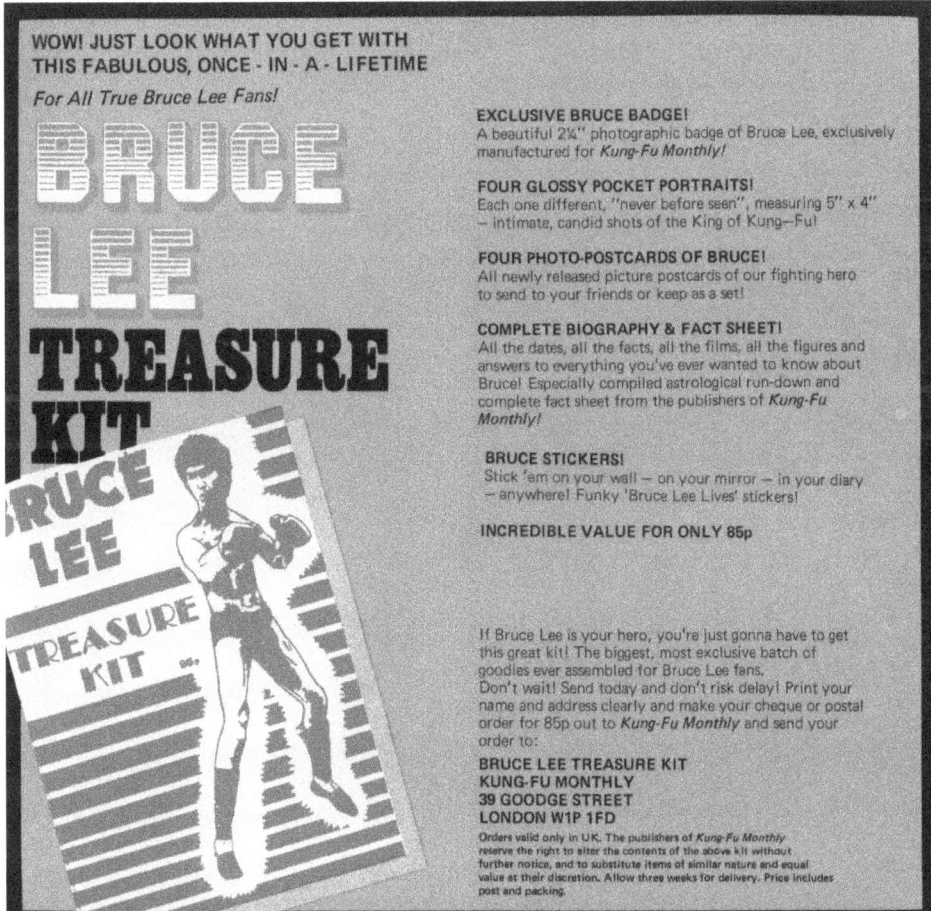

fanatic called Jeff Cummins from Holywell in Wales took a gamble and wrote to *Kung-Fu Monthly*. "I sent a letter to Felix Dennis or Felix Yen as it was at the time," laughed Cummins, "And amazingly Felix called me. He wanted to use the artwork for a poster offer with *KFM* and would pay me money!" Dennis said he was prepared to sell the posters though the magazine marketplace and offered to pay a grand sum of £70, which was quite a lot to the young artist. "I was earning £35 a week at the time so £70 was a great deal of money to me at the time," said Jeff. Copies of that poster are still for sale today through various martial arts equipment suppliers, though Cummins does not receive any royalties.

The success of the poster led Dennis to commission Cummins to paint two more paintings to be used as front covers for *Kung-Fu Monthly*, which would appear in No.9 and No.20. Cummins would go on to have a very successful career as a professional illustrator and has worked on many projects including *Doctor Who* and album covers for Paul McCartney, Rick Wakeman, Jon Anderson, Elvis Costello, Whitesnake and others, as well as creating unused pre-release poster artwork for the classic movie *Back to the Future*. "I'm grateful to Felix. He gave me my big break and I have him to thank for taking a chance on me."

BRUCE LEE DRAGON POSTER !!!

Especially painted for KFM by Jeff Cummings, here is a magnificent full colour poster of the Dragon King of Kung-Fu, Bruce Lee! Only available through KFM .. cannot be bought in shops! Printed on glossy art paper, this is probably the best action poster of Bruce you will ever see . . . but don't take our word for it, rush your P.O. or cheque for 90p (includes all post and packing) made out to Kung-Fu Monthly to: BRUCE LEE DRAGON POSTER OFFER, KFM Mail Order, 39 Goodge Street, London W1P 1FD.

Chris Rowley, a former writer and ad salesman also remembered how Felix had a far-fetched idea to create a Kung Fu board game, where players went around the board collecting cards and trading blows, but the idea never came to fruition. However, the first session descended into chaos after, while playing other board games for research purposes, they got sidetracked and a regular Friday night get-together to play board games began.

One of the only criticisms of *Kung-Fu Monthly* was the size of the text and colour of the print, both of which were partly down to designer Richard Adams. "There's a long tradition of that," explained Adams. "Whenever you mention *Oz* to anybody who knew the magazine at that time, they'll always say that it was completely illegible. That was an exaggeration; it just wasn't true. However, it has to be said there were certain pages that were quite challenging. But *Oz* magazine, unlike the other underground magazines like *IT* and *Friends*, established a tradition for using colour and made it a key feature of the magazine. The intention was to blast the reader with colour that was often testing to read, so something of that tradition would have been brought to *Kung-Fu Monthly*. The colours used were primary in nature, blue, red, green, yellow, orange, purple, black. There was nothing very subtle about the use of the colour. It was purposely used and applied as an attention grabber. I mean, you couldn't miss that on the news stand, or anywhere else it was displayed. Sometimes they worked and sometimes they didn't but in a number of instances, it's really quite hard to read, I would accept. Even the size of the type was quite testing to read but that was partly to do with the fact that the lead features were often lengthy but if you want to get everything onto the page, and want to combine that with large format photographs, then there's a cost and that is the size of the type."

The Kickback page in *Kung-Fu Monthly* was a direct link between the magazine and the fans. With very little information out there on Bruce Lee at the time and as a lot of the information was inaccurate, the Kickback Letters page was extremely popular with *Kung-Fu Monthly* readers. On hand to answer just a handful of the thousands of letters that poured in, was Jenny Lee, whose identity has always remained a mystery and her entire existence had been called into question on several occasions but Don Atyeo claimed that she did exist. "Jenny Lee did exist, but her last name wasn't Lee though I suspect. Felix met Jenny Lee, I think, in the Chinese Restaurant at the end of Goodge Street and she was just this girl he took a shine to. She might have been part Chinese but I can't swear to it. From memory, he invented a whole persona for her, like she was Bruce Lee's long lost cousin or something. She actually legitimately sat down and replied to a bunch of letters which

Letters editor Jenny Lee poses at her desk in the Goodge Street office in early 1974.
Photograph © Copyright Richard Adams 1974.

I'm sure she did that for a while. She was good. It wasn't a piss-take. Jenny wasn't Bruce Lee's cousin obviously, but she did her research when she was replying to letters and so on. I don't know how long she did that for but she was a real person. She might have lasted a couple of weeks. I can't remember but she was legitimate." Richard Adams also had good words to say about Jenny Lee and corroborated Don's views. "Jenny was very dedicated and finding her was a complete fluke. Felix picked her up in a Chinese restaurant that we used to go to just around the corner in Charlotte Street, I expect, and brought her back to the studio late one night and asked her if she would like to be the letters editor. We showed her the magazine which was in mid-production, and she jumped at the prospect of earning some easy money for very little effort. She was no fool, probably a student and keen to earn some extra money. She was paid but how long she lasted for I couldn't tell you. I think she was half Chinese which was part of the attraction. She was very attractive and actually good fun." After the departure of Jenny Lee, *Kung-Fu Monthly* carried on the Kickback page but had someone else writing under her guise. The third and final editor of the magazine, Colin James recalled, "As far as I know, it was Bruce Sawford. It was probably before my time but as far as I remember, I'm pretty sure it was the previous editor Bruce Sawford. I don't remember at all ever forwarding mail on to someone called Jenny Lee."

A big year for H. Bunch Associates was 1975 for two reasons; the first being that *Kung-Fu Monthly* went international. Dennis wrote, "The very first foreign edition of *KFM* was the Dutch edition, edited and published in Gouda - home of the famous cheese - in the summer of 1975." The Netherlands were quickly followed by Ger-

A rare candid shot of letters editor Jenny Lee at Kung-Fu Monthly's Goodge Street office in early 1974. *Photograph © Copyright Richard Adams 1974.*

many, France, Italy and Spain. The international editions had a varying degree of success; the Spanish edition of *Kung-Fu Monthly* was exported in great numbers to Spanish speaking countries in South America, while the French version was quite short-lived. While the foreign poster magazines kept the *Kung-Fu Monthly* branding, the foreign-language counterparts of the English books adopted the Super Kung-Fu branding. The USA edition was initially titled *Kung-Fu Monthly*, but later became Bruce Lee & *Kung-Fu Monthly* before finally becoming Bruce Lee Monthly. H. Bunch Associates never really had any involvement in the foreign issues of *Kung-Fu Monthly* and it appears they were printed under license. "We certainly didn't print copies and send them to America. We've never done that," recalls Pountain." I imagine we just sold a license to them for that. And I don't know who it was that we licensed it to. And they probably did that in a lot of several other countries as well." This theory is backed up by the content inside the magazine, especially the advertisements.

For *Kung-Fu Monthly*'s venture into America, Felix headed off there on a business trip with his *KFM* in his hand and dropped in to see Marvel Comics legend Stan Lee, who quickly showed him the door. Though Stan Lee would later confess to being a fan of Lee, he wasn't exactly a fan of the poster magazine format. Unperturbed, Felix headed off to a small business run by Peter Godfrey and Bob Bartner, on advice from his friend Tony Elliott. Godfrey recalled his feeling when Felix showed him a copy of *Kung-Fu Monthly* for the first time, "He explained what a poster magazine was and I thought, 'God, that must be a money-making gem of an idea!'"

A partnership would be formed where H. Bunch Associates would provide the almost-completed poster magazine and the American company would print and then distribute it under a new company, Paradise Publications. It was the start of a very successful partnership for the trio and one that

would continue for a number of years on a number of ventures. During its tenure, *Kung-Fu Monthly* was published in fourteen countries in eleven languages.

On the receiving end of a few lawsuits and copyright claims, Dennis also had to hire a solicitor for several offensive things, as he recalled, "Many 'pirate' editions of *Kung-Fu Monthly* were produced in Greece by unscrupulous publishers after a quick buck. After several threatened lawsuits and much international wheeling and dealing, we finally managed to get a reputable publisher to produce the real thing on a regular basis." As well as Greece, unauthorised duplication was also taking place in Hong Kong, such was the popularity of the magazine.

Not only were *Kung-Fu Monthly* reproduced without permission, so was Dennis and Atyeo's *Bruce Lee King of Kung Fu* book. Don Atyeo remembered, "We went to Mexico on a holiday with my wife, and were tootling around it. We weren't really big book readers but I imagine there was some sort of Spanish bookshop somewhere. It mainly had these booths with comics hanging out on something like clotheslines which seemed to be full of all sorts of action comics, magazines and so on. I looked up and thought, 'That looks familiar' - it was our book. There were thousands and thousands of the damn things everywhere; every city we went to, there were these pictures these books which had just been ripped off."

After a year, designer Richard Adams parted company with Bunch Books for pastures new as he explained, "I left after about a year, a time when things were really heating up. We were earning more money than at any time in our respective lives. After working for the underground press we often got paid, but it wasn't a fat lot and not always. Working on the underground press was about political commitment as well rather than for financial return. So when *Kung-Fu Monthly* appeared, closely followed by other one-shot magazines and spin off books, it became a very busy studio, a time when I had one talented assistant, Mikki Rain. We worked in a cork-lined basement with a great sound system, a state of the art Agfa process camera and dark room, at 39 Goodge Street. Dick Pountain, Felix and others were upstairs on the top floor. We were producing different magazine titles at a furious rate: *Crossroads Monthly*, *TV Sci-Fi*, Bjorn Borg and one-shots of bands like Earth, Wind and Fire. It was all happening but I was actually sick to death of it all because it gave me little time to do anything else. Although it was really nice to earn that kind of money, Don and I agreed to work for Felix, H. Bunch Associates, which then became Bunch Books, for one year. At the end of the twelve months, I split and so did Don. He went off to become editor of *Time Out* and I dropped out for a second time and found a studio in Notting Hill, where I started an anarchist publishing partnership with a writer called Heathcote Williams. We called it Open Head Press and went back to being skint again!"

Kung-Fu Monthly going international was one big milestone in 1975 but another, even bigger milestone, was just around the corner.

The Official Bruce Lee Fan Club had closed down just after founder Rhona McVay returned from her pilgrimage trip due to the pressures of work. A chance visit to the *KFM* office around that time by Pam Hadden, a twenty-four year lady from Streatham in London, would kick off a whole new chapter for *Kung-Fu Monthly* - the birth of the legendary Bruce Lee Secret Society.

The Bruce Lee Secret Society was first featured in Kung Fu Monthly No. 20 from 1976, telling fans that, "*KFM* is planning to start its own Bruce Lee fan club!" and to "Hold on...

THE BRUCE LEE SECRET SOCIETY.

HI — it's Jenny Lee here and am I happy to be writing these few words! Thanks largely to a lot of persuasion from you, the KFM readers, I am delighted to announce the grand opening of the *Bruce Lee Secret Society*. Yes, your own Kung-Fu Monthly is taking up the reins along with Pam Hadden and Carmella Rapa (who will be joint presidents of the club). They'll handle all the letter writing and day-to-day running of things ... good luck Pam and Carmella, I know you're going to need it! OK, I've said my piece so it's back to the mail bags for me. Over to you ...

Thanks for the intro' Jenny — we couldn't have done it better ourselves! Because we've got so much to tell you, I hope you'll forgive us if we itemise everything — that way we'll be able to squeeze more in.

1) On application you'll receive your membership card and a number, plus the fabulous *Society Kit*, containing your very own official certificate of membership (for framing), a *Bruce Lee Secret Society* badge and sticker, an autographed Bruce Lee pic and *four incredible photos of the Little Dragon in action that we promise have never been published in the world before!* All this plus news, views, facts and info — what a great package!

2) Then, once every three months, we'll post to you the quarterly Society news sheet — brim full of the latest chit-chat, letters, pen-pals, club offers and much more.

3) In every single issue of KFM you'll find your very own *Bruce Lee Secret Society* corner ... we'll be handling that!

4) All members will soon be able to get a discount on most KFM mail order offers.

5) On top of all that, there'll be lots of special Bruce Lee mail order products exclusively on offer to club members.

6) We are very sorry, but we have to point out that there is NO connection whatsoever between this and the previous Bruce Lee Fan Club. Regretfully therefore, we shall not be able to enter into any correspondence in regard to problems arising from its closure.

7) Sorry again! ... but we do really have to restrict membership to the United Kingdom only.

8) Finally, may we say here and now that we shall *not* be replying to letters that come without stamped addressed envelopes — you have been warned!

So there it is — what a great line-up and all for an annual subcription of only £2.95 — not bad eh?

Judging by the mail deluge that comes in through Jenny's door we think we have a fair idea of what we are letting ourselves in for — it's a good thing we're gluttons for punishment! But remember, if you've got any bright ideas on what you'd like to see in your club, don't hesitate to write ..., we promise you ALL letters will be answered. And by the way, don't forget that's exactly what it is — your club. After all, what's a club without members? The old Bruce Lee Fan Club apparently had around five thousand members when it closed ... let's see if we can double it — and keep open!

DON'T DELAY

Just send your £2.95 to:

The Bruce Lee Secret Society
Kung-Fu Monthly
39 Goodge Street
London W1P 1FD

(Cheques/Postal orders made out to Kung-Fu Monthly please.)

We'll get your Society Kit and membership card off to you as quickly as possibly. See you soon — *Pam and Carmella*.

don't write in yet. Full details in *KFM* No. 21."

It seemed that in No. 21, the editor didn't have time to put full details together, instead opting for a full page advert on the back page stating that "Full details will be in the next month's issue."

Kung Fu Monthly No. 22 boasted on the front cover, "NOW OPEN! THE BRUCE LEE SECRET SOCIETY," with the back page of the magazine carrying a full page advert.

The Bruce Lee Secret Society (later just The Bruce Lee Society) was jointly run on behalf of *KFM* by Pam Hadden and Carmella Rapa, though the latter would resign within the first six months due to work commitments, leaving Pam as the sole president of the Society. Andrew Hadden, the son of Pam Hadden, recalls, "I guess my mum got involved with *Kung-Fu Monthly* because there was no fan club at the time and I think my mum wanted one. So the people at Kung Fu Monthly were like, 'Let's set one up and you can run it.' Her motivation for running the society was that it took on a life of its own and she ended up in a little circle of Bruce Lee enthusiasts, all kind of feeding each other's interest. I think my mum originally became a Bruce Lee fan after seeing Enter the Dragon on a date sort of thing. I guess she admired the sort of the artistry and the skill and the speed of his martial arts."

The Bruce Lee Society was as successful as *Kung-Fu Monthly*, and throughout the eight active years of the Bruce Lee Society, it boasted over three and a half thousand members. While *Kung-Fu Monthly* was a magazine with limited fan interaction, the Bruce Lee Society was a buzzing pre-internet hub of news, reviews, letters, petitions, pen pals and more, all culminating in a quarterly newsletter which members relished dropping through their letterboxes. It was a community where friendships were forged, some of which continue to this day. The task of running The Bruce Lee Society was not an easy one. Pam Hadden tried to make an active effort to respond to each and every single letter that the Bruce Lee Society received, while single-handedly holding down a full time job as a secretary for British Airways. "Pam Hadden was a wonderful president of The Bruce Lee Society," recalled Dennis, "Quite simply, Pam worshipped the ground that Bruce Lee walked on and did more than anyone to keep Bruce Lee's memory alive - not to mention answering hundreds of letters from members of the Society personally." *Kung-Fu Monthly* editor Bruce Sawford also remembered Pam fondly. "She was the absolute fan and put lots of work into it. One day, she returned to her Mini in Tottenham Court Road and the engine wouldn't start. She took off a shoe and used it to hold the throttle down while she tinkered with the engine. When she got back, a man who was helping her had done a runner and nicked her shoe. Funny how some things you never forget!"

Future *Kung-Fu Monthly* writer and Hong Kong film expert Bey Logan shared the same sentiments. "I had some minor interactions with the late Pam Hadden," said Bey. "She seemed to be quite a character, deeply dissatisfied with everyone except Bruce and Elvis! Regardless, she worked tirelessly to allow fans to receive and share information on their idol, and for that she has a special place in the UK's Bruce Lee fan community."

Spread across five pages in *Kung-Fu Monthly* No.21 and No.22 was an advertising feature for an upcoming book, *The Wisdom of Bruce Lee*. Written by Felix Dennis with former *Oz* and *International Times* colleague Roger Hutchinson, *The Wisdom of Bruce Lee* was to be one of the very first books to focus primarily on Bruce Lee's philosophy.

Though *The Wisdom of Bruce Lee* was credited to Dennis and Hutchinson, it was primarily Hutchinson who did the writing, having been commissioned by Dennis to do so. Felix obviously expected it to sell well and featured it across the five pages in two issues of *Kung-Fu Monthly* as a sort of advertorial. After those two issues, several other issues mentioned a delay and that it was coming soon, though in 1976, *The Wisdom of Bruce Lee* had still not been released, a fact which was somewhat unknown to Hutchinson. Even four decades later, fans were still asking what happened to *The Wisdom of Bruce Lee*. To the surprise of many people, including the author Roger Hutchinson, it emerged that the book was released in 1976 by Pinnacle Books in the USA as a small paperback book with black and white image inserts in the middle. Thanks to the success of *Kung-Fu Monthly*, Felix had started other magazines which would also be successful which would explain how he wound up relocating to the US. Bruce Sawford says, "He sidled off to America with a load of money he made from selling *Personal Computer World* to VNU. Once over there, he launched *Mac User USA*."

Another intriguing tit-bit about *The Wisdom of Bruce Lee*, is apart from the US paperback, a shorter, larger, full colour abridged version was released in the Netherlands, Germany and Spain in their native languages. The layout and design of those books followed the layout and design of the usual *Kung-Fu Monthly* books such as *The Secret Art of Bruce Lee*, The *Unbeatable Bruce Lee*, and the rest of the *Kung-Fu Monthly* library.

At the height of *Kung-Fu Monthly*'s popularity, Bruce Lee Society member and regular contributor Martin Hughes made the trip to visit the publication's offices in London's Goodge Street, only to leave disappointed, He recalled, "I was in London on a school trip in late 1977 with friend and fellow Bruce Lee Society member Mark Burns. We had a couple of hours free, so Mark and I thought we'd visit the *KFM* offices. We worked out the way to 39 Goodge Street as it didn't look to be too far from the museum we were there to visit and I think we wrote to Pam Hadden et al to announce our visit. I expected a pagoda at the very least, rows of typewriters and telex machines, manned by rabid fans like ourselves plus a hotline to Raymond Chow at Concord for the latest on *Game of Death*. Felix Yen and Don Won Ton would beam down from their bamboo thrones and the fair maidens of *KFM* would wait upon us with cups of jasmine tea or some such. Nope. Just an alley, some whiffy bins and a doorway with a push button. We tried the button. '*Kung-Fu Monthly?*' we asked tentatively. 'Er, yeah,' came the reply. 'It's us!' we said, 'Can we come in? PAM..?' 'Pam's not in,' said the voice at the other end,

BRITAIN'S FIRST BRUCE LEE CONVENTION 1979

THOUGH THE MASTER IS GONE HE WILL NOT BE FORGOTTEN

Saturday May 19th at the Acklam Hall, Acklam Road, London W10.
Tickets £3.25 (Society members £3.00) from Kung-Fu Monthly, 14 Rathbone Place, London W1
BE QUICK -- THERE'S VERY FEW LEFT!

'There's nobody here.' 'Er, um. Oh well,' we thought and finding the door unlocked, we pushed it open. We found a long uncarpeted stair case, bare walls and box after box of *KFM*'s latest album of Bruce Lee quotes and pictures. I wish that we'd nicked a few boxes now, but we were a fair walk away from the train station and notionally under the supervision of a slightly camp RE teacher."

In March 1977, H. Bunch Associates moved out of their offices at 39 Goodge Street and moved into new, larger offices at 14 Rathbone Place. As Dick Pountain explained, "We'd run out of space after *Kung-Fu Monthly* and *Hi-Fi Choice* became successful and we wanted to acquire or launch more magazines like *Which Bike* and *Personal Computer World*. It tripled the amount of space we had."

Kung-Fu Monthly, with the help of The Bruce Lee Society, organised the UK's First Official Bruce Lee Convention in 1979. Originally it was scheduled to be held at The Acklam Hall in London's Notting Hill Gate on Saturday 19th May 1979 but was later changed to the larger capacity London University Union building, due to the sheer number of applications for tickets. The event was sold out and the hundreds of people who showed up on the day without tickets had to be turned away.

As well as tables of merchandise and films shown on the big screen, Felix thought it would be a great idea to feature a martial arts demonstration. As Bruce Sawford remembers, "We decided to hire a local Kung Fu club to do a demo on stage and halfway through they summoned me onto the stage to hold this concrete slab that someone was going to

A merchandise stall at the Second Annual Bruce Lee Convention held at the Gaumont State Theatre, Kilburn High Road in London on Saturday 19th July 1980. *Photograph courtesy of Tony Lundberg.*

kick in half. I was holding onto it and had no idea how to do it, because there is a technique to it, and this guy went flying across the stage, jumped into it and went smack into my face." Instead of enjoying the rest of the convention, Sawford spent the majority of it being patched up in the local hospital.

The event was an enormous success, both in terms of fan satisfaction and in revenue. After the convention and back at the office, illustrator Mikki Rain, who once worked at H. Bunch Associates and attended the convention recalled, "He was sitting there at his desk with bags of money around him, with a picture of Bruce Lee in the background and this sort of insane grin on his face."

More successful conventions and film festivals followed, until a late cancellation of the 1981 convention, put a halt on future events.

Bruce Sawford was more involved with the second convention held in 1980 but even that was not without incident. Bruce recalled, "I organised the second convention in Edgware Road. The highlight was that we had a Chuck Norris imitator and a Bruce Lee imitator and they recreated the Coliseum fight on stage. When it finished, the Norris imitator turned to me as he left the stage and asked, 'Where's my money?' Felix was busy counting it back at the office and 'Chuck' was last seen boarding a cab in that direction. I understand he got paid. We also had Bruce Lee's brother Robert singing along to backing tracks from his latest album at the time. My wife (to be), Nicola, created a thousand Bruce Lee Snack Boxes, all containing a boiled egg which unfortunately had not been hard boiled. We had to dispense with a thousand eggs by the end of the evening."

So successful were the events of 1979 and 1980, other companies began to organise rival conventions to take place weeks before the *Kung-Fu Monthly* ones.

As well as the convention, 1979 was the year of another major milestone in the history of *Kung-Fu Monthly* - the publication of the fiftieth issue of the magazine. With *Kung-Fu Monthly* No.50, was a flexible 7" vinyl disc containing an interview with actor James Coburn, which they decided to include after receiving so many requests for it after it was played at the 1979 convention.

The Seventies had been a mixed bag for H. Bunch Associates. The start of the decade foretold disaster but by the end of it, Felix Dennis was richer than even he possibly imagined.

KUNG-FU MONTHLY
THE ARCHIVE SERIES

THE POSTER MAGAZINES - VOLUME ONE

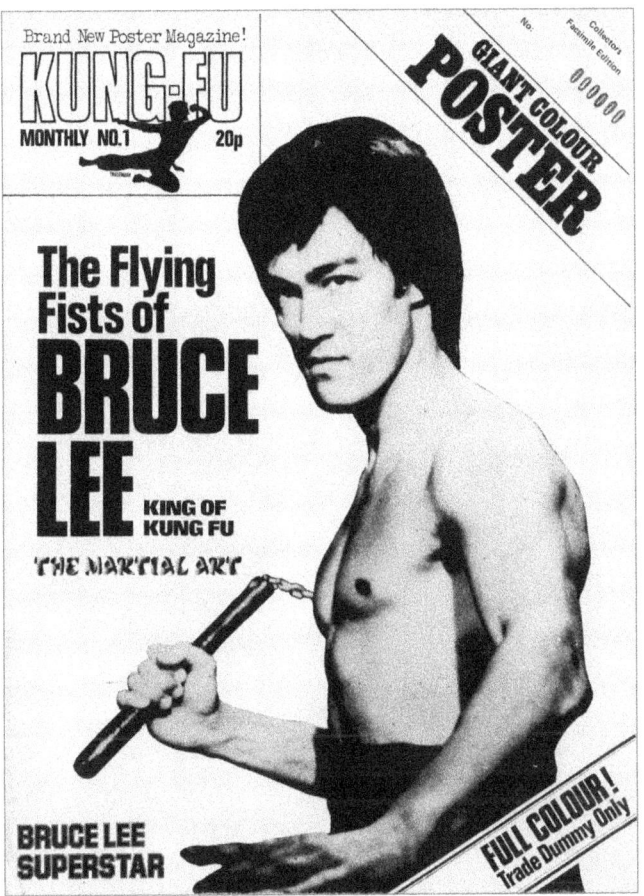

1974

EDITORIAL

Hi there Kung Fu fans...
Well, here it is... your very first issue of *Kung-Fu Monthly* - and what an issue!
In the wise words of our featured fighting superstar, Bruce Lee, "It has to be real and natural..." and that's exactly what we aim to bring you every month - Kung Fu, real and natural with no holds barred!
Real information, real facts, real tips and expert hints on the Chinese 'martial art' of attack and defence. Not forgetting the incredible poster pictures and photographs we have lined up to batter your eyeballs and bludgeon your brain in this and all our forthcoming issues. Action shots, exclusive stills and portrait pin-ups - you'll find 'em all in *Kung-Fu Monthly*, naturally!
It's natural, too, that we should have chosen the late great "Little Dragon," (Bruce Lee's Chinese name literally translated), to feature in *Kung-Fu Monthly* No.1. Bruce was undis-

putedly the global King of Kung Fu. More than any other fan, Bruce Lee was responsible for bringing the mysterious secrets and deadly art of Kung Fu to the Western World.

A master Kung Fu fighter whilst still in his teens, Bruce always believed in his eventual success. Born in America and raised in Hong Kong, he alone understood the tremendous potential that the Oriental 'martial arts' possessed in the West. By a combination of grim determination, unbelievable fitness and unshakeable faith, he persuaded first, the Hong Kong movie industry, and finally, Hollywood itself, to sit up and take notice.

Had he lived, Bruce would undoubtedly have been the biggest movie star to have emerged for many years. Tragically, though, as you will read for yourself, Bruce Lee is now dead. In his thirty short years, he had climbed from the gutters of Hong Kong to the heights of superstardom. In this first issue of *Kung-Fu Monthly* we salute Bruce "Little Dragon" Lee - the fittest man the world has ever known.

That's all from me this month...

Felix Yen
Editor-in-Chief

BRUCE LEE: THE KING OF KUNG FU

For untold centuries, the deadliest martial art of them all - Kung Fu - was the lethal secret code riding the lives of countless millions throughout the mysterious East. Known only to the iron-fisted monks of China's legendary Shaolin Temple, Kung Fu was kept closely hidden on pain of death from the eyes of outsiders eager to learn its awesome powers.

But in less than a year, Lee Hsiao Lung - better known as Bruce Lee, the 'Little Dragon' - single-handedly plucked Kung Fu from the undiscovered temples of the Orient and unleashed it around the globe in what has now become the Kung Fu Revolution.

It took Bruce Lee - the boy from Hong Kong who grew up into the fittest, and deadliest, man in the world - just one film to gain the elusive fame and riches which most actors only dream of. But then again the Little Dragon was far more than a mere actor. Bruce Lee was the King of Kung Fu!

Born in San Francisco in 1940, the son of a famous Chinese opera singer, Bruce moved to the teeming capital of Asia, Hong Kong, where he became a child star in the growing Eastern film industry. Strangely enough, his early producers decided to call Bruce's very first film *The Birth of Mankind*. Little did they know how right they were!

Those who knew Bruce as a child say that he was a cheeky, stubborn lad, but also very clever. More important still though, the Little Dragon was always a loner and it was this fact which drew him towards the personal training and discipline of the martial arts.

It was the famous Kung Fu master Yip Man who taught Bruce most of his basic skills, but it was not long before the youngster was matching skills with his teacher. Whenever the serious young student learned a new skill - or thought he had - he would prowl the rough and ready streets of the city looking for a fight so he could try out what he had just

been taught. Often he would lose to bigger and older opponents, but even at this early stage of his incredible fighting career, Bruce was never afraid to enter a fight.

Yip Man, acknowledged to be one of the greatest authorities on the subject, was a master of the Wing Chun branch of the Chinese martial arts, which Bruce mastered before going on to develop his own personal style. This he dubbed Jeet Kune Do, or Quick Fist.

At the age of 19, Bruce left Hong Kong to study for a degree in philosophy at the University of Seattle in America. As he was quite poor at this time, he decided to earn some extra money by putting to use Yip Man's expert training and teaching the martial arts. But Bruce soon found himself using his skills to survive! By the time his school was established he had taken on - and beaten - the leaders of several Japanese Karate colleges already operating in Seattle who had tried to force the 'new boy' out of their territory.

It was while studying at Seattle that Bruce met a young American girl called Linda, the girl he would eventually make his wife.

After graduating, Bruce won several parts in Hollywood movies, but his real love was Kung Fu and his martial arts school. As more and more Americans heard of his fighting fists and saw his plank smashing exhibitions, his fame exploded and stars such as James Coburn, Steve McQueen and Lee Marvin were travelling long distances to sit at the feet of the Little Dragon.

At one of his famous displays - in Long Beach, California - Bruce was spotted by a Hollywood producer and immediately signed up to play Kato in the long-running *Green Hornet*

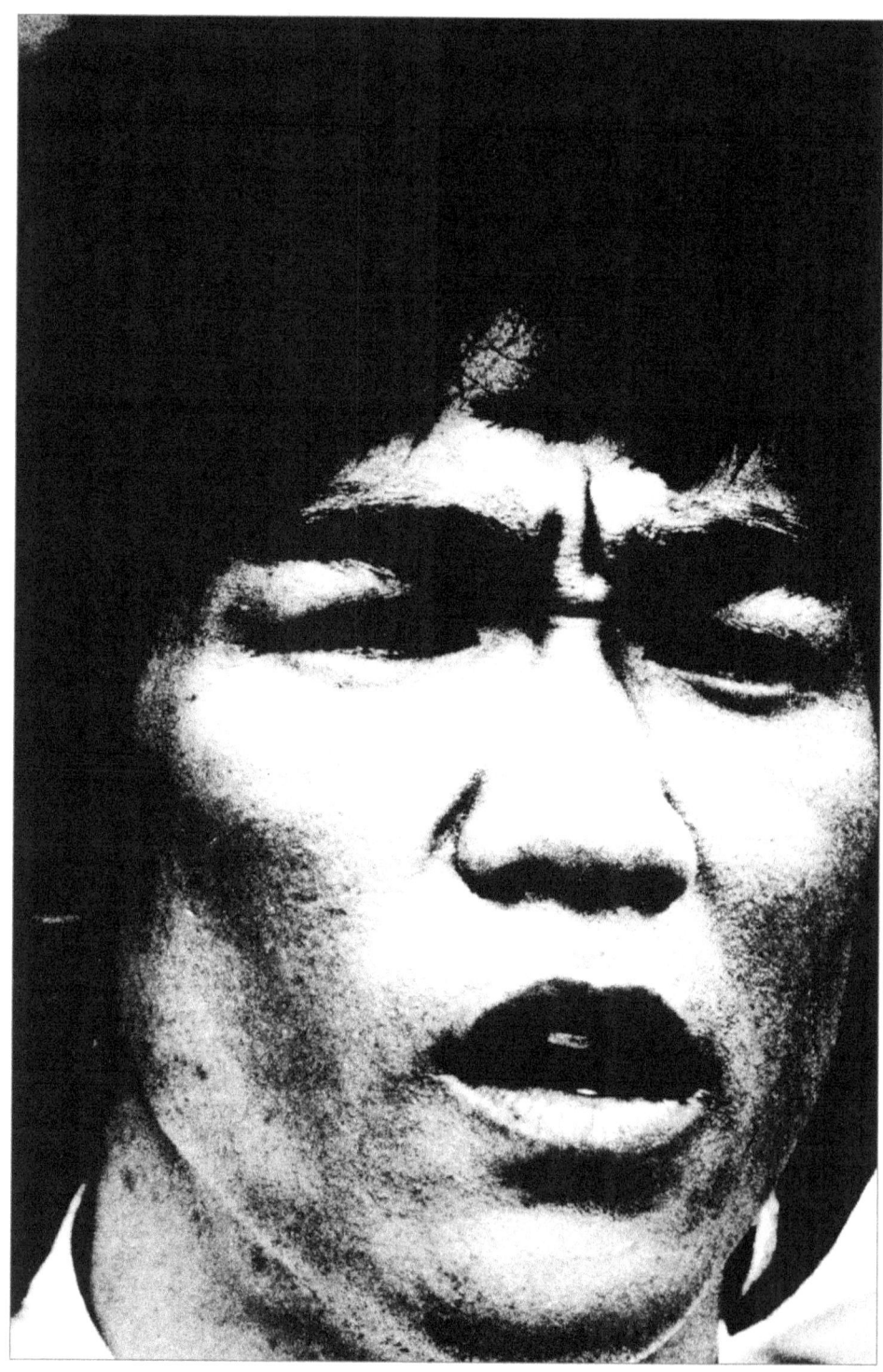

television series. A success in the States, the series caused havoc in Hong Kong when it was shown and the Bruce Lee legend was born.

With the Hong Kong fans crying out for a glimpse of their idol, Bruce and Linda returned 'home' in 1968. "It sure was an experience," said Bruce, overwhelmed by his homecoming welcome. "I made several appearances with the largest radio and television stations. People flocked around me wherever I went."

Bruce returned to the States for more television appearances until the ecstatic screams from Hong Kong became too loud to ignore. "One day a radio announcer asked me if I would do a movie there," he recalled. "When I replied that I would if the price was right, I began to get calls from producers in Hong Kong and Taiwan."

Back to Hong Kong, to producer Raymond Chow of the Golden Harvest film company, and to the biggest movie ever made in the whole of Asia... *The Big Boss*!

"I didn't expect *The Big Boss* to break any kind of record," confessed the sensational new superstar, "but I did expect it to make money." Make money it certainly did... 3.2million Hong Kong dollars in that city alone. And box office records the length and breadth of the Far East smashed like they'd been hit with a blow from those flying fists.

Next came the fabulous *Fist of Fury* which immediately set about destroying all the records recently set by *The Big Boss*. On opening night in Singapore, ticket touts were getting £15 for £1 seats and eventually the movie had to be put off for a week because the fans had caused a huge traffic jam outside the cinema! Bruce, who sat in at the premiere as an unrecognised paying customer, had this to say about it: "The fans hardly made any noise in the beginning, but at the end, they were in a frenzy and began clapping and clamouring."

With each new Bruce Lee movie setting the East alight, Hollywood was not slow to realise the mistake they'd made in allowing the Little Golden Dragon to return to his homeland. Every week they flew into Hong Kong waving multi-million dollar contracts and fighting over Bruce's signature.

The lucky company - and how lucky they were - was Warner Bros. Sparing no expense, they laid the finest Hollywood film experience and know-how at the feet of the Little Dragon, giving him full opportunity to amaze the world with Kung Fu. The rest is history. *Enter the Dragon* exploded onto cinema screens around the globe, making the lonely boy from the crowded streets and alleys of Hong Kong the highest paid superstar of all time!

How did he do it? How did this small - just 5'7" - innocent-looking young man rise sensationally almost overnight to a fame unmatched even by kings?

The simple answer is that Bruce was real; everything he did on the screen he could have done to enemies out on the streets. Unlike James Bond and the other glamorous cinema super heroes, Bruce scorned the cheap gimmicks and trick photography of Hollywood. "Everything must be real," he would say, "Everything must be natural."

Bruce lived as tough and demanding a life off-screen as he did while thrilling movie fans of the world. His secret was his superb body, as graceful and supple as it was rock hard. When Bruce slashed out with his iron muscles he was unbeatable... by anyone!

Once on Hong Kong television, a movie director, Lo Wei, claimed Bruce had threatened him with a knife. "If I had wanted to kill Lo Wei," the Little Dragon replied, "I would not have used a knife; two fingers would have been enough."

Bruce's mansion in Hong Kong was really nothing more than a luxurious gymnasium where he would tune his body, developing his strength and reflexes for hours on end. Each day his tortuous work-out included a three mile run.

One device he was especially fond of was a box which strapped to his waist with two electrodes connected to his head. When switched on it would make the wearer extremely tired after just five minutes of training, thus helping to build up stamina.

"Some martial artists are now going to Hong Kong to be in the movies," said the Fittest Man In the World after he had reached the pinnacle of fame. "They think they can be lucky too. Well, I don't believe in pure luck. You have to create your own luck. Some guys may not believe it, but I spent hours perfecting what I did."

"I don't want to do anything half way, it has to be perfect. To be good, I have to spend a lot of time practicing. My minimum daily training is two hours; this includes running, special weight-training, kicking and hitting the light and heavy bags. I really dig exercise."

"I feel that I want to be The Best Martial Artist, not just for the sake of the movies but because this is my interest."

Tragically, this very fitness proved to be the fatal chink in the Little Dragon's iron-clad armour, and on July 20th this year - the same day that *Fist of Fury* opened in London to a packed house - the world was stunned by the death of Bruce Lee.

Doctors in Hong Kong were at first baffled and could find no apparent reason for his death. However it soon became painfully clear that Bruce had suffered a brain haemorrhage caused by an accidental overdose of body-building pills. The fittest man in the world had pushed his physique to the limits, and for the first time in his fantastic career, had lost.

Bruce had two funerals; the first a symbolic one in Hong Kong where 120,000 distraught fans packed the streets which he loved, to catch a final glimpse of the Little Dragon. A special plane flew his body back to Seattle where he was buried. Among his pall bearers were his former pupils Steve McQueen, James Coburn and Lee Marvin.

The Little Dragon - movie superstar, athlete, artist - died for his art; an art which will live on in legend far into the future. On a *Fist of Fury* poster in London, one of his millions of devoted fans scrawled the ultimate tribute to the King of Kung-Fu; above Bruce's name he added one line which read: "The Late Great..."

BRUCE LEE: SUPERSTAR

Never in the glittering history of world cinema has there been such a sensation as Bruce Lee.

From the first stunning shot to each breathtaking climax, the fantastic Kung-Fu action grips the audience in a steel vice. When Eastern fans rioted in the streets after a taste of the Little Dragon's deadly power, movie producers in the West shook their heads and said, "No, it couldn't happen here."

But happen it did! One giant close-up of Bruce's brain-piercing battle stare is enough to drive anyone into a frenzy... no matter which part of the globe you come from!

It was *The Big Boss*, a gripping story of gang warfare in the Far East, which overnight turned Kung-Fu champion Bruce Lee into the screen idol of millions throughout the world.

Shot on location in the streets of steamy Bangkok, the tough, violent capital of Thailand, it tells how one man takes on the Big Boss of a huge drugs and vice ring... and wins!

In some of the most exciting action ever filmed, Bruce - playing a young factory worker Cheng - chops and hacks his way through an army of hired killers until he finally comes face to face with the Big Boss. In the final scene, Bruce, unarmed but for the deadly power of Kung Fu, kills the boss and smashes his empire.

Although already immensely popular on Hong Kong television for his portrayal of Kato in *The Green Hornet* television series, the film rocketed Bruce to superstardom throughout the East, breaking all-time box office records in every country it was shown.

FIST OF FURY

With *The Big Boss* playing to packed houses and Kung Fu sweeping a dozen countries, it was no easy task for Bruce to come up with a second film that would better his first starring role. But better it he did, and *Fist of Fury* immediately smashed every box office record that had been set only months before by *The Big Boss*!

Set at the turn of the century in Shanghai, *Fist of Fury* is based on a true story - the murder of a Chinese martial arts teacher by treachery, and his student's fight to bring justice and revenge to the assassins. However Bruce, as the student Chen, finds himself up against not just two murderers, but a whole Japanese Kung Fu school! Secretly he enters the school, defeats both the chief instructor and a famed Russian Kung Fu expert, and fights a savagely violent duel with the school principal.

Using for the first time the famous 'toggle clubs' - two heavy 18 inch long wooden clubs and joined by a foot of iron chain (a Bruce Lee trademark in later films) - Chen avenges his master's death by killing his opponent. "I had to use some sort of weapon," said Bruce after the release of the movie. "After all, that guy was coming for me with a sword, and no man can use bare fists against swords." *Fist of Fury* sealed Bruce's success. Made for just 200,000 dollars, it grossed a million dollars in Asia alone... and it's still going strong!

Although Bruce's third film, *Way of the Dragon*, has not as yet reached Western screens, we can assure you it is every bit as exciting as the other Little Dragon classics.

Forming his own film production company, Bruce moved the stare 'n' tear Kung Fu action to international Rome to stand against an ugly army of Italian gangsters and American Karate killers.

In two hours of high-powered beatings and battles, Bruce single-handedly scatters a gang of standover henchmen armed to the teeth with iron bars and chains, escapes death at the hands of hired assassins and leads a band of Chinese waiters against a criminal stronghold. As a climax, Bruce fights a gladiator battle in the famous Coliseum against an international Karate expert.

THE WAY OF THE DRAGON

When Bruce told the public he expected *Way of the Dragon* to make more than five million dollars in Hong Kong alone, the movie critics thought he was mad. But it did - a record $5,400,000.

"It was different from the other movies," explained Bruce. "I wrote the script, had the starring role, directed it and produced it!" The Little Dragon was learning other tricks to add to his Kung Fu skills!

With Bruce a national hero and millions of fans in the thrilling grip of Kung Fu, Hollywood's top producers were beating on the Little Dragon's door and waving multi-million dollar contracts.

In 1972, Bruce signed with Warner Bros, for a record budget movie produced by his old friend Fred Weintraub. The biggest film crew ever assembled in Hollywood was flown out to Hong Kong and the most breathtaking Martial Arts epic of them all - *Enter the Dragon* - was born.

THE ENTER DRAGON

Bruce, playing Lee, the top student at Hong Kong's Shaolin Temple, is recruited by an international intelligence organisation to crack an enormous vice and opium racket controlled from a sinister island fortress.

With the help of American Karate stars John Saxon and Jim Kelly, Bruce explodes into Kung-Fu action far below the steel fortress in an amazing network of underground caves and secret passages. In a hair-raising chase after vice king Han through the maze of tunnels, Bruce carves a bloody path through an army of highly trained guards... all with his famous flashing fists of fury and his heart-stopping battle cry!

Finally, he fights to the death with Han, a one-armed monster with a lethal steel claw, and leaves him speared on a huge stake, his criminal empire in ruins.

Tragically, *Enter the Dragon*, the greatest exhibition of Kung Fu techniques ever filmed, was to be Bruce's last film. On its release in England and America, it took the western world by storm and, if he had lived on, Bruce Lee would have been the highest-paid star in cinema history!

Never was a film made like *Enter the Dragon*, and with the Little Dragon now gone, there will never be another.

"If I wanted to kill a man, I wouldn't have to use a knife... just two fingers."

As the fittest man in the world, Bruce's feats of strength soon became legendary. One famous example occurred on Hong Kong television when he was asked to demonstrate Tameshiwari - breaking technique. When interviewed, Bruce said it was easy to break a plank with a chop. He then held his hand only four inches from a board and calmly smashed it with a straight thrust of his fingertips!

THE MARTIAL ART

Kung Fu Wu-Su - to give the deadliest art of them all its full title - began more than 4000 years ago when Huang Di, ancient China's ferocious Yellow Emperor, started searching for a quick way of training his own private army. He hit on Kung Fu, and from then on for a dozen centuries, Huang Di and his sons ruled supreme which was no easy job considering the hordes of bandits and cut-throats roaming the land.

But after 2000 years, the fearsome art was forgotten by the people of China - that is until an Indian monk named Dat Mor Jo Si happened to visit the now legendary Shaolin Temple, perched high on the Lau Fou San mountain in Southern China, in the year 900. Jo Si (meaning in English 'First Master') found the Shaolin monks weak and helpless, living in constant fear of roving pirates and robber barons.

He taught them Kung-Fu so they could protect themselves. As the monks travelled

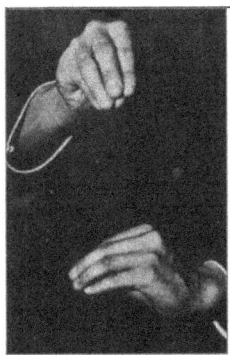  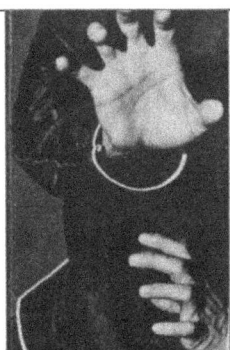 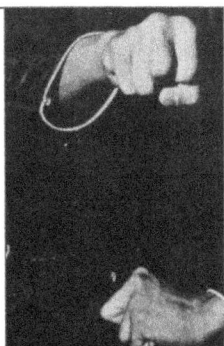

Crane's Beak *Snake Strike* *Tiger Claw* *Dragon's Head*

the length and breadth of China, the Martial Arts once more became a way of life for millions.

Although no-one could ever match his Kung Fu combat skills, Bruce was always willing to pass on the secret of his fighting success to others. "You must be fierce, but have patience at the same time," he would tell his pupils. "Most important of all, you must have complete determination. The worst opponent you can come across is one whose aim has become an obsession. For instance, if a man has decided that he is going to bite off your nose no matter what happens to him in the process, the chances are he will succeed in doing it. He may be severely beaten up too, but that will not stop him. That is the real fighter."

Now thanks to the Little Dragon, Bruce Lee, this secret code, known only to the Chinese for so many centuries, has been revealed to the world.

But what exactly is Kung Fu? In point of fact, Kung Fu Wu-Su is the general term used to explain all the Chinese Martial Arts. This includes fencing, Chinese boxing, sword and stick fighting, together with the well known foot and fist defences. The term Kung Fu is used in the same way that Karate describes

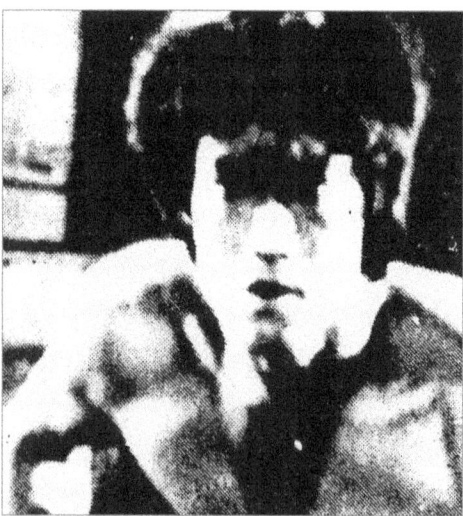

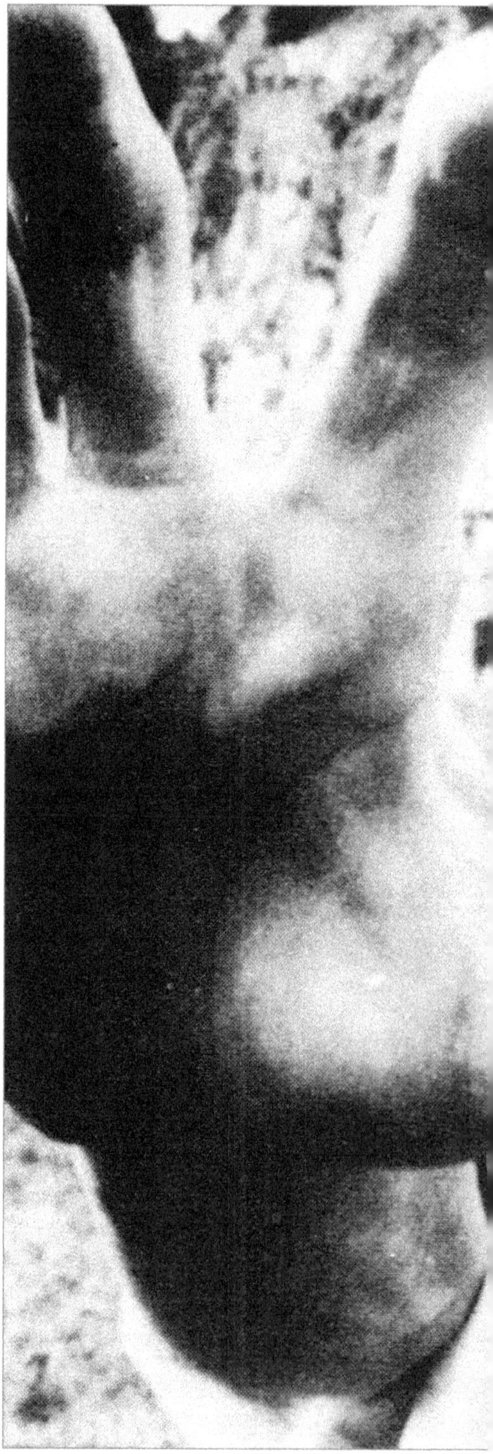

the whole range of the Japanese Martial Arts.

Translated, Kung Fu Wu-Su means a weapon master - Wu-Su, to use one's body, stick or sword as a weapon, and 'Kung Fu,' a person who has mastered his weapons. When applied to the Martial Arts though, Kung Fu Wu-Su means something far more than just a weapons expert. It describes a whole way of life based on a strict, unbreakable code.

And the code is this: No disciple shall kill or injure anyone deliberately, even though he has the power to easily do so.

Kung Fu is not a child's game but rather an art which takes years of study and practice to master. An example of how serious it is can be seen in the traditions of the fighting monks of the Shaolin Temple. When each monk had reached a certain level of training, he would hug a red hot cauldron so that the marks of the tiger and the dragon would be burnt into his arms forever!

Today the Chinese Martial Arts can be roughly divided into two different schools - the North and South Chinese. In the North where the people are big and strong, the Kung Fu style is mainly kicking and gouging. On the other hand, the people of the South are lighter, so they mainly use the fist.

In addition to these two schools there are of course several less important Kung Fu training courses, such as Korean Kempo and Hapkido (often called Aikido).

Bruce's own style - Jeet Kune Do - takes the best from all the different Kung-Fu schools. And as Bruce owned the world's biggest Martial Arts library, he certainly knew what to pick!

Jeet Kune Do, based on the North Chinese style, uses kicking rather than punching. But the real secret of its super deadliness is where you aim the kicks.

Bruce once explained this on Hong Kong television, "There are lots of places on the human body which are obvious spots to attack such as the stomach or the head," said the Little Dragon. "But if you aim for somewhere unexpected, then your opponent can't defend himself in time.

"A kick of only 60 pounds pressure on the kneecap can dislocate the leg. Do it harder and you can smash the kneecap. Your opponent is as good as dead."

This then is the secret behind Kung Fu. But of course there is far more to the Martial Arts than knowing just that. There are over 325 movements alone which have to be learned and practiced, practiced, practiced.

The main kicks Bruce used to destroy opponents often twice his size were the Groin Kick, the Front Through the Heart Kick, the Shovel Leg Kick and the Tiger Tail Kick. With his fists, he used the Crane's Beak, the Snake Strike, the Tiger Claw and the Dragon's Head. His stances included the Deer, the Bird and the Monkey.

Pretty names... but all pretty deadly!

The King of Kung Fu was always being challenged to fight in the streets of Hong Kong by those who thought his deadliness was only for the screen. Mostly he would ignore the challengers, but occasionally he would decide to teach them a lesson. Once on a movie set, a young karate student walked up to him and said, "I don't think you're so fast. I can beat you." Bruce raised his hands and stamped his feet three times - the signal he was ready to fight - and with one lightning kick to the face, laid his opponent on the floor.

1974

EDITORIAL

Hi there Kung Fu fans...
Well, here it is... your very first issue of *Kung-Fu Monthly* - and what an issue!
In the wise words of our featured fighting superstar, Bruce Lee, "It has to be real and natural..." and that's exactly what we aim to bring you every month - Kung Fu, real and natural with no holds barred!
Real information, real facts, real tips and expert hints on the Chinese 'martial art' of attack and defence. Not forgetting the incredible poster pictures and photographs we have lined up to batter your eyeballs and bludgeon your brain in this and all our forthcoming issues. Action shots, exclusive stills and portrait pin-ups - you'll find 'em all in *Kung-Fu Monthly*, naturally!
It's natural, too, that we should have chosen the late great Little Dragon, (Bruce Lee's Chinese name literally translated), to feature in *Kung-Fu Monthly* No.1. Bruce was undis-

putedly the global king of Kung Fu. More than any other fan, Bruce Lee was responsible for bringing the mysterious secrets and deadly art of Kung Fu to the Western World.

A master Kung Fu fighter whilst still in his teens, Bruce always believed in his eventual success. Born in America and raised in Hong Kong, he alone understood the tremendous potential that the Oriental 'martial arts' possessed in the West. By a combination of grim determination, unbelievable fitness and unshakeable faith, he persuaded first the Hong Kong movie industry, and finally, Hollywood itself, to sit up and take notice.

Had he lived, Bruce would undoubtedly have been the biggest movie star to have emerged for many years. Tragically, though, as you will read for yourself, Bruce Lee is now dead. In his thirty short years he had climbed from the gutters of Hong Kong to the heights of superstardom. In this first issue of *Kung-Fu Monthly*, we salute Bruce "Little Dragon" Lee - the fittest man the world has ever known.

That's all from me this month...

Felix Yen

Felix Yen
Editor-in-Chief

BRUCE LEE: THE KING OF KUNG FU

For untold centuries the deadliest martial art of them all - Kung Fu - was the lethal secret code riding the lives of countless millions throughout the mysterious East. Known only to the iron-fisted monks of China's legendary Shaolin Temple, Kung Fu was kept closely hidden on pain of death from the eyes of outsiders eager to learn its awesome powers.

But in less than a year, Lee Hsiao Lung - better known as Bruce Lee, the 'Little Dragon' - single-handedly plucked Kung Fu from the undiscovered temples of the Orient and unleashed it around the globe in what has now become the Kung Fu Revolution.

It took Bruce Lee - the boy from Hong Kong who grew up into the fittest, and deadliest, man in the world - just one film to gain the elusive fame and riches which most actors only dream of. But then again the Little Dragon was far more than a mere actor. Bruce Lee was the King of Kung Fu!

Born in San Francisco in 1940, the son of a famous Chinese opera singer, Bruce moved to the teeming capital of Asia, Hong Kong, where he became a child star in the growing Eastern film industry. Strangely enough, his early producers decided to call Bruce's very first film *The Birth of Mankind*. Little did they know how right they were!

Those who knew Bruce as a child say that he was a cheeky, stubborn lad, but also very clever. More important still though, the Little Dragon was always a loner and it was this fact which drew him towards the personal training and discipline of the martial arts.

It was the famous Kung Fu master Yip Man who taught Bruce most of his basic skills, but it was not long before the youngster was matching skills with his teacher. Whenever the serious young student learned a new skill - or thought he had - he would prowl the rough and ready streets of the city looking for a fight so he could try out what he had just

been taught. Often he would lose to bigger and older opponents, but even at this early stage of his incredible fighting career, Bruce was never afraid to enter a fight.

Yip Man, acknowledged to be one of the greatest authorities on the subject, was a master of the Wing Chun branch of the Chinese martial arts, which Bruce mastered before going on to develop his own personal style. This he dubbed Jeet Kune Do, or Quick Fist.

At the age of 19, Bruce left Hong Kong to study for a degree in philosophy at the University of Seattle in America. As he was quite poor at this time, he decided to earn some extra money by putting to use Yip Man's expert training and teaching the martial arts. But Bruce soon found himself using his skills to survive! By the time his school was established he had taken on - and beaten - the leaders of several Japanese Karate colleges already operating in Seattle who had tried to force the 'new boy' out of their territory.

It was while studying at Seattle that Bruce met a young American girl called Linda, the girl he would eventually make his wife.

After graduating, Bruce won several parts in Hollywood movies, but his real love was Kung-Fu and his martial arts school. As more and more Americans heard of his fighting fists and saw his plank smashing exhibitions, his fame exploded and stars such as James Coburn, Steve McQueen and Lee Marvin were travelling long distances to sit at the feet of the Little Dragon.

At one of his famous displays - in Long Beach, California - Bruce was spotted by a Holly-

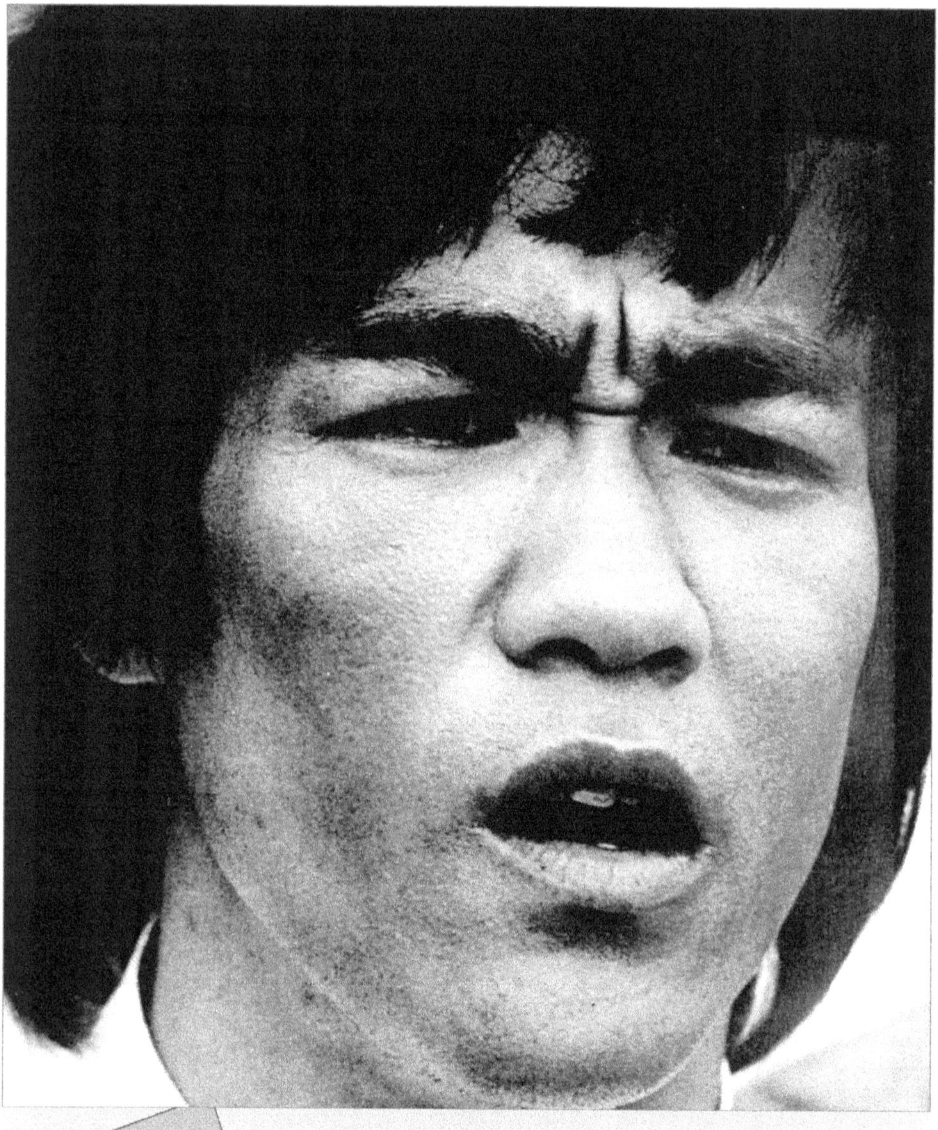

Special Offer!
FABULOUS GIANT SIZE GLOSSY
PHOTOGRAPHS OF
BRUCE LEE

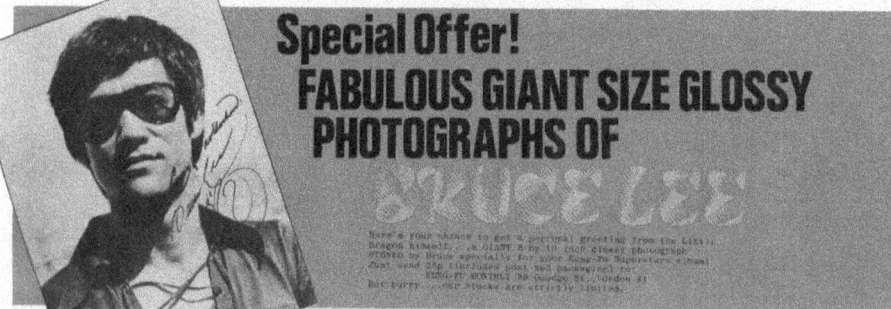

wood producer and immediately signed up to play Kato in the long-running *Green Hornet* television series. A success in the States, the series caused havoc in Hong Kong when it was shown and the Bruce Lee legend was born.

With the Hong Kong fans crying out for a glimpse of their idol, Bruce and Linda returned 'home' in 1968. "It sure was an experience," said Bruce, overwhelmed by his homecoming welcome. "I made several appearances with the largest radio and television stations. People flocked around me wherever went."

Bruce returned to the States for more television appearances until the ecstatic screams from Hong Kong became too loud to ignore. "One day a radio announcer asked me if I would do a movie there," he recalled. "When I replied that I would if the price was right, I began to get calls from producers in Hong Kong and Taiwan."

Back to Hong Kong, to producer Raymond Chow of the Golden Harvest film company, and to the biggest movie ever made in the whole of Asia... *The Big Boss*!

"I didn't expect The Big Boss to break any kind of record," confessed the sensational new superstar, "but I did expect it to make money." Make money it certainly did... 3.2million Hong Kong dollars in that city alone. And box office records the length and breadth of the Far East smashed like they'd been hit with a blow from those flying fists.

Next came the fabulous *Fist of Fury* which immediately set about destroying all the records recently set by *The Big Boss*. On opening night in Singapore, ticket touts were getting £15 for £1 seats and eventually the movie had to be put off for a week because the fans had caused a huge traffic jam outside the cinema! Bruce, who sat in at the premiere as an unrecognised paying customer, had this to say about it: "The fans hardly made any noise in the beginning, but at the end they were in a frenzy and began clapping and clamouring."

With each new Bruce Lee movie setting the East alight, Hollywood was not slow to realise the mistake they'd made in allowing the Little Golden Dragon to return to his homeland. Every week they flew into Hong Kong waving multi-million dollar contracts and fighting over Bruce's signature.

The lucky company - and how lucky they were - was Warner Bros. Sparing no expense they laid the finest Hollywood film experience and know-how at the feet of the Little Dragon, giving him full opportunity to amaze the world with Kung Fu. The rest is history. *Enter the Dragon* exploded onto cinema screens around the globe, making the lonely boy from the crowded streets and alleys of Hong Kong the highest paid superstar of all time!

How did he do it? How did this small - just 5'7" - innocent-looking young man rise sensationally almost overnight to a fame unmatched even by kings?

The simple answer is that Bruce was real; everything he did on the screen he could have done to enemies out on the streets. Unlike James Bond and the other glamorous cinema super heroes, Bruce scorned the cheap gimmicks and trick photography of Hollywood. "Every thing must be real," he would say, "Everything must be natural."

Bruce lived as tough and demanding a life off-screen as he did while thrilling movie fans of the world. His secret was his superb body, as graceful and supple as it was rock hard. When Bruce slashed out with his iron muscles he was unbeatable... by anyone!

Once on Hong Kong television, a movie director, Lo Wei, claimed Bruce had threatened him with a knife. "If I had wanted to kill Lo Wei," the Little Dragon replied, "I would not have used a knife; two fingers would have been enough."

Bruce's mansion in Hong Kong was really nothing more than a luxurious gymnasium where he would tune his body, developing his strength and reflexes for hours on end. Each day his tortuous work-out included a three mile run.

One device he was especially fond of was a box which strapped to his waist with two electrodes connected to his head. When switched on it would make the wearer extremely tired after just five minutes of training, thus helping to build up stamina.

"Some martial artists are now going to Hong Kong to be in the movies," said the Fittest Man In the World after he had reached the pinnacle of fame. "They think they can be lucky too. Well, I don't believe in pure luck. You have to create your own luck. Some guys may not believe it, but I spent hours perfecting what I did.

"I dont want to do anything half way, it has to be perfect. To be good, I have to spend a lot of time practicing. My minimum daily training is two hours; this includes running, special weight-training, kicking and hitting the light and heavy bags. I really dig exercise.

"I feel that I want to be The Best Martial Artist, not just for the sake of the movies but because this is my interest."

Tragically, this very fitness proved to be the fatal chink in the Little Dragon's iron-clad armour, and on July 20th this year - the same day that *Fist of Fury* opened in London to a packed house - the world was stunned by the death of Bruce Lee.

Doctors in Hong Kong were at first baffled and could find no apparent reason for his death. However it soon became painfully clear that Bruce had suffered a brain haemorrhage caused by an accidental overdose of body-building pills. The fittest man in the world had pushed his physique to the limits, and for the first time in his fantastic career, had lost.

Bruce had two funerals; the first a symbolic one in Hong Kong where 120,000 distraught fans packed the streets which he loved, to catch a final glimpse of the Little Dragon. A special plane flew his body back to Seattle where he was buried. Among his pall bearers were his former pupils Steve McQueen, James Coburn and Lee Marvin.

BRUCE LEE: SUPERSTAR

The Little Dragon - movie superstar, athlete, artist - died for his art; an art which will live on in legend far into the future. On a *Fist of Fury* poster in London, one of his millions of devoted fans scrawled the ultimate tribute to the King of Kung Fu; above Bruce's name he added one line which read: "The Late Great..."

Never in the glittering history of world cinema has there been such a sensation as Bruce Lee.

From the first stunning shot to each breathtaking climax, the fantastic Kung-Fu action grips the audience in a steel vice. When Eastern fans rioted in the streets after a taste of the Little Dragon's deadly power, movie producers in the West shook their heads and said, "No, it couldn't happen here."

But happen it did! One giant close-up of Bruce's brain-piercing battle stare is enough to drive anyone into a frenzy... no matter which part of the globe you come from!

It was *The Big Boss*, a gripping story of gang warfare in the Far East, which overnight turned Kung Fu champion Bruce Lee into the screen idol of millions throughout the world.

Shot on location in the streets of steamy Bangkok, the tough, violent capital of Thailand, it tells how one man takes on the Big Boss of a huge drugs and vice ring... and wins!

In some of the most exciting action ever filmed, Bruce - playing a young factory worker Cheng - chops and hacks his way through an army of hired killers until he finally comes face to face with the Big Boss. In the final scene, Bruce, unarmed but for the deadly power of Kung Fu, kills the boss and smashes his empire.

Although already immensely popular on Hong Kong television for his portrayal of Kato in *The Greent Hornet* television series, the film rocketed Bruce to superstardom throughout the East, breaking all-time box office records in every country it was shown.

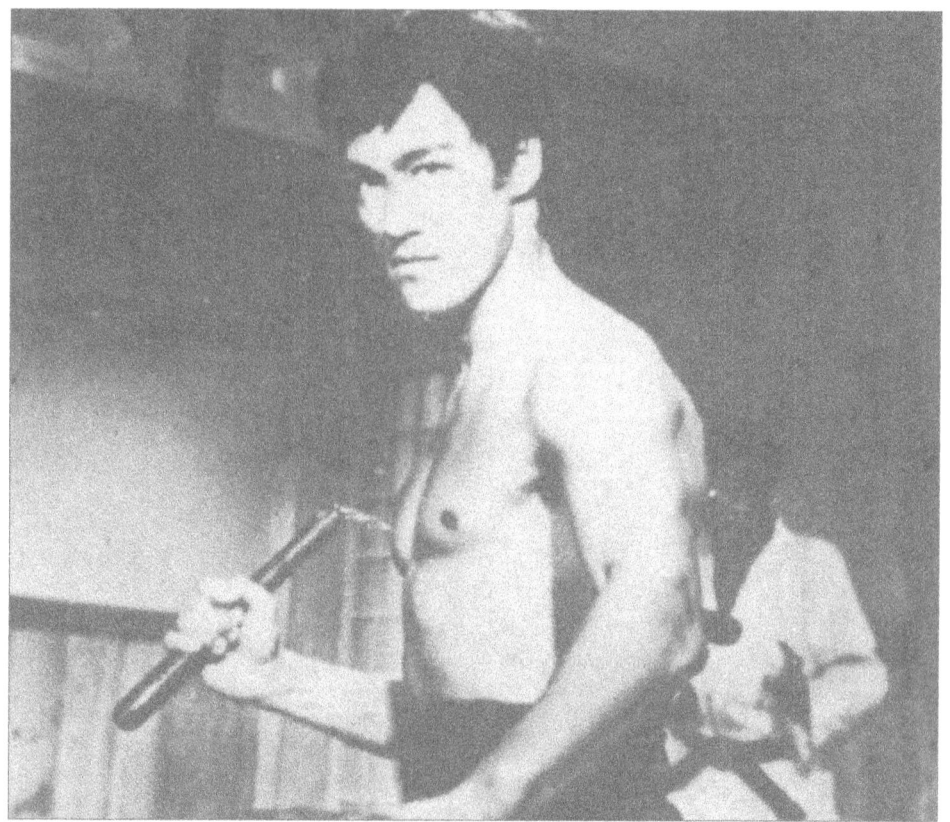

FIST OF FURY

With *The Big Boss* playing to packed houses and Kung Fu sweeping a dozen countries, it was no easy task for Bruce to come up with a second film that would better his first starring role. But better it he did, and *Fist of Fury* immediately smashed every box office record that had been set only months before by *The Big Boss*!

Set at the turn of the century in Shanghai, *Fist of Fury* is based on a true story - the murder of a Chinese martial arts teacher by treachery, and his student's fight to bring justice and revenge to the assassins. However Bruce, as the student Chen, finds himself up against not just two murderers, but a whole Japanese Kung Fu school! Secretly he enters the school, defeats both the chief instructor and a famed Russian Kung Fu expert, and fights a savagely violent duel with the school principal.

Using for the first time the famous 'toggle clubs' - two heavy 18 inch long wooden clubs and joined by a foot of iron chain (a Bruce Lee trademark in later films) - Chen avenges his master's death by killing his opponent. "I had to use some sort of weapon," said Bruce after the release of the movie. "After all, that guy was coming for me with a sword, and no man can use bare fists against swords." Fist of Fury sealed Bruce's success. Made for just 200,000 dollars, it grossed a million dollars in Asia alone... and it's still going strong!

Although Bruce's third film, *Way of the Dragon*, has not as yet reached Western screens, we can assure you it is every bit as exciting as the other Little Dragon classics.

Forming his own film production company, Bruce moved the stare 'n' tear Kung Fu action to international Rome to stand against an ugly army of Italian gangsters and American Karate killers.

In two hours of high-powered beatings and battles, Bruce single-handedly scatters a gang of standover henchmen armed to the teeth with iron bars and chains, escapes death at the hands of hired assassins and leads a band of Chinese waiters against a criminal stronghold. As a climax, Bruce fights a gladiator battle in the famous Coliseum against an international Karate expert.

When Bruce told the public he expected *Way of the Dragon* to make more than five million dollars in Hong Kong alone, the movie critics thought he was mad. But it did - a record $5,400,000.

"It was different from the other movies," explained Bruce. "I wrote the script, had the starring role, directed it and produced it!" The Little Dragon was learning other tricks to add to his Kung Fu skills!

THE WAY OF THE DRAGON

With Bruce a national hero and millions of fans in the thrilling grip of Kung Fu, Hollywood's top producers were beating on the Little Dragon's door and waving multi-million dollar contracts.

In 1972, Bruce signed with Warner Bros, for a record budget movie produced by his old friend Fred Weintraub. The biggest film crew ever assembled in Hollywood was flown out to Hong Kong and the most breathtaking Martial Arts epic of them all - *Enter the Dragon* - was born.

THE ENTER DRAGON

Bruce, playing Lee, the top student at Hong Kong's Shaolin Temple, is recruited by an international intelligence organisation to crack an enormous vice and opium racket controlled from a sinister island fortress.

With the help of American Karate stars John Saxon and Jim Kelly, Bruce explodes into Kung Fu action far below the steel fortress in an amazing network of underground caves and secret passages. In a hair-raising chase after vice king Han through the maze of tunnels, Bruce carves a bloody path through an army of highly trained guards... all with his famous flashing fists of fury and his heart-stopping battle cry!

Finally, he fights to the death with Han, a one-armed monster with a lethal steel claw, and leaves him speared on a huge stake, his criminal empire in ruins.

Tragically, *Enter the Dragon*, the greatest exhibition of Kung Fu techniques ever filmed, was to be Bruce's last film. On its release in England and America, it took the western world by storm and, if he had lived on, Bruce Lee would have been the highest-paid star in cinema history!

Never was a film made like *Enter the Dragon*, and with the Little Dragon now gone, there will never be another.

As the fittest man in the world, Bruce's feats of strength soon became legendary. One famous example occurred on Hong Kong television when he was asked to demonstrate Tameshiwari - breaking technique. When interviewed, Bruce said it was easy to break a plank with a chop. He then held his hand only four inches from a board and calmly smashed it with a straight thrust of his fingertips!

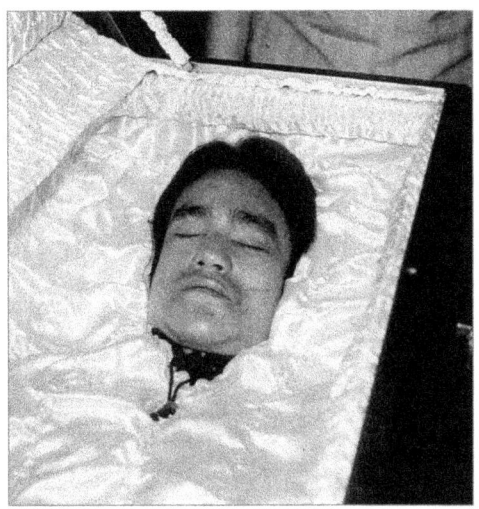

THE MARTIAL ART

Kung Fu Wu-Su - to give the deadliest art of them all its full title - began more than 4000 years ago when Huang Di, ancient China's ferocious Yellow Emperor, started searching for a quick way of training his own private army. He hit on Kung Fu, and from then on for a dozen centuries, Huang Di and his sons ruled supreme which was no easy job considering the hordes of bandits and cut-throats roaming the land. But after 2000 years, the fearsome art was forgotten by the people of China - that is until an Indian monk named Dat Mor Jo Si happened to visit the now legendary Shaolin Temple, perched high on the Lau Fou San mountain in Southern China, in the year 900. Sijo (meaning in English 'First Master') found the Shaolin monks weak and helpless, living in constant fear of roving pirates and robber barons.

He taught them Kung Fu so they could protect themselves. As the monks travelled the length and breadth of China, the Martial Arts once more became a way of life for millions.

Although no-one could ever match his Kung Fu combat skills, Bruce was always willing to pass on the secret of his fighting success to others. "You must be fierce, but have patience at the same time," he would tell his pupils. "Most important of all, you must have complete determination. The worst opponent you can come across is one whose aim has become an obsession. For instance, if a man has decided that he is going to bite off your nose no matter what happens to him in the process, the chances are he will succeed in doing it. He may be severely beaten up too, but that will not stop him. That is the real fighter."

Now thanks to the Little Dragon, Bruce Lee, this secret code, known only to the Chinese for so many centuries, has been revealed to the world.

But what exactly is Kung Fu? In point of fact, Kung Fu Wu-Su is the general term used to explain all the Chinese Martial Arts. This includes fencing, Chinese boxing, sword and stick fighting, together with the well known foot and fist defences. The term Kung Fu is used in the same way that Karate describes the whole range of the Japanese Martial Arts.

Translated, Kung Fu Wu-Su means a weapon master - 'Wu-Su,' to use one's body, stick or sword as a weapon, and 'Kung Fu,' a person who has mastered his weapons. When applied to the Martial Arts though, Kung-Fu Wu-Su means something far more than just a weapons expert. It describes a whole way of life based on a strict, unbreakable code.

And the code is this: No disciple shall kill or injure anyone deliberately, even though he has the power to easily do so.

Kung Fu is not a child's game but rather an art which takes years of study and practice to master. An example of how serious it is can be seen in the traditions of the fighting monks of the Shaolin Temple. When each monk had reached a certain level of training, he would hug a red hot cauldron so that the marks of the tiger and the dragon would be burnt into his arms forever! Today the Chinese Martial Arts can be roughly divided into two different schools - the North and South Chinese. In the North where the people are big and strong, the Kung Fu style is mainly kicking and gouging. On the other hand, the people of the South are lighter, so they mainly use the fist. In addition to these two schools there are of course several less important Kung Fu training courses, such as Korean Kempo and Hapkido (often called Aikido).

Bruce's own style - Jeet Kune Do - takes the best from all the different Kung Fu schools. And as Bruce owned the world's biggest Martial Arts library, he certainly knew what to pick! Jeet Kune Do, based on the North Chinese style, uses kicking rather

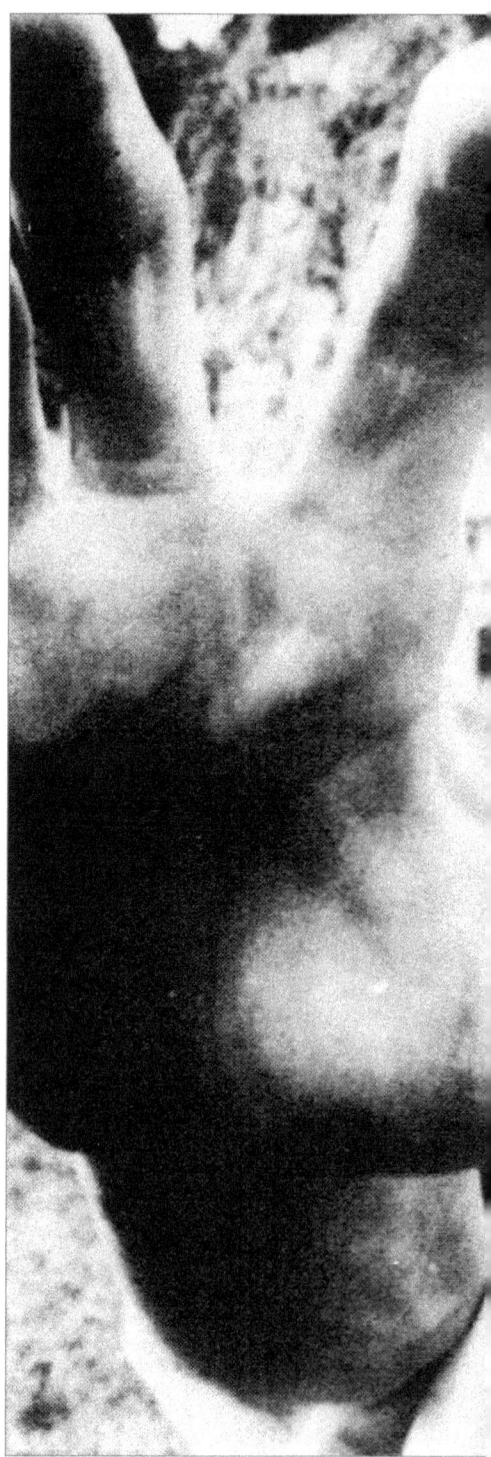

than punching. But the real secret of its super deadliness is where you aim the kicks.

Bruce once explained this on Hong Kong television, "There are lots of places on the human body which are obvious spots to attack such as the stomach or the head," said the Little Dragon. "But if you aim for somewhere unexpected, then your opponent can't defend himself in time.

"A kick of only 60 pounds pressure on the kneecap can dislocate the leg. Do it harder and you can smash the kneecap. Your opponent is as good as dead." This then is the secret behind Kung Fu. But of course there is far more to the Martial Arts than knowing just that. There are over 325 movements alone which have to be learned and practiced, practiced, practiced. The main kicks Bruce used to destroy opponents often twice his size were the Groin Kick, the Front Through the Heart kick, the Shovel Leg Kick and the Tiger Tail Kick. With his fists, he used the Crane's Beak, the Snake Strike, the Tiger Claw and the Dragon's Head. His stances included the Deer, the Bird and the Monkey. Pretty names... but all pretty deadly!

The King of Kung Fu was always being challenged to fight in the streets of Hong Kong by those who thought his deadliness was only for the screen. Mostly he would ignore the challengers, but occasionally he would decide to teach them a lesson. Once on a movie set, a young karate student walked up to him and said, "I don't think you're so fast. I can beat you." Bruce raised his hands and stamped his feet three times - the signal he was ready to fight - and with one lightning kick to the face, laid his opponent on the floor.

  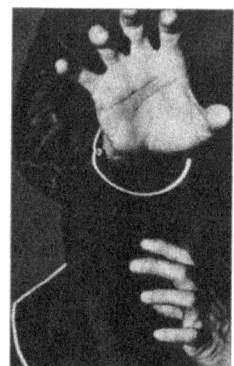 

Crane's Beak　　　Snake Strike　　　Tiger Claw　　　Dragon's Head

02

1974

EDITORIAL

Hi there Kung Fu fans..

Well, here it is... the second issue of *Kung-Fu Monthly*! Our first issue has taken the publishing world by complete surprise! Again and again from newsagents across the country we have heard the same cry: 'Sold Out!' We'd truly like to thank all of you for making *KFM* such an incredible success story, and at the same time apologise to the thousands of you who were unable to obtain copies.

Remember that for *KFM* to have sold out our first issue is proof that although Bruce Lee the man, may be sadly dead, the Spirit of Bruce Lee Lives On! And who is there who would dare to quarrel with that sentiment!

This month we have divided our pages between Bruce Lee and David Carradine, the man who as Caine, has enthralled millions of TV viewers around the world in the Warner Bros/ITV series *Kung Fu*.

David is certainly a very controversial figure, and in one way or another seems to have been a rebel for most of his life. 'Hippie Superstar,' they call him in the press, but there's much more to David than many reviewers and critics would have you believe. Very much the loner in both real life and as Caine, David believes strongly in the profound Kung Fu maxim, "Avoid rather than confront." Over and over again, both in his TV series and in interviews, he has sought to stress the spiritual and mental disciplines of Kung Fu rather than emphasise its physical side. In his own words, "Anyone who I talks about how well he can do Kung Fu, is simply proving he can't do it at all."

Which leads me to a word about the hundreds of requests I have received for information concerning martial arts clubs in Britain. In the next issue of *KFM*, we will be publishing a list of all clubs in the British Isles open to the general public, together with their addresses. Those of you who are genuinely interested in taking up Kung Fu can then write and apply for membership.

Lastly, some really exciting news: Cathay Films have finally authorised the UK release of *Way of the Dragon*, a film produced, written, directed by and starring Bruce Lee! It's showing to packed houses in London's West End at this very moment and we understand that the movie is due to go on general release some time in June. The Way of the Dragon is a superb movie, packed with explosive stare 'n' tear Kung Fu action throughout. Bruce is in devastating form, and personally I rate this as the best Lee film I have ever seen. Don't miss it!

That's all from me this month,

Felix Yen

Felix Yen
Editor-in-Chief

DAVID CARRADINE: THE HIPPIE CROWN PRINCE OF KUNG FU

When a shocked world awoke, barely twelve months ago, to the tragic news of the death of Bruce Lee, the Little Dragon of Kung Fu, millions of devoted fans from every nation were cast into mourning. The Master of the Martial Arts, the man who, virtually single-handedly, had brought the East's deadliest secret out of its age-old seclusion, the Fist of Fury himself, had fought his final bout. Who, asked countless grieving fans, could replace the Master?

Their answer came speedily enough. For while Bruce Lee's Kung Fu prowess was taking the East, and soon the West, by storm, thousands of miles away from Lee's Hong Kong studios, in Hollywood, California, another man was preparing to hold high the banner of the Kung Fu Revolution - David Carradine, Kwai Chang Caine.

Kung Fu is the continuing saga of the adventures of Kwai Chang Caine, played by David Carradine. He is the orphan child of an American father and Chinese mother, who has

been brought up in a Shaolin Temple, the cradle of the Martial Arts, where he has been inducted into Taoist philosophy and the deadly skills of Kung Fu; skills of which his teachers are commanded by ancient ritual, "This art is never to be taught to the people, for it is dangerous in their hands."

Caine is a man filled with humility, versed in the teachings of the temple - avoid before confront, maim before kill - but he is a strong man and a proud one too. Forced, in self-defence, to use his peerless fighting skills against a Prince of the Imperial House, Caine flees China, the home of his mother, his faith and his lighting ability, for his father's land; the distant, and still very wild West of America.

Every so often David goes on a fast which usually lasts up to 21 days. But David is honest about the reasons for it. "It isn't because of any Oriental philosophy," he says. "It's because of my little pot belly." Even a Kung Fu hero has to work at keeping himself in trim!

Once in America, Came begins his personal odyssey through the rugged country of the emerging South-West. Armed with the Taoist philosophies and the Kung Fu martial skills he has learnt in the Temple, Caine goes from town to town dealing with the many and varied problems he encounters. As he has been taught, words must be his first line of defence. Nevertheless, harsh reality decrees that rarely are they effective. Inevitably, men's refusal to accept the truth of his teaching means that Caine must fall back on another set of unshakeable facts: the deadly skills of Kung Fu, against which no opponent can hope to battle for very long.

"I have sworn on the altar of God eternal hostility toward all forms of tyranny over the minds of men. That's always been important to me," says Carradine.

Likewise, Carradine and Caine share a desire for a Libran harmoniousness with the world around them. The aim is for balance, not extremes, for peace, rather than aggression. The very principles of a Shaolin Temple, the perfect basis for a student, and a master of Kung Fu.

If the Caine of the series is above all a loner, then Carradine must, if for none other of his qualifications, be an ideal man to play that demanding role. Son of a Hollywood star, with all the material and social benefits that such a childhood brings with it, David Carradine spent a youth diametrically opposed to the 'good life' available to him.

It would be hard, studying the life of David Carradine the man, not to see the obvious similarities to David Carradine, the actor, playing the role of Kwai Chang Caine.

Like Caine, David Carradine is a vegetarian; he eats no meat whatsoever. His house is filled with vitamin bottles and neither Barbara nor Free eat meat. It is all part, he fells, of his refusal to kill living creatures, even for food. He does, on the other hand, have one definite obsession when it comes to his stomach: around thirty cups of coffee every day!

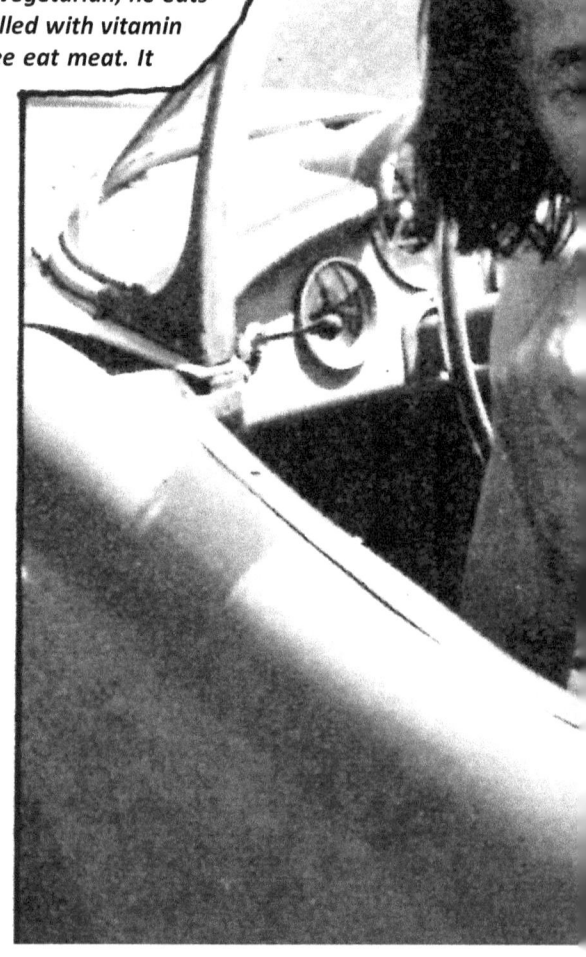

Astrologically a Libra, (born October 8th 1936) David Carradine, both in person and as star of *Kung Fu*, is very typical of his sign. The most outstanding facet of the Libran person is his over-whelming respect for, and insistence on justice. No one who's watched Kung Fu could deny that Caine is above all a man dedicated to that very thought. In his own life David is equally devotion to the principles of truth, and he quotes the founder of the American state, Thomas Jefferson.

Thrown out of six schools, including the famous Stockbridge Academy in Massachusetts, specifically designed to deal with wayward genius, David found his way to a seventh-reform school. After a spell there, his father found his rebel son a private tutor. It was harder for young David to play truant with a man watching him and him alone.

David is steadfast in his approach to violence. "I am an individual," he says. "I am not sure that I would resist if someone tried to kill me. Maybe it would be better for the salvation of my soul than to strike back and take someone else's life."

His academic career ended at San Francisco State College, officially to study music, but, as might be expected, David found more of an interest in a subject outside his own course - drama. As he remarked in an interview recently, "In the student cafeteria, the musicians all had their tables and the drama students all had theirs, and I just naturally gravitated to the theatre kids."

It was a move that David was never to regret. Although at first, things were by no means easy for the fledgling actor. He spent a couple of years at college and then left to start acting in earnest. While on the one hand performing Shakespeare and other classic plays all over California, he developed another lifestyle; playing the guitar, reading poetry, and just talking in the cafes and bars of San Francisco. He was one of the original San Francisco beatniks - 50's forerunners of today's hippies. "There were only about fifty of us. The rest were hangers-on and completely phoney," he recalls. To keep himself alive, when audiences and parts were slim, he sold sewing machines and encyclopedias door-to-door.

David's final brush with officialdom, his compulsory army service, brought out the rebel almost as soon as the camp gates had shut behind him. In two years at Fort Eustis, Virginia, he was court-martialled three times! Though he did like the uniforms: "I didn't even make Private First Class so the result was my uniform was very bare, like an officer's. Guys would salute me thinking

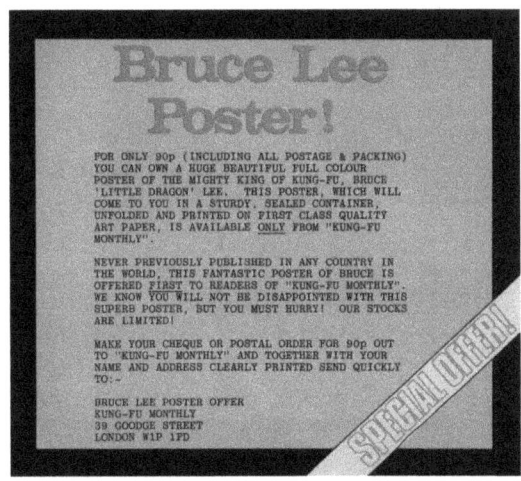

that's what I was."

If people were sitting up and taking notice of the rebellious soldier for all the wrong reasons, then it wasn't long before they were doing just the same thing for something much more worthwhile. After his discharge from the army, David went to New York and played Laertes in *Hamlet*. His father watched the show, didn't think much of it, and put on his own production, still using David. But the critics had seen the first show, and they liked it. Parts in long-running TV westerns like *Wagon Train* and *The Virginian* followed. It looked as if David Carradine, veteran beatnik and coffee bar soloist was really on his way this time.

But his truly big break, the role that in the end led to Kwai Chang Caine and the superstardom of Kung Fu, was as Atahualpa Capac, the Inca chieftain, in the Broadway production of *The Royal Hunt of The Sun*. The critics raved and the show, with David, stayed on Broadway for six months.

More TV followed, and movies too - *Macho Callahan* and *Taggart* among others - but it was not until a couple of scriptwriters at Warner Brothers put together the original story of Kung Fu, that David Carradine's star truly rose in the sky.

Naturally, a major TV series cannot be launched without one very important person - it's star. As Jerry Thorpe scanned the available talent, his mind kept returning to a show he had seen some years before, in New York. The star had been filled with the characteristics that Thorpe was looking for in his hero. "He had just the kind of dignity and lyricism that we wanted," said Thorpe. When Thorpe contacted David Carradine, the actor in question, his future star 'simply flipped,' and Kwai Chang Caine was born.

The scripts that had fascinated a few men in Hollywood were soon claiming literally millions of converts to Kung Fu, the most authentic of all the Martial Arts, in America and soon all over the globe. Says Thorpe, "Audiences are sated with police shows and lawyer shows. A vast segment of our audience is looking for some moral standard. That's why there's so much interest in the Eastern philosophies."

The audience themselves are more forthright. "I would like to learn Karate and Judo", explained one viewer, "Because kids are always trying to beat me up at school." Carradine himself disclaims the material success that this runaway hit, surely one of TVs greatest ever smashes, has brought him.

Living 2,000 feet up in California's lush Laurel Canyon, home of many Hollywood stars both in the film and music businesses, he is more concerned with his baby, Free, his mistress, Barbara Hershey Seagull, with whom he starred in *Boxcar Bertha*, than with "more money than I know what to do with." His main outlays are on his own films, such as *You and Me* and *I'll Come Home in the Spring*, but even their budgets don't make much impression on an income estimated at near £4,000 every week.

"I would like to throw this whole life away and go on to something that was actually more unconventional but less flamboyant and simpler." That's how David Carradine is thinking these days, but it will be a while before the success and popularity of *Kung Fu*, both as a programme and a Martial Art, will permit him to vanish. The mantle of the Little Dragon, Bruce Lee, has fallen about David Carradine's muscled shoulders; if for no other reason, he will not give up the role of Kwai Chang Caine. A role which, in his own life as well as in front of the cameras, fits so perfectly with the old Shaolin description of a Kung Fu master:

"Listened for, he cannot be heard; looked for, he cannot be seen; felt for, he cannot be touched."

David is famous in California for his offbeat behaviour. He has been known to turn cartwheels during Press conferences, walk into the lounges of plush and expensive hotels in bare feet, dressed only in a ragged T-shirt and jeans. And once, when a reporter tried to interview him in his tiny wooden house, David climbed up a rafter and hung there, dangling from the roof for five minutes! The reporter left, baffled at these eccentric antics, and convinced that David was a madman!

When David was spending his two years with the U.S. Army at Fort Eustis, there was one thing that interested the much-punished private. It was the talent competitions that the Army arranged, open even to the 'bad boys.' In one such show, the actor-to-be managed to reach the finals. He recited the soliloquy from Shakespeare's Richard II. But he still didn't come first. The star of the Army show was a man who could twirl two batons at the same time!

Many magazines and newspapers have commented on David Carradine's earlier life as a hippy, and on his drug taking habits. But David has long since given up LSD and other kinds of hallucinatory drugs. He says that he doesn't need them now, although he admits that in his past, he took up to four or five hundred acid trips on LSD.

While David Carradine has two cars - a '58 Packard and a Lancia - a dog named Buffalo and many other possessions, there is no television in his Laurel Canyon home. Once he did have one, but soon gave it away. "TV," says David, "Is poisonous. It pollutes the consciousness."

Barbara Hershey Seagull is not David Carradine's first lady. In '61, while still in the Army, David met and married Donna Brecht, who became the mother of his first child, Celesta. Unfortunately the marriage was not fated to last, and everything collapsed on the first night of David's hit performance in The Royal Hunt of the Sun. He and Barbara are not married, and they aren't thinking of it. Says David, "To marry just for the children's sake is not enough today... the important thing is truth at all costs."

Much of Caine's unique style comes from David Carradine himself. At the start of the series, the wardrobe department had Caine wearing shoes, but Carradine refused to put them on. "I just took them off and left them off," recalled Carradine, "I realised that Caine wouldn't need shoes, and wouldn't wear them." The same thing went for Caine's hairstyle, or lack of it. While staid studio bosses find his increasingly long hair shocking, Carradine is standing firm. "I'm just letting my hair grow. I haven't cut it since we started and I'm not going to. I had to fight them on that and I won."

CATHAY FILMS: AN APOLOGY

The publishers of Kung-Fu Monthly wish to apologise to Cathay Films Ltd for unauthorised use of photographic material advertised for sale in the last issue of KFM. The copyright of that photograph was, and remains, the sole and exclusive property of Cathay Films Ltd.

THE MARTIAL ART

Kung Fu is not a game. Kung Fu is a highly skilled art which, if misused by the untrained, can be deadly! It took Bruce Lee many years of back breaking training to master the art of Kung Fu, and when he died, he was still learning. Bruce never used Kung Fu against anyone in anger in his life. He knew only too well its dangerous power - the same power that the fighting Shaolin Monks swore never to use to deliberately kill or injure any opponent.

So if you are thinking of taking up the martial arts, and who isn't after a glimpse of the Little Dragon's exploits on the silver screen, be prepared to devote a large part of your daily life to its study and practice. Also, make sure you join a reputable club run by someone who knows what they're talking about.

And if you're not prepared to become a Kung Fu disciple, then leave the fighting to the experts!

RISING ELBOW STRIKE

- Arms are held across the body, with fists clenched to give tension to striking arm. The striking arm is held uppermost.
- The elbow is brought sharply upwards in a circular movement. The blow is made with the point of the elbow. The other arm is drawn back, the fist held at chest height.
- This strike is used to the opponent's face, neck and chest.

FORWARD KNIFE HAND STRIKE

- Right hand is held behind the ear and the strike is made with a semi-circular movement.
- The left hand, held across the body, is brought back across the body and held at chest height.
- This strike is used to the opponent's face or neck.

These illustrations by Paul Simmons are from a book to be published later this year called *The Beginner's Guide to Kung Fu*. We hope to be featuring further extracts from this excellent book in future editions of *Kung-Fu Monthly*.

Warning: A little knowledge is often a dangerous thing! Read the Kung Fu Code at the beginning of this book before lifting a finger... even in fun!

KICKBACK: THE LETTERS

Uggghhhhh! Whheeeeew! Why the groans and sighs? Well, the editorial offices of *Kung-Fu Monthly*, (or *KFM* as we all call it for short), are located on the fourth floor of a building that unfortunately doesn't have a lift! And you guessed it, our postman has absolutely refused to carry another sack of mail up the stairs! Not that we can blame him really. Thousands of letters from all over the country have been pouring in from eager and enthusiastic *KFM* fans, and the weight of those sacks might even have strained Bruce's incredible muscles!

My name is Jenny Lee, (no relation him sorry to say!), and your editor, Felix Yen, has given me the fantastic fob of sorting through all your mail. I'll be doing my best to answer your queries when I can and selecting a few of the more unusual and interesting letters to print every issue. We love to know how you feel about *Kung-Fu Monthly*, about the martial arts in general and of course, your thoughts on Bruce, David, Angela Mao and all the other Kung Fu superstars are always welcome. Keep writing and be happy!

WE DON'T THINK HE'S DEAD!

Dear *KFM*,
My friend and I are doing a project on Kung Fu. Most of it is centred around Bruce Lee, but as yet we have not got any pictures of him. I wonder could you send any information about Bruce to us to help us? We are ardent Bruce Lee fans but we don't think he's dead! And the picture you published of him in his coffin has made us almost certain! Can you help us?
Mark Palmer, Preston, Lancashire

Dear Mark,
You are only one of hundreds of people who have written to us asking whether it is possible that Bruce is still alive. Sadly, the answer is that Bruce is indeed dead. He died in Hong Kong last year on the 20th of July. Amidst great mourning by millions of his Chinese and Western fans alike, Bruce was buried firstly (symbolically) in Hong Kong, and finally in the city of Seattle in the United States.

LUCKY GIRL

Dear *KFM*,
I am a Chinese girl and lived in Hong Kong before moving to England. It is wonderful to see the English people come to love Bruce Lee, as many of my friends (and I!) have done for years. Once, three years ago, I actually met Bruce after waiting for hours and hours outside of his house. I was so nervous when he passed us that I almost forgot to ask him to sign his name in my book. Just as he was getting into his car, I shouted, "Bruce, please sign this for me!" and without saying a word, he scrawled his signature right across an entire page! Then he smiled at me and I fainted! How stupid of me! But at least I have his signature, and I will never, ever part with that book!
Betty Leung, Hounslow, Middlesex

Dear Betty,
I don't think you were stupid at all! Anyone who has seen Bruce in any of his movies will know what a stare from those deep, dark eyes could do, and if he was smiling just for you at the same time, well, I'm not surprised you fainted!

ROOM FULL OF BRUCE

Dear *KFM*,
When I saw your No.1 issue of *Kung-Fu Monthly*, I hastily rushed back to my newsagent and bought 8 more copies for the fabulous posters which now hang all over my room. I'd like to congratulate you on publishing my kind of magazine, and in fact, if I could, I would like to shake your hand to thank you. Keep up the good work!
S. Farrell, London N.16

Dear S. Farrell,
Glad you liked it, and I hope you'll be keeping up the good work at your end! In fact, it was probably 'bulk-buying' from fans like yourself that led to such a shortage of copies of Kung-Fu Monthly in many parts of the country. We're sorry that so many of Bruce's fans were unable to get a copy of KFM No.1, but how were we to know that it would sell out! First come, first served!

DARLING DAVID

Dear *KFM*,
I am a great Kung Fu fan and really like Bruce Lee, but I do wish you had printed some pictures and information about darling David Carradine. My brother showed me an interview with David in a music magazine and I could not believe a lot of the things that they printed about him. I'm sure they are all lies! Please, please print the real story of David with lots of pictures and facts about him. Why do magazines and newspapers always print such horrible things about people? It just isn't fair! I hope you will put the record straight for David, who seems such an honest and sincere person.
Lucy Thompson, Farnborough, Hants

Dear Lucy,
This Issue should cheer you up I think! You shouldn't take everything you read in the newspapers and magazines at face value though. I have a fair idea which magazine you are talking about, and without naming names, I'll happily agree with you that I thought that particular interview and article was largely untrue and 'slanted.' Some people will print anything to sell copies, Lucy, and there's not much we can do about it! Hope you liked the article in this issue on David. I can promise every word it is true and factual.

ANGELA MAO

Dear *KFM*,
I have just bought your first issue of *Kung-Fu Monthly* and found it very good. Previously, I have had to buy Chinese film magazines for information. Could you tell me, will you be doing any articles on Angela Mao, with photos from her films, such as *Hapkido*?
Peter Gilham, Rainham, Essex

Dear Peter,
Glad you asked that, Peter! Along with Bruce, as always, the next issue of Kung-Fu Monthly will be featuring a whole article on Angela containing biographical information and as many photographs of the first lady of Kung Fu as we can cram into the pages. By the way, Hapkido is showing now in the West End and it's a really great movie!

A GOAL TO AIM FOR

Dear *KFM*,
I have followed Bruce Lee for a long time, but unfortunately have never been able to find out all the true facts. Thanks to your new monthly magazine I now have a little more insight into Bruce's life. I have realised and found a goal to aim for from your magazine as I hope all your readers have, and together, (as Bruce would have wanted) to find a real and natural way in everything, but to be patient in finding that way.
F. Hailing-Keep, Leckhampton, Cheltenham, Glos.

Dear F. Hailing-Keep,
You don't give your first name so you'll have to forgive me being so formal! Seriously, though, I'm so glad that the 'inner' message of Bruce's wonderful example in his life, his films and his whole career have given you a goal to aim for. Patience is a virtue that few of us master easily, but it's certainly worth striving for!

WHO IS RIGHT?

Dear *KFM*,
We hope you can settle an argument. My brother says that Bruce Lee is Chinese and I say that he was born in America, (which I read in a magazine), and he is therefore really an American. Who is right? Please settle this before we come to blows!
P.S. We both think Bruce Lee is the King of Kung Fu by the way!
Sally & Robert Feldman, Great Yarmouth

Dear Sally & Robert,
Bruce was born in San Francisco, but his parents were both Chinese! There is a very large Chinese community in San Francisco, and has been for many, many years. Both Bruce's parents were in show business, and returned to Hong Kong shortly after Bruce's birth. He grew up in Hong Kong and did not return to the U.S.A. until his late teens.

BRUCE LEE FACT SHEET

Born: November 27th 1940, San Francisco
Died: July 20th 1973, Hong Kong
Father: Li Hoi Chun (Died February 1965).
Mother: Grace Li
Siblings: Agnes, Phoebe, Peter and Robert.
Wife: Linda Emery
Children: Brandon and Shannon
Height: 5' 7½"
Weight: 140 lbs
Sign: Scorpio

Education: Several schools in Hong Kong before enrolling in St Francis Xaviers College. Following that, visited USA to attend Edison Vocational High School and finally majored in philosophy at Seattle, Washington University for three years, although he never completed his course.

Resident: Cities in which Bruce lived for any length of time include: San Francisco, Hong Kong, Los Angeles, Seattle, Oakland, and finally Kowloon Tong in Hong Kong.

Films: Tears of San Francisco (made when Bruce was still a tiny baby). This was followed by a number of Cantonese movies in which Bruce starred as a young child, made in Hong Kong, including *Kid Cheung*, *Birth of a Boy*, *Orphan Ah Sam* and *The Long and Winding Road*. In the 1960's, in the USA, Bruce starred in several TV series including *The Green Hornet* and *Longstreet*. He also made guest appearances on other TV shows including *Ironside*, *Blondie*, and *Here Comes The Brides*. He co-starred with James Garner in the MGM film *Marlowe* and finally returned to Hong Kong where he made the following Kung Fu movies: *The Big Boss* and *Fist of Fury* for Golden Harvest, *Way of the Dragon* for Concord and *Enter the Dragon* for Warner Bros and Concord jointly. Bruce had begun shooting Game of Death, but had not completed the film when he died.

Martial Art: As a boy in Hong Kong he learned Tai Chi Chu'an and aged 13 he undertook Wing Chun Kung Fu under Yip Man, a respected and revered master of the art. Later Bruce developed his own style of Kung Fu which he termed Jeet Kune Do (literal interpretation: The Intercepting Fist). In the USA he founded three Jun Fan schools of Kung Fu in Seattle, Oakland and Los Angeles which attracted many pupils, several of them famous (Steve McQueen, James Garner etc). He closed these schools following return to Hong Kong. In 1972 he was awarded a place in Black Belt magazine's 'Hall of Fame.'

EDITORIAL

Hi there Kung Fu fans...
Well, here it is... the third issue of *Kung-Fu Monthly*!
This month we have a really fascinating lead article from our editor, Don Won Ton, who has flown thousands of miles to Hong Kong and back on a fact finding mission in search of the real story behind the untimely death of Kung Fu's most famous son, Bruce Lee!

In answer to the thousands of letters we have received here from readers and fans all over the United Kingdom, Don has unearthed the stranger than fiction chain of events that lead up to the Little Dragon's departure from this world. Like a plot from one of Bruce's own thrilling movies, you will read of the pressures, omens and ill luck that culminated in Bruce's death.

It is a sad story. A moving and heartbreaking story that every real fan of the King of Kung Fu will read with a sense of loss and pain. Bruce was a champion; the toughest, fastest and fittest man the twentieth century has produced, but he was also a human being, not a god! Like the rest of us, Bruce was burdened with the frailties of human nature. And like the rest of us, when fate beckoned, he was powerless to resist!

Passing on to happier subjects, a word is due here on the new movie *Black Belt Jones*, currently showing in London's West End. Starring the up and coming martial artist/actor Jim Kelly (who you will remember played opposite Bruce Lee in *Enter the Dragon*), this film is a must for all Kung Fu fans. Jim is a born fighter, and like Bruce himself, he is a top champion in his own art of Karate. Made by the same team that filmed *Enter the Dragon*, *Black Belt Jones* is a fast and furious movie, packed with excellent fight scenes and some first class workouts between martial artists.

Angela Mao fans will be pleased to hear that next issue we plan a feature on the first lady of Kung Fu. We also hope to include an amazing scoop on Bruce Lee! It's a surprise item, and I won't spoil it by hinting at the contents just now, but I'd advise our regular readers to place their order for *KFM* No.4 with their newsagent right now. When it reaches the newsstands, I'm absolutely convinced we will have sold out in a few days!

This month, along with other offers, we are inviting pre-publication subscriptions on two books to be published later this year. By subscribing now, you will ensure that copies of these books, both of which have been approved by *KFM*, will reach you on the day of their publication! You will find the order forms for *Bruce Lee: King of Kung Fu* and *The Beginner's Guide to Kung Fu* underneath this month's poster. These books are not hurriedly thrown together rehashes of previous publications. I want to assure you that they are both beautifully produced, intelligently written, authoritative books you will be proud to own and treasure. I urge those of you interested in Bruce Lee's life, or in the martial art of Kung Fu, to send off for them now!

That's all from me this month...

Felix Yen

Felix Yen
Editor-in-Chief

EXCLUSIVE FROM HONG KONG!
BRUCE LEE'S LAST HOURS

What killed the Little Dragon? This is the burning question which has been on the lips of Bruce Lee disciples the world over ever since that tragic midsummer's night of July 20th, 1973 when the Man with the Golden Fists passed from life into legend.

To this day, many of Bruce's millions of devoted admirers are still mystified as to the true story behind their idol's shocking death. Facts have become lost in a flood of rumours sparked by grief-stricken fans trying to guess how the 'fittest man in the world' could possibly die at the age of 32.

Some devotees believe Bruce died from an accidental blow to the stomach while filming a furious stare 'n' tear Kung Fu fight scene or that he finally succumbed to an incurable childhood disease. Others feel that some sinister organisation may have had a hand in Bruce's last hours - perhaps a rival business organisation, a renegade martial artist jealous of the Little Dragon's enormous fame, or the vicious secret 'mafia' of Hong Kong, known to its deadly members simply as the Triad Society.

Another popular rumour blames followers of the outlawed Japanese murder gang - the Ninja Society - and claims that Bruce was pushed from the seventh floor of one of Hong Kong's many tower-skyscrapers. Practitioners of the incredible Art of the Vibrating Palm have also been mentioned as a possible killer group wishing to do Bruce evil. These mythical Eastern fanatics have the amazing power to destroy a victim by a 'delayed death strike,' converting their internal energy into lethal shock waves and murdering, by simply placing their open palm on their intended victim.

"Let him rest in peace. Do not disturb his soul." - Linda Lee.

A tribe of Malaysians even believe that Bruce is in fact alive and is being hidden by his film company as a macabre publicity stunt!

However none of these bizarre theories come anywhere near the real truth which itself is far stranger than fiction! To unravel the mystery, I flew to the harbour city of Hong Kong - homeland of the legendary Li Siu Loong, better known as Bruce Lee.

The events leading up to Bruce's last hours actually began almost two months before that fatal July night, in a small room attached to the now-famous Golden Harvest film studio. The Golden Harvest lot was Bruce's movie home; the location where he edited *The Big Boss*, and *Way of the Dragon* and where *Fist of Fury*, *Enter the Dragon* and the unfinished *Game of Death* were actually filmed. Walking around the sun-baked, dusty lot, it is hard to imagine that this is the place which inspired the Little Dragon to the heights undreamed of in the film capitals of the world. But Golden Harvest has now become a part of the Bruce Lee legend.

When Bruce's famous film star friends learned of his death, they were heartbroken. "Why is it always the good guys who go first," cried Australian actor George (James Bond) Lazenby. At Bruce's graveside, James Coburn made this eulogy: "Farewell my brother. It has been an honour to share this space in time with you. As a friend and as a teacher, you have brought my physical, spiritual and psychological lives together. Thank you. May peace be with you." He then, together with Bruce's other pallbearers, threw his white gloves into the open grave as a mark of respect.

On the afternoon of May 10th, Bruce was dubbing the soundtrack to his latest martial arts epic *Enter the Dragon* in one of these very buildings. All Hong Kong movies are shot without sound equipment and the voices are dubbed in later; a tricky job as no outside noise can be allowed during recording in case it shows up on the final print. On that day, the air-conditioning was turned off in Bruce's dubbing studio so as not to break the silence and, under the blazing Hong Kong summer sun, the atmosphere in the little room was stifling.

Late in the afternoon, following many hours of exhausting work, Bruce excused himself and went to the studio bathroom. His assistants in the dubbing room waited patiently for his return, but when he still hadn't reappeared after 20 minutes, they began to feel anxious and sent a helper to find out what the delay was. To his horror, the young boy found Bruce lying semi-conscious on the bathroom floor and, after timidly shaking him awake, helped the star to his feet. Bruce staggered back to the furnace-like dubbing room, but almost immediately collapsed a second time.

Raymond Chow, the Golden Harvest chief who gave Bruce his first break into the Chinese film world with the record breaking sensation *The Big Boss*, rushed from his office to where Bruce lay shaking and fighting for breath. Mr. Chow immediately telephoned Dr. Charles Langford of the near by Baptist Hospital who ordered that Bruce be rushed by ambulance to the emergency ward. "Lee was brought in by several men from the studio," remembers Dr. Langford. "First there were breathing noises, then they stopped. There was a series of convulsions."

As he lay unconscious on the hospital stretcher, Bruce's life seemed to be slowly ebbing away and doctors fought a frantic battle against death to revive the young star. Two and half hours later they succeeded and Bruce Lee lived!

According to Dr. Langford, Bruce's recovery was a drama in itself. First, the Little Dragon opened his eyes and moved around slightly and then, although he could not speak, he made a sign of recognition to his attractive young American wife Linda, who had hurried to his side. When he was able to talk, it was only with a slurred accent, but by the time he was transferred to another hospital, he was able to joke and laugh about his brush with death. When they examined Bruce, the doctors at the Baptist Hospital found his brain had swollen, but they were unable to pinpoint the cause of the near-fatal swelling.

Bruce was very fond of pop music and it was his wish that all the music played at his funeral, be numbers he had loved during his lifetime. His request was not forgotten. During the ceremony, there were recordings of Frank Sinatra's 'My Way,' the Tom Jones hit 'The Impossible Dream,' Sergio Mendes' 'Look Around' and the Blood, Sweat and Tears number 'When I Die,' to speed the Little Dragon on his way. Linda herself closed the service with a line from 'When I Die:' "And when I'm dead, and when I'm gone, there'll be one child more in this world to carry on, to carry on."

After fully recovering, Bruce admitted that he had taken cannabis on the day of his collapse and he was warned against using the drug. But when he flew to Los Angeles shortly afterwards for a complete medical check up by a team of medical experts, he was told that cannabis in moderate doses, was harmless. Team leader Dr. David Reisbord diagnosed the collapse as a form of epilepsy and presented a seizure-control drug called Dilantin. He added that Bruce seemed in perfect health and had the body of an 18-year-old!

Bruce returned to his bustling homeland in high spirits despite the frightening shock he had undergone and immediately threw himself into a heavy filming schedule. While he had been away, movie offers had been pouring into the Golden Harvest studio from all four corners of the globe. With the enormous overseas success of his Kung Fu epics, Bruce was the hottest property the film industry had ever known and the salaries he was promised would have rocketed him to the position of highest paid actor in the world if he had lived!

But before these golden offers could be considered, there was still Bruce's own *Game of Death* to complete. Ace American basketball star Kareem Abdul-Jabbar had jetted in to Hong Kong to visit his old friend Bruce and, a martial arts student himself, he readily agreed to appear in the film. After a week of shooting, Bruce had hundreds of feet of extraordinary Kung Fu footage in the can and the basis of what looked to be his most spectacular movie yet; 5 foot 7 inch Bruce Lee pitted against Kareem Abdul-Jabbar, who scrapes seven foot! Tragically the film was destined never to be finished.

Without warning shortly before midnight on July 20th, film fans and martial artists around the world were struck a devastating blow. Bruce Lee, the greatest hero of modern times, toughest superstar in cinema history, the Man with the Golden Punch, was dead at the age of 32!

On the afternoon of that shattering day, Bruce and Raymond Chow had visited the apartment of glamorous Taiwanese starlet Betty Ting Pei to discuss with her, a part in *Game of Death*. At around 7.30 pm. Bruce complained of a headache and beautiful Betty had made the well-meaning but ghastly error of giving the superstar a pain killing tablet called Equagesic. Half an hour later, Bruce lay down in Betty's bedroom, promising to meet Raymond Chow and Australian actor George Lazenby (the former James Bond) for dinner after he had rested for a short time. When Bruce failed to keep the appointment, Raymond Chow hurried back to Betty Ting Pei's apartment where he found the Little Dragon unconscious.

Once more, Bruce was rushed to the emergency ward of a Hong Kong hospital and once more, doctors fought feverishly to pull him out of the coma. This time they were too late. At 11.30 pm, Raymond Chow walked out of the hospital to tell the waiting throng of reporters and spectators, "He's gone." Bruce's wife Linda, who had sat anxiously outside the ward during the desperate life or death struggle, was led home weeping.

Several days after Bruce's death, Hong Kong said its last goodbye to its most famous son with a symbolic funeral which turned into a riot. Twenty thousand distraught fans packed the narrow streets surrounding the Kowloon Funeral Home where Bruce lay in state in an open bronze coffin. Many had camped all night on the street, in the hope of catching a final glimpse of the King of Kung Fu and others climbed onto rooftops and advertising signs high above the frenzied crowd. Three hundred police linked arms in an attempt to restore order, but many more reinforcements were needed. Women and young children were repeatedly plucked from behind steel barricades to prevent them from being crushed, and ambulances ferried dozens of injured spectators to hospital.

Inside the parlour, more than 600 film stars, friends and photographers were jammed together in a tight mass before Bruce's HK$40,000 coffin. Linda, the 28-year-old widow, who was dressed in a white Chinese mourning robe, broke down several times during the ceremony and many of the mourners wept with her.

Bruce Lee was gone Hong Kong had lost its hero. Never before had so many people gathered in the city to pay tribute to one man, and it is unlikely that they ever will again!

Dressed in the blue suit he wore in *Fist of Fury*, Bruce's body was flown to Linda's

American hometown of Seattle, where he was buried in the Lake View Cemetery, overlooking Lake Washington. Among the pallbearers were Bruce's old Kung Fu pupils Steve McQueen and James Coburn. Even today, thousands of Bruce's disciples make the pilgrimage up the cemetery's grassy slopes to kneel at their master's graveside.

Back in Hong Kong however, a flood of rumours had sprung up around the Little Dragon. Many stories were claiming that Bruce had been killed either by Betty Ting Pei, Raymond Chow or the boss of a rival film company who had wanted Bruce out of the way so he could corner the Kung Fu movie market. Incredible as they seemed, these foul rumours were actually believed by thousands of Chinese in the seething colony.

To put a stop to the terrible gossip which was sweeping Hong Kong, the government ordered a full inquiry into the mysterious death of the Little Dragon. No expense was spared in getting to the true facts and medical experts were flown in from as far away as London!

The inquest opened on September 3rd and lasted for a mammoth 21 days! Dozens of the top stars of the Chinese movie industry, friends, doctors and relatives of Bruce, all appeared in the witness box to tell what they knew of Bruce's last heartbreaking hours. The first shock which shook the courthouse - and indeed the whole of Hong Kong - came when it was learned that particles of cannabis had been discovered in Bruce's stomach during the autopsy examination.

For days, hundreds of questions were asked whether it was possible for cannabis to kill a person, but eventually the argument was crushed by the weight of medical evidence which found that Bruce couldn't have died from a drug overdose.

What the inquest did find, however, was even more startling. After a thorough examination of all the facts and evidence, the Coroner ruled that Bruce had died because of one tiny pill; the Equagesic tablet that Betty Ting Pei had given him to help ease his headache!

When they heard the verdict, the hundreds of spectators who had kept a constant vigil outside the courthouse during the long, weary investigation, couldn't believe their ears. How could one small pain-killing tablet have done what no man alive could have managed... killed Bruce Lee, the most lethal human being in the world?

And so the rumours flooded on. Not even Linda's heartbreaking plea to the people of Hong Kong could halt them.

"It is my wish that the newspapers and the people of Hong Kong will stop speculating on the circumstances surrounding my husband's death," said Linda.

"Although we do not have the final autopsy report, I hold no suspicions of anything other than natural death. I myself do not hold any person or people responsible for his death. Fate has ways we cannot change.

"The only thing of importance, is that Bruce is gone and will not return. He lives on in our memories and through his films. Please remember him for his genius, his art and the magic he brought to every one of us.

"For those who knew him very well, his words and thoughts will remain with us forever and influence the rest of our lives.

"I know the people of Hong Kong loved Bruce and are proud of his achievements which have brought world attention to Hong Kong. So I appeal to all of you to please let him rest in peace and do not disturb his soul.

"These are my personal feelings and those of his close friends and I would appreciate it if you will honour and respect my wishes."

But no-one was listening. The colony's four million Chinese just couldn't accept the fact that their hero had been struck down in so tragically simple fashion and, to this very day, most of the population still firmly believes that sinister forces were at work that fatal summer's night in the home of Betty Ting Pei!

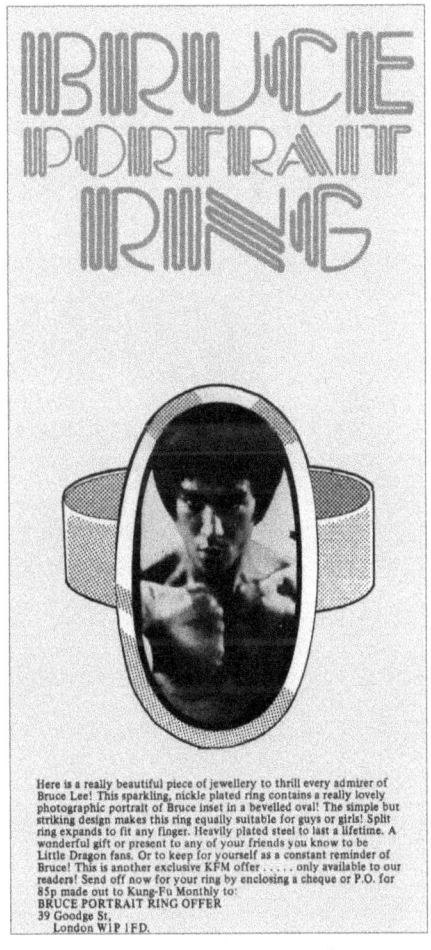

BRUCE PORTRAIT RING

Here is a really beautiful piece of jewellery to thrill every admirer of Bruce Lee! This sparkling, nickle plated ring contains a really lovely photographic portrait of Bruce inset in a bevelled oval! The simple but striking design makes this ring equally suitable for guys or girls! Split ring expands to fit any finger. Heavily plated steel to last a lifetime. A wonderful gift or present to any of your friends you know to be Little Dragon fans. Or to keep for yourself as a constant reminder of Bruce! This is another exclusive KFM offer . . . . . only available to our readers! Send off now for your ring by enclosing a cheque or P.O. for 85p made out to Kung-Fu Monthly to:
BRUCE PORTRAIT RING OFFER
39 Goodge St,
London W1P 1FD.

The facts, however, speak for themselves. Bruce has gone - a brilliant light shockingly eclipsed purely by accident - and all the speculation and rumours in the world won't bring him back. But on movie screens around the globe - in the gymnasiums of five continents - in fact wherever there is a Little Dragon fan who carries in his or her heart, a treasured memory of the greatest martial artist of them all, Bruce Lee Lives!

JIM KELLY: KARATE CHAMP TURNS ACTOR!

Jim Kelly, the star of the new Warner Bros. martial arts movie, *Black Belt Jones*, is no newcomer to either fighting or acting! Best known to Kung Fu film fans as Bruce Lee's co-star in *Enter the Dragon*, Kelly to a rugged, dynamic black performer who has gone to the top of one career, to now moving quickly to the top of another. In 1971, Jim won the International Middleweight Karate Championship and has gone on from that triumph, to appear in several television and motion picture productions. Born in Paris, (that's in Kentucky, America - not France!) and raised in San Diego, California, Kelly became a major athlete at the Bourbon County High School in Kentucky. He was an All-Star in four sports: football, basketball and track! After high school, Kelly went on to play football at the University of Louisville.

Whilst at the University of Louisville, Kelly began to study Karate. Within a few short years, he had won several trophies and finally the championship. During this time, Kelly returned to sunny California and opened a Karate school in Los Angeles - the same town

where Bruce Lee established one of his own Jeet Kune Do schools early in his career!

Kelly's chance to swap the ring for the studio came first with modelling and television commercials. Then, while technical advisor for fight scenes on Melinda, Jim was asked to play a role in that film. It was a long, sweeping jump from there to his featured role in the record breaking *Enter the Dragon*, his real motion picture debut, which, like *Black Belt Jones*, was also filmed by the trio of Fred Weintraub (Producer), Paul Heller (Producer) and Robert Clouse (Director). Although Jim Kelly devotes a lot of his time to Karate and acting, an exhausting combination by any standards, he does have time for relaxing diversions. Those he pursues most actively are tennis and girls!

Black Belt Jones is a fast, action packed movie featuring master Karate expert Jim Kelly and beautiful, deadly Gloria Hendry. Without wishing to compare *Black Belt Jones* with any of the inimitable Bruce Lee movies, we can promise *Kung-Fu Monthly* readers that the same team who made *Enter the Dragon* have come up with another blockbuster!

THE MARTIAL ART

These illustrations by Paul Simmons are from a book to be published later this year called *The Beginner's Guide to Kung Fu*. We are inviting subscriptions to this book for *KFM* readers and you will find an order form for a pre-publication subscription to *The Beginner's Guide to Kung Fu* at the foot of this month's pin-up poster!

MIDDLE LINE CIRCULAR BLOCK

- Keeping the feet square, the blocking arm is brought across the body until the fist reaches the opposite armpit, bringing the shoulders of the attacking arm forward. (When the arms cross, the blocking arm is underneath).
- Keeping the shoulder forward, the blocking arm is swung back out.
- Deflecting the opponents punch away from the body. This block is used against blows to the chest and body.

LOW LINE BLOCK

• As with all Kung Fu blocks, this is a deflection and a blow as well as a block. The force of the opponents blow is diverted, still bringing him forward into range for a counter attack. The blocking arm is brought up to behind the ear.
• The blocking arm is swept down across the body, deflecting the kick.
• The other arm is drawn sharply back, fist held at chest height, creating a counter force, and leaving you in a position to counter attack. Using the bony edge of the forearm, this block is used against kicks and blows to the lower body.

Warning: A little knowledge is often a dangerous thing! Read the Kung Fu Code at the beginning of this book before lifting a finger, even in fun!

KICKBACK: THE LETTERS

Hi there! This is Jenny Lee again with another collection of your letters, queries and questions to *Kung-Fu Monthly*. Really, the response from *KFM* readers has been unbelievable! Thousands of letters have been piling up on my desk, and it's impossible for me to help all of you, but I'll be doing my best to keep up in the weeks ahead, and I hope you'll be as patient as you can! One point I'd like to correct from an answer I gave to a reader in the last issue, is that our Angela Mao feature was really scheduled for *KFM* No.4 and not for No.3 as I'd promised. So hang-on there all you fans of the first lady of Kung Fu; Angela will be appearing without fail next month. Lots of letters to cram in this issue, so I'll leave you with the plea to address your letters and replies to our special offers very carefully. We want to answer your mail as quickly as we can, and to do that we need your help. Please, please be sure to put the purpose of your letter on the envelope, be it 'Poster Offer,' 'Enquiry,' 'T-Shirt Offer,' or whatever! Now on with the show...!

WHATS THE WORD?

Dear *KFM*,
I thought I'd just write and say how thrilled I was with the Bruce Lee photo in *KFM* No.1's special offer. But could I ask what the third word after "Peace, Love..." is please? I can read his signature; it's just the words after "Love" I can't make out!
J. Clark, Bedfordshire

Dear J.,
I'm afraid that I can't read your signature (!) John, James, Jimmy or June... but I do know that the words you couldn't make out were "... and Brotherhood". By the way, I'll take this opportunity of reminding all KFM readers to print their names and addresses carefully and clearly when ordering any of our offers. It really helps us to reply quickly!

WRONG SIGN!

Dear *KFM*,
I would like to subscribe to your incredible magazine. Please tell me, can I do this? Also, I noticed a small mistake in your fact sheet on the back of *KFM* No.2. You said that Bruce was a Scorpio, although his birthday really makes him a Sagittarius. Isn't that right?
Brenda Lennon, Sunderland, Co. Durham

Dear Brenda,
I'm afraid we don't take subscriptions here for KFM. The best way to be sure of getting a copy, is to place an order with your newsagent. As to our 'small mistake,' I'm pleased to tell you that along with about a thousand other readers (who all wrote to us!) you've caught us out. The birth date given was absolutely correct, but the sign we gave had been typed wrongly! No marks to our sub-editing department!

CAN DAVID FIGHT?

Dear *KFM*,
I have just read *KFM* No.2 and really enjoyed it! Especially the article on David Carradine, who I always watch on the television series *Kung Fu*. Was David a real Shaolin Monk turned 'drop-out?' And does he really fight like that? Or is it just trick-photography? Although I like David Carradine, I don't think he would have been much of a match against Bruce Lee, do you?
Bob Turner, Upminster, Essex

Dear Bob,
No, I don't think he would have! David Carradine is a sincere and honest person, and he has always stressed that he knows little about the martial arts. Many of the fight scenes in the television series Kung Fu are done using trick-photography, or a stand in for David. David is pretty fit, however, and much of the simpler movements he does himself. He was never a Shaolin Monk though! David was born in America and has been an actor for the better part of his life.

QUESTIONS, QUESTIONS!

Dear *KFM*,
I have some questions of the death of Bruce 'Little Dragon' Lee that I would like you to answer if you could. Firstly, I have heard that he committed suicide by taking a pill, but I do not believe this and would like to know the facts. Secondly, is that picture you printed of him in the coffin in *KFM* No.1 really Bruce? Lastly, could you tell me if Bruce's teacher, Yip Man, is still alive or not? Sorry I have so many questions but *KFM* is the only place I can turn to for the real answers.
Lynne Smith, Bagshot, Surrey

Dear Lynne,
Well, right away, let me assure you that Bruce did not commit suicide! The complete story of his tragic death is the main feature of this issue and you can get all the information you need from Don Won Ton's article direct from Hong Kong. Bruce was not the kind of man to kill himself, Lynne!
Now, as to that picture of Bruce in his coffin we published in KFM No.1, I did actually answer this question in 'Kickback' last month and the answer is still the same! It is Bruce, although I admit that his face looks very different from the powerful staring features we have come to recognise in his pictures. Lastly, Bruce's teacher Yip Man, a revered and respected master of the Wing Chun school of Kung Fu died a couple of years back in Hong Kong. As a devoted pupil, Bruce attended the funeral ceremony and signed the ceremonial register.

THE MISSING FILM

Dear *KFM*,
I have bought Nos.1 and 2 of *KFM* and I think it is a great magazine. In the first two issues of *KFM*, you have only had pictures from Bruce's first four films. I would like to know if you will be having any information and pictures from his last film, *Game of Death*?
Paul Keay, Grangetown, Cardiff

Dear Paul,
The only picture I've personally seen from Game of Death, is the scene where Bruce is fighting Big Lew, (Kareem Abdul-Jabbar), an old friend of Bruce's from the U.S.A. These shots are pretty amazing as Big Lew stands over seven feet tall and is a professional basketball star in the States! I'll see if we can print one of these pictures in a forthcoming KFM.

04

1974

EDITORIAL

Hi there Kung Fu fans.

This month we have two feature articles; both of which I know are going to please many thousands of readers! To kick off with, Don Won Ton, our resident editor has culled a collection of the best, wittiest and most profound quotes from the late great Bruce Lee!

Bruce was more than just the world's top Kung Fu fighter and cinema star. As those who knew him during hit short but meteoric and turbulent life will testify, Bruce was an intelligent and perceptive judge of the world around him. His humour and quick wit were legendary amongst interviewers in Hong Kong and America. But Bruce was not a man to tolerate fools easily, and his criticisms of those people who incurred his displeasure were often sharp and to the point.

Our second feature this issue is for all fans of the first lady of Kung Fu, Miss Angela Mao. Angela is fast gaining popularity throughout the Western world with her tremendous performances in films such as *Hapkido* and *Enter the Dragon*. From the letters we have been receiving at *KFM*, I know that many of you feel that Angela Mao is going to be as big a star in Britain as she now is, in the Eastern world. And after a glimpse of the Lady Whirlwind in action on the screen, I'm inclined to that view myself! Angela has all the ingredients that go to making a top martial artist in Kung Fu movies. She is dedicated to her art, the Korean school of Hapkido, besides being an excellent actress who obviously loves her work! Although very different in character, as our article clearly shows, from Bruce Lee, Angela shares with Bruce, the convincing mastery of her goal in life. She knows where she is going, and come what may, she will attain her objectives!

By the time you read this, (*KFM* is prepared for the printer some weeks prior to publication), the publication date for one of the two books I mentioned in my last editorial, will nearly have arrived! *Bruce Lee King of Kung Fu*, an authentic, fully researched and illustrated biography of Bruce Lee's life and career written by F. Dennis and D. Atyeo is due for publication in July by the publishing company Wildwood House Ltd. Those of you who have already ordered this book, which contains 100 pages crammed with exclusive photographs and 40,000 words on the Little Dragon's incredible life and death, can look forward to receiving your copy very soon! If you haven't already ordered one, then I can only suggest that you do so as soon as possible to avoid disappointment or delay!

Order forms for *Bruce Lee: King of Kung Fu* and for another book, *The Beginner's Guide to Kung Fu* (by the same artist whose work you will find on our 'Martial Art' page each issue), can be found at the foot of this months pin-up poster. I advise those of you who are interested in Bruce Lee's life or in taking up the martial arts, to send off now!

That's all from me this month...

Felix Yen

Felix Yen
Editor-in-Chief

THE SAYINGS OF BRUCE LEE

Some superstars make their way up the ladder of success almost with their eyes closed, blinded to everything around them except that golden top rung. Not so Bruce Lee! As in everything which the Little Dragon turned his hand to, Bruce was fully aware of what was happening to him during his meteoric rush to superstardom. And, assisted by his university training in psychology, Bruce was able to capture his thoughts, feelings and emotions and put them into words for interviewers around the world.

In this selection of the finest of Bruce's many sayings, his charm and wisdom shine through time and time again. They paint a portrait of a man swept along by a glittering whirlwind of public acclaim, yet a man who is wise enough not to be fooled by his position but who devotes much of his time to thought and analysis.

Someday somebody will undoubtedly collect together in a book, the Sayings of Bruce Lee. Chairman Mao, you have been warned!

PHILOSOPHY

Bruce's philosophy on life was a wise and complex mixture of both the mysteries of the East and the beliefs of the West. Although he did not believe in God, he was certain of the inner power which is in all of us, and he spent his life tapping that power, both in his martial arts and his film career.

"Man is a self-made product. If there is a God, he is within. You don't ask God to give you things, you depend on God for inner theme."

"You must learn defeat. Like most people, you want to learn to win. To learn to die, is to be liberated from it. When tomorrow comes, you must learn to die and be liberated by it."

"I never believe in the word 'star.'"

"You don't ask God to give you things..."

"Some martial artists are now going to Hong Kong to be in the movies. They think they can be lucky too. Well, I don't believe in pure luck. You have to create your own luck. You have to be aware of the opportunities around you and take advantage of them. Some guys may not believe it, but I spent hours perfecting whatever I did."

"I'm not the type of guy who can sit in the office doing the same routine day in and day out. I have to do something creative and interesting. I don't want to do anything half way; it has to be perfect. I feel that I want to be the best martial artist. Not just for the sake of my movies, but because this is my interest."

THE FILMS

Although, as Bruce himself says below, his Mandarin films were not intended for Western consumption, he was still extremely proud of his efforts.

"What I hope, is that the movie will represent a new trend in Mandarin cinema. I mean people like films that are more than just one long armed hassle. With any luck, I hope to make multi-level films; the kind of movies that where you can just watch the surface story if you want, or you can look deeper into it if you feel like it."

On *Way of the Dragon*: "It's really a simple plot of a country boy going to a place where

he cannot speak the language; but somehow he comes out on top because he honestly and simply expresses himself by beating the hell out of everybody who gets in his way."

On Enter the Dragon: "This is definitely the biggest film I have ever made. This is the movie that I'm proud of because it is made for America as well as Europe and the Orient. I'm excited to see what will happen. I think it's going to gross $20 million in the U.S."

THE MARTIAL ARTS

"The martial arts is more than fighting. It's a way of thinking, of feeling - it's a whole new lifestyle."

"It's an art, and like any art, the martial arts are ultimately self-knowledge. A punch or a kick is not to knock hell out of the guy in front, but to knock the hell out of your ego, your fear, or your hang-ups. Once that is clear, then you can express yourself clearly."

"In building a statue, a sculptor doesn't keep adding clay to his subject. Actually, he keeps chiselling away at the unessentials until the truth of his creation is revealed without obstructions."

"Classical forms, rituals and unreasonable stances are useless. They are just too artificial and mechanical and don't really prepare a student for actual combat. A guy could get clobbered while getting into his classical mess!"

"I don't have any (honorary) belt at all... that is just a certificate. Unless you can really do it, that belt doesn't mean anything. It might be useful to hold your pants up, but that's about all."

"I never believe the word 'star.' That's an illusion, man, something the public calls you when you become famous. It's very easy to be blinded by all these happenings. Everybody comes up to you as Mr. Lee when you have long hair and they'll say 'Hey man, that's the in thing,' but if you have no name, they'll say, 'Look at the disgusting juvenile delinquent.'

"You must ask yourself how can you honestly express yourself at that moment? When you punch, you must really want to punch, not that you want to punch to avoid getting hit, but to really be in with it and express yourself. It doesn't matter how you are built or how you are made; you must go in there and be that punch."

ACTING

Bruce Lee was the greatest actor of all time. How did he see his role on the screen?

"I don't play the superhero, but the audience wants to make me one. I don't always play the same kind of role. Each role is different, although when I fight, I come out the same - like an animal!"

"I never depend solely on my fighting skill to fulfil any of my film roles, although the audiences in South East Asia seem to think so. I believe it is more my personality and the expression of my body and myself. I am not acting, I am just doing my thing. When somebody tries to mimic my battle cries or grimaces, he makes himself look ridiculous."

"I don't call the fighting in my films violence; I call it action. Any action film borders

somewhere between reality and fantasy. If I were to be completely realistic, you would call me a bloody violent man - I would simply destroy my opponent by tearing him apart or ripping his guts out. I wouldn't do it artistically."

"When I first arrived, I did *The Green Hornet* and as I looked around, I saw a lot of human beings, and as I looked at myself, I realised I was the only robot there because I was not being myself. When I look around, I learn something, and that is to be yourself, to express yourself, to have faith in yourself."

WOMEN

"I advise a female learning Kung Fu, that if they are ever attacked, hit 'em in the groin, poke 'em on the shins or the knee, and run like hell!"

"Women fighters? They're all right but they are no match for the men who are physiologically stronger except for a few vulnerable points. My advice is that if they have to fight, hit the man at his vital spots and then run."

"Women are more likely to achieve their objectives through feminine wiles and persuasion."

THE CHALLENGES

As the world's greatest martial artist, Bruce was plagued by challenges from many people anxious to win his crown. But Bruce Lee never doubted his own ability.

"When I first learned martial arts, I too challenged many established instructors, and what I have learned is this: If you are secure within yourself, you treat it very, very lightly because you ask yourself, 'Am I afraid of that man? Do I have any doubt within me that he is going to get me?' If I do not have such doubt, I treat it very lightly, just as today the rain is going on strong, but tomorrow maybe the sun is going to come out again."

"All the time people come up and say, 'Hey Bruce, are you really that good?' I say, well, 'If I tell you I'm good, probably you'll say I'm boasting, but if I tell you I'm no good, you'll know I'm lying!'"

"I have no fear of an opponent in front of me. I am very self-sufficient, they do not bother me. I make up my mind, and that's it, baby, you'd better kill me before I get you!"

HOLLYWOOD

"Film producers in Hollywood thought they could make use of my martial art and hoped that I would act in their films. *The Green Hornet* is one of the examples that I was being made use of. I discovered at that time, acting in that kind of film was meaningless because the roles didn't fit me. That didn't mean that I could not play such roles, the situation was only because of my yellow face."

"I guess I'm the only guy who ventured away from there and became an actor. To most people, including the actors and actresses, Hollywood is like a magic kingdom. It's beyond everyone's reach and when I made it, they thought I'd accomplished an incredible feat."

Bruce also had a few words about his famous Hollywood friends.

"James Coburn, definitely, is not a fighter; a lover, yes! I mean he's really a super nice guy, a very peaceful man who learns the martial arts because he finds it is like a mirror to reflect himself. I personally believe that all types of knowledge - I don't care what it is - ultimately means self-knowledge, and that is what he is after. Now Steve McQueen can be a very good martial artist, but I hope that it will cool him down a little bit, maybe make him a little bit more mellow and more peaceful like Jim."

FAME

Although Bruce strove continually to reach the top in everything that he attempted, when he was rocketed into fame and fortune, he discovered that kings are lonely people.

"It's like I'm in jail. I am like the monkey in the zoo with people looking at me and things like that. Basically I like the simple life and I like to joke a lot and all those things, but I cannot speak as freely as I could before because misinterpretation comes in and all kinds of things."

"The biggest disadvantage of success is losing your privacy. It's ironic but we all strive to become wealthy and famous, but once you're there it's not all rosy.'

"There's hardly a place in Hong Kong where I can go to without being stared at or people asking for autographs. That's one reason I spend a lot of time at my house to do my work. Right now, my home and the office are the most peaceful places."

ANGELA MAO: FIRST LADY OF KUNG FU!

Although the 'Little Dragon,' the incomparable Bruce Lee it dead and gone, the Kung Fu armies march ever onwards. With the spirit of Bruce to guide them, that code of personal control and disciplined perfection that gave his martial arts performances their immortal cutting edge, millions of fans are learning, loving and living Kung Fu. The ancient Eastern fighting systems are more popular today than ever before and this new wave of popularity is also world wide. From the palm skirted shores of the China Seas to such decidedly non-oriental locations as Battersea and Manchester, the Kung Fu message has gone home, with all the power of a back-swinging high kick by the 'Little Dragon' himself. And its not only the boys who've taken up the martial arts, for now thousands of girls have before them, the amazing example of Lady Kung Fu herself, Angela Mao, to show them just how deadly the female of the species can become.

Of all the contenders for the throne now so sadly left empty by the mysterious tragedy of the death of Bruce Lee (see *KFM* No. 3), the little Chopsocky Queen from Taiwan, a bundle of fury that tips the scales at no more than one hundred and five pounds and stands just a shade over five feet tall, is perhaps the most directly connected claimant to the throne. Not only that but her chops and kicks have a power numbing accuracy and speed that even the mighty Bruce would have been amazed to see! Indeed his advice to Angela, during the beginnings of both their Kung Fu screen careers was, "Do good to someone, and that person will never be able to forget you."

Born the third of seven in the Mao family, on September 20th 1950, she was enrolled at the age of five in Taiwan's prestigious Fu Shing Academy. In this residential school where the ancient Chinese traditions and arts are taught, Angela flourished. Despite the strictness of the discipline and the tight regiment under which the pupils lived at Fu Shing, Angela enjoyed her education there. Right away, her abilities as an actress and singer were noted by her teachers. She was awarded sought-after roles in the Peking Style Opera, the great Chinese Classical combination of music, singing and dancing - including highly elaborate and formalised Kung Fu! When she was twelve, she even went on a world tour with the Opera during which she made her only visit to the United States. The following year, she left school and joined the famous Hoi Kwan theatrical troupe and worked all over the

far eastern Chinese world.

It was while she was with the Hoi Kwan troupe that she caught the eye of one of Golden Harvest's top directors, Huang Feng and in 1969, he approached her with an offer to begin her career in Kung Fu films. Huang Feng had seen immediately the potential for stardom in this diminutive lady and when she accepted the company's offer they installed her in a flat in crowded Hong Kong and put her on a regular salary. She's never looked back. With Huang Feng directing, she made her screen debut in *Angry River* which has yet to be released in the West. Several more films followed, all shot under Huang Feng, to whom Angela has become devoted, and finally she got her first starring role in *Lady Whirlwind*. After this picture had proved highly successful on the Far Eastern Mandarin Movie Circuit, it was opened in the United States as *Deep Thrust, Hand of Death* and almost overnight, Angela became an international Kung Fu star. *Deep Thrust, Hand of Death* has since proved one of the most successful Kung Fu pictures ever made.

Still, Angela had yet to really cement her image with the public and now she began to seriously study her chosen school of the oriental martial arts. Hapkido is a Korean system and she originally began her work upon it when filming *Angry River*, but now she really got down to the test! After a few months' study, she so impressed top Hapkido master

Chi Han Tsai with her skills, that he awarded her a second degree black belt. An almost unheard of rate of progress, a black belt after just a few months intensive study! Angela had really begun to accept the martial arts way of life by now and for her, Hapkido became a philosophy, a physical culture and a way of living.

In her next movie, convincingly titled *Hapkido*, Angela really caught on with the public's imagination and her spitfire displays of fighting prowess was soon knocking out audiences in the West, in America, even in the middle eastern Arab countries. She was fast catching up on big brother Bruce already! In *Hapkido*, she played the indomitable Yu Ying and with the assistance of her martial arts teacher, she wipes out an entire enemy school of Kung Fu students.

The thing about Angela's fight sequences in her films that really socks it home to audiences, is the intense realism she projects. You just know that she really can do all that death defying, acrobatic Hapkido.

After Hapkido, which was shot on location in Korea, Angela filmed *When Taekwondo Strikes*, sharing the star billing with the American Taekwondo expert Jhoon Rhee; once again under the sure hand of director Huang Feng.

The film that most English fans will remember seeing her in for the first time was *Enter the Drago*n; the epic, large scale Kung Fu classic, that was Bruce Lee's last completed film. Her part in the film was short but certainly dynamic In a flashback sequence she played Bruce Lee's little sister, out walking with her aged father. A gang of thugs attack and the old man is beaten to the ground. Angela flees, pursued by the villains and after a number of frantic battles where she whirls through their ranks dealing out tremendous hammer blows right and left, she is finally confronted with no other choice but suicide. She stabs herself with a huge piece of glass and dies. It was a powerful sequence and but a foretaste of Angela Mao's amazing screen presence. *Lady Kung Fu* really arrived here with the re-

lease of *Hapkido* a few months later. As well as these, there are a number of other films that her British fans are waiting to see. *Deep Thrust, Hand of Death* (or if you prefer the Hong Kong title, *Lady Whirlwind*) in which she plays a revenge seeking sister, *Black Alley Princess* which she says is her own personal favourite and the film she considers to include her best performances so far and *The Fate of Lee Khan* in which she co-starred with another Kung Fu star in Hong Kong, King Hu. There can be little doubt that over the next few months we will be seeing a lot more of the fighting queen of Kung Fu!

What kind of girl is this remarkable *Lady Kung Fu*? Not surprisingly, she spends most of her spare time in dedicated practice of her martial art. Her instructor or 'Sensei' is one of her closest companions and everyday, she spends at least a couple of hours at work, perfecting the astonishing speed and lightning movements of Hapkido. Another fairly continuous occupation for lovely Angela is attending the Studio Doctor. Filming Kung Fu tends to leave her with any number of bruises and sprains, produced by tiny mistakes made in executing some of the more dangerous manoeuvres that are so exciting on screen. After filming Thunderbolt a few years back, she was out of action for more than two weeks; hospitalised by a fall during a particularly outrageous leap. After a hard day working in the studios and practicing in the gym, Angela normally has little energy left over for lavish socialising. In fact, she prefers the quiet life every time; its just the way she was brought up to be. The ideal of classic Chinese culture is for women to be modest, quiet and good mothers. But Angela is kept so busy making films and getting over them, that she seems to have

lost out somewhat in the area of her social life. Her favourite leisure time occupations are reading, watching sport on TV, (particularly football which she finds filled with grace, power and skill not too unlike Kung Fu itself) or just staying in for the evening and asking a few friends to drop round. Certainly you won't find her out for the night in any of Hong Kong's infamous bright lights districts, nor hanging out at wild parties or glittering society engagements. She's a homebody, and even when she does decide to go out, it's just as likely to be to play basketball or go bowling as anything else. However Angela does like to see some Western Movies. Her favourite actor is Marlon Brando, although she'll never see *Last Tango in Paris*, with all its explicit sex scenes because the censors in Hong Kong completely banned it.

Hapkido itself is a newcomer amongst the codified fighting systems in use in the East. Recently organised along easily taught lines, it is a development from thirteen hundred years of Korean fighting skill. The origins are obscure but certainly the dreaded Hwa Rang Do, the fighting samurai style warrior knights of Korean yesteryear, were the most likely originators of the style. The art was then refined further by isolated Hermit Monks who, forbidden by the Emperors to carry arms, were often attacked and killed by wandering bandits. To protect themselves, the monks took up the skilled martial arts of the warrior knights and perfected the 'circular motion' and the 'water principle,' both of which are so important in modern day Hapkido.

Naturally enough because this Korean school of Kung Fu relies so much on kicking, its exponents must be superbly fit. To get a kick placed in the right place, say on the chin, means the foot must travel several feet. Obviously an opponent will have longer to see it coming and take evasive action. Also, it is harder to avoid 'telegraphing' by facial movements and shifts of the body to your opponent that you are about to launch a kick. To overcome this difficulty, the Hapkido masters stress that the body must be in absolute tip top condition so that these blows will travel with the highest possible speed. That is one good reason why Angela, the First Lady of Kung Fu and the Queen of Hapkido, spends so much of her time in the gym, training under the eyes of her 'Sensei.'

So, what will Angela, at present, superbly fit and constantly at work, be doing in the future. She will probably move on to less physically exhausting and mentally satisfying movie roles but her Kung Fu skills will always be a part of her life. Her code of conduct and her daily observance of the ancient rites of her martial art will ensure that!

Tong Inch'iek

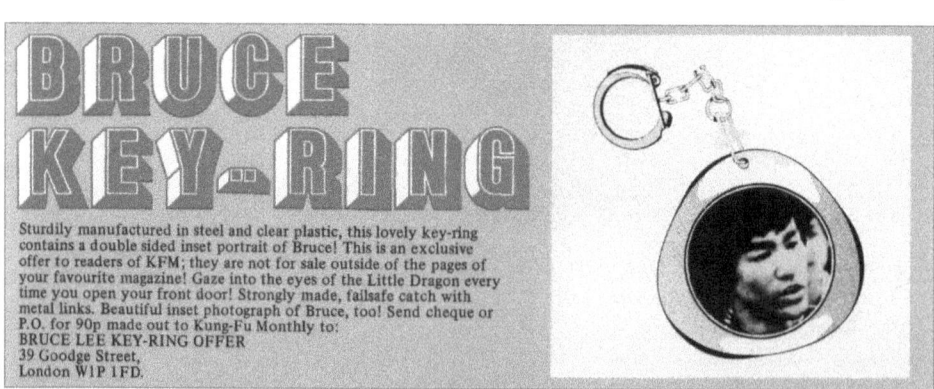

BRUCE KEY-RING

Sturdily manufactured in steel and clear plastic, this lovely key-ring contains a double sided inset portrait of Bruce! This is an exclusive offer to readers of KFM; they are not for sale outside of the pages of your favourite magazine! Gaze into the eyes of the Little Dragon every time you open your front door! Strongly made, failsafe catch with metal links. Beautiful inset photograph of Bruce, too! Send cheque or P.O. for 90p made out to Kung-Fu Monthly to:
BRUCE LEE KEY-RING OFFER
39 Goodge Street,
London W1P 1FD.

THE MARTIAL ART

These illustrations by Paul Simmons are from a book to be published in October of this year by Wildwood House of London. The book is to be called *The Beginner's Guide to Kung Fu*. You will find a detailed description of the book and an order form at the foot of this month's pin-up poster!

Warning: A little knowledge is often a dangerous thing! Read the Kung Fu Code at the beginning of this book before lifting a finger. Better still, write to one of the organisations listed elsewhere in this book to find out about joining a reputable Kung Fu club!

ACHILLES TENDON EXERCISE

- From basic stance (A) bend the knees and drop into a squatting position (B) Rock back onto heels keeping the fists at the hips (C).

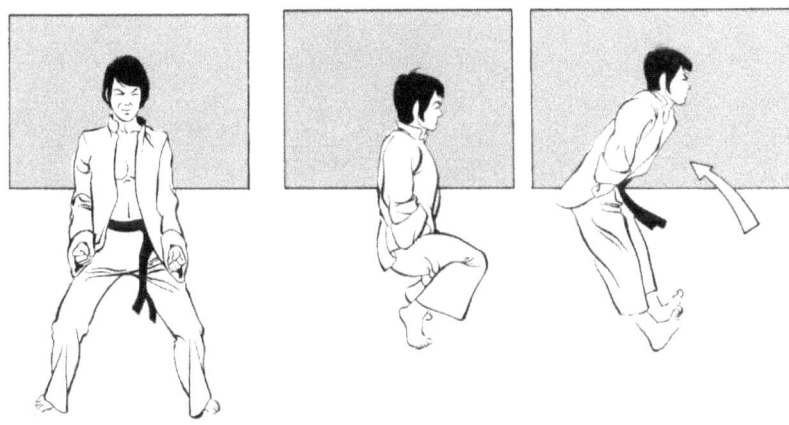

LEG EXERCISE

- From basic stance (A) bring the feet together. Draw the knee up to the abdomen (D) and push the straight out in front until leg is straight, horizontal to floor (E) This exercise is for the muscles and ten-in the back of the leg.

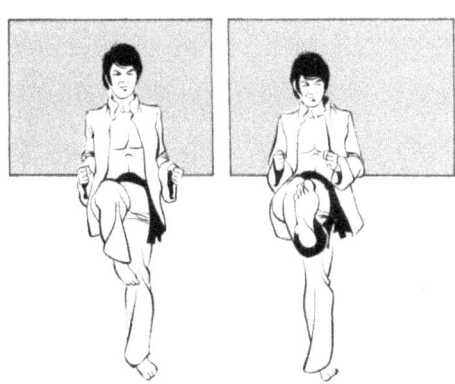

DEFENCE & COUNTER ATTACK

- Up until now, the various techniques of blocks and strikes have been dealt with separately. But in this chapter we will demonstrate how to put them in application.

- Opponent leads with right punch to the chest. Forearm Middle Line Block.
- Side Snap-kick to the abdomen with the left foot. This can be followed up if necessary with a Rising Elbow strike to the throat.

KICKBACK: THE LETTERS

Hi there! Jenny here with more of your letters, questions, queries and comments! We're still ploughing our way through all the suggestions and good advice we've had from many of you about subjects for future issues! In fact, we've had so many suggestions, that it's difficult to know where to begin! I think that we might be running a really great piece I sneaked a preview of on the editor's desk last week about the Kung Fu movie industry and all the people, companies and stars that produce those films we're just beginning to get a glimpse of in Britain! Just before we get onto the letters, I'll leave you with my usual pleas to mark the envelopes of your letters clearly, whether you're writing for information, or sending off for any one of the Special Offers. It really helps us sort your mail quickly!

REAL NAME PLEASE!

Dear *KFM*,
I am very confused about Bruce's name because in your magazine, you call him Lee Hsiao Lung, but in the Sunday People, his name was given as Lee Yuen Kam. Could you please tell me who is right and what is his correct name?
Jackie Brown, North Walsham, Norfolk

Dear Jackie,
Bruce was born with the name Lee Yuen Kam, but he changed his name on several occasions in his life. The Chinese spelling of 'Lee' is, in fact, 'Li.' Also, the first or Christian names of a person in China, are put after their surname. So both The Sunday People and our article were right! Many people in Hong Kong, still spell Bruce's name as Bruce Li!

BRUCE LEE AUTHOR

Dear *KFM*,
I want to know: Did Bruce Lee ever write any books or publications of any kind? Especially on the martial arts? If he did, I would pay any price to get hold of a copy. I am just learning Kung Fu at a local club; Wing Chun style. Your magazine inspired me to join this club and I practice my exercises every day. Congratulations *KFM*. All your staff should be given medals for producing such a great magazine!
Nigel Thomas, Chelmsford, Essex

Dear Nigel,
I thank you for your overwhelming praise! I don't think we quite run to medals, but we do all wear our Bruce Lee badges here in the KFM offices! Now, as to your question about Bruce's writing. I have asked the authors of the new book to be published in July called Bruce Lee King of Kung Fu, whether or not Bruce ever wrote any books or articles. They have told me that apart from the film scripts he worked on, Bruce wrote a book called The Tao of Jeet Kune Do, which he was going to publish at one time. It was a manual on his own fighting style and martial art! However, after much thought, he decided not to publish the book, and I doubt if his widow, Linda Lee, will ever allow it to be published!

AGE LIMITS

Dear *KFM*,
As I am only writing to ask you about one thing, I will make this letter short and to the point. Do you think Bruce Lee's films should be shown to people under the age of 18? As I am only 14, I think they should!
Martin Brook, Thornhill Lees, Dewsbury

Dear Martin,
Many, many other readers have written to me saying much the same thing as you! They all desperately want to see Bruce on the screen but they are too young to attend the movies! Unfortunately, there is nothing that can be done while the laws stay as they are! I have seen Bruce Lee movies where there were very young people attending, but they were all outside of this country. I'm afraid that until you reach the right age, Martin, you'll just have to be patient which isn't much of a consolation I know!

KUNG FU CLUB

Dear *KFM*,
I have enquired about local Kung Fu clubs around where I live but have only found Judo and Karate clubs, which I do not want to join. Until I can find a club to join, or until one opens in my area, could you advise me of a book or reading material on Kung Fu? By the way, my heartiest congratulations on *KFM* - in my house, we have taken to buying two copies per issue to save the fighting and squabbling over who gets to read it first and keep the poster!
Nick Weymouth, Newcastle-under-Lyme, Staffs

Dear Nick,

Hope you managed to win the fight for the poster of last month. That's my favourite picture of Bruce in KFM No.3! As to a Kung Fu book, I would suggest that you fill in the order form for The Beginner's Guide to Kung Fu elsewhere in this issue. I've seen proof pages of this hook and as you can tell from Paul Simmons drawings on the 'Martial Art' page of each Issue of KFM, it really is going to be a super book and a very practical one too. It's a shame that the publishers can't get it out before October, but I can promise you it'll be worth waiting for!

BRUCE LEE FAN CLUB

Those of you who wish to join the Bruce Lee Fan club should write to the following address enclosing a stamped addressed envelope. Mark your letter, 'Application for Membership.' You might like to mention, too, that you are a reader of *KFM*!

The Legendary Bruce Lee Fan Club, 62 Milton Road, London, W.7.

The club is run by Miss Rhona McVay and is an official club, with the backing of Cathay Films Ltd. Please be patient if your letter is not answered immediately; remember there are delays in the postal services in London at present, and Rhona has many thousands of letters to deal with each week!

IMPORTANT NOTICE

Many of you have contacted us informing us of late delivery of your orders for Treasure Kits, Poster, T-Shirts and other items. We apologise sincerely to those of you inconvenienced in this way. However, the situation is really out of our hands at present. The G.P.O. (General Post Office) has confirmed that due to shortage of staff and a dispute at their Central London sorting office, all incoming mail, (that means your orders to us!), is being delivered anything up to 14 days late! We have, in fact, received orders from outside of London that were posted three weeks previously! The G.P.O. assures us that the situation is slowly improving, however. We ask for your patience and cooperation; all our staff work very hard to despatch your orders within a few days of receipt. We can only hope that you agree that the waiting is worthwhile!

EDITORIAL

Hi there Kung Fu fans...

Welcome back to another issue of *Kung-Fu Monthly*... and this time we feel we've outdone ourselves! First off, we have another feature article by our resident editor Don Won Ton tracing the full history of Kung Fu back to its earliest roots plus a detailed look at Bruce Lee's revolutionary contribution to the Martial Arts. As you may remember from *KFM* No.3, Don visited Hong Kong to uncover the true facts about Bruce's extraordinary life and career and, while there, he spoke to many of Bruce's fellow martial artists. Just how much he learned can be seen from the story on this page!

Bruce, of course, was far more than just the greatest action movie superstar of all time. His life was devoted to the Martial Arts and, in fact, to Bruce, the glamour of the film world ran a poor second to Kung Fu. But to many of his fans who only knew Bruce from his movies, the Martial Arts often seem to take a back seat to his spectacular acting ability. In his article this month, Don sets the record straight.

Next up we have an exclusive report from our Hong Kong correspondent Peter Woo on the Kung Fu stars who are is the running to take over Bruce's vacant throne. Some of the faces that Peter has collected will probably be familiar; others you may not know so well, if at all! But certainly, none of them can be discounted as future Kings of Kung Fu. In later issues we hope to publish more contenders, so stand by!

Back in London, it has been a busy month for the Martial Arts. Cathay Films, who brought you three of Bruce's Kung Fu epics, are to release two new action dramas: *One-Armed Boxer*, starring Wang Yu, and *Stoner*, starring Angela Mao and Australian star George Lazenby. What's an Australian actor doing in a Kung Fu movie? Well George, who rose to fame as James '007' Bond, went to see a Bruce Lee film in Los Angeles a year ago and decided that he must co-star with the Little Dragon. He flew out to Hong Kong and was signed up by Bruce's producer Raymond Chow to star in *Game of Death*. Tragically, a week later, Bruce was dead. But George, by now a fully-fledged Kung Fu addict, stayed in Hong Kong, and *Stoner* is the result! With Angela to help him out of the tight spots, it should be some movie!

As you will see by our advertisement, we still have some stocks left of the Bruce Lee Treasure Kit but you'd better hurry as the response has been fantastic. We're still taking orders for the two book offers - *Bruce Lee: King of Kung Fu* and *The Beginner's Guide to Kung Fu* - but again you'll have to be quick!

That's all from me this month...

Felix Yen

Felix Yen
Editor-in-Chief

HOW BRUCE LEE SPARKED THE KUNG FU REVOLUTION

There is no doubt in the minds of film fans around the world that Bruce Lee - the man they called The Little Dragon - was the greatest action movie star of all time. In countless far flung cinemas from London to Kuala Lumpur, Boston to Bangkok, Bruce was the unchallenged Prince of the Flashing Fists, thrilling audiences of every race, colour and creed with his stare 'n' tear film fury. Movie producers hounded him, martial artists envied him and his enthralled fans worshipped him. If Bruce Lee had lived, he would have been the highest paid movie actor in the world!

But how much did Bruce really do for the martial arts? Will he be remembered as a legendary fighter by the Kung Fu disciples of tomorrow? Or will he go down in history merely as a superb film actor?

To answer these questions, we must first trace back to the roots of Kung Fu to discover how it developed up until the spectacular arrival of Bruce Lee.

As with any tradition or art founded before the birth of civilisation as we know it today, the origins of Kung Fu are extremely blurred. Some scholars believe that it was first developed 4,600 years ago by Hung Di - the 'Yellow Emperor' - who required a fast method of training his army. The next mention of the art comes in The Book of Rites (1066-403BC), but unfortunately it is only a mention and no details of its practice are given. After this date, Kung Fu seems mysteriously to have been forgotten in China for 1,000 years.

According to popular Chinese legend, the re-birth of the deadly art was the work of an Indian monk - the legendary Bodhidharma (sometimes known as Daruma and Sifu). While on a journey through China around the year 525 AD, Bodhidharma stopped off at a monastery in the Honan Province known as the Shaolin Temple. Bodhidharma stayed at the monastery and taught the resident monks many lessons in Zen Buddhism. However, he noticed, much to his dismay, that the unfit monks were nodding off during his classes, unable to stay awake for even a few hours at a time. What was worse, Bodhidharma learned that the monks, as they wandered throughout the country, were in great peril for their lives; easy prey for the many roving bands of cut-throats and brigands who controlled large areas of China.

In order to keep his pupils awake and to provide them with some means of defending themselves (at that time it was forbidden by law to carry weapons on pain of death), Bodhidharma taught them a set of eighteen physical and mental exercises which he called Eki-Kinkyo. Later, these eighteen exercises were expanded to seventy-two movements by a wealthy young disciple named Yen, and later still another set of 'soft' movements were added. From these, the deadly lightning-bolt we now know as Kung Fu was born.

Suddenly, China became Kung Fu crazy! As the Shaolin monks travelled across the land, so too did they take with them their lethal secret, spreading the invincible knowledge of Kung Fu to dozens of Chinese temples and cities. And Shaolin Kung Fu has remained one of the most popular forms of the art, right up to this very day. Although more than 100 different Kung Fu styles have sprang up over the centuries, the Shaolin school and its five main branches (named after their founding monks: Hung, Low, Li, Choy and Mok) are still the most widely respected!

The reason for this lasting respect lies in the incredibly rigorous training which the Shaolin style demanded. In the recently published biography of Bruce by F. Dennis and D. Atyeo titled *Bruce Lee: King of Kung Fu*, James Yee, a Shaolin disciple in China until the Communist takeover of the country, recounts his boyhood training in a Shaolin temple.

By constantly practicing his exercises every single day without fail (exercises which included slamming his fists into bags of rice for hours on end, kicking at boards and clinging to a pole with his knees in the rain for twenty minutes and more), Yee could slice a melon thrown in the air with a sweep of his hand, break bricks with his fist and kill a man with one blow; all at the age of 16! Eventually Yee was allowed to take on the training for the Iron Fist technique, the famous Shaolin method of invincible combat. Many years after, his fists are still lethal weapons.

Had he continued training at the Shaolin Temple, Yee would have been initiated into the secrets of internal power whereby a disciple can seemingly perform feats of unbelievable 'magic.' With what small amount of instruction in internal power Yee did receive, he learned the ability to bend swords using just his throat! Later, he would have found out how to make himself literally as light as a feather, how to see for several miles, hear the tiniest sound and break a dozen bricks with one blow!

To become a fully-fledged Shaolin Kung Fu Master, disciples had to undergo the fearsome Test of the Four Rooms. Each room was designed to test the novice in a different way: for example, in the Dark Room, the disciple had to sit on the floor in total darkness and then suddenly a knife would be thrown directly at him. The disciple had to be so alert that he could actually hear the wind made by the knife so as to be able to duck or block it. In the Power Room, the student had to lift a 200lb rock, pull back an enormous strong bow and carry two 400lb baskets.

The final test was the Revenge Room. "All they gave you was this long chair," writes Yee. "Then you had to defend yourself against ten guys with sticks bundled together to start whipping you. If you could defend against them without injuring any of them, then you'd made it."

In the book, Yee relates many more torturous physical disciplines required by the Shaolin Masters, but from these few examples, it is easy to see why Shaolin Kung Fu is revered by martial artists as the ultimate form of traditional Kung Fu!

As a permanent and lasting badge of his ordeals, the Shaolin Kung Fu Master, once he had passed through the Test of the Four Rooms successfully, he picked up a red hot urn with his forearms to brand an indelible symbol into his flesh! In the T.V. series *Kung Fu*, David Carradine carried the mark of the Dragon on his forearm which, if he had been a real Shaolin monk, he would have got by lifting the urn.

But apart from Shaolin Kung Fu, many other Kung Fu styles and schools were founded. As can be expected from the musical names of many of their movements, (Monkey Grabbing the Peach, Tiger Descending the Mountain etc.), many of these schools were based on the movements of animals and insects. In fact, animal, bird and insect actions were responsible for entire new fighting styles.

For example, legend teaches that the founder of the Tong Long (Praying Mantis) school, first discovered his style while watching a praying mantis fighting a grasshopper 300 years ago in the Chinese province of Shantung. So impressed was he by the praying mantis' attack and defence systems, that he captured it and took it home. By prodding it with a small stick, he was able to work out its various stances, which he quickly transferred to paper. So too was how the Bak Hok Pai (White Crane) school founded. It is a long range Boxing style for use against several attackers and it closely resembles the flapping wings of a large crane.

By the 16th century, Kung Fu in China had become an established and firmly rooted method of defence. However, sometime during that century, the whole martial art of

Kung Fu was overturned and revolutionised by the ideas of one person; a woman by the name of Yim Wing Chun! Madam Yim, while studying the martial arts under a Shaolin nun, Ng Mui, decided that traditional Kung Fu had become bogged down by too many unnecessary stances and movements. She set about developing an entirely new, close quarter method of combat by cutting down the number of 'sets' or 'Katas.' Kung Fu schools often require a knowledge of over a hundred Katas (Shaolin has 38), but Madam Yim paired her style down to just three! She called her new school Wing Chun Kung Fu, a name that would sweep martial arts colleges throughout the Far East!

What Madam Yim hoped to do was to balance the traditional 'harder' Kung Fu with a new 'soft' method of fighting which actually used the opponent's strength rather than tried to dominate it. By flowing with his opponent, the Wing Chun disciple is capable of defending himself even when he has been blindfolded! Gradually Madam Yim's new martial art of Wing Chun was handed down from generation to generation of star students until finally it was given to a disciple from China's Kwantung Province. This was the legendary Yip Man, the martial master who discovered and instructed the great Bruce Lee!

Yip Man realised that in the modern world, fighting styles had to be adaptable to any form of attack, whether it be Western Boxing, wrestling, Thai kick Boxing, sword fighting and so on. He believed that Wing Chun, with its stripped-down movements and no-non-

sense lightning fast attack system, was the ideal Kung Fu school for modern defence. He passed on this conviction to his many pupils, one of whom was a young 13-year-old street fighter and teenage gang-leader who joined his class one day, in the hope of learning a few new savage tricks to try out on the vicious streets of seething Hong Kong.

Instead of becoming bored by the monotonous routine and drifting away from the class after one or two lessons, as most of the other tough street punks did, the young Bruce became fascinated by Wing Chun Kung Fu and he struck up a lasting friendship with his ageing master, Yip Man. When the old man died in 1973, Bruce, by now a famous movie superhero and an extremely busy man, took time off to attend his master's funeral and to sign the register.

Yip Man taught Bruce everything he knew about Wing Chun, but still the young man demanded to know more about Kung Fu! Finally, even the few limitations of the stripped-down Wing Chun style became a burden to the lethal young fighter and Bruce decided to do something about it. In doing so, like Madam Yim three centuries before him, Bruce Lee sparked another Kung Fu revolution!

Why not, figured Bruce, throw away all styles and schools and restrictions and try for total fighting freedom? The traditional teachers thought he was mad. "How can you do away with style?" they asked dumbfounded.

But that is exactly what Bruce did. He took the rule book and threw it out the window and invented his own form which was, in fact, no form at all. He called it Jeet Kune Do - 'The Way of the Intercepting Fist!'

"I am no styles, but I am all styles," he told the many rich and famous pupils who flocked to his Jeet Kune Do academies in later years. "You don't know what I am going to do and even I don't know what I am going to do. My movement is the result of your movement; my technique is the result of your technique."

To become 'no style yet all styles,' Bruce devoted his life to studying almost every fighting technique the world could offer. In his U.S. apartment, he would sit glued to the T.V. watching the Boxing and wrestling bouts. It got so, that he could tell his friends what punch a particular boxer was about to throw even before the boxer had actually started to move! His library in Hong Kong was reputed to be the largest collection of martial arts literature ever collected by any one man!

By studying all these different styles and learning their rules, Bruce was able to break them at will and add them piece by piece to his own invention - Jeet Kune Do. Watch again the action in any of Bruce's movies. Compare his 'non-style' against that of the rigid and formalised movements of his traditional Karate opponents. One minute Bruce is fighting like a Shaolin School disciple, using hard, sharp punches; the next he is dancing around his opponent like Muhammad Ali! "I am all styles...!"

This then, is Bruce's astonishing gift to the world of the martial arts.

Not only did he become the swiftest, deadliest, most damaging exponent of the lethal Wing Chun Kung Fu school, but he broke through the barriers of Wing Chun to open up a whole newer, wider horizon for the martial arts.

It is for this gift, the gift of Jeet Kune Do, that the spirit of Bruce Lee will live on in the hearts and minds of all those who tread the enlightening path of the martial arts!

WHO'S THE NEW KING OF KUNG FU?

For countless centuries, this age-old traditional cry has rung out from British palaces with the passing of each monarch. When a king dies, the people mourn, but another is always there to take his place.

In the exploding world of the martial arts, with the passing of Bruce Lee, The Little Dragon, the King is truly dead. But unlike the British monarchy where the next-in-line to the throne is chosen long before he has to take up the crown, just exactly who will fill Bruce's shoes is far from certain.

In Hong Kong at this moment, there are more than a dozen contenders for the crown - both male and female - all of whom have staked a claim to it with their fighting prowess. Several stars such as Wang Yu, Angela Mao and David Chiang you will have already seen in films such as *Hapkido*, *The One Armed Swordsman* and *The Chinese Boxer*. Others you may not have even heard of as their films, though wildly successful in their native Hong Kong, are still waiting for release in this country, America and Europe.

Our man in Hong Kong, Peter Woo, with the help of our own ever-ready cameraman Paul Chang, has brought you this first selection of title contenders. In the near future we plan to run pictures and information on many more of the up-and-coming martial movie stars.

Also, Cathay Films are planning to release two more fighting Kung Fu epics in the very near future. The first is *The One Armed Boxer*, starring the fantastic Wang Yu. The second is called *Stoner*, and stars ex-007 James Bond George Lazenby. Both movies should be a knockout!

So here they are, in pictures and in words, the men and women who are fighting (literally!) for Bruce Lee's Kung Fu crown. If you think there is a worthy successor amongst them, drop us a line here at *KFM*, telling us who you chose and why.

The man with the flying fists in this picture is none other than former James Bond George Lazenby! In this, his first Kung Fu movie, Stoner, George plays a narcotics agent who teams up with Lady Kung Fu herself, Angela Mao, to smash a drug gang headed by the sinister Mr Sinn. Incidentally, the co-star is Betty Ting Pei, Bruce Lee's close friend.

With a line-up like this, *Stoner* should put George well on the way to Kung Fu stardom!

It was Wang Yu who in fact starred in the first Kung Fu movie; a Shaw Bros. production called *The Chinese Boxer*. In Hong Kong, the film was an immediate hit (as it was later in the Western world) and it made Wang the hottest movie property in the East. However, when Bruce Lee made *The Big Boss*, Wang was overshadowed by The Little Dragon, although he could still command an enormous fee. Finally, Wang decided to leave Shaw Bros., and now, as his latest production shows, he has joined up with Raymond Chow's Golden Harvest company. This picture is taken from the soon-to-be-released *One-Armed*  *Boxer*, co-starring Tien Yen and Tang Shin. Before his death, Bruce said that he would like to make a film with Wang, but added that any battle between the two stars would have to come out a draw as both were, in the eyes of the fans, evenly matched. High praise indeed, coming from The Little Dragon!

Lo Lieh's latest film is with Lee Van Cleef and one of the first Eastern/Western co-productions to come out of Hong Kong. Titled *Blood Money*, it is produced by Shaw Bros., and Carlo Ponti. You may remember Lo as the star of *The Killer*, one of the first Kung Fu movies to explode in Britain.

Fu Sheng is a new rising star in the Kung Fu galaxy. Watch for him in the Shaw Bros. *Friends*, co-starring with David Chiang and Peter Cushing. If his fighting talents match his looks, we're certain of seeing much more of Fu Sheng on the big screen.

Carter Wong is also no stranger to Kung Fu fans. Co-starring with Angela Mao has boosted his career no end, and if he can show the same fighting form in his own films,

Carter could be a force to be reckoned with!

This off-camera shot is of David Chiang and veteran British actor Peter Cushing. Together they star in the new Shaw Bros, epic *Friends*. Hong Kong film men strongly tip David as Bruce's successor.

KICKBACK: THE LETTERS

Hi there! Jenny here once again with some more selections from our overloaded mailbag. And I'm not kidding when I say overloaded either! Honestly, It's a full time job just opening all your hundreds of letters which I receive each day. It's even reached the stage where readers are answering other readers' questions before they're even asked! For instance, B.K. Thompson of Oakham wrote in to tell us the details about the Enter the Dragon title music, "Just in case any of your readers are interested." The next day, we had two enquiries about the track! If this keeps up, I'll be out of a job! (Incidentally, the soundtrack - complete with Bruce's battle cry - is by Lalo Schifrin on the Warner Bros. label, No. K4627S.) Letter of the Month goes to Miss Gina Lawson of Williamson Street, Holloway. I showed Gina's letter to our editor Don Won Ton, who was so impressed with her suggestion that he dug into the files and came up with the feature in this issue. Good work, Gina. Well, that's about it from me this month, but before we get onto the letters, I'll ask you to remember to mark your envelopes clearly, whether you're writing to me or for a Special Offer. Now, on with the show!

LETTER OF THE MONTH

Dear *KFM*,
Although I am an avid Bruce Lee fan (and your articles and pictures are really great) I still enjoy watching other Kung Fu artistes such as Alex Lung, David Chiang etc. I know as yet it is 'early days' for *KFM*, but will you in time, be covering all the different stars? It might be a good idea to publish a chart showing 'Who's Who in Kung Fu' (and it rhymes) with pictures of the actors, some personal info and the films they've been in. I know I, for one, would find this very interesting and helpful.
Gina Lawson, Williamson Street, Holloway

Dear Gina,
A great idea as Don Won Ton and I both agree. I hope this month's story gives you some help in recognising the up and coming stars of Kung Fu. In future issues, Don Won Ton has promised to feature more 'greats' of the martial movie scene, so watch out for that.

BRUCE AND LINDA

Dear *KFM*,
Thank you for producing such a fantastic magazine. I have enjoyed reading all three, especially Issue No.3. Now, at last, we know the truth of how Bruce really died. It was a very touching account and I cried myself to sleep that night and I'm sure many other *KFM* readers felt the same. Although Bruce is dead he will never be forgotten. Please, if it is possible, print some pictures of Bruce with his wife. Also in *KFM* No.3, you printed a picture of Bruce with a Chinese man. Can you tell me who it is?
Bruce Lee Fan, Stockingford Nuneaton

Dear Bruce Lee Fan,
Thanks for the praise about Don Won Ton's article from Hong Kong. Although it is a relief to know the truth, I agree that it was also very sad. As you will see from the picture in this issue, we were able to help you out with a shot of Bruce and his wife Linda, which was taken while they were relaxing in an airport lounge. Hope you like it. As for the Chinese man standing with Bruce in No.3, he is Mr. Raymond Chow, the movie producer who gave Bruce his first break into the Chinese film world with The Big Boss. After their first overwhelming success, the two men became business partners and were firm friends right up to the day of Bruce's tragic death.

BRUCE'S BACKGROUND

Dear *KFM*,
I am a great fan of Bruce Lee. Although I get *Kung-Fu Monthly*, there are many things I don't know. These are some things I would like to know. What car did Bruce drive? Did he make any films for children? How many attacking men could he cope with at once? Has he actually been cut or bruised in a fight? Keep up the good work.
Gian Rizzi, Middlesbrough, Teeside

Dear Gian,
Bruce was a very complex man and there are a lot of things which I don't know about him! But I put your questions to the authors of the new Bruce book titled BRUCE LEE: KING OF Kung Fu and this is what they came up with. Bruce drove several cars during his career, but his favourite and last one was a huge red Mercedes which he had imported to Hong Kong. At the time of his sad death, he was in the process of buying a Rolls Royce, complete with a gold nameplate. Unfortunately, Bruce did not make any A-rated films. When in a fighting mood, I doubt if an army could have stopped Bruce, but in answer to your third question, I think the most opponents Bruce ever took on was in the film Fist of Fury, where he single-handedly beats up the entire rival Karate academy! Funnily enough, Bruce was injured in a fight during filming of Enter the Dragon. His co-star Bob Wall, lunged at Bruce with a bottle and held on to it for just a second too long. The result was a nasty cut in Bruce's hand which held up shooting for twelve days.

THE LITTLE DRAGON

Dear *KFM*,
First we would like to thank you for your wonderful magazine. We missed the first issue but we have bought the last two and we will continue to do so faithfully for as long as it lasts! Thank you for the article in *KFM* No.3 about the sad story of Bruce Lee's last hours; it answered many questions, but could you please tell us exactly what his real name was? Two more questions about Bruce. Was he a vegetarian, and did he really take cannabis? We found that strange, especially as he was a non-drinker and a non-smoker. We hope you can supply the answers to our questions and keep up the good work with *KFM*!
Carole Smith & Jeanette Campbell, The Crossways, Sheffield

Dear Carole and Jeanette,
You are just two of the hundreds of Bruce fans who have written in asking about his name! Bruce was born with the name Li Yuen Kam (meaning Protector of San Francisco, where Bruce was actually born), but after a film which he made while only a small boy (Bruce was also a child star in his homeland of Hong Kong, a fact which many people do not know!) his fans began calling him Li Hsiao Lung, which means literally The Little Dragon. This stuck until Bruce returned to the US where he changed his name yet again to plain old Bruce Lee! Bruce was not exactly a vegetarian, but he did follow a unique diet which consisted mainly of raw minced beef, milk, eggs and treacle all mixed up in a blender and drunk from a glass! Not very appetising I must admit, but if you want to become the fittest man in the world... As to your last question, Bruce did take cannabis occasionally after checking with a medical specialist that it wouldn't harm his fitness. Incidentally, two free copies of Issue No.1 are on their way out to you.

HIS TRUE STORY
HIS LIFE HIS ART HIS FILMS HIS DEATH

BRUCE LEE
KING OF KUNG-FU

100 PAGES LONG!
CONTAINS OVER 40,000 WORDS!
SCORES OF EXCLUSIVE PHOTOGRAPHS!
FULLY RESEARCHED BY THE AUTHORS IN HONG KONG AND U.S.A.! THIS IS THE ULTIMATE BRUCE LEE BOOK!

INCREDIBLE BOOK OFFER!
BRUCE LEE: KING OF KUNG-FU
This is the legendary story of Bruce Lee, Yuen Kam, The Little Dragon. Lavishly illustrated with scores of exclusive photographs, this book is to be published in August by a major London publisher, Wildwood House Ltd. Every aspect of Lee's incredible career has been covered throughly and exhaustively researched: His childhood, his teenage gangs, his family, his early martial training, his life in America, his role as kung-fu champion and teacher and his bid for world fame on the silver screen.
The book also investigates deeply into the real cause behind Bruce Lee's death, and reports on his lasting effect on the Chinese people and his place in movie fans' hearts around the world. Here is a book that will thrill every real fan of Bruce Lee; a book to be kept, to be read and re-read a thousand times. It contains *everything* you ever wanted to know about Bruce and together with the big, beautiful photographs, (the format of the book is large—over 11" x 8"), it is a worthy tribute to the invincible King of Kung-Fu.
We are inviting pre-publication subscription offers on this book to KFM readers *only*! Your copy of what will probably become the classic version of Bruce Lee's life will be sent to you on the very day of publication this August. Avoid disappointment and send off now! Mail £1.25 by cheque or postal order made out to Kung-Fu Monthly and enclose your carefully written name and address. All orders to: BRUCE LEE BOOK OFFER, Kung-Fu Monthly, 39 Goodge Street, London W1P 1FD. You won't be disappointed!

THE POSTER MAGAZINES - VOLUME ONE

06

1974

EDITORIAL

Hi there Kung Fu fans...

Here we go again with another bumper issue of *Kung-Fu Monthly* and even if I do say so myself, I think this one's a winner! To start the ball rolling, we have another in-depth investigation by our own Don Won Ton into Bruce Lee's Hollywood years. As you shall see, the time Bruce spent in Hollywood left an indelible mark on the young fighter. Sometimes the movie capital was kind to Bruce, but at other times it was cruel! In his article, packed with quotes from Bruce's Hollywood friends and colleagues, Don looks at just how Bruce became the highest paid actor in the world!

Also in this issue, our Hong Kong bureau chief Peter Woo has scoured the movie studios of the Far East to bring you yet another array of the top Kung Fu film stars in action today. You'll no doubt remember last month's 'Who's Who' feature with its line-up of such incredible names as Wang Yu, George Lazenby, Carter Wong and David Chiang.

And while we're talking about popular choices, have you got your copy of our *KFM* Special - the Giant Bruce Lee Scrapbook? From start to finish this - our first *KFM* Special took us many weeks of hard work to prepare, sorting through our photo library, chasing off to Hong Kong and America for more material, pestering film companies for action film stills. And what a job the *KFM* team has produced, but don't just take my word for it. Rush out and get your own copy as this one's sure to become a red hot collector's item in the not too far distant future! Back on the cinema circuit, it's been a good month for Kung Fu fans, what with the release of the first East/West co-production *Legend of the Seven Golden Vampires*, as described by Don Won Ton in this month's Hollywood feature but it looks like being an even better one next month! Cathay Films have informed me that they have no less than four films all on the starting blocks - *One Armed Boxer*, *Beach of the War Gods*, *Kung Fu Girl* and *When Taekwondo Strikes*. A knockout bunch if ever I saw one!

This month we have several brand new special offers for you to select. First up is the Bruce Lee souvenir coffee mug, a lovely gift for any Bruce fan and a treasured memory for you. Also, for martial art enthusiasts, we have an incredible Kung Fu suit offer imported direct from China especially for *KFM*.

And last - but certainly not least - let me recommend to you all the latest Cathay release in this country, Wang Yu's *One Armed Boxer*. Produced by Raymond Chow, the man who brought Bruce Lee back to Hong Kong, and directed by Wang Yu himself, *One Armed Boxer* is the story of a disabled kung fu fighter's revenge on a gang of martial artists led by a deadly Judo master. It's great stuff!

That's all from me this month...

Felix Yen

Felix Yen
Editor-in-Chief

HOW BRUCE LEE TAMED HOLLYWOOD

For those who make it to the top in the cutthroat business of international film making, Hollywood - movie capital of the world - is a lush paradise, crammed with an endless supply of parties, social events and million dollar jobs.

But for every 'star' in Hollywood, there are a hundred others struggling to break into the big time, and for them, Hollywood is not a paradise but a nightmare, cruelly driving them to desperation and defeat. And such is the power of Hollywood, that it almost crushed the finest martial artist the world has ever seen - Bruce 'Little Dragon' Lee!

This is the story of how Bruce rose to the challenge and fought on until he had Hollywood in the palm of his hand!

Even as a teenager roaming the streets of Hong Kong, Bruce was irresistibly drawn to the magical fairyland of Hollywood. The son of a famous Cantonese opera stage star, from his earliest childhood days, Bruce had been a popular screen attraction in Hong Kong. With the release of his finest childhood movie *Kid Cheung*, Bruce, or 'Little Dragon' as his

Chinese fans now began to call him, rose to the position of top child actor in Hong Kong.

For any other youngster, reaching the top at such an early age would have been a satisfying achievement but not for Bruce Lee! Realising that he was really only a local attraction, known to only a limited number of fans, Bruce became bored and disillusioned with his child acting career. To break away, he took to running with teenage gangs in the rough and tough Hong Kong streets, which led him into contact with an old Wing Chun Kung Fu master called Yip Man. What resulted from this chance meeting is martial history! But again, even though by the age of eighteen, Bruce had rocketed to the status of a junior martial arts master, he knew that the world awaited his special talents and that he couldn't give himself solely to Hong Kong. With $100 in his pocket, Bruce jumped ship for America and ultimately, Hollywood! "To most people, including actors and actresses, Hollywood is like a magic kingdom," he told one interviewer many years later. "It's beyond everyone's reach..."

Including the reach of the great Bruce Lee, or at least for the moment! For his first few months in America, Bruce chose to stay in California, close to his goal - Hollywood. For the moment he was content to work as a waiter in a friend's Chinese restaurant in the hope that he would be spotted and signed up by one of the large film companies based in California. But breaking into the glittering Hollywood dream world is not that simple, as Bruce soon realised!

Eventually he tired of the restaurant business and moved on to Seattle and the Washington University to take on a Philosophy degree. And to help pay his way, he began teaching Kung Fu classes, at first instructing in car parks and then moving to basements and empty rooms.

But all thoughts of becoming a philosophy scholar vanished when Bruce met a beau-

tiful young medical student by the name of Linda Emery. It was love at first sight and in 1964, Linda Emery became Mrs. Linda Lee. They both dropped their studies and Bruce took up martial arts instruction seriously to provide for his wife. He opened his first Jun Fan Gung Fu Institute in Seattle and such was its success, that, soon after, he moved once again to California and set up a second school in San Francisco.

And then it happened! While giving a Kung Fu demonstration - consisting of smashing thick planks with his fists to the delight and amazement of his audience - Bruce was spotted by a friend of top Hollywood TV producer William Dozier who had put together the enormously popular *Batman* series. When Dozier heard about Bruce's board busting stunts, he signed him up and Bruce Lee had his chance at fame and fortune!

It was originally planned that Bruce would star in a remake of the old Charlie Chan television series as Charlie's *Number One Son*, but instead, he was scheduled to star alongside veteran Hollywood actor Van Williams in *The Green Hornet* series. "I'll tell you why I

got that job," he once remarked after the series had long since vanished. "The hero's name was Britt Reed and I was the only Chinese guy in the whole of California who could pronounce Britt Reed. That's why!" But whatever the reason, Bruce had the part and it was to work wonders for his career, even if he didn't realise it for many years after.

The Green Hornet ran for thirty episodes in the States and was a flop. The *Batman* show had been too similar and viewers had become bored with comic strip TV shows. But when The Green Hornet was released in the Far East, it was a smash hit. 20th Century Fox hastily organised a publicity tour for Bruce and he found himself aboard a plane bound for his old homeland. When he arrived, he was overwhelmed by the star treatment he received. "It sure was an experience," Bruce remembered later. "I made several appearances with the largest television and radio stations. People flocked around me wherever I went." While in Hong Kong, Bruce was approached by several Mandarin film makers anxious to sign up the new star which the Chinese people had taken to their heart as a hero. But despite the tempting offers to stay and have his pick of the Hong Kong film world, Bruce was still hooked on Hollywood. "Now that I've done something successful," he thought to himself, "It should be easy to reach the top in Hollywood."

But when Bruce returned to California, his hopes were shattered. Now that *The Green Hornet* had finished, the Hollywood movie moguls could not, or would not, find him a part. The reason was, of course, the colour of his skin and the slant of his eyes. At that time, it was unheard of for a Chinese actor, even such a skilled and attractive performer as the Little Dragon, to be given a starring role in the US. Although in his native Hong Kong, Bruce's ancestry made him a legend but in the USA, it was the thing which blocked his every move in the film world. Hollywood was suddenly a cold and cruel city for Bruce Lee.

Sickened and disgusted, Bruce gave up his dream of stardom, but only for the moment, and turned once more to his beloved Kung Fu instruction. And if he couldn't reach stardom, at least the stars were more than willing to come to him! Even the top names of Hollywood had never seen anybody defend himself quite like Bruce, and they began signing on in droves for Bruce's instruction classes. "It was a very profitable thing to do," said I Bruce. "I used to charge $500 for a ten hour course and people flocked to the schools. I even doubled the price and people still kept coming. I had no idea so many people were interested in Chinese Boxing!"

Interested they certainly were! Names such as Steve McQueen, James Coburn, James Garner, screen writer Stirling Silliphant, all came knocking at the Little Dragon's door seeking help. And after class, they stayed to chat and joke and soon Bruce was close friends with the cream of the Hollywood acting set!

It didn't take Bruce's famous friends long to realise his talent and charm, and they acted accordingly. First off, James Garner persuaded MGM to include Bruce in a movie he was shooting called *Marlowe*. Unfortunately it was only memorable for Bruce's role - which had him playing a Chinese thug called Winslow Wong - but it did get him noticed once more by the men who rule Hollywood; the all-powerful producers.

Next, Bruce's old friend Stirling Silliphant engineered him a part in a TV series he was writing titled *Longstreet* which starred James Franciscus. Many of you may have seen *Longstreet* and if you have, I'm sure you'll agree that it is a masterpiece. Certainly the critics thought so and they raved about it, urging the studios to give Bruce his own show. Bruce himself even liked his part; the first time since he had arrived in Hollywood!

Suddenly everyone in the Hollywood boardrooms were talking about Bruce Lee! Warner Bros, had him in mind for no less than FIVE parts in the one movie - *The Silent Flute* - which had been written by Bruce, James Coburn and Stirling Silliphant The movie, the story of a man searching for his soul, was Coburn's brainchild and he was strongly pressing Warners for the green light.

Warner Bros, were also considering a Kung Fu television series to be called, simply, *Kung Fu*. Bruce was extremely anxious to have the part of the wandering monk Caine and he too was pressing Warners for a 'Yes.'

In time, both these ventures would fall through for Bruce, showing once more how Hollywood - the maker or breaker of the film world - grossly overlooked Bruce's startling talent for so long. When the news came that Bruce had missed out on the Kung Fu part, he was bitterly disappointed and he must have remembered a conversation he had had some time before, where Bruce mentioned to a top Hollywood producer that he was going to follow in the footsteps of Charles Bronson and Clint Eastwood. The producer laughed in his face and replied, "You're Chinese. The Western fans won't accept you."

But even before the news that he had missed out on the role of Caine reached him, Bruce had again become disillusioned by the way in which Hollywood could not make up its mind on his talent. When a Trans-Pacific telephone call from Hong Kong was put through to him, in which the chief of Hong Kong's Golden Harvest movie studio, Raymond Chow, offered him a deal to star in a Hong Kong production, he snapped it up and once again quit Hollywood.

What Bruce achieved in Hong Kong and how he went about doing it is another story. But it is enough to say that when Bruce arrived for the second time in his homeland and put together *The Big Boss*, *Fist of Fury* and *The Way of the Dragon*, he became a living legend, taking the whole of South East Asia by storm. Before he left Hollywood, he wrote down on a scrap of paper for Linda his goal: To become a film star, bringing out the best qualities of the Chinese martial arts and showing them to the world. With one film, he

more than achieved this goal!

Such was the success of Bruce's three Hong Kong films throughout the East, that it was impossible to confine him to the Chinese population. Although he was their messiah, Bruce was too big to be tied down by one group of people, no matter how devoted they were. He was the property of the world, and once again this meant Hollywood.

But this time it was different. This time it was Hollywood which came on bended knees

BRUCE LEE T-SHIRT

AT LAST! An official Kung-Fu Monthly T-Shirt featuring the legendary Bruce Lee. Printed in glowing red on fine quality cotton T-Shirt, this bold portrait of the King of Kung-Fu will be in big demand from all Bruce's many fans, so . . .
Don't DELAY! Send off NOW to avoid disappointment as supplies are limited! Choose from any three sizes: Small (34 - 36 ins), Medium (36 - 38 ins) and Large (38 - 42 ins).
PLEASE indicate clearly which size you require when ordering. Send your cheque or postal order for £1.40 made out to Kung-Fu Monthly to:
BRUCE LEE T-SHIRT OFFER
39 Goodge Street,
London W1P 1FD.

THE KUNG-FU MONTHLY ARCHIVE SERIES

to Bruce's door! When *Fist of Fury* - the first of Bruce's films to be shown in the West - was given a world wide release, Hollywood realised what it had let slip through its fingers. Suddenly the rush was on to sign on Bruce Lee, the hottest property in show business!

Cables, express letters, phone calls and top Hollywood film personnel flooded into the Golden Harvest studios in Hong Kong, swamping the Little Dragon with gilt-edged offers and gold-bound movie contracts. It was a satisfying feeling for Bruce. After all those closed doors and blind turnings of his early Hollywood career, he was now the man at the top, opening and closing his door at will!

Eventually he accepted the huge offer from Warner Bros., to make a film with John Saxon titled *Enter the Dragon*. The result, as every movie and martial arts fan in the world knows, is a classic. Warners poured huge amounts of money into the film, building lavish sets to equal the plush James Bond films, and flying in to Hong Kong, the largest camera crew ever assembled outside Hollywood! "*Enter the Dragon* should make it," predicted Bruce, and once again he was not wrong! Cinema audiences had never before been treated to such martial scenes on the wide screen and they packed theatres around the world. *Enter the Dragon*, which has already made something like 20 million dollars - will run for years to come!

But besides being simply a superb example of masterpiece film making, *Enter the Dragon* is an important milestone in cinema history for another reason; it was the first Hong Kong/Hollywood co-production. With his talent and skill, Bruce, by making Enter the Dragon, irrevocably welded together East and West cinema and forged another link in the chain, binding together the two different cultures.

Just how important this feat is can be seen by the growing influx of East/West co-productions which are being introduced into movie houses the world over. After *Enter the Dragon*, we now have the brilliant *Legend of the Seven Golden Vampires* which is a joint effort between the famous Hammer Studios in Britain and the giant Shaw Brothers Studio in Hong Kong. *The Legend of the Seven Golden Vampires*, which stars veteran horror actor Peter Cushing and the new Kung Fu star David Chiang, tells the gripping and horrific story of the legendary battle between the forced of good (Peter Cushing, David Chiang and Robin Stewart) and the terrifying Seven Golden Vampires - each wielding a golden sword above their head - who lead an army of killer zombies.

The film is a thrilling mixture of British horror and Chinese martial arts and as such, is a fitting successor to Bruce Lee's *Enter the Dragon* - even if it is without the Little Dragon himself. There will be many more Hong Kong/Hollywood co-productions in the future, thanks to the pioneering work of the greatest superstar of all time - Bruce Lee! Such is Bruce Lee's legacy to Hollywood, the city which for so long turned its back on the Little Dragon, ignoring the brilliant flame of talent which glowed so brightly before their very eyes for so many years.

Bruce's brush with Hollywood - the story of his manhood film career - is an epic legend of courage and fortitude in the face of soul-destroying ignorance and prejudice. Single-handedly, a young Chinese actor grabbed the most powerful movie capital by its throat and forced it to recognise te potential of those people outside its own narrow view.

In doing so, Bruce Lee irrevocably changed the whole face and history of Hollywood.

WHO'S WHO IN KUNG FU

Well, you asked for it, so here it is; the second collection of Kung Fu heroes with their eyes on Bruce Lee's glittering martial crown! The last issue, which we featured such 'greats' as Wang Yu, Lo Lieh, David Chiang and Carter Wong, seems to have stirred up a postal storm with hundreds of *KFM* readers writing in to let us know just who they think is today's top film fighter and the worthy successor to the late, great Little Dragon.

Now *Kung-Fu Monthly*, with the invaluable assistance of our intrepid Hong Kong photographer Paul Chang, Hong Kong Bureau Chief Peter Woo, Golden Harvest Films and Cathay Films here in London, proudly present a new galaxy of rising Kung Fu stars.

Some of the faces will undoubtedly be familiar (Angela *Lady Whirlwind* Mao seems like one of the family here at *KFM*!). Others, you will probably not yet have seen, although we can promise you that each star pictured here will bestriding across your local cinema screen sometime in the near future! Watch for coming Cathay/Golden Harvest releases *One Armed Boxer* starring Wang Yu, *Beach of the War Gods* also with Wang Yu, *Kung Fu Girl* with Cheng Pei Pei and James Tien and, finally, *When Taekwondo Strikes* starring Angela Mao.

So, as we said before, here they are; the cream of the martial arts film world. Last issue's fighters were all male martial masters, so this month we have added several touches of glamour to the line-up. And if you think these girls can't hold their own against the competition, just take a glance at their credentials!

JAMES TIEN

Although this young man's face may seem familiar, most of you will probably require an introduction before he finally clicks. He is James Tien, the artist who played alongside none other than the immortal Bruce himself in *Fist of Fury*.

Now James has carved out for himself an impressive career in Hong Kong co-starring with Wang Yu in such box office smashes as *Wang Yu: Seven Magnificent Fights*, *A Man Called Tiger*, and *One Armed Boxer*. His latest film, *Kung Fu Girl* in which he stars with Cheng Pei Pei, should greatly enhance James's chance at the Kung Fu Crown in the eyes of his Western audiences!

ANGELA MAO

If you don't recognise this pretty face, you must have spent the last six months locked away in a Shaolin Monastery! Yes of course it's none other than *Lady Whirlwind* herself, Angela Mao, or to credit her with her full Chinese name, Angela Mao-ying. Just as her face needs no introduction, neither do her movie and martial arts credentials. Hapkido Black Belt and *Back Alley Princess*, *Hapkido*, *Lady Whirlwind*, *Stoner*, *Enter the Dragon* etc. etc.! Now the First Lady of Kung Fu has tied another knot in her belt in the shape of *When Taekwondo Strikes*, soon to be released by Cathay Films. Incidentally, since we ran the Angela Mao Story way back in *KFM* No.4, Angela's life has changed pretty drastically; one day she ducked out of the Golden Harvest Studio in Hong Kong and got herself married!

CHUCK NORRIS

What's the greatest fight scene ever captured on film? The epic battle between Bruce Lee and Chuck Norris in the Coliseum at the climax of *The Way of the Dragon*? Just that one fight would have been enough to write Chuck Norris into the martial arts record books, if he hadn't been there already as the seven-time winner of the US Karate championships! Filmwise, Chuck seems to be resting on his laurels somewhat, but Cathay Films in London have received such a landslide of Chuck Norris fan mail, that we wouldn't be at all surprised if 'The Ironman' once again graced the silver screen in the very near future.

CHENG PEI PEI

Here's another young lady who is going places fast when it comes to flashing fists and flying feet; Cheng Pei Pei. A long-time favourite with film fans in her native Hong Kong, Miss Cheng is all set to take the West by storm with her latest movie offering, *Kung Fu Girl*, in which she stars alongside James Tien.

FOUR GUYS

Here's a shot you won't see too often; four top martial artists standing together peacefully for the camera! This is the famous Shaw Brothers Studio's Kung Fu stable which has become known in the Hong Kong film industry as the 'Four Tigers.' Off the set, these four stars (From left: Wong Chung, Cheng Kuen Tai, David Chiang and Ti Lung) are close friends; a change from the deadly rivalry they often find themselves engaged in on the set.

CHENG KUEN TAI

Cheng Kuen Tai may not be immediately recognisable to Western film and martial arts fans, but to audiences in his hometown Hong Kong, he is a very big name indeed. Now the

balance seems to be being restored with the release of Cheng's super-bloody Men from the Monastery. Hopefully many more of his movies will soon be crossing the waters to thrill British fans.

KICKBACK: THE LETTERS

Hi there! Jenny here again with the *KFM* Mailbag,. or should I say bags? there's been such a terrific response to our 'Who's Who in Kung Fu' feature from Issue 5! Really, you have all been great, writing in to tell us who your favourites are; after the King himself, the Little Dragon, of course. Some of you seem a bit worried that we might be forgetting Bruce in favour of the newcomers. No chance!! Bruce Lee IS Kung Fu, or in the offices of *KFM* at least! Anyway, that said, have a close look at this month's star collection, pick your successor to Bruce, and drop me a line. We'll let you know the results in a coming issue. Please don't forget, that when writing to me or to the Mail Order Department, mark your envelopes clearly. Well, that's enough talk from me this month. Now on with the show!

KING BOXER

Dear *KFM*,
In *KFM* No.3 the poster is of Bruce Lee wearing Boxing gloves. Would you please tell me if it is a clip from the film *King Boxer*. If it is not, which film is it from? Also would you tell me why Bruce has his hand up in the poster from *KFM* No.4?
Christopher Mulvey, Edinburgh

Dear Christopher,
No, Chris, the photo of Boxer Bruce doesn't come from King Boxer, which was a Shaw Bros. film starring Lo Lieh and one of the very first Kung Fu films ever made. It is a shot from the opening sequence of Enter the Dragon, Bruce's Hollywood epic. And so too is the poster in KFM No.4. Bruce Lee fans who have seen Enter the Dragon, will certainly well remember the deadly battle below Han's island fortress. Bruce's upraised hand is spelling big trouble for his opponents in that battle.

SHAOLIN LADIES

Dear *KFM*,
I think your monthly magazine is really fantastic. Through your magazine, I learnt the true meaning of the martial art and how deadly it can be, yet there are a few questions that I haven't had answers for, such as: 1. Was Bruce Lee taught Kung Fu in a Shaolin Temple? 2. Are women allowed in a Shaolin Temple? 3. In the old days, in the Shaolin Temple, after passing the tests of the four rooms, the Kung Fu disciples had to hug a huge red cauldron. Do the disciples of today still do this? Thanks very much and keep up the good work.
Lubna Ul-Hasan, Ilford

Dear Lubna,
Thanks for the kind words. No Bruce was not trained in a Shaolin Temple, but he had the next best thing. His martial arts master was Yip Man, the undisputed leader of the Wing Chun Kung Fu school in Hong Kong. With regards to your second question, Lubna, you can breathe a little easier. Yes, women definitely are allowed in Shaolin Temples. It was, in fact, a Shaolin nun - Madame Wing Chun - who founded Bruce's and Yip Man's Wing Chun school. Now that the Communists are in power in China, many of the ancient Temples have disappeared, but perhaps somewhere on the Chinese mainland there is a Temple which carries on the tradition of the red hot cauldron.

WAR CRIES

I find your magazine tells the real truth about Bruce Lee and his life. A few weeks back, my girlfriend bought me the theme music from *Enter the Dragon* and it would please me very much if you could tell me if it is or isn't Bruce Lee making the battle cries on this record?
John Whitehouse, Cardiff

Dear John,
Yes, that is the Little Dragon in person whose ear-splitting war cry appears on the soundtrack record. Enter the Dragon was the only film which Bruce made, in which he used his own voice. In all the others, Bruce's 'voice' was dubbed in by an English studio actor after the film had been completed. However, even in his Hong Kong masterpieces, Bruce always insisted on recording his own war cries in person.

LETTER OF THE MONTH

Dear *KFM*,
I have quite a few questions that I hope you can answer: 1. Could you please publish something on Chuck Norris and Bob Wall as they deserve it. Also, what are their next pictures going to be? 2. I read somewhere that Bruce Lee never liked Chuck Norris. Is this true? 3. I bought the Bruce Lee book and it says that Bob Wall caught Bruce with a bottle, but it was not in the film. Why? 4. When is *Game of Death* going to be released? Thanks a lot.
David Jones, Splott, Cardiff

Dear David,
Congratulations on making Letter of the Month, and I hope I can do your questions the justice they deserve. First up, I hope you like the picture of Chuck Norris in this issue. And I agree, he and Bob Wall certainly do deserve their own special features. Our editor, Don Won Ton, promises that there'll be more on these two gentlemen in the near future. As for Bruce not liking Chuck, it's the first we've heard of it here. Sometimes tempers frayed a little between Bruce and Bob, but all three martial arts masters were close friends out of the ring. Unfortunately the bottle scene in Enter the Dragon, although it was filmed, was cut out of the final print. And a release date on Game of Death? Well, that's the $64 question which millions of Lee fans around the world are pondering. But as I mentioned before, I'll keep you posted.

1975

EDITORIAL

Hi there Kung Fu fans...

What a month it's been for martial art disciples! In countless cinemas and in bookshops throughout the country, Kung Fu and its galaxy of superstars are enjoying more popularity than ever before. Just take a look at the fantastic fighting films which have been released by such companies as our old friend Cathay Films. *One-Armed Boxer* with the mighty Wang Yu (more about him later), *The Skyhawk* with Carter Wong and Bruce Lee's favourite female co-star Nora Miao, *Back Alley Princess*, *Legend of the Seven Golden Vampires* and so on.

In this issue of *KFM*, we're sure that we have brought you a mountain of straight facts and vital information which will shed yet more light on the martial arts and its leading practitioners. For starters, there's the in-depth article on the great Bruce Lee's prowess and many-faceted talents. It is only now - a year after the Little Dragon's tragic death - that the majority of the world is realising just how overwhelming were Bruce's skills and I am certain that this month's lead story is a fitting tribute and a vivid appraisal of the man and his art.

Next up, we have the story which I know many of you have been waiting anxiously for - the story of Wang Yu, the master whom many of the world's most renowned film and fight critics believe is the true successor to the Little Dragon's Kung Fu crown. With the release by Cathay of Wang's sizzling *One-Armed Boxer*, our feature could not have come at a better time!

Besides all this, we have our regular features and facts such as the Jenny Lee Kickback page and our exclusive *KFM* mail order offers. Also we have devoted another page to the brilliant work of artist Paul Simmons, co-author of the book The Beginner's Guide to Kung Fu.

That said, all that's left for me to do, is to wish you all, on behalf of the *KFM* staff, a very Happy New Year in 1975!

Felix Yen

Felix Yen
Editor-in-Chief

THE DEADLY ART OF BRUCE LEE

Like any genius, Bruce Lee made his art look easy. It is only when you try to imitate it that you realise how difficult it is. The swiftness, the balance, the accuracy may seem impossible to master. It is as if the Little Dragon possessed some secret knowledge.

But Bruce always told his followers that there was nothing mysterious about his fighting art. His particular skill was called *Jeet Kune Do*. In Chinese, *Jeet* means *To Stop* or To Intercept, *Kune* means Fist and *Do* means The Way. So his art can be called *The Way of the Stopping Fist*, or as it is more commonly known, *The Way of the Intercepting Fist*. Like any good craftsman, Bruce depended on his tools. "My hands, my feet and my body are the tools of my trade," he said. And like any good craftsman he would make sure that his tools were always at their sharpest. And before we go on to look at his special skills - finger-jabbing to the eye, kicks to the groin, hand-trapping and the nunchaku - we should see first of all just how he kept those tools so sharp.

If you study one of his films closely - *Fist of Fury* is an excellent example - you will notice that sharpness. He is able to guess which way his opponent will turn. His reactions are sudden, flexible and sharp.

So how do you sharpen up? Think of the way a boxer trains. He uses a skipping rope, goes on long plodding runs, hammers away at a punch bag.

Then compare any boxer you have seen in the ring with Bruce Lee. A boxer seems slow, obvious. You can tell where his punch is going to be aimed. Apart, possibly, from Muhammad Ali and Ken Buchanan, there are hardly any boxers who seem able to change their tactics suddenly.

Now, when Bruce warmed up, he tested every muscle in his body. Not just his biceps or his thigh muscles, but every one.

Like many athletes, he would do press-ups. But he would do them using only two fingers and one thumb of each hand. To strengthen his shoulders and upper arms, he would use only two fingers of one hand! It was one of his favourite warm-up exercises.

Of course, he would run to keep fit, too. Often in the early mornings, you would see him and his Great Dane, Bobo, jogging along together. He used to run six miles a day. First he would jog, then gradually increase his speed to a sprint.

To strengthen his legs, he would exercise with a high bar. You have probably seen ballet-dancers using one of these bars. Bruce would raise one leg high, keeping it completely straight in front of him and resting on the bar, then he would stretch down to touch his toes. Simple, you might think, and Bruce would agree. He was always keen that his followers should understand the basic skills of his art and realise how simple they were.

Bruce also used a dummy as his sparring partner. It was about six foot tall and a foot in diameter. It had two 'hands' made out of wood below the 'neck' and another one at waist height. It had one metal 'leg' that stretched out as if bent at the 'knee.' It was on this 'leg' that he would perfect his art of groin-kicking. In this way he could practice his blocking and pulling skills without hurting anyone.

A large bean bag nailed to the wall was another of Bruce's favourite sparring aids. It helped him develop accuracy and speed in his punches.

He also liked to use a round pad held by one of his students. This taught him how to time his blows and how to outwit his opponents by hiding his blows til the last possible moment.

You have all seen the punch bags used by boxers. Bruce used one, too, but in a very different way. He would try out his kicks in the same way that a boxer would try out his left hooks.

He would kick the bag again and again to develop the speed necessary to make a kick effective. A slow kick is useless. You will know yourself from watching an ordinary scrap that a man on one leg is easily thrown to the ground. So Bruce always taught people to kick swiftly so that they could get their balance back and be ready for another move.

BRUCE LEE DRAGON POSTER !!!

Especially painted for Kung-Fu Monthly by Jeff Cummings, here is a beautiful full colour poster of the Dragon King of Kung-Fu, Bruce Lee. Printed on quality art paper, this brand new poster is only available through KFM. Sent in a sturdy cardboard container, we are offering this poster to our readers for 90p including all postage and packing. Never previously published in any country in the world — as usual, KFM offers its readers first choice! Send your cheque or P.O. for 90p to: BRUCE LEE DRAGON POSTER OFFER, KFM Mail Order, 39 Goodge Street, London W1P 1FD. Superb Quality — a gift to treasure!

Bruce didn't believe in jumping and kicking at the same time. He used it for dramatic effect. Watch the last part of *The Big Boss* and you will see just how deadly that 'dramatic effect' can be.

To perfect his finger-jabbing skills, Bruce would practice on a leather strip. Few sparring partners would be willing to submit themselves to the Master for this sort of training! Before we leave the subject of sparring and look at some of Bruce's skills in detail, we should remember his advice: "Like water, sparring should be formless. Pour water into a cup, it becomes part of the cup. Pour it into a bottle; it becomes part of the bottle. Clutch it and it will yield without hesitation. How true it is that nothingness cannot be confined. The softest thing cannot be snapped."

And it is worth remembering, too, the very basis of Kung Fu fighting comes from what we know as the Yin and the Yang. Yin can stand for gentleness, darkness, night. Yang can stand for activeness, firmness, brightness, day. What Bruce always remembered was that Yin and Yang were not two separate things. They exist together. So fighting is not just attack, but also defence. Not just speed and action, but also timing and patience.

Let's start with the stillness and patience first. Take the stances for instance.

Bruce learnt early on to adopt the correct, balanced stance. This is based on something called 'Joan Sien' which means 'The Centreline' in English. It is an imaginary line drawn down the centre of the body. He would distribute his weight evenly on both feet and place his hands over that imaginary line with the right hand just in front of the left.

The Right Stance is just a variation of that basic stance. The right leg is placed forward but most of the weight is kept on the left leg. And, of course, The Left Stance is just a reverse of this.

The Right Sitting Horse Stance - 'Jor Mah' - means that you take up a position as if sitting on horseback with the weight mainly on the right leg. The left hand is kept at waist height with the palm to the ground. The right hand remains in the same position as for the other stances. Once again, The Left Horse Sitting Stance is just the reverse of this. Like a sprinter in his starting blocks, Bruce would adopt these stances to give him the best chance of sudden movement.

From these positions, Bruce felt most confident when defending himself against an opponent. And since he always taught his students that Kung Fu was not an aggressive art, it is important that we look closely at his methods of defence. This, after all, is the principle of Jeet Kune Do.

For instance, if an opponent lunged at Bruce with his fist, Bruce would wait as long as possible before using his Left Slap Block ('Pak Sao'), and follow it up with a right fist kept vertical to the ground. What about kicks?

That surely was another area where Bruce excelled. One of his favourites was the High Straight Kick. This was aimed for an attacker's face. Of course he would vary it depending on the attack. Sometimes he would use the Middle Straight Kick.

Or he would often shift his body to the side of an opponent, pivot round on one foot and deliver the famous Downward Side Kick. That's when all those hours spent on the bars in the gym would pay off.

Kicks can be used both for attack and defence and many's the time that some unwise fighter would lunge at Bruce, ready for any attack from Bruce's fists of fury, only to find himself felled by a sudden Downward Kick.

Bruce used his feet in other ways, too. On one occasion when he was attacked from

behind and grabbed in a bear-hug by an attacker much larger than himself, he let himself go completely limp. Then he turned and struck out with his elbow. At the same time he stepped hard on the attacker's toes. Of course all this was done before you could say *Big Boss*.

He used his knee with the same effect. If an opponent tried to rush him, Bruce could skip slightly to one side and throw him off balance by striking him at waist height with his knee. This requires a lot of practice. You can easily dislocate a knee by using it too soon or too late on an opponent.

Another of Bruce's special skills was that of using the nunchaku. That's the name of the two-part club linked together by a chain. It is an ancient martial arts weapon that was mainly used by Kung Fu fighters who were attacked by two or more people at once.

It took Bruce ten years before he felt he had mastered it entirely.

But after ten years, he was able to use nunchaku as if it was an extra arm. He could spin it round his head and trap it under his arm. He could whip the sword from an opponent's hand and send him spinning to the ground. But he always warned his students against studying this art unless they were dedicated and disciplined fighters.

Nunchaku in the hands of someone who only wants to use Kung Fu aggressively is just a dangerous weapon and often the person who tries to use it, is the person who gets hurt!

Of all his skills, Bruce felt that the nunchaku was one where he had to learn and study before trying to use it in a real fight. So he would listen first to what is known in the martial arts as his 'Si Hing.' That means someone who has learnt the art before you; a senior or a brother in the martial arts.

There has been a lot of talk recently about the values of the various different forms of the fighting arts. People have even suggested putting a boxer in the ring with a Kung Fu fighter! Without wishing any disrespect to our Boxing friends, that would seem a bit like putting someone on a tricycle and asking them to race a Ferrari.

No, Bruce Lee's fighting arts did not come from brute strength or from magic. They came from dedication, humility, practice, discipline and inner peace.

If Bruce had been an angry, bitter person he could never have been the fighter he was. He needed his inner calmness to be able to fight the way he did. He could not afford to lose his temper like a street fighter. He knew his strength too well.

We know Bruce as the Little Dragon. The dragons of legend used to have fire coming from their noses. Bruce had fire in his belly.

JIMMY WANG YU

No, it's not Bruce Lee! The man's name is Wang Yu. He is known to his friends as Jimmy, and without his influence, it might have taken Bruce a little longer to achieve universal fame and adulation.

Back in 1968, the Hong Kong film industry was in trouble. For years, the only fight films they'd produced had been Japanese samurai movies - glorifying the ancient Japanese art of fighting with long, lethal, razor-sharp swords. But the Chinese audiences began to tire of this, and the samurai movies were dealt a death blow by the words of Red Chinese politician Chou En-Lai. In 1968, Chou accused Japan of being the new imperialist force in the East, and urged Chinese everywhere to seek their own identity.

They took those words to heart in Hong Kong's teeming Chinese population, and the great producer Run Run Shaw, sensing the mood of his audience, began to look around for a Chinese martial art to replace the Samurais. He studied the Boxer Rebellion, and stumbled across the carefully guarded, age-old secret of Kung Fu.

Run Run Shaw decided to bring out a film based on this martial art, called *The Chinese Boxer*. He chose as his director and star, a respected actor and Karate expert - 'Jimmy' Wang Yu. Run Run could not have made a better choice.

The Chinese Boxer swept the East. In cinemas from Indonesia to Taiwan, audiences stood up on the backs of their chairs, leapt into the aisles and roared their approval. Kung Fu was here to stay. Enough box office records were broken to make Jimmy Wang Yu richer beyond his wildest dreams and to ensure that he need never have worked again.

But Jimmy is, in life as on screen, a man of action. He built a glorious home in Taiwan's Grass Mountain for his beautiful wife Jeannette and their three daughters, and then his love of Kung Fu and the movies drew him back to the big screen. His output of stare 'n' tear action since then has been huge, and has provided the cinema with some of its greatest moments.

The One-Armed Swordsman, for instance, set a new standard of martial arts action; where the hero is opposed not only by skilful, vicious mercenaries, but also by his own physical disabilities - the loss of an arm. The anti-Japanese feelings were still running high in Chinatown, and Wang Yu inevitably cast Japanese as the villains. *In One-Armed Swordsman*, eight Japanese invade Wang Yu's village and cut off the right arm of every male inhabitant. Wang Yu accepts his maiming and waits, with ferocious patience, until his one remaining arm is strong, skilled, and ready to extract fitting revenge.

"He swoops down on his enemies like a silver white toe; no one has survived a duel with him."

These words were spoken of a Chinese fighter who, among other things, launched the Kung Fu Movie Revolution, performed some of the greatest martial arts mastery on celluloid, did all his own stunts, became accepted as one of the most brilliant actors in Asia, and thus became the first Chinese actor-millionaire.

Jimmy Wang had joined that industry when he was twenty-one, in 1963. Born and raised near Shanghai, he was the swimming champion of that city before moving to Hong Kong and becoming an extra in the studios of Run Run Shaw. Run Run was quick to recognise the modest young fighter's potential, and he and Jimmy worked happily together until 1970, when Raymond Chow invited Jimmy to work on a film in Taiwan. Chow gave Wang the script that he wanted to do, and it was the script of Zatotchi and the *One-Armed Swordsman*. Even though it meant breaking contract with Run Run Shaw, Jimmy could not turn down that script. Run Run was so heartbroken when he heard of the defection of his favourite star, that he put adverts in the Taiwan press warning locals that Wang Yu could not legally work! Fortunately for us all, Wang Yu did work!

Like Bruce Lee, and the other Kung Fu greats, Jimmy Wang always insists on doing his own stunts, however dangerous and he knew that the trained eyes of the world could tell what was real and what wasn't! So he took on the whole package, not only the fights but

also the dramatics - which have meant him falling two hundred feet from a cable car into a shallow river, jumping from a third floor window, and dodging speeding motorbikes in *A Man Called Tiger*. As his hobbies include horseback riding, swimming, and automobile racing (he owns a Porsche, a BMW, and a Mercedes Benz), Wang Yu is perhaps better qualified to risk his neck than most!

In Australia recently, however, Jimmy may have for a moment, regretted his bravery. While filming an action scene for his latest movie, *The Man From Hong Kong*, Wang broke both his wrists. Panic swept through the mandarin film industry, but only briefly. Like one of his screen characters, Jimmy worked hard and patiently at the injured bones and was miraculously able to resume filming within two weeks! The most recent of Wang Yu's films to excite Western audiences has been *The One-Armed Boxer*. It is Wang Yu's hard, fast and bloody style of Kung Fu at its rip-roaring best. Jimmy plays the impatient star pupil of a martial arts school who gets into a tea-house fight with some local thugs. The leader of the thugs, Shao, demands of Wang's teacher, that Wang should be handed over. The old man refuses, and beats Shao out of the school.

Shao returns, with the most impressive array of martial arts mercenaries ever assembled. They include two Thai boxers, a Taekwondo expert, a fanged satanic Japanese Karate master, an Indian Yogi (who introduces himself by plunging a knife into his own heart and beaming at everybody), and two wily Tibetan priests. The assorted skills of the mercenar-

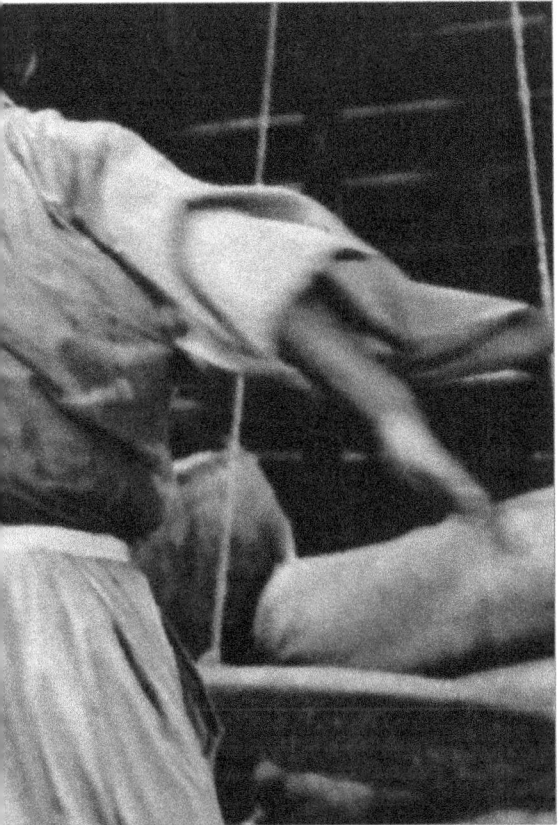

BEAUTIFUL BRUCE LEE SOUVENIR MUGS

We are proud to offer fans of Bruce Lee this handsome earthenware coffee mug which has been especially manufactured for KUNG-FU MONTHLY readers by Panorama Studios in Devon! With a great photograph of Bruce fired permanently into the glaze, this half pint mug is made to the very highest standards and finished with a platignum rim. Here is a momento of Bruce that will truly last for years, and due to bulk purchasing we are able to offer our readers this mug for only £1.25. This price includes all post and packing charges. The mug will be despatched to you direct from the manufacturers in a specially designed container to avoid any possibility of breakage. Only available from KFM, cannot be bought elsewhere! Would make a wonderful present for any Bruce Lee fan! Send your order enclosing your cheque or P.O. for £1.25 made out to Kung-Fu Monthly together with your name and address clearly printed to: **Bruce Lee Coffee Mug Offer, KFM Mail Order, 39 Goodge Street, London W1P 1FD.** Delivery within three weeks.

ies are enough to massacre the entire school. The hapless Wang crawls away from the carnage without a right arm, and is discovered by a herbalist and his daughter who nurse the young man back to health. The herbalist then teaches Wang the iron fist technique, which has Wang killing off the nerves in his remaining arm by plunging it into a white-hot fire, and then treating the burnt, hard limb with herbs. It is an unbeatable weapon, and Wang tracks down his enemies with confidence. He eventually meets them all in the dusty bowl of a lime quarry, and one by one, outdoes their unique styles.

The Thai boxers are punched senseless, the Taekwondo fighter torn apart. The Tibetans inflate their bodies and lumber monstrously towards Wang, who deftly deflates them with two jabbing fingers. The Yogi attempts to confuse Wang by running around him on his hands. Wang himself stands, first on one arm, and then hops towards his enemy on one finger. The Yogi cannot cope. Wang's final enemy, the Japanese, inflicts terrible punishment on Wang, taking out one of the boy's eyes, before being hammered into extinction by that deadly left fist.

Typically, Wang leaves the blood stained arena in no attitude of triumph, but with a strange worldly sadness as he picks his way through the remains of his vengeance.

The One-Armed Boxer is the kind of excitement and filmic quality that Jimmy Wang has consistently given us. His genius, we can rest assured, will continue to expand and create.

THE MARTIAL ART

These illustrations by Paul Simmons are from a new book published by Wildwood House of London. The book is called *The Beginner's Guide to Kung Fu*. You will find a detailed description of the book and an order form at the foot of this month's pin-up poster!

KUNG FU DEFENSIVE STANCES

- Both the stances shown here are good basic defensive stances. The man on the left is in the Cat Stance; a ready-for-action position good for fast movement. 75% of the body weight is placed on the back leg, which is bent to lower the body. The man on the right is in the Horse Stance, feet two shoulder widths apart, knees bent.

- There are an infinite number of hand positions, but the position shown here is best recommended for beginners. The leading hand is inclined forward at 45°, elbow down to cover the ribs. The rear hand is held back at the abdomen or at belt height. N.B. Beginners are advised to keep the fists clenched at first.

BLOCKING IN THE HIGH LINE

- High Line Rising Block (Leaping Deer). Used against a straight punch or thrust to the head and shoulders, the forward arm is brought slightly across the body, upwards, and outwards, deflecting the intended punch to high left. Lean the body weight slightly into the block.
- Inset A. Contact is made with the hard outside edge of the forearm, driving into the soft inside face of attacking arm at 90°. If using knife hand position it is imperative to tense both fingers and wrist as tightly as possible.

HIGH INNER KNIFE HAND OUTSIDE BLOCK

• Used to counter hook punches, or roundhouse thrusts and kicks, this technique uses both arms. The blocking forearm is held vertically, the palm of the other hand placed against it, and is driven across the body and slightly upwards to block the intended blow.
• Inset B. This technique uses the hard inside edge of the forearm as the blocking area, the hand held in the inner knife hand position, palm facing towards the body, wrist and fingers tightly tensed.

KICKBACK: THE LETTERS

Hi there! Jenny here again to wade through the stacks of mail which still pour Into the *KFM* offices and to select some of your questions and queries on the martial arts. Unfortunately, because of space reasons, it's impossible to answer any more than just a tiny, tiny fraction of the letters which arrive on my desk, so if yours doesn't appear, that's the reason and I'm truly sorry. But don't give up. I love to hear from you all out there in Kung Fu land and even if you don't get into print, you've kept me happy and busy! Hope you liked the four-page spread our editor Don Won Ton gave me in our *KFM* special, *The Book of Kung Fu*, which went a long way towards cutting down our mailbag backlog! As usual, I'll take this opportunity to remind you to please, please mark your letters plainly on the envelope. On with the show!

TOO FAR?

Dear Jenny,
All I want to know is do you think Kung Fu Wu Su has been taken too far? Whenever people who seriously know about this old Chinese fighting technique mention the word Kung Fu, people laugh and I think it has been taken too far. There are a lot of people making money out of something they know nothing about.
Alan Blowers, Zulu Coy 8 TRP, 45 Commando RM

Dear Alan,
I know exactly what you mean. Whenever I tell people who aren't versed in the martial arts that I work for KFM, more often than not, their reaction is to start laughing or leaping about in the air making grunting noises! The reason is that when Bruce and Kung Fu burst onto the British scene, it became an overnight fad, which most people thought would die out as quickly as it had arrived. But of course, this isn't the case - Kung Fu is here to stay, and, like Karate, Judo, Boxing, wrestling and so on, the art has established itself as a legitimate part of Western life. As the months go by, people will recognise this. In fact, they are doing so now and Kung Fu will be granted the respect it so richly deserves. In the meantime, just ignore those who are ignorant of the martial arts. After all, you're the one who knows the real truth! As for people cashing in on Kung Fu, it's easy to pick the genuine article from the cheap imitation. Needless to say, KFM imitates nobody!

NO ARGUING

Dear Jenny,
After seeing and reading the Who's Who In Kung Fu, it gave me an idea; now that Bruce Lee is no longer the King of Kung Fu, all the other top exponents should compete against each other in a world wide tournament which should be held in somewhere like the Empire Pool, Wembley. The one that wins should, and will, be the new King of Kung Fu. It would also save a lot of arguing.
Steven White, Cheshire

Dear Steven,
An excellent suggestion and with luck, one of the martial arts promoters in this country may take you up on it! Although it would be a mammoth task bringing the big names of the martial arts world together under one roof, now that Kung Fu has more than established itself in this country, there is a good chance that it could come off. In the future, several Kung Fu stars will be visiting Britain - one of them being the fabulous first lady of Kung Fu, Angela Mao, no less! - so keep your fingers crossed. And watch out for more of Angela, in KFM; my editor has a special surprise for you soon.

CHINESE PEN PALS

Dear Jenny,
We are two ardent readers of your great magazine from Scotland and we are writing to you as a last hope of finding two nice Chinese male pen-friends. Our names and addresses are: Irene Neill, Glasgow and Jean Wright, Glasgow. All letters will be answered - especially if photographs are enclosed. PS: Keep up the good work!

Dear Irene and Jean,
You're the first two of our readers to have pen pal requests published in KFM. Hopefully we'll publish one or two names and addresses each issue to help bring Britain's Kung Fu family closer together, so if you're short of a martial arts pen friend, drop me a line here at KFM and mark on the front of the envelope, 'Pen Pal.'

BRUCE CUT

Dear Jenny,
I think *KFM* is the best magazine in Britain, but I am very concerned over the Bruce Lee film *The Way of the Dragon*. I have come to the conclusion that some of the film has been cut. I do not think it is the cinema's fault as I have seen it six times altogether in two different cinemas. I believe the film has been cut in every fighting scene except the last and the one in the syndicate's office. I am very disappointed in missing some of the best parts of the film.
A.J. Lea, Cardiff

Dear A.J.,
Sadly you are right. The Way of the Dragon, as shown to British and American audiences, was cut. This was done by the distributors, Cathay Films, who knew that the censors in this country would not allow certain scenes to be shown here, especially scenes with Bruce using nunchakus. I think that it is a great pity that the censors can't realise that Bruce's action scenes are not just pieces of degrading violence, but art in its highest form - the art of the mind and body working together in unison. Perhaps one day, everyone will realise just how beautiful Bruce was in action and then we'll be able to see his work exactly as he intended it to be seen, with no cuts!

FAST FOOTWORK

Dear Jenny,
Let's start straight away with question time: 1. Was *Hapkido* speeded up? 2. Could you have a poster of Angela Mao fighting from a clip of *Hapkido*? 3. Were any of Bruce's films speeded up? I would like this letter to be printed and I also think Bruce would have liked that as well.
Stuart Thompson, Bentley, Doncaster

Dear Stuart,
No, Hapkido was not speeded up and nor were any of Bruce's classics. Both Bruce and Angela never had any use for trick photography and in fact went out of their way to make their films as true a reflection, of their art as possible. When Bruce's movies took Hong Kong by storm, several local actors thought that all they had to do was to stand around and look pretty while the camera did all the fighting. But this idea was short-lived; when their films were released audiences soon realised that the 'stars' were little more than flat footed flops worthy of only a passing glance. Bruce was first and foremost, a martial artist and a movie actor second, and it shows in all his celluloid works. As for Angela, as the Far East's reigning Hapkido champion, what does she need with fancy camera work? As mentioned before, our editor Don Won Ton has promised a new, detailed look at Lady Kung Fu in a coming issue, which just might include an action poster!

CHINESE PUZZLE

Dear Jenny,
I have been a devoted fan of *Kung-Fu Monthly* ever since the first issue, but one thing has been puzzling me for a long time. if, as you say, Kung Fu is an ancient Chinese art which began in the provinces of China all those thousands of years ago, why is it that all the best fighters seem to come from places such as Hong Kong and Taiwan which are not really part of China? For instance, the late great Little Dragon was born and lived most of his life in Hong Kong and Angela Mao comes from Taiwan. Also, one more personal question: I saw your picture in *The Book of Kung Fu* and you looked Chinese. Are you from China? Keep up the good work and as long as *KFM* keeps appearing, I will be your best fan.
Geraldine Maguire, London

Dear Geraldine,
Thanks for the compliments, and I hope we will be pleasing you for a long time yet! Yes, Kung Fu did originate on the Chinese mainland, but after the communist revolution, the cream of the martial artists fled to other countries such as Hong Kong and Taiwan, where they established themselves and carried on the fighting traditions of their forefathers. One of these masters was the leader of the Wing Chun school of Kung Fu named Yip Man, who settled in Hong Kong and started to teach his skills to the enthusiastic local population. His star pupil just happened to be a youngster by the name of Bruce Lee! I hope you enjoyed my feature in The Book of Kung Fu. No, I am not Chinese or at least, not all Chinese. My grandfather was born in Hong Kong's Clearwater Bay district - the same place that houses the mammoth Shaw Brothers film studio - but he migrated to this country many years ago and married my grandmother, who comes from Scunthorpe. My only regret is that I am related to Bruce only in name.

THE BEGINNER'S GUIDE TO KUNG-FU

The title of this book is self explanatory. The graphic, easy to understand illustrations by Paul Simmons and the carefully conceived step by step instructions make this the perfect book for beginners wishing to take up kung-fu. Unlike certain other publications on the market, this book has been carefully planned and meticulously executed. We claim it to be the best book of its kind for kung-fu novices in the world! Chapters include: HISTORY AND ORIGINS, EXERCISES, STRIKES, KICKS, BLOCKS, DEFENSE AND COUNTER ATTACK and STANCES.

Many thousands of KFM readers have already ordered their copy of this exciting book. If you are genuinely interested in taking up kung-fu then our advice to you is to order your copy today! Only an order through KFM can *guarantee* you will obtain a copy. Mail £2.00 by cheque or postal order made out to Kung-Fu Monthly and enclose your carefully printed name and address. All orders to: **KUNG-FU BEGINNERS BOOK OFFER**, Kung-Fu Monthly, 39 Goodge Street, London W1P 1FD.

THE POSTER MAGAZINES - VOLUME ONE

EDITORIAL

Hi there Kung Fu fans!

Well, here we are well into the second year of publishing *Kung-Fu Monthly*, and to think that some sceptics predicted we would never last beyond an issue or two! Thanks to the marvellous support we have received from all *KFM* readers, I can report that *Kung-Fu Monthly* is by far the world's biggest selling martial arts publication. Already, *KFM* is published in three languages, (English, German and Dutch), and plans are underway right now to spread the word in French, Spanish, Turkish and Italian! If only Bruce were alive today to witness the world wide revolution in the appreciation of his art that his energy and genius has produced.

I'm keeping my editorial short for this issue to give more room for the great features and there are only two points I must bring to your attention. Firstly, no new orders please for the Back Issue Bonanza advertised in past issues. We are rapidly running out of early issues, (which were themselves reprinted!) and, for the moment, cannot deal with any further orders.

Secondly, I want you to know that the advertisement for the Summer Bruce Lee Pilgrimage holiday offer in this issue has my full consent and backing. The travel company, with whom the holiday has been arranged, are a highly reputable and competent organisation who have been flying people in and out of the Orient for many years. In fact, they are the official travel organisers for the Anglo-Chinese Families Association, and we at *KFM* have every confidence in them! Hope you can make it with us on our pilgrimage to Hong Kong as it's going to be great fun! That's all from me this month!

Felix Yen

Felix Yen
Editor-in-Chief

THE DEADLIEST ART

What does the word Karate mean? What is the difference between the Chinese martial arts and those of Japan? What is Thai kick Boxing or Burmese Bando? Which is the deadliest martial art of them all?

These are just a few of the questions that flood in every month to the *KFM* offices from the hordes of new, western Kung Fu fans. Many people inspired by the amazing skills of Bruce Lee, perhaps the greatest ever martial artist, are confused by a bewildering array of different Asian martial arts. Every country seems to have its own speciality and in some countries, there are hundreds of different schools within any one of the arts.

One of the most frequent questions concerns the powerful fighting art known as Karate. Many people think of it as a Japanese art while in actual fact, it derives in a roundabout way from the original Kung Fu of mainland China. Perhaps the reason that we get so many questions about Karate, is that Bruce Lee was often pitted against Karate experts in his films. Do you remember the tremendous sequence in Fist of Fury, when Bruce, discovering that members of the rival Karate school have attacked and slain his venerable teacher, goes to his enemies' establishment and shows them once and for all that no longer were the Chinese martial arts, the arts of the 'Sick Men of Asia.' In a devastating display of his own Jeet Kune Do style, Bruce whirls through the ranks of the Karate students, leaving them behind him like chaff, thrashed with a pair of flailing nunchakus! The solid, angular movements of the Karate students make an odd comparison with Bruce's fluid, 'all styles' approach.

Then again, there is that amazing sequence in *The Way of the Dragon* when Bruce comes up against Chuck Norris, seven times winner of the United States' Karate Championships. At first, the massive strength and brutal speed of the chunky American seems likely to prevail! Using a roundhouse Japanese high kick known as the 'Mawashi Geri,' he slams Bruce again and again, right back into the wall! But even then, when it all seemed to

be up for the King of Kung Fu, Bruce suddenly switched tactics completely and turned the tables on Chuck by turning on a light, prancing, practically 'western' style of Boxing, staying out of reach of the heavier man until with the incredible speed that made the 'Little Dragon' famous, he took the fight back on his own terms. As Bruce used to say when asked about 'Black Belts,' 'Brown Belts' and the honours of Karate, "I don't have any honorary belt at all. That belt doesn't mean anything. It might be useful to hold your pants up with but that's about all!"

Karate is very much a modern form of the martial arts, although it can be traced back to the Kung Fu of China during the T'ang Dynasty. At that time, the people of the island of Okinawa, which lies off the coast of China about five hundred miles south of Japan, absorbed the ancient martial arts teaching of China. They practiced both empty hand systems and weapons systems under the name 'Te' or 'Hand.' Then the island was conquered by the warlike Japanese. The conquerors prohibited the islanders from carrying any weapons at all and so the Okinawans had to rely on their empty hands for survival when faced with marauding bandits or drunken Japanese soldiers. At the same time, they developed the use of the 'nunchakus,' the deadly rice flails connected by a length of chain.

Soon there were several schools of Okinawan 'Te,' all underground andd kept secret from the Japanese and similar to the different schools of classical Chinese Kung Fu Wu Shu, with one big difference, however. At an early date, the Okinawans moved away from the traditional 'animal' fighting patterns used so extensively by the Chinese. The ancient Dragon, Tiger, Leopard, Snake and Crane systems went out of use on the island. Their 'te' became a vigorous, often brutally hard system with a lot of concentration going into hardening the fingers and the sides of the hand.

The next important date in the history of Karate is 1890, when the warlord Shoguns were toppled in Japan. The newly restored Japanese Emperors now decided to complete-

ly integrate Okinawa with Japan and accordingly, the ban on the martial arts was lifted. The Japanese forms Judo and Kendo were introduced and taught to the islanders. The Okinawans quickly picked up these foreign arts and began to win competitions with the mainland Japanese. A sharp-eyed Japanese doctor is credited with noticing that many of the Okinawan recruits for the army were possessed of tremendous physiques, which they credited to their 'te.' The Japanese investigated the long secret 'Te' and were so impressed that they incorporated it into their own schools! By 1932 all Japanese universities had 'Dojos' or training gyms for the art of Okinawan 'Te.'

The Okinawans had to choose a new word for their art and they came up with 'Kara-Te-Jutsu.' The reason for this is that the 'Te' was represented by a Chinese symbol that also meant 'T'ang Dynasty.' This very same symbol was read by the Japanese as 'Kara' which also meant Chinese. So to the original 'Te,' was added the Japanese 'Kara' and then the symbol of 'Jutsu' which means 'Arts' in Japanese. In this way, the Okinawans cleverly avoided upsetting their Japanese overlords while respecting their own culture and complimenting that of China from whence they had originally learned the art. So 'Karate-Jutsu' means Chinese Hand Art!

Of course, Karate isn't the only martial art for which the Japanese are famous. In the

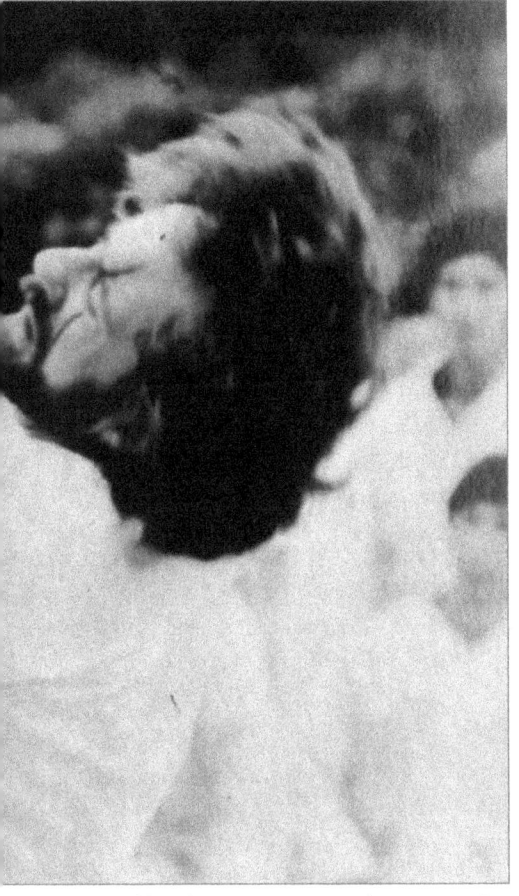

West there are many schools of Judo, Kendo and Aikido. All of these are spotting developments of the older 'Jutsu' of the Samurai.

To understand how these Japanese fighting forms developed, we have to understand a little about Japanese society and history. As we have said, the Chinese 'Empty Hand' systems came to the Japanese islands in the twelfth and thirteenth centuries. They had been invented in China, where the warrior was a well-paid person but one who was low in the social scale. He had all the weapons he could need and plenty of money for his warlike efforts, but the ruling of China was done by the Emperors and a huge government of civil servants. The martial arts were mainly practiced by the poor monks and ordinary people, for self defence.

In Japan, on the other hand, society was ruled by a high class of warriors, known as the 'Bushi' or 'Samurai,' who prohibited anyone else from carrying weapons. These warriors controlled Japanese life so tightly that they prevented the spread of Kung Fu knowledge amongst the ordinary people. The weapon skills practiced by the Samurai were known as the various 'Jutsu', such as Ken-Jutsu, the sword art, or Ju-Jutsu, the hand art. When the warriors lost their grip on Japanese society in the last century, these 'Jutsu' became less important; in their place new forms with a sporting emphasis were developed, like Judo, which was invented by Jigoro Kano, who also invented the system of grading by coloured belts, of which Bruce was so scornful. The vital difference between the 'Jutsu' forms and the 'Do' forms, is that the 'Jutsu' were for war. They taught the Samurai how to kill. The difference between Ken-Jutsu and Ken-Do is that Ken-Jutsu is a lethal art practiced with the deadly Japanese sword and Ken-Do is a sport practiced with a bamboo sword!

With the introduction of Karate from Okinawa, the Japanese forms became more organised and scientific. In the 1920s, a new school was begun named 'Aikido,' which is a combination of physical exercise, combat, sport and education. This system was invented by Morihei Ueshiba, a student of more than 200 different styles of Japanese hand art. His invention, also called 'Hapkido' in China, includes techniques from Korean 'Taekwondo' or 'empty hand', as well as the native Japanese forms. So after being refined by the Japanese warrior caste for several hundred years and then given a new, sporting twist by modem Japanese martial artists, the ancient Wu Shu of Twelfth Century China has returned to its homeland in the shape of Hapkido!

Far away, on the other side of China, from the islands of Okinawa and Japan, lies Burma, birthplace of one of the most ferocious fighting forms ever. They call it Bando and it numbers twelve offensive striking forms with names such as 'Boar,' 'Cobra,' 'Eagle,' 'Panther,' and so on.

Bando has come down from the ancient Burmese skills of 'Thaing,' which developed from both Chinese and Indian sources, the two giant countries that lie on either side of Burma. Buddhism also played a part as it was the Buddhist teachers, following in the footsteps of Bodhidharma, who taught the Burmese the skills of Kung Fu Wu Shu.

During the war, Burma was occupied by the Japanese, who organised contests between their own Karate champions and the Burmese Bandoists. During this period, Bando came to borrow quite a few skills from the Japanese forms of Judo and Aikido, not to forget Karate. In 1948, the Burmese held their first National Championships and since then, they have made giant strides with their art. Several organisations now exist to promote the sporting side of Bando.

In Bando fighting, there is a great deal of close quarters combat and consequently, they have developed techniques for striking with almost every part of the body; flips, shoulders, knees, feet and of course the elbows and fists! They have developed a special 'midget' punch for this close quarters fighting and also a method of 'climbing' up an opponent's thighs and ramming a knee into his face!

Next to Burma at the southern end of the Asian continent, lies Thailand, the home of that remarkable martial 'sport' called Thai Boxing. Originally taken from the Chinese some time in the Fifteenth Century, it has gradually become less of an 'art' in the manner of Chinese Kung Fu, and more of a sport. The fights are professional competitions and the fighters wear gloves and bandages around their ankles and feet. However, because the Thais have played down the grappling and throwing side of the sport, Thai Boxing has become more and more like Western Boxing except that in the Thai version, you are allowed to punch, knee, kick or elbow your opponent. It's a very spectacular thing to see and in recent years, it has become popular in Japan and Hong Kong, where professional bouts are held.

So which is the deadliest art of them all? Well, remembering one of the most important of all the sayings of Bruce Lee, still the unquestioned King of the Martial Arts in most people's minds, "When in actual combat you're not fighting a corpse. Your opponent is a living, moving object. Deal with him realistically and not as though you're fighting a robot.

Don't indulge in unnecessary moves. You'll get clobbered if you do, and in a street fight, you'll have your shirt ripped off you. In other words, when someone grabs you, punch him. To me, a lot of this fancy stuff is not functional."

But Bruce was so confident because he spoke from a position of towering knowledge. He collected books on the fighting arts just as avidly as his fans collect pictures of him! And he didn't just keep this mountain of knowledge in his extensive Kung Fu library, but actually took it into the gym and worked it out so that he knew the ins and outs of Thai Kick Boxing, Burmese Bando and many Japanese forms. It was from first hand experience that he could criticise so strongly, the classical forms that emphasise training by 'Kara.' The Kata systems rely on practicing over and over again, certain set piece movements, either in attack or defence. Eventually these become so thoroughly ingrained that the student responds automatically with the correct Kata in the correct situation. Unfortunately for such a student confronted with a loose, all styles fighter like Bruce Lee, he was unlikely to find himself in any of the 'correct' positions for his well learned Katas. Bruce could keep such a person totally off balance until they were so confused they'd be unable to stop the shower of thunderbolts he would then unleash.

To Bruce, the object of the martial arts was not simply to arm yourself for combat, but to learn to understand yourself. His Jeet Kune Do system, because it is totally dedicated to fluid movements and constant flexibility, is perhaps the most important step forward this century for the martial arts. Set-piece 'Katas,' tediously repetitive training systems and over elaborate rituals are no longer attractive to the modern day martial artist. By combing through the mass of different schools of skill on the Asian continent, Bruce led the way to all-styles Kung Fu; it only remains for those who come after him to live up to his awesome beginning!

Join us on Kung-Fu Monthly's...
BRUCE LEE PILGRIMAGE

The Excelsior Hotel, Hong Kong.

Kung-Fu Monthly, in co-operation with F.E.T.C. (Far East Travel Centre) are proud to announce the package holiday of a lifetime! Here is your chance to visit Hong Kong, the home town of Bruce Lee and mecca of contemporary Kung-Fu films and clubs! You will be travelling and staying with other Kung-Fu and Bruce Lee fans, and we have no hesitation in promising you that this will be an experience you will never forget!

Hong Kong is an incredible city, a melting pot of Eastern and Western cultures with air-conditioned superstores standing right next to colourful street markets containing every conceivable kind of merchandise from around the world! Hong Kong is famed for the breathtaking variety it offers to visitors, and we have arranged an extensive programme of free guide tours during your stay, ranging from visits to Bruce Lee's gymnasium, location scenes from "Enter The Dragon" and "The Big Boss", Bruce Lee's house, the "Golden Harvest" and "Shaw Bros." studios, introductions to Lee's associates and pupils with kung-fu demonstration sessions, viewings of brand new kung-fu films and much much more!

The cost of this holiday will be approximately £325.00. This will include accommodation and breakfast at the first class Excelsior hotel, return direct DC8 jet flight by Thai International Airways, coach transport to and from London Heathrow airport and Hong Kong Kai Tak airport and free guided coach tours during your stay. The holiday runs from 30th August 1975 (depart Heathrow airport) to 12th September 1975 (return to Heathrow from Hong Kong). A qualified tour courier will be at the party's disposal throughout the stay in Hong Kong.

We are expecting an enormous response to this holiday of a lifetime from Bruce Lee fans across the U.K. Our advice to those of you who wish to take advantage of the low, low cost and book early is to send a large, stamped, self addressed envelope (with no obligation) immediately to: **PILGRIMAGE KFM BRUCE LEE HOLIDAY, Kung-Fu Monthly, 39 Goodge Street, London W1P 1FD.**

Do **not** send money at this stage and be certain to indicate how many booking forms you might require.

WAS BRUCE LEE THE GREATEST?

Who was the Greatest? You are probably familiar with that kind of argument. Would Muhammad Ali have beaten Joe Louis in his prime? Was Georgie Best as difficult to tackle as the late Alex James? Would W.G. Grace have been able to handle the Australian fast bowlers of today?

Sometimes such discussions are pointless. In football, for instance, styles and tactics have changed so much that it would be impossible for us to say now, who was the Greatest.

But such is not the case with the martial arts. The basic rules have been laid down over the centuries. So it is possible for us to look at some of the great names of the past and ask: If the Little Dragon had met those old legendary fighters, who would have triumphed?

Let us imagine that we are the promoters of a contest to find out just who was the Greatest. First of all, we must travel back through time, to the end of the last century, in China.

It was then that Huo Yuan-chia was carving out a mighty reputation for himself as one of China's most skilful fighters ever. He was strong, too. Legend has it, that when he worked in the Tientsin docks, he was able to lift weights of four hundred pounds in each hand. That is like being able to pick up two men with one hand, and fat men, too!

Huo is never known to have been beaten and there is every reason to believe that he never was.

There would have been no shortage of news if such a defeat had been in public. But how would he have fared with Bruce?

Perhaps we should first make sure that Bruce would have agreed to such a contest. Certainly, if a challenge was made, Bruce would not flinch from it.

Another great fighter who would have kept the little Dragon on his metal was Shang Yun-hsian. This shaven-headed well-muscled athlete was born just over a hundred years ago and died in 1938. He came from Shantung, which is well-known in China as a place that produces fine fighters, much like the East End of London and the docklands of Liverpool and Glasgow are well known in this country for breeding successful boxers.

BRUCE LEE DRAGON POSTER !!!

Especially painted for KFM by Jeff Cummings, here is a magnificent full colour poster of the Dragon King of Kung-Fu, Bruce Lee! Only available through KFM .. cannot be bought in shops! Printed on glossy art paper, this is probably the best action poster of Bruce you will ever see . . . but don't take our word for it, rush your P.O. or cheque for 90p (includes all post and packing) made out to Kung-Fu Monthly to: BRUCE LEE DRAGON POSTER OFFER, KFM Mail Order, 39 Goodge Street, London W1P 1FD.

Shang had an amazingly strong belly. Probably you have come across people who can make their stomach muscles so tight that, however hard you punch them, you cannot hurt them. Well, Shang went one step further. He could break a man's wrist with his belly!

But watch Bruce Lee carefully in *The Way of the Dragon*. See how he looks closely at each opponent before he allows himself to be drawn. Bruce had too much 'noy sing' (patience) to allow himself to be lured into going for Shang's stomach in this way.

However Shang was a strange man. He was responsible, it is said, for the death of one of his students. That is unforgivable and something that would have made Bruce full of fury. Bruce would have been so keen to avenge the good name of Kung Fu that Shang would have stood little chance in a straight fight.

Having sent Shang spinning on his way, who can we find next to stand up and face Bruce?

Now Shang's teacher was a man named Li Ts'ub-i who died fifty years ago exactly. He was so respected in China that he had as many as five thousand students in Peking.

We know that Li was fond of the classical style of Boxing. So perhaps it is best to hear what Bruce had to say about that: "Classical forms and rituals are just too artificial and mechanical and don't really prepare a student for combat. A guy could get clobbered while getting into his classical mess." So we can mark up that contest to Bruce.

Another martial artist fighting at the same time as Li was a former carriage driver called Ch'e I-chai. He was a remarkably gentle man with a drooping moustache and a very peaceful nature. So would Ch'e have beaten Bruce? More likely that he would have told him that they had no quarrel and so there was no reason to fight. Bruce, being the artist that he was, would respect that. In many ways, in their respect for other people and for life, Bruce and Ch'e were very similar. No contest!

Tu may have been a humble carriage driver but another of the Greats, Li Neng-jan, was also poor in his youth. He worked as a farmer in Shansi and it was not until he was aged 47 that he became a complete fighter.

One of Li's special skills was his ability to do a complete flip in the air. How would he have fared in combat? It seems likely that Bruce would have been too swift for him and would have taken advantage of the fact that Li came late into the martial arts while Bruce had been tuning up his body since his teens.

Now Li's first pupil, Kuo Yun-shen might have been a different kettle of fish or should we say a different bowl of king prawns?

His nickname meant 'Divine Crushing Hands.' The name was not given idly. Once, in the Hopei province, he had actually killed an opponent by crushing his hand. For this crime, he was jailed for three years. A tough customer, certainly.

But we do know that Ch'e I-chai did defeat him once and so did another fighter called Tung Hai-ch'uan. If those two could master him, it would be impertinent for us to suggest that Bruce could not. Anyway, it would have been a brave man who tried to crush Bruce's hand knowing the strength of his fingers and his famous 'seong chi' (double sticking hands).

We have limited our matches to the martial arts. We have not tried to pick a fight for Bruce with Indian wrestlers or Thai boxers or Russian bare-knuckle fighters. Or American prize-fighters! Do we have any idea of how Bruce might have fared with fighters like those in the past?

John Tunney, the son of the great American Boxing champion, Gene Tunney, had dinner with Bruce once. He asked Bruce if he thought he could have defeated his father.

"To tell you the truth," said Bruce, trying to be as honest as he could without appearing boastful, "I could beat anyone in the world. Of course, if I sat still and your father hit me, forget it. The question is, could he ever get close to me?"

That is the key question. How do you get 'close' to a piece of greased lightning?

So who was the Greatest?

Bruce would probably have said that such a question was unimportant. He felt no need to travel round the world proving himself to others. He let his art speak for itself! And it spoke louder than any words that we can write here!

THE MARTIAL ART

These illustrations by Paul Simmons are from a new book published by Wildwood House of London. The book is called *The Beginner's Guide to Kung Fu*. You will find a detailed description of the book and an order form at the foot of this month's pin-up poster!

BLOCKING IN THE MIDDLE LINE: OUTSIDE BLOCK

- Used against a straight punch or thrust to the chest or solar plexus, from fighting position (*KFM* No.6) the forward arm is brought round across the body, the forearm deflecting the opponent's attack away, carrying him slightly past. Fighting the natural tendency to lean away or move backwards, it is often very effective to step inwards towards the opponent while simultaneously performing the block, from which position a counter can be immediately executed, in this case an inverted Fist Strike (Fig 2), using the Blocking Arm.
-

BLOCKING IN THE MIDDLE LINE: BLOCK AND TRAP

- The Inside Block is equally effective against both Straight and Hook or Roundhouse Thrusts, the hard edge of the forearm being applied to the attacker's inside forearm.
- From this position, the attacking arm can be 'trapped' after the block, by immediately hooking onto the arm or sleeve with the same hand (Figs A & B). Fingers and

wrist must be held tightly tensed to avoid injury to the hands.
- Having trapped the arm, a Straight Counter can be used (as in Fig 2) or alternatively, as a slightly more advanced technique, the opponent's forward leg can be 'swept' away, if correctly performed, throwing him to the floor.
- All movements are effective only if performed at speed and without hesitation.

KICKBACK: THE LETTERS

If I didn't enjoy reading your letters so much, I'd ask you to stop writing so many! The editor's told me that if I need any more cupboards to keep your mail in, he'll make me buy them myself! But seriously, it's wonderful to see your letters come pouring in - nothing cheers me up in the mornings (after a grim ride to work on the tube) more than a huge pile of envelopes all addressed to me, in your friendly handwriting. You mustn't be disappointed if your letter doesn't get printed. If we were to print every good letter that comes to me, we'd have to bring out a daily Kung Fu newspaper!

Well, I'm waffling on a bit this month; this is your page, so let's get on with what you have to say.

CONTENDER FOR THE TITLE

Dear *KFM*,
I have the answer to a problem of yours. Everybody's looking for a new King in the martial arts; what about Jim Kelly, star of the films *Enter the Dragon* and *Black Belt Jones*? I have seen him four times, and am convinced that he is good enough for the vacant crown. In an American magazine called Fighting Stars I recently collected, there was an interview with Jim Kelly and he said that he has challenged the famous boxer Joe Frazier to an all-in fight, but has got no reply yet. He also predicts that he will make a bigger impact on martial arts movies than Bruce Lee in three years from now. So who knows what could happen in the next few years. I hope you have more articles on Jim Kelly, and also on my favourite martial arts of Taekwondo. Thanks for a superb magazine.
Jim Kelly Fan, Hove, Sussex

Dear Jim Kelly Fan,
You're certainly not alone in plugging big Jim as the next great martial arts master. Hundreds of readers have suggested the same thing and here at KFM, we're certainly not surprised that Joe Frazier hasn't replied to Big Jim's challenge! You can be sure that we'll be covering his career with interest In future issues of KFM.

LETTER OF THE MONTH

Dear *KFM*,
Regarding Bruce Lee's title 'The Little Dragon,' I happen to know that your Chinese horoscopes are based on different animals and last one year and one month. Naturally, Bruce Lee was born under the year of the seventh Dragon. His name also amounts to a number seven, and this number crops up several times in his date of birth. Seven is a mystic number and I believe that Bruce was a mystic.
I am also sure that he was aware of the influence of the Dragon, and adopted that name as rightfully belonging to him. If you watch his fights very closely, his high battle pitch is not a roar but the sound of a dragon, so are his movements. In fact, I almost expect him to spit fire! Dragons, as a myth, are of course invincible. So the Little Dragon, Bruce Lee, or his spirit, will be here to stay but he should really be handled with care.
Miss G.F.J. Schwarzfeld, Chelsea, London.

Dear Miss Schwarzfeld,
Well, you obviously don't need KFM to tell you much about Bruce Lee! It's always nice to get further information about the life of the Little Dragon, so thanks for going to the trouble of sharing, your thoughts on his mystic influences with us.

BRUCE LEE SPORTS AND SHOULDER BAGS!

Here's a fine new offer from KFM, the world's best selling martial arts mag! We have licenced a reputable bag manufacturer to produce for us these fantastic sports and shoulder bags for all our Bruce Lee fans! Whether you need something to carry your kit to kung-fu class or just to stash your make-up or books and stuff to school and college, these bags are for you! And if you're an older Bruce Lee fan (we know plenty of mums and dads who fight their sons and daughters over who reads KFM first), well, take the load out of shopping with the fun power of the King of Kung-Fu!
The sports bag is the bigger of the two, but both are manufactured to a high standard from durable canvas backed with PVC to keep them showerproof. The zips are metal (not plastic) and the straps are sewn with double stitches to really last. We're proud of these bags and we know that you'd be proud to own one too! The printing is of an exceptionally high standard, four colours on each bag, and you have a choice of red, blue or green canvas.
To order, mail us £1.50 for the shoulder bag and £2.00 for the sports bag (not forgetting to include your name and address and choice of colour) made out to Kung-Fu Monthly. Orders to: **BRUCE LEE BAGS OFFER**, KFM Mail Order, 39 Goodge Street, London W1P 1FD. Price includes all post and packing.

Waterproof! Strongly Made! Metal Zipper!

BRUCE ON RECORD

Dear *KFM*,
I would like to know if it is possible to get the record theme from *The Way of the Dragon*? I have been all over the record shops in my area but I've had no luck. I think I should say that Chan Yiu Lan would do well as Bruce Lee's successor so tell me if he's in the running. Keep up the good work.
Mark Binns, Stafford, Staffs

Dear Mark,
Our old friends at Cathay films tell us that they're not surprised you couldn't find the record, as it hasn't been released. They have some good news though. It may be released at some point in the future, and Cathay will certainly be releasing the soundtrack from Game of Death, Bruce Lee's last film, when Game of Death is released this autumn. You can, of course, console yourself meanwhile, by buying the soundtrack of Enter the Dragon by Lalo Schifrin on Warner Bros. No. K4627S.

HIGH-FLYING BRUCE!

Dear *KFM*,
Please can you tell me how high Bruce used to be able to jump? My uncle said he used to be able to jump 12ft, but I say he could jump 7ft. Could you please sort out our problem, and keep up the good work.
Paul O'Hagan, Wythenshawe, Manchester

Dear Paul,
Unfortunately, there is no definite answer to your question, as Bruce's superb leaps were seen at their best in his spontaneous fight scenes, and were never properly measured. Thinking back though, he did jump about twice the height of the Big Boss in that memorable last fight on the lawn, didn't he? That's some leaping.

CHIANG IS THE GREATEST!

Dear *KFM*,
I have just read *KFM* No.5. At last you have woken up. Your magazine has always been good but this one was brilliant. You showed for the first time, an interest in other martial artists. Although Bruce Lee was the best, he is unfortunately dead. So it is time to concentrate on the men who will carry his torch. I would like to point out that David Chiang is a fantastic actor. You did not mention that he starred in *Chinese Vengeance* or *Hellfighters of the East*, but both of these films were brilliant. Nor did you mention the phenomenal Alex Lung ('King of Kung Fu.') In that film he was as good as Bruce Lee himself. So how about a big pin-up of Alex Lung, Carter Wong and David Chiang in action in your magazine very shortly? I look forward to more magazines like No. 5.
M. Sharp, Newton Abbot, Devon

Dear M. Sharp,
Well, we try to please, and you can be assured that we've been keeping our eyes on the gentlemen you mention for many months. But we can only get so many pictures into one KFM, and while I promise you that any fighting star worth their salt will get full coverage, you may have to wait for an issue or two to see all of them given the KFM treatment!

KFM PEN PALS CORNER

Hmmm! I didn't know what I was letting myself in for when I mentioned the magic words 'pen pals' in last issue! We've had so many fans writing in asking for Chinese pen pals to write to them, that I can't possibly print them all, however, here are a few names and addresses of Bruce Lee or Kung Fu fans who would like to hear from any of our Chinese readers!

Yvonne Carter, Gillingham, Kent. Lorraine Baines, Westvale Kirkby, Nr. Liverpool, Lancashire. Anne White, Oakdale, Poole, Dorset. Helen Hunter, Canford Heath, Poole, Dorset. Trevor Preston, Landkey, Nr. Barnstaple, North Devon. Ivan Mortis, Rayleigh, Essex. Mrs. June Mitchell, Bilton, Hull. Pam Jones, Trevor, Caernarvon, N. Wales. Carl Humpage, Newcastle, Staffs. Linda Williams and Diane Webb, Whyteleafe, Surrey. Carol and Liz Leckie, Glasgow, Scotland.

Note to Chinese readers! Unless otherwise stated, all addresses of readers are In England!

THE BEGINNERS' GUIDE TO KUNG-FU
Graphic, easy to understand illustrations by Paul Simmons and carefully conceived step by step instructions make this the perfect book for beginners wishing to take up kung-fu. This book has already introduced thousands of KFM readers to the martial arts and it can do the same for you! It is a serious and carefully planned instructional guide which we claim to be the best of its kind for kung-fu novices in the world. Chapters include: HISTORY AND ORIGINS, EXERCISES, STRIKES, KICKS, BLOCKS, DEFENSE AND COUNTER ATTACK and STANCES.

If you are genuinely interested in kung-fu then you should order your copy today! Mail £2.00 by cheque or postal order made out to Kung-Fu Monthly and enclose your carefully printed name and address. KUNG-FU BEGINNERS' BOOK OFFER, Kung-Fu Monthly, 39 Goodge Street, London W1P 1FD.

BRUCE LEE: KING OF KUNG-FU
This is the legendary story of Bruce Lee, Yuen Kam, The Little Dragon! Contains scores of exclusive photographs and over 40,000 words covering the entire span of Lee's amazing life story. The authors delve deeply into Lee's early life, his passion for the martial arts, his meteoric rise to world fame and the real cause of his tragic death. Here is a book that will thrill every real fan of Bruce Lee: a book to be kept, to be read and re-read a thousand times. Sales already exceed a quarter of a million copies and Bruce Lee: King of Kung-Fu is sure to become the classic published version of the Little Dragon's life. To obtain your copy mail £1.25 by cheque or P.O. made out to Kung-Fu Monthly enclosing your name and address to: BRUCE LEE BOOK OFFER, Kung-Fu Monthly, 39 Goodge Street, London W1P 1FD. You won't be disappointed!

THE BOOK OF KUNG-FU
One hundred pages packed with photographs and articles featuring the superstars of Kung-Fu! This is Kung-Fu Monthly's own special book, with articles on Angela Mao, David Carradine, Bruce Lee's secret training methods, The origins of kung-fu, The power of Ch'i, The wit and wisdom of the Little Dragon and much, much more! Many pages in full colour and absolutely jam packed with facts, figures, action, comics, illustrations and tremendous photographs. Would you like to speak the language of kung-fu or learn the Ten Commandments of the ancient art? Can you solve the Bruce Lee quiz? Don't miss this book! Rush your cheque or P.O. for only 95p made out to Kung-Fu Monthly to: THE BOOK OF KUNG-FU OFFER, Kung-Fu Monthly, 39 Goodge Street, London W1P 1FD.

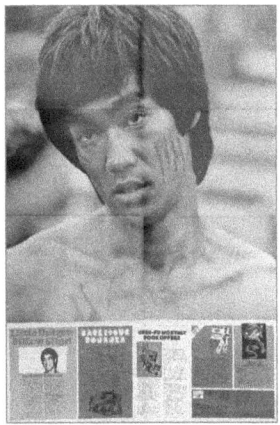

EDITORIAL

Hi there Kung Fu Fans!

Just the other day, we received some news, which frankly I found difficult to believe. It seems that *KFM* is so popular in Hong Kong, that a local pirate printer has turned his hand to printing up 'bootleg' copies of our magazine and selling them there! They say that imitation is the highest form of flattery, so I guess we'll just have to gracefully accept the 'compliment.' But it's a strange world where Chinese 'bootleggers' choose to steal articles and photographs from a European magazine about the Oriental arts, isn't it?!

This month's lead article is an answer to all those critics currently jumping on the 'anti-Kung Fu' bandwagon. As usual, it only takes a couple of rotten apples for the more sensational of our newspapers to condemn the whole barrel. Those critics who moan about the growing influence of Kung Fu in Britain and elsewhere, really get my goat! If only they would take the time and trouble to find out what Kung Fu is really all about, they'd soon be eating their words!

On to happier subjects and you'll be glad to hear that we are offering a brand new poster of Bruce Lee by Jeff Cummins, the artist who painted the tremendously popular 'Dragon' poster. Also, there are still some places left in our plane load of *KFM* fans already booked for 'The Bruce Lee Pilgrimage' to Hong Kong this August. That certainly promises to be a trip of a lifetime!

Lastly, I'll let you into a secret! *KFM* is planning to publish a new martial arts comic! It is tentatively titled, *When Kung Fu Strikes!* With luck, it will be on the stands in a few weeks, but please don't send in for copies just yet. I'll keep you posted in my next column on the launch date for WKFS.

That's all from me this month!

Felix Yen

Felix Yen
Editor-in-Chief

THE KFM INTERVIEW: RHONA MCVAY BRUCE LEE FAN CLUB PRESIDENT

Rhona McVay must be the ultimate Bruce Lee disciple. Ever since their two paths crossed, Rhona, a young lady born and bred in London, has followed the Little Dragon with unrivalled devotion. Eighteen months ago, Rhona, assisted by three friends, started the world's first Bruce Lee Fan Club. The response was overwhelming. After the legendary Raymond Chow - Bruce's Hong Kong film producer and close friend - recognised the club

as an official organisation, letters poured in from all over the globe - Australia, America, Algiers, Kenya, Tanzania, Cyprus and even Hong Kong! Now the membership books stand at a massive 22,000 and today Rhona is busier than ever! *KFM* invited Rhona to join us for a chat about what's happening in her own special Bruce Lee life.

KFM: Rhona, you've just returned from a pilgrimage to the United States, Could you tell our readers a bit about what you saw on your travels?

Rhona: Well, first of all, I flew to Los Angeles. There I saw the film *The Green Hornet* which I had never seen before. That's here in London at this moment, by the way, but I am having trouble with the film to get them to release it because his part is so small they think it might spoil his image. But he does have a couple

of good fights and it is definitely worth a release. There's a possibility it will be released here if I lean hard enough on the film company.

KFM: What is *The Green Hornet* about?

Rhona: Well, they've joined up three episodes of Bruce's old television show and they're showing that as a film. They've just done it again in the States but it hadn't been released when I was there. I suppose, as long as people keep going to see them, they will just keep joining episodes together. If you're a Bruce Lee fan, it's worth going to see, but if you're not, it's not worth going because it's as ridiculous as *Batman* and just as corny.

KFM: It's a kid's film.

Rhona: It's definitely a kid's film. But then again, I get so many letters saying, "I am under 18 and is there anything I can do to see Bruce in action?" For the sake of the younger ones, it would be a marvellous chance for them to see what they wouldn't normally see, because there's no blood or nunchakus or anything. I get hundreds and hundreds of kids joining because of your magazine or pictures or books, who have never even seen Bruce on film!

KFM: In Los Angeles, you also saw members of Bruce's family.

Rhona: Yes. I met his brother Robert, who's fantastic and has just made a fantastic album. He's got such a voice! The album, called *The Ballad of Bruce Lee*, will be released here later this year. Robert adores Bruce. He trains every day. Bruce used to make him

train. Now he does it 'cos he says Bruce would have wanted him to. He says he's going to come over and spend two weeks with us here later this year. But he doesn't look at all like Bruce; no resemblance at all.

KFM: What else is happening in LA?

Rhona: I missed Linda Lee, Bruce's wife, because she was moving; now she lives next door to Chuck Norris. There's a committee in LA with Linda, Robert, Stirling Silliphant and the publisher of Black Belt. They're making a film of Bruce's life. Barbra Streisand owns the film company and her boyfriend is going to direct it. There are auditions going on at this moment to choose a double for Bruce. If they can't find one in LA, they'll go to Hong Kong.

KFM: How did this come about?

Rhona: Linda tried to get *Super Dragon* banned but she couldn't, so I suppose she thought that if she couldn't beat it, she would make her own version. *Super Dragon* is really bad. The guy is quite a good double with shades on, but without sunglasses he doesn't look a bit like Bruce Lee. The girl who plays Ting Pei is absolutely Ting Pei's double. The girl who plays Linda is so ugly! She's meant to be the villain. Ting Pei is the heroine. They've changed the names slightly except Bruce is called Li Siu Lung.

KFM: You wouldn't recommend it?

Rhona: No. Definitely not!

KFM: You also went to Seattle when you were in the States?

Rhona: Yes. I went to Bruce's grave every day. The flowers that arrive there all the time! One day I was there a bouquet arrived from Australia! The caretaker says it's the best kept grave he has ever known. Pilgrims are always there. It's a beautiful grave. There's a photograph of Bruce very cleverly embedded in the marble. But I was told that maybe the family will be digging Bruce up to take him to LA. All his family is in LA now - Robert, his mother, Linda, the children - and he's way out in Seattle. They are just waiting on permission from the church, and it's still not definite.

KFM: You also saw Bruce's old friend Taky Kimura?

Rhona: He's very nice. He has a big supermarket in Seattle. Underneath the supermarket is Bruce's old martial arts school with pictures of Bruce still on the wall, all the same equipment, philosophies that Bruce had written that are still on the wall. The school has about forty students but only six are into Jeet Kune Do. The rest are on Wing Chun style. These six were trained by Bruce himself. Also, Taky says you cannot teach somebody Jeet Kune Do; Jeet Kune Do is Bruce Lee and you can only teach the basics because you have to develop it yourself. They all still wear the same jackets Bruce designed. They made me an honorary member and gave me one of the original application cards Bruce had designed. He was a very good artist.

KFM: Bruce is still remembered in the States?

Rhona: Well, Taky is 52 and he told me, "Many people have asked me why a guy my age spent so much time with a guy less than half my age. But listening to Bruce, you'd have thought our two ages were the other way around." Everybody in LA and Seattle said, "Anything you've ever read or heard about Bruce Lee is an understatement; he was that good and better." I said to Taky that probably there are a few Sifus in Hong Kong better than Bruce and he said, "No way! He was absolutely the finest!"

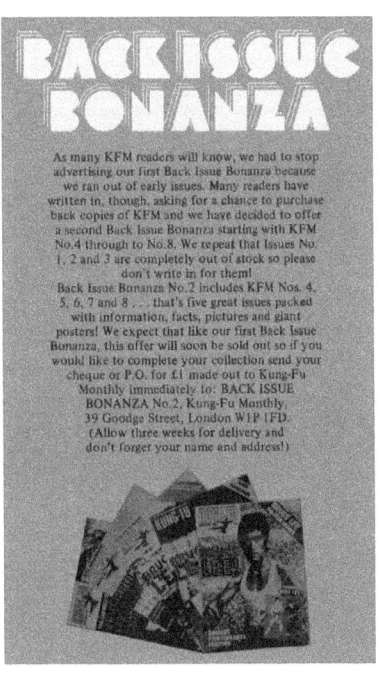

KFM: It sounds like you had a fabulous time in the States. Will you be returning in the near future do you think?

Rhona: If they really do dig him up, I'll go back for that.

NEWS FLASH

There will be a Memorial Service for Bruce Lee at St. Paul's Church in Covent Garden, London WC2 on Sunday 20th July. All are welcome.

Note: Many of you who turned up for last year's service went mistakenly to St. Paul's Cathedral. Please be sure to come to St. Paul's in Covent Garden. Thank you.

WHO'S KNOCKING KUNG FU?

As the fame and influence of Kung Fu and other Eastern martial arts sweeps the western world, as every town seems to be opening its own martial school and every cinema showing a Kung Fu spectacular, in other words, as the martial arts establish themselves as an essential part of western life; perhaps we ought not to be surprised to hear the critics go to work. It seems that for everything fresh and startlingly different there must be moaners and pessimists, whining to anyone who'll listen that the 'fad' cannot last, or if - like Kung Fu - it is obviously here to stay, that it is dangerous, useless, irresponsible, etc etc. What they mean, of course, is that they don't understand it and do not want to try and understand. As yet, the campaign against Kung Fu is in its early days and with any luck it will never see old age. But *KFM* is outraged and alarmed by some of the slanders recently printed against the martial arts, and in an attempt to set the record straight, we'd like to answer some of the charges.

Let's start with an article recently printed in one of the old-fashioned national papers. A director of a London-based cinema group, who after seeing just one Kung Fu film, came out ranting that watching such films makes people dangerously violent. All right then...

Q. Do Kung Fu films turn their audiences into vicious psychopaths?
A. Obviously, as any student of the martial arts knows too well, a person who uses violence at random, who fights without thought or reason, is not a healthy person (nor, incidentally, is such an opponent difficult to beat). There are and always have been people

of this sort. They existed before Kung Fu films, indeed, they existed before films were ever invented; and they are not pushed into pointless violence by watching a ninety minute film. If our cinema director can come up with any solid facts to support his claim, if he can find someone who came straight out of, say, *Enter the Dragon*, and immediately begun beating up innocent passers-by (which we doubt), then let him examine their history and background. He will find a person whose inner violence was bred not by the movie, but by a malevolent character and unhappy mind. Bruce Lee was constantly having to face such opponents. His films make it perfectly clear that they are not admirable people. We are reminded of the story from Bruce's childhood, when a local thug, desperate for a fight, finally pushed the Little Dragon into accepting his challenge to fight on the roof of a nearby tenement block.

"The winner," said Bruce's challenger, "May push the loser off the roof to his death." Bruce nodded quietly. They reached the roof, and Bruce almost instantly disabled his maniac opponent with a sharp kick to the ribs. Then, instead of extracting the final punishment, he carried the loser down and got an ambulance to take him to hospital.

This is the spirit of the Kung Fu films, as exemplified by their greatest star.

Many critics, however, accept that the films have nothing to do with street violence, but suggest that the teaching of the martial arts is a risky business, so...

Q. Should people be encouraged to teach of learn Kung Fu?
A. Since the beginning of time, man has tried to perfect everything that he is capable of doing. We have great painters because men wanted to develop their art, great writers because they worked and studied to make writing not just something they were good at, but something which could bring pleasure and enjoyment to millions. No less important, we have great martial artists because they trained and persevered to take their art to a peak of perfection. This is the reason for Kung Fu schools, and for martial arts schools of any type. They are not training grounds for muggers and thugs.

To understand how true this last statement is, a small examination of the philosophy of Kung Fu is necessary. To quote from a 'Warning' at the front of the excellent *The Beginner's Guide To Kung Fu*:

"If you are serious about taking up Kung Fu, then it is essential that you find yourself a reputable teacher and school. Be prepared to devote a considerable amount of time and effort to the art's study and practice.

"Above all, never use Kung Fu in anger. To protect yourself against unwarranted attack is, of course, justifiable. But to attack without provocation or necessity is at once dishonourable and indefensible.

"Remember, often the greatest courage a man or woman can display, is in retreat from an antagonist they know they can defeat."

The point is that Kung Fu is much more than just a way of fighting. It is a way of looking at the world, a way of understanding the forces of life and of death, of good and evil. It is no more possible to learn the fighting art without understanding the philosophy than it is to eat chips without vinegar. The same cannot be said of, for instance, Queensberry Rules Boxing.

Kung Fu has its roots in the wisdoms of ancient China, where, to be a great fighter was simply not good enough. Patience, kindness, and restraint were necessary; they made up the development of that inner energy known as 'Ch'i' - without which, nobody, ancient or modern, can become a Kung Fu fighter. Let us quote from the Ten Commandments of Kung Fu, laid down in the early Sixteenth Century by the great master Chueh Yuan:

"2nd Commandment - Fighting must be used only for legitimate self-defence.

"5th Commandment - In travelling, a fighter should refrain from showing his art to the common people, even to the extent of refusing challenges.

"6th Commandment - A fighter must never be bellicose.

"9th Commandment - Fighting should not be taught rashly to non-Buddhists, lest it produce harm. It can only he transmitted to one who is gentle and merciful.

"10th Commandment - A fighter must eschew aggressiveness, greed, and boasting."

Any worthwhile teacher at any worthwhile school is fully versed in such philosophy, and we may be sure that the art can never be taught to or by somebody who does not accept or understand its meaning.

But still the critics find something to knock. What with all those broken bones in the average Kung Fu film, they say...

Q. Isn't Kung Fu a particularly nasty form of fighting?

A. All fighting is violent. We should be under no illusions about that. Whether it's wrestling, rapier-fencing, or pistol-duelling, people get hurt. And once the codes of Kung Fu have been obeyed with regard to who fights who and why, there is going to be some pain involved in the conflict. Both combatants recognise this. But let's listen to the critics for a moment. One gentleman objected to the film he'd seen because, "It was not just a question of victims getting a bloodied nose or bruised jaw. Here, they deal in breaking arms and backs, with terrifying cracks, and jumping at people to kick them in the throat."

Apart from this interesting interpretation of Kung Fu, perhaps we should consider what it was that offended that viewer. Had he never seen the slow and terrible tortures practiced by Hollywood Indians in Hollywood Westerns? Or the vicious and artless beatings-up from many an American gangster film? Or even the merry massacre of boatloads of unfortunate pirates by 'gentleman' Errol Flynn? Let's be sensible; Violence has always been a mainstay of the movies, and what our critic is objecting to, is not the fact that somebody is getting hurt, but that they are being hurt in an unusual manner.

But Kung Fu films are about a style of fighting that is lethal. It would be simply dishonest to make a film pretending to depict Kung Fu in which the combatants patted each other around like playful spaniels, then shook hands and forgot it. But at the same time, it is not the cracking of bones and the spilling of blood that Kung Fu fans go along to admire. These are incidental. What is important is the speed, agility, grace, and accuracy of the fighter. Bruce Lee's films attracted so many more fans than any other martial artist, not because there was more gore and blood spilt in them than in any other film (there was not), but because he was the greatest fighter the world has ever seen. A star of such power could not help but attract satellites.

Q. Does Kung Fu encourage racial violence?

A. This question may seem odd to our readers, but it has been suggested, and we should answer it once and for all. The accuser's actual words were, "I have been told that the popular theme is a confrontation between Orientals and White men and that seems to me, a subtle encouragement to racial violence."

Of course, this is silly, inaccurate nonsense. For a start, the popular theme is not confrontation between whites and non-whites; the popular theme is between forces of good and evil. Facial colour is secondary to this. Where white Europeans do enter into the films, they are not particularly on the side of good or of evil. The roles of Bob Wall in *Enter the Dragon* and Peter Cushing in the Kung Fu/Horror films are almost heroic roles. The truth is that the Chinese have no particular reason to dislike and fight Europeans.

The Japanese, however, are a different matter. Although our white/yellow conscious critic may not have noticed, there is much more conflict between Chinese and their similarly coloured neighbours, the Japanese, than between Chinese and whites. And there are reasons for this. In the 1930s, while Europe and America were anxiously watching Hitler's tyrannical steps draw nearer, the Chinese were watching the Japanese Empire with equal concern. Under the corrupt and careless rule of Chiang Kai Sh'ek, China had come to be described as 'the sick man of Asia,' and Chinese national pride was at an all-time low. The Japanese, long-time rivals (and occasionally enemies), were quick to exploit this weakness, in many different ways. They invaded China, hoping to colonise part of the mainland, and they took to treating the Chinese much as Hitler did the Jews, as an inferior species. Their films reflect this; the famous Samurai films and other Japanese martial arts epics invariably depict Chinese as an unmanly, cowardly race of peasants and servants.

As we know, things were to change. Mao Tse-Tung's troops swept like an avenging dragon through China. The tide was turned by the end of World War II, with the Japanese defeated and the new Chinese era firmly underway. A sense of pride began to return, gradually, to those of Chinese origin, an idea that, perhaps, they were no longer the 'sick men of Asia.'

And no-one could confirm that feeling better than Yip Man's pupil, the Little Dragon, Bruce Lee. Can you imagine the feelings that swept through his Chinese audience when, in Fist of Fury, Chinese Bruce Lee outwits and outfights the supposedly invincible Japanese school. In the same film, there is a notice up above a park entrance which reads 'No Dogs or Chinese Allowed.' With one mighty leap and one ferocious kick, Bruce smashes the sign to smithereens, and with it, the myth of Chinese inferiority.

So there is, undoubtedly, racial violence in Kung Fu films, though not between whites and non-whites. It is the kind of racial violence that is shown in such English war films as Sink The Bismarck and The Great Escape, where the Germans are portrayed as the wicked oppressors, soon to be beaten. It is understandable, such emotion and pride, and all nations are guilty of it.

Those are the principle objections that have been raised in the occasional petty tirade against the art of Kung Fu, As you have seen, they are not difficult to deny and dismiss. But the press, always anxious to find some sensational story, some drama, will continue to pick straws and to quibble. The only answer, in the long-term, lies with you, the genuine Kung Fu artists and fans, to prove that the style and philosophy of Kung Fu is a good, unconquerable one. It has nothing to do with the lunatics who make 'Kung Fu Stars' - the sharp throwing weapons - and hurl them at innocent policemen. These people know nothing, repeat nothing, of true Kung Fu; they are more in the style of the ugly, vicious thugs from the evil school, the kind that Bruce Lee's Ch'i quite easily overcame. They have a hatred of peace and life that the true Kung Fu believer must always oppose.

Remember the skills of the old masters, the Shaolin priests? As observers have put it, "I remember punching Di Sum Si in the stomach, and he caught my fist in his stomach. I pulled and pulled, but I couldn't get my fist out. When I tried to hit his face, he would block the punch with his shoulder. He moved his shoulder that far up!

"The monks had this hang gung (light power) whereby they could make their bodies light. I remember this demonstration where they took a small match box and laid it on its side. The guy jumped right on top of it, and it didn't break."

The true qualities of Kung Fu are tolerance, gentleness, and a sense of peace.

Q. Is Kung Fu here to stay?
A. Yes.

KICKBACK: THE LETTERS

While we've been on our holidays here at *KFM*, the mail has been mounting up once again on my desk! There's an awful lot of interest these days in up and coming Kung Fu stars and I've persuaded our editor to begin a new feature next issue which will introduce some of these new stars to you readers. Watch out for it in *KFM* No.10!

SUPER DRAGON

Dear Jenny,
I recently had the misfortune to see a film in London called *Super Dragon*. This film pretended to be the 'true story' of Bruce Lee's life and death, but it was absolute rubbish! It had doubles playing the parts of Bruce and his wife and friends, though their names were changed. I just thought I'd let you know to warn your readers what a horrible, distorted movie it is, and I hope you'll print my letter as a warning.
Mr. J. Pickett, Brixton Hill, London, SW2

Dear Mr. Pickett,
I'd better not express my own opinion of this movie or I'll get carried away with rage! There's an old saying about how, if you sling enough mud, some always sticks. Let's just leave it at that! Thanks for your letter.

MARTIAL ARTS BOOK?

Dear Jenny,
Could you please recommend a book outlining all of the martial arts, not just Kung Fu, that I would be able to buy or borrow from a library? Most of the books in the shops seem to be very specialised. Keep up the really great work in *KFM*. Your page is always the first I turn to!
Michael Barrett, Stretford, Manchester

Dear Michael,
The book you're after is definitely *Asian Fighting Arts* by Donn F. Draeger and Robert W. Smith. I know that it is available in libraries and many bookshops. I always keep a copy of this first rate 'encyclopaedia' of the martial arts in the office. You'd be amazed at the number of arguments it resolves!

GAME OF DEATH RELEASE DATE

Dear Jenny,
I am going crazy waiting for the release of *Game of Death*. When will it be out? What's all the delay? I thought Bruce had finished the movie just before he died. By the way, my nomination for the new King of Kung Fu is Barry Chan. I've seen him in *The Dragon's Vengeance* and he is just absolutely incredible. Let's have pictures of him please.
Leslie Hobbs, Melling, Liverpool

Dear Leslie,
Agree with you about Barry Chan - he's very, very good. I'll do some arm-bending in our editorial department to get a picture of him in KFM very soon! As for Game of Death, I'm afraid we'll all just have to be patient. I'm sure that Golden Harvest and Cathay are doing their utmost to complete that movie. As soon as we have a definite date, you'll find it here first!

JEET KUNE DO

Dear Jenny,
I want to ask you a question about Jeet Kune Do. Firstly, why is it called that in the first place? Secondly, what makes it so different from any of the other styles of Kung Fu? Lastly, did Bruce Lee invent it all on his own and is there anyone who still teaches it now that he is dead? I've tried writing to other magazines, but they didn't (or couldn't) answer my questions. Can *KFM* do better?
Robert Austin, East Molesey, Surrey

Dear Robert,
You should have tried KFM first and saved yourself the postage! To answer your questions in full, would take a book or two, especially the bit about 'what makes it different?' Briefly, Jeet Kune Do means The Way of the Intercepting Fist. But as Bruce himself once said, "It's just a convenient name - nothing more."
Yes, Bruce did invent Jeet Kune Do on his own and yes, there are (a very few) teachers of it who studied under Bruce in America. As to that big question, 'what makes it different,' I guess the best thing to do is to let Bruce explain it in the words he used in an interview with Black Belt magazine in the USA some years ago: "Let it be understood once and for all that I have not invented a new style, composite or modification. Unlike 'classical martial art,' there is no series of rules or classification of technique that constitutes a distinct 'Jeet Kune Do' method of fighting." If you want to know more Robert, I suggest you ready Issues 5 & 6 of KFM and the biography, Bruce Lee: King of Kung Fu.

FIST OF UNICORN

Dear Jenny,
One of my pen pals in America mentioned that Bruce Lee appeared in a movie over there called, *Fist of Unicorn*. I know that in America, they often change the names of films, and I was wondering whether or not this *Fist of Unicorn* movie might be *The Big Boss* or *Fist of Fury* in disguise. Can you help?
David Clayton, Dublin, Eire

Dear David,
Well, this one kept me guessing for a few days. I can tell you! Finally, though, I managed to contact a Kung Fu film addict in New York and he explained the mystery. Apparently, Fist of Unicorn was produced by the Shaw Brothers in Hong Kong and does indeed feature a fleeting glimpse of Bruce Lee. But when I say fleeting, I mean fleeting! My New York friend informed me that if you so much as blinked a couple of times in the wrong place, you might easily miss the Little Dragon's appearance!

HONG KONG PILGRIMAGE

Dear Jenny,
I would like to go on your Bruce Lee Pilgrimage to Hong Kong which you advertised in the last issue. But I wondered if that would be allowed seeing as I'm only 15 years old? Please let me know if I'd be able to join you on that holiday of a lifetime, which it would be. By the way, *KFM* always arrives late up here, north of the border. Can't you deliver it any quicker? My newsagent gets tired of me asking him, "Is it in yet?" every day!
Angela Argyle, Aloah, Scotland

Dear Angela,
Providing your parents agree, you will be very welcome to join us on the Pilgrimage. As explained in the advertisement, you'll receive a brochure, a leaflet and order form with all the relevant details. I shouldn't wait too long though as there's only so many seats on our flight! We're sorry if copies of KFM sometimes take a few days longer to reach you in Scotland but better late than never!

KFM PEN PALS CORNER

Here are a dozen or so *KFM* readers taken at random from the hundreds of you who are after Kung Fu pen pals. Wish we had more space. By the way, we can't promise to find you Chinese pen pals, though we have heard from several people who were lucky enough to find pen pals from Hong Kong and other areas through *KFM*.

Liz and Bernadette McConkey, Belfast, N. Ireland. Henry Jacques, North Watford, Herts. Marion Bostock and Linda Fraser, Basildon, Essex. Christine Rogers, Laughton, Sheffield. Robert Anderson, Giffnock, Glasgow, Scotland. Arthur and Duncan Ramagge, Glacis Site, Gibraltar. Teresa Brown, Great Yarmouth, Norfolk. Carolyn Campbell, Falkirk, Stirlingshire, Scotland. Kim Toon, Whitwick, Coalville, Leicester. Malcolm Rogers, Littleworth, Stafford. Cathryn McKinven, Corby, Northants.

EDITORIAL

Hi there Kung Fu Fans!
This month we have two really informative and exciting articles for you. Firstly, we take a close look at the violent and treacherous world of Chinese Secret Societies! For centuries, these deadly organisations have ruled throughout the Orient and their close historical connections with the martial arts, makes fascinating reading!
In Hong Kong, you will still find many thousands of Chinese people who remain convinced that Bruce Lee was murdered on the orders of one of these dreaded societies! Before you scoff too loudly, it's worth remembering that the very fact that such rumours are believed and repeated so widely just goes to show the power these societies wield over the lives of the Chinese community even today!
Our second article is concerned with a man who probably did more to expose the genius of Bruce Lee to the world than any other. Raymond Chow, the brilliant movie producer

who founded Golden Harvest Films, is an extraordinary man whose talents and energy have revitalised the Chinese film industry. Under Chow's guiding hand. Golden Harvest Films has grown from a small company into a multi-million dollar organisation! It was with Raymond Chow that Bruce decided to work throughout his Kung Fu movie career. Although the Little Dragon was often tempted with huge sums of money by rival film companies, Bruce trusted and respected Raymond Chow and the two forged a uniquely successful partnership. In this issue of *KFM*, we salute Mr. Chow as the man who gave us the legend of Bruce Lee! Lastly, I'd like to thank the hundreds of fans who write regularly to *KFM* with suggestions, questions and information. We're sorry if we can't always get the time to reply personally, but your letters are always appreciated.

That's all from me this month.

Felix Yen

Felix Yen
Editor-in-Chief

CHINESE SECRET SOCIETIES

Two years ago, the most famous of Hong Kong's sons died suddenly in mysterious circumstances. Out of the blue, the Hero of Kowloon, the 'Little Dragon' had gone, the victim of a ghastly mistake, involving one tiny pain-killing tablet!

Naturally enough, in such a close knit, overpopulated place as Hong Kong, the rumours started sweeping the streets as soon as the news had sunk in.

Amongst the superstitious, a lot was made of the name of Bruce's very last film, *Game Of Death*.

Astrologers mumbled over mystery numbers and linked his death with everything from the imaginary monsters that were supposed to rule the district in which he lived in Kowloon, the '9 Dragon Pond,' to the name of that last film! Others believed that he had been slain by an unknown Kung Fu master, jealous of the young man's brilliant success.

One of the most persistent rumours, and one that is still current in Hong Kong despite the results of the official inquest, despite Linda Lee's pleas to the people to stop the rumours, concerns the shadowy figures of the Secret Societies.

Names like the 'Green Pang,' 'The Triad Societies' and 'The 14K' were often quoted as being at the root of Bruce's death and when you consider the overwhelming power and secret influence wielded by the Secret Societies and the widespread graft and corruption in Hong Kong, who can ever say for sure that somehow they weren't involved? Even the black garbed Ninjas of Japan, the dreaded murder squad of soft footed assassins were blamed by some Hong Kong residents. It was almost as if the people of the Crown Colony, used as they are to the activities of the Secret Societies, just couldn't bring themselves to believe that they weren't implicated in the 'Little Dragon's' death in some way.

In that same year, 1973, the notoriously corrupt Hong Kong Police Force smashed 77 organisations involved in protection racketeering, drug smuggling and the like. And of

course, that was only the tip of the iceberg of Triad Society activity.

The Secret Societies of China and Japan are a maze of strange sounding names and rituals. Curious initiation rites, bloodthirsty gang wars and, of course, intense devotion to the Kung Fu Wu Shu. The two are inextricably mixed, the martial arts of China and the Secret Societies. Indeed the major force for the growth of the societies at one time was the subtle influence of the monks of the Shaolin Temples!

There was the 'White Lotus,' who were responsible for over-throwing the Mongols and placing the Ming dynasty on the throne in the fourteenth century. Then there was the 'Eight Diagrams Society,' who almost managed to murder and overthrow the Manchu Dynasty in 1814. The names are laced with mystery images, 'The Single Hearted Celestial Principles,' 'The Small Daggers,' 'The Yellow Turbans', 'The Dragon Flowers,' 'The Nine Mansions Society,' and, of course, the 'Fists of Righteous Harmony,' which we know of here as the 'Boxer' Society. The Boxers rose up at the end of the last century against the increasing aggression of Western powers in China. Anyone who's seen that classic of the Kung Fu screen *King Boxer* will know of their amazing feats. But despite their beliefs in their invulnerability, the Boxers were eventually to fall victim to Western weapons, even though for a while, it looked as if this fighting Kung Fu society might single-handedly free China from foreign exploitation.

It remained however for another Secret Society, one that was and still is, the most powerful of all, to finally overthrow the Manchus and rid China of the excessive influence of the West, and infamous Triads. Even the President of the Republic of China proclaimed in 1911, Sun Yat Sen, was a member of the Triads. Both Chiang Kai Shek and Mao Tse Tung had dealings with this awesome secret society and devoted to a fanatical organised crime throughout the Far East with a mixture of ruthlessness and secrecy without equal anywhere.

The Chinese societies are said to have begun as long ago as AD 9, when the early Han Dynasty was interrupted by the usurper Wang Mang. A society calling itself the 'Carnation Eyebrows,' because they painted their eyebrows red, rose up against this usurper and in AD 25, overthrew him and restored the Han and began a confused period when many warlords and petty tyrants struggled for supremacy.

It was during the period that Bodhidharma or Ta-Mo came to China and introduced the

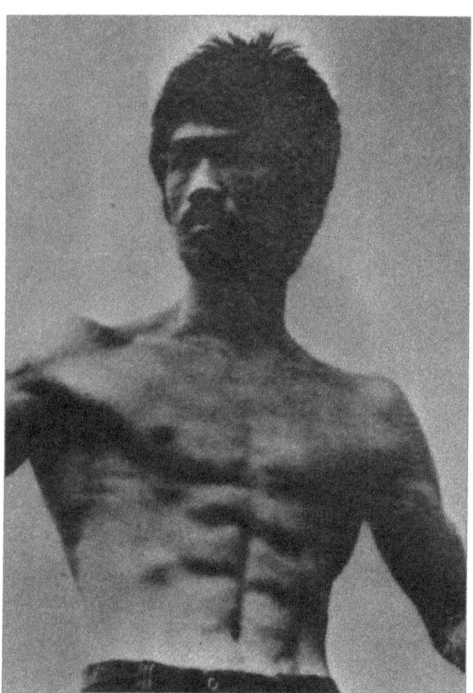

'muscle change classic' that revolutionised Kung Fu. About the same time, an event occurred that is still very important in the lore of Secret Societies, the 'peach garden oath,' sworn by the blood brothers Kwan Yu, Liu Pei and Chang Fei. They were great generals and popular leaders and Kwan Yu was later deified as Kwan Ti and made the patron God of War and of all Secret Brotherhoods.

It was also during this early period of unrest that the most important of all Chinese Secret Societies was founded, the mysterious 'White Lotus.' Originally, it was a Buddhist meditation sect, similar in nature to the Shaolin Temples but when the T'ang Emperors began persecuting Buddhists, the White Lotus was driven underground. There they invented a host of cryptic rituals and secret passwords and signs designed to protect themselves from the attentions of the Imperial forces.

Down the centuries, the White Lotus has continued, popping in and out of the History of China like an enigmatic shadow. Under a hundred different names, this society has contrived many rebellions against unpopular rulers while increasing its influence quietly in the vast population of China. At various times, the White Lotus has been known as the 'White Yang Sect,' and the 'Incense Smelling Sect,' while at other times its influence has been felt in offshoot organisations like the 'Eight Diagrams,' the 'Nine Mansions,' and most important of all, the 'Heaven and Earth Society,' from which has sprung today's Triads and American Tongs.

Sometime in the seventh century AD, the White Lotus was imported into Japan by one of the founders of Japanese Buddhism and certainly Japan has been riddled throughout its history by Secret Factions and Societies. Most famous of all Japanese secret societies are, of course, the Ninjas, the practitioners of Ninjitsu, the 'Way of the Spies.' The Ninjas were originally a hereditary cult, considered outcasts by the rest of society and devoted to a fanatical self discipline in the art of espionage and assassination. They developed the 'Shuriken,' a star-shaped throwing blade which they could use them with a deadly accura-

cy. At various times in Japanese history, Ninjas were employed in great numbers to eliminate the enemies of the stable or to increase the power of a great warlord. Today they are said to still be in existence; a mysterious, secret organisation skilled above all others in the arts of assassination and spying.

The origins of the Triad Society, or 'Hung League' as it is sometimes called, are said to lie in the Shaolin Temple of Fukien. During the reign of K'ang Hsi, one of the first Manchu Emperors, a rebellion broke out on the western borders of the Empire. The Emperor called for volunteers to help put down the rising and 128 brave monks from the Shaolin Temple at Fukien responded. So skilful in war and the martial arts were these monks, that they succeeded in routing the enemy without suffering a single casualty themselves. Led by Cheng Kwan Tat, the victorious monks declined the Emperor's offers of titles, wealth and official posts at the Imperial court and instead chose to return humbly to their temple. The Manchu Emperor was persuaded by jealous officials that the Fukien monks were secretly rebels, perhaps even members of the persecuted and feared White Lotus Society itself. With the aid of an unfrocked monk, the Imperial troops surrounded the monastery and set fire to it. Only five of 128 monks survived this blaze and by means of legendary feats and the intervention of the heavens, they escaped and eventually reached sanctuary in a place known as the White Stork Grotto. There they founded the Triad Society with its motto, still in use today, of 'overthrow Ch'ing restore Ming.'

The martial arts are another vital part of the Triads, the Green Pang and the other societies. Training in T'ai Chi and in the Wu-Shu is a common part of the education of a young member of the Triads. In the ceremonies that precede opening a meeting, all the members present go through a complex Boxing routine, during which they each make the hand sign appropriate to their rank. For example, a 489 Official will make the sign for 'Head of Dragon and Tail of Phoenix.'

In Hong Kong, Singapore, California, everywhere that has sizeable Chinese communities, the Secret Societies flourish. In America, the Triads arrived with the coolies and other immigrant workers who came to the West Coast in the nineteenth century. There they became known as 'Tongs,' named after the tong or hall in which they met. The Tong wars in San Francisco were ferocious affairs that lasted well into the twentieth century as the various groups fought for supreme control.

In Hong Kong, there are innumerable Triads and other groups and their membership is vast. Many young men join the Triads from the street gangs, such as the one that Bruce Lee fought with in his younger days. Every year there are thousands of street battles between these gangs and hundreds of deaths and the gangs make up a ready pool of youngsters for recruitment to the Societies.

Perhaps such hidden powers were really observing Bruce Lee. Perhaps the Shaolin based Secret Societies, the shadowy White Lotus or the criminal Triad gangs were really jealous of the 'Little Dragon.' It may be, that even now, David Chiang and Angela Mao, the reigning King and Queen of Kung Fu, are being quietly observed by those influences that have sought power through stealth and murder for so long!

RAYMOND CHOW
THE MAN BEHIND BRUCE LEE!

At 11.30 pm on the night of July 20th, 1973, a slight, elegantly dressed elderly man stepped out of the main doors of Hong Kong's Queen Elizabeth Hospital. There was a great sadness in his eyes as he quietly spoke two words to a crowd of reporters: "He's gone."

The "He" referred to, was Bruce Lee. The elderly man was someone who had understood, loved, and helped the Little Dragon perhaps more than any other living person. His name is Raymond Chow, and his story is a fascinating one.

Raymond Chow was born in pre-war Hong Kong, the son of a banker. His father wanted Raymond to have a Chinese education, however, in 1939, the family moved to Shanghai. It was the beginning of an interesting ten years for the young Raymond, indeed the start of an action-packed career. In 1940 the Japanese bombed Pearl Harbour, and the Chows found themselves stranded in China for the remainder of the war. Raymond took the opportunity to continue his education there, studying journalism at the American Christian University. His extraordinary talent soon showed, and he found himself working part time for the United Press, as well as running his own English and Chinese language school papers.

In 1949 the Communists took Shanghai, and Raymond, equipped with a Bachelor's Degree, returned to Hong Kong, where he immediately became the star reporter for the English language Hong Kong Standard. He was offered a scholarship to study at the University of Missouri, but in his own words, "I had my family to support. My father had died and my two younger brothers hadn't finished school, so I gave that up." Who knows what might have happened to Hollywood had Chow been able to go to America!

In 1951 came Raymond Chow's first big break. He joined the 'Voice of America,' and within seven years he had founded and managed their radio and movie-production section, especially for Chinese overseas.

It was inevitable that his path should sooner or later cross the path of Run Run Shaw. Run Run Shaw had, with the help of his family, introduced talking pictures to the East, before the war decimated his growing empire. After the war, he picked up the pieces once again and, instead of importing western movies, began to make his own. By the middle-to-late '50s, Shaw Brothers was the Hollywood of the East. But something was missing, something that Run Run realised. In 1958, he says, "The Chinese film industry was at its lowest level. Films were made in seven or ten days and were of very poor quality."

Shaw Brothers had just opened up in Hong Kong in '58, and were looking for an advertising and publicity manager. Raymond, curious about this industry and anxious for a change, took the job. After two months he saw the first film that Shaw brought out in Hong Kong. "I was horrified," remembers Chow, "and told him I wanted to quit. I felt so appalled, that I felt sure I couldn't sell the film." Run Run Shaw smiled gently at his talented new recruit and said, "Well, that's exactly why you have to come to take over production, because they are so bad!" Out of this inspired piece of 'casting' by Run Run Shaw, was born the Kung Fu Movie! Because, after spending several years organising Shaw Bros studios and producing spectacular films of quality, Raymond Chow got one of his new directors to make a film based on the martial arts, entitled *Come Drink with Me*. It was an instant success, and the era of eastern action films was underway. *Come Drink with Me* was quickly followed by other, more celebrated films, and stars such as Wang Yu began to appear in such epics as *The One-Armed Swordsman*. Under the management of Raymond Chow, Shaw Bros were now virtually without competition in the Mandarin film industry. Three of their films had won the Best Picture Award at the Asian Film Festival, and their rivals were sinking into oblivion. But things were to change. Raymond Chow was once more becoming restless.

In 1970, Raymond Chow left Shaw Bros to set up his own production company, Golden Harvest. Run Run Shaw was heartbroken, and angry. Ronnie Poon, Chow's replacement at Shaw Bros, told the authors of Bruce Lee - King of Kung Fu, "Don't ask the old man (Run Run Shaw) anything about Chow. You will make him sick to the guts for the whole day if

you mention Raymond Chow." And Golden Harvest's Andre Morgan added, "It's more than just a question of face. Run Run feels that Raymond was a trusted younger son and that Raymond was ungrateful by leaving. Raymond's attitude is that if Run Run wasn't such a goddam penny pincher, he wouldn't have had to leave."

Harsh words, perhaps. But an incident that occurred just a few months after the split-up helps to explain Chow's point of view. It was certainly the most important incident in the history of Mandarin films, perhaps in the history of worldwide cinema. A young actor named Bruce Lee, who had achieved some fame in America through various TV series, was visiting Hong Kong to publicise his latest serial *The Green Hornet*. He had mentioned on Los Angeles radio that he would consider working for the Mandarin film industry "if the money is right."

Obviously, Shaw Bros made an offer. But it was not exactly a golden handshake! Andre Morgan says, "All Shaw's offered was a trainee actors job, and Lee never forgot it." Raymond Chow saw his chance, and telephoned Lee back in Los Angeles with a more realistic offer. Lee accepted over the phone, and Chow sent the wife of his top director, Lo Wei, to America to clinch Bruce's signature. She got the treasured contract, and was followed back to Hong Kong by the Little Dragon-to-be! When he left, Bruce left a note for his wife Linda. It said that he wanted to be a film star, bringing out the best of Chinese martial arts and showing them to the world.

It would be possible, then, to proclaim Raymond Chow as a genius among film men; the producer who discovered and launched the greatest movie star of our times. But Chow is typically modest about his achievements. Looking back, he says, "I did not discover Bruce Lee, just as much as he did not discover me, as many people are now saying. What I really did was remember him; his charisma stuck in my mind. I kept thinking of a screen vehicle for him. It would have to be a starring part, I was sure. I couldn't have seen him doing anything less."

The starring part that Chow eventually decided upon for Bruce was, of course, *The Big Boss*. Although neither Chow nor Lee were expecting too great a response from Bruce's

first effort, they (and the rest of the world) were to be happily surprised. *The Big Boss* smashed records like they were eggshells. In its first 19 days on the Hong Kong circuit, it grossed HK$3,200,000, surpassing by HK$800,000 the previous record held by *The Sound of Music* since 1966. The China Mail writes, "It is generally believed among local film businessmen that *The Big Boss* has done so well that its record is unlikely to be equalled by any film in the future."

Golden Harvest's fortunes boomed. From being a one-horse race, the Mandarin film business was suddenly competitive again! Shaw Bros had good cause to worry about Golden Harvest, who were soon bringing out thirteen to fourteen films a year. Run Run recognised his mistake, and occasionally tried to get Bruce Lee away from Chow, but to no avail. Andre Morgan

says, "Shaw would be on the phone for the better part of the day to get Lee over. He never went because Bruce had been in the business long enough to know that people will promise you anything to get what they want."

So the golden partnership of Lee and Chow continued to grow, in quality and success. *Fist of Fury*, their second film, even broke the records set by *The Big Boss*. They were innovating and experimenting all the time, the agile brilliance of Bruce Lee inspiring and being inspired by the practical genius of Raymond Chow. They developed a new way of shooting fight scenes, mainly because the Little Dragon's martial prowess demanded a new way, and continued taking the Mandarin industry to new heights and setting new standards.

After *Fist of Fury*, so many offers were coming in for Bruce Lee that Chow had to take him to one side. "I told Bruce," Raymond recalls, "That it would be difficult - impossible in fact - for me to match the huge offers he was receiving. It would be unfair to him and it would have been unfair to me." But Bruce would not leave his cherished partner. Instead, they formed a new company and agreed to split the profits from the Little Dragon's films 50/50. Then, together, they entered upon the co-productions with Warner Bros that was to produce *The Way of the Dragon*, *Enter the Dragon*, and *The Game of Death*.

Now, as we are all only too aware, Bruce Lee has left us; taken his great genius to another world. But the man who recognised that genius at its true value, and who nurtured and developed it, works on. Raymond Chow's Golden Harvest is reaping bigger and better crops with every season that passes. Occasionally Chow looks back on the days when the successes that he built were just dreams and talks about the dreams that he will make into future reality, "At the moment, we are producing a lot of Won Ton Westerns, as they are called, but I think that particular tide will pass very shortly. What will be left, will be a market for the better of the Hong Kong films. Now the door is open, it is easier for the distributors to be receptive to the idea of Chinese films. You have no idea of the trouble we ran into when we first started to push our films overseas. The reaction was, "What! A Chinese film!" Then Bruce Lee changed all that."

Bruce Lee, with a little help from Raymond Chow.

KICKBACK: THE LETTERS

Hello there! Another bulging sack of mail for, me to answer the best I can. In addition to your questions, we are also receiving lots of letter from out new European readers. Unfortunately, French, German and Italian were never my strong points so I'll have to ask our Common Market friends to be patient! Many of you have written to say that you're looking forward to the Kung Fu comic that Felix Yen mentioned in his editorial last issue. Well, like he said then, we will let you know as soon as its published, but don't go bothering your newsagent too hard yet!

BRUCE LEE GLOVES AND NUNCHAKUS

Dear Jenny,
Could you please tell me where I could get a pair of nunchakus, the Boxing gloves Bruce was wearing in your poster a couple of issues back and Kung Fu throwing stars which I read about in the paper? I am interested in Kung Fu weapons and wish you would do an article about them in *KFM*.
Richard Townshend, Warrington, Cheshire

Dear Richard,
No, I do not know where you could buy such weapons, and even if I did know, I'm afraid that I would not pass on the information. It may be that your interest in these deadly weapons is purely scholarly, but I doubt it! Kung Fu is not a game Richard! The nunchakus and throwing stars you're after can maim or blind somebody for life if used carelessly by a novice! If you're really interested in Kung Fu, then find yourself a class to join or write to the British Kung Fu Council. Forget about weapons, is my advice!

BRUCE LEE'S MUSICAL BROTHER

Dear Jenny,
Is it true that Bruce has a brother who has just released a record about Bruce's life? Where could I get it, if this is true? I'm sorry to bother you with this silly question but there's nobody else who can tell me. Thanks for your great magazine, and especially your letters page.
Tony Fisher, Parkhead, Glasgow

Dear Tony,
Your question is not in the least silly; that's what I'm here for! Yes, it is true that Bruce's brother, Robert Lee, has just released an album called 'The Ballad of Bruce Lee.' It has not yet been released in this country. I have written to the States to obtain a copy and will report on it next month. Robert is quite a pop star in Hong Kong, where he has had five hit singles. As yet, he has not had this kind of success in the Western world, but I'm sure that it will come!

HOW LONG?

Dear Jenny,
I've just started learning Kung Fu at a local class. It's hard work but well worth it! Could you tell me, how long will it take if I practice say two or three nights a week before I will be really proficient? My teacher wouldn't answer that question. How long, for instance, did Bruce Lee have to practice before he became a master?
Gordon Ford, West Ealing, London

Dear Gordon,
I'm afraid I can't really give you an exact answer as it all depends on your own natural abilities and talents. Bruce Lee always said that he was still learning every day of his life. He started learning when he was just a young boy and by the age of 25, he was certainly a qualified expert. Just keep up the practice and the mastery will come all by itself!

BRUCE LEE BIOPIC

Dear Jenny,
I hear that Linda Lee, Bruce's widow is making a film about Bruce in America. Have you any more information on this please? By the way, *KFM*'s article last issue on 'Who's Knocking Kung Fu?' was a real winner. I showed it to one of my teachers at school who is always on about how dangerous Kung Fu is and we even debated the questions in class. The title of the debate was, 'Is Kung Fu in Britain a dangerous menace to society?' The motion was defeated by 37 votes to 3!
Joy Peterson, Maidstone, Kent

Dear Joy,
I'm glad to hear that you liked our article and won your debate. As for Linda Lee's plans for a film about Bruce, I can confirm that this is true and that the provisional title for the film is 'Bruce Lee - His Life & Legend.' Auditions were recently held in Burbank, California, to try to find an actor to play the part of Bruce in the movie. As you can imagine, that is a pretty tall order! Still, I understand that they had dozens of applicants and that further auditions are planned in New York and maybe, even in London! Robert Clouse, who directed Enter the Dragon, will also be directing this film, so all in all, we can look forward to a worthy tribute on film in a year's time or so.

SHAOLIN KUNG FU: THE GREATEST?

Dear Jenny,
Before I bombard you with my questions, may I congratulate you on producing such a fantastic a worthy tribute to Bruce? I have heard that Shaolin Kung Fu is the greatest of all martial arts and one of the hardest to master. Did Bruce study Shaolin Kung Fu at any time? Would it be possible to print some photos of Bruce from the Long Beach Tournament in 1964? Once again, thanks for a great magazine - *KFM* is the best 25p worth in the world.
Joe Delargy, Coventry, Warks

Dear Joe,
Compliments, compliments - they work on me every time! Firstly, the term Shaolin Kung Fu is a little too general to give you a specific answer. As you can read in the chapter on the origins of Kung Fu in The Beginner's Guide to Kung Fu, most forms originated from the Shaolin Temples in China many, many centuries ago. There is no one particular style, them, that can claim to be Shaolin Kung Fu as all branches of the art spring from that source. As to the photographs, I have seen pictures from that Long Beach Tournament in 1964 but they were printed in the excellent Black Belt magazine in the U.S.A. Our editor tells me that we would not be able to reprint them for copyright reasons. Perhaps you could write and ask if they have any back issues. If you write to me, I'll give you their address.

SO MANY ARTS

Dear Jenny.
I especially liked your article in *KFM* No.8 on 'The Deadliest Art.' It made me wonder how many different arts there are! I would like to know more about Burmese Bando. There doesn't seem to be any books or films around containing information about Bando. Could you send me some information please?
P.S. *KFM* is like the legendary Bruce Lee - unbeatable!
Malcolm Sharp, Chiswick, London

Dear Malcolm,
Thanks for the compliment! I've had several letters asking about books on different martial arts. Firstly, I can find no book, I'm afraid, published in the UK, which is specifically concerned with Burmese Bando. All I can suggest is that you invest in a copy of 'Asian Fighting Arts' by Donn F. Draeger and Robert W. Smith, which has a section on Bando.

For Tony White of Newcastle, who wrote asking about a book on Japanese Kempo, I would suggest the book 'Shorinji Kempo: Philosophy & Technique' by Doshin So.
For Alex Donner of Newhaven, who wrote asking about Wing Chun Kung Fu, I suggest the book 'Wing Chun Kung Fu' by R. Clausniter and Greco Wong.
All of these books are published in Britain and your library or bookshop should be able to order them for you.

KFM PEN PALS CORNER

KFM Pen Pals Corner has been postponed for this issue but it will be back next month - hopefully with an expanded amount of space!

Hi there Kung Fu fans...
What a line-up we've got in store for you this month! First off we have what we think is a major scoop - probably the last full-length interview with Bruce Lee ever made. How we managed to obtain a tape of this historic event would fill a magazine all on its own! All I'll say now is that the *KFM* editorial team all deserve long holidays for their persistence! I'm sure you'll agree that their efforts were not in vain after you read Bruce's own words in print for the first time.

And if that is not enough, *KFM* is proud to present the life and career of a young man from Hong Kong who seems destined to capture martial hearts throughout the world - David Chiang! Already David's premiere movie *Legend of the Seven Golden Vampires* (in which he starred with veteran Hammer superstar Peter Crushing) has led the way for future Hong Kong/Hollywood co-productions, and we are certain that it will not be long before David graces silver screens in this country again!

Well, that's all from me this month. Hope you enjoy this issue and if you do, why not drop Jenny Lee in our Kickback department a line? She'd love to hear from you and so too would the rest of us here at *KFM*.

See you next month.

Felix Yen
Editor-in-Chief

This month, *Kung-Fu Monthly* is proud to publish an historic piece of the Bruce Lee legend - an exclusive interview with the Little Dragon himself! Taped by Radio Hong Kong in Hong Kong shortly before Bruce's tragic death, this interview provides a rare and remarkable glimpse into the private life of Bruce Lee - superstar, Bruce Lee - martial arts master, and Bruce Lee - human being. Some sections of the interview have been reprinted before in books and in previous editions of *KFM*. But this is the first time the complete interview has appeared in print anywhere in the world! Although Bruce's English sometimes falters, we have left his words largely unchanged. We are sure you will agree that, despite a language barrier, the wit, charm and wisdom of one of the greatest men of our - or indeed anytime shines through!

Interviewer: Bruce, now that you're the screen tough guy, you must have to suffer what all screen tough guys suffer - challenges from exhibitionists and nuts. It's already begun to happen hasn't it?

Bruce Lee: Yes it has.

Interviewer: How do you deal with it?

Bruce Lee: When I first learned martial art, I too challenged many established instructors. But what I have learned is that challenging means one thing; it is 'What is your reaction to it? How does it get you?' Now if you are secure in yourself, you treat it very, very lightly because you ask yourself, 'Am I really afraid of that man? Do I have any doubts that that man is going to get me?' And if I do not have such doubts and such fear, I would certainly treat it very lightly, just as today the rain is going on very strong but tomorrow the sun may come out again.

Interviewer: But they can't lose really can they? Even if you win, they still get the publicity.

Bruce Lee: Well, let's face it. In Hong Kong today can you have a fight? I mean a no-holds-barred fight? Is it a legal thing? It isn't, is it? And for me, I am always the last to know about these challenges, man. I mean, I always find out from newspapers, reporters, before I personally realise what the hell is happening.

Interviewer: Bruce, you were teaching martial arts in the States and two of your pupils were James Coburn and Steve McQueen. Do you find them tough people as they are portrayed on the screen?

Bruce Lee: No. First of all, James Coburn is definitely not a fighter. Lover, yes! He is really a super-nice guy. Not only that, he is a very peaceful man. He learns martial arts because he finds that it is like a mirror to reflect himself. I mean like, I personally believe that all type of knowledge - I don't care what it is - ultimately means self knowledge. And that is what he's after. Now Steve, Steve is very uptight, Steve is very high strung. Now Steve, he could be a very good martial artist but I hope that martial art would cool him down a little bit; maybe make him a little bit more mellower and be more peaceful, like Jim.

Interviewer: Do you feel that you are achieving that? That he is learning something?

Bruce Lee: No, definitely not yet. First, because of shooting schedule and all that, he cannot have it on a regular basis. And secondly, he is still on the level right now of enjoying it as an excitement, like his motorcycle and his sports car; some form of release of his, whatever, anger, whatever, you name it.

Interviewer: How much of your screen personality is really you? You teach martial arts, but often teachers are not the best exponents. Are you able to take care of yourself would you say?

Bruce Lee: I will answer first of all with a joke, if you don't mind. All the time people come up and say, "Bruce, are you really that good?" I say, "Well, if I tell you I am good, probably you will say that I'm boasting. But if I tell you I'm no good, you'll know I'm lying." Okay, going back to being truthful with you. Let's put it this way: I have no fear of an opponent in front of me. I am very self-sufficient and they do not bother me. And should I fight? Should I do anything? I have made up my mind that, baby, you had better kill me before I get you.

Interviewer: In *The Big Boss*, you play a man who is very slow to anger, who stays out of fights in the early stages because of a promise you made to your mother. Is that a little bit like you?

Bruce Lee: This is definitely a screen personality because as a person, one thing that I have definitely learned in my life - a life of self-examination, self-peeling bit by bit, day by day - is that I do have a bad temper. A violent temper, in fact. (Laughs) So that is definitely a screen personality; some person I am portraying and not Bruce Lee as he is.

Interviewer: As well as being a very successful film in terms of finance - it grossed more than any picture has done in Hong Kong - *The Big Boss* does show some very explicit sex scenes doesn't it? What's your reaction to being in bed with a lovely young movie star in front of the whole studio crew? Does it worry you? Does it intimidate you?

Bruce Lee: Well it certainly would not intimidate me, I can tell you that! (Laughs) It's alright as long as the script justifies it. But I do definitely not agree to put something in there just for the heck of it because it is exploitation. For instance, when I started shooting *The Big Boss*, the first question that was asked was how many thousands of feet of film is it going to be? My reaction is first of all, why do I start fighting? You see what I am saying?

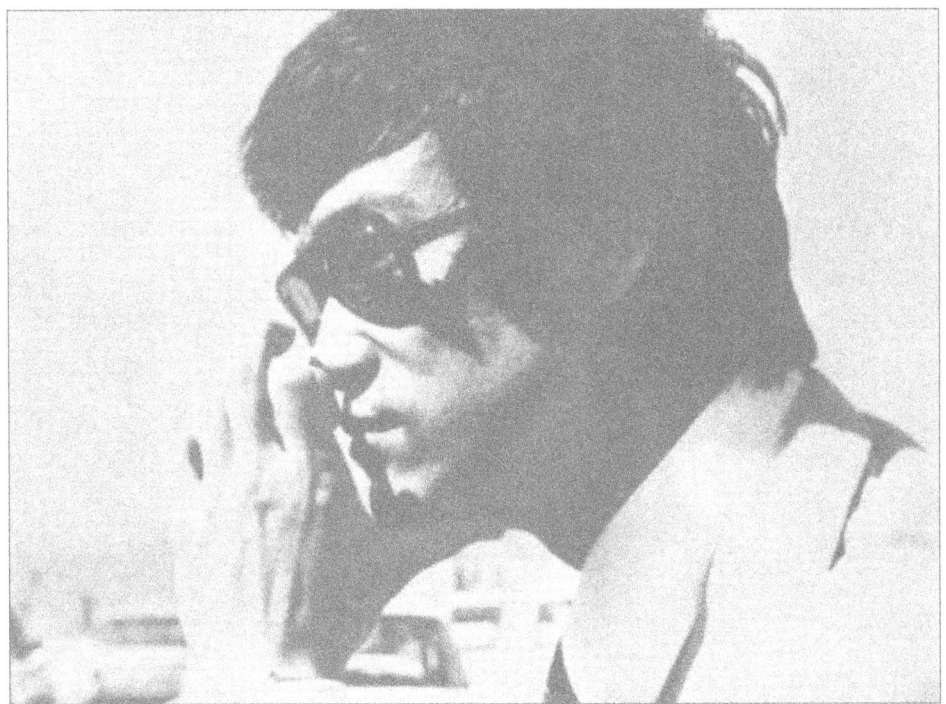

It seems to be the thing now; they go for sex, blood, just merely for the sake of sex and merely for the sake of blood.

Interviewer: One question about the film; at the time when you decide you are going to get revenge, obviously leading up to the climax, you suddenly go and make love to a girlfriend in a bordello. What's the motivation for that?

Bruce Lee: Now, the way I look at that; that was a suggestion of the director. I accept it in such a way which is, him being such a very simple man, when all of a sudden he has made up his mind he is going to go and either die - kill or be killed. It is kind of a sudden thing of a human being, that a thought just occurs that, well, such is the basic need of a human being that I might as well enjoy it before I kick the bucket, like that kind of an attitude. It is just an occurrence, you know?

Interviewer: I think that you would agree with me Bruce that one of the things which has limited the appeal of Chinese films in the past is that it is very difficult to find a Chinese actor who can act in a Western style, I mean. You seem to have crossed that barrier. How do you think you've achieved it? Do you think it had to do with your time in the United States?

Bruce Lee: Oh yes. It really has. When I first arrived, I did *The Green Hornet* television series back in '65 and as I looked around, man, I saw a lot of human beings and as I looked at myself, I saw I was the only robot there. I was not being myself, and I am trying to accumulate external security, external technique, the way to move my arm and so on, but never to ask what Bruce Lee would have done. When I look around, I always learn something, and that is to be yourself! And to express yourself; to have faith in yourself. Do not go out and look for a successful personality and duplicate him. That seems to me that

that is the prevalent thing happening in Hong Kong. They always copy mannerism, they never start from the very root of his being, that is, "How can I be me?" You see, I never believe the word 'Star.' That's an illusion, man, something the public calls you. When you become successful, when you become famous, it's very, very easy to become blinded by all these happenings. Everybody comes up and calls you 'Mr Lee.' When you have long hair they all say, "Hey man, that's *in*; that's the *in* thing." But if you have no name they all say, "Look at that disgusting juvenile delinquent!" I mean, too many people are 'Yes, yes, yes' to you all the time, so unless you realise what life is about and that some game is happening and realising that it is a game, fine and dandy, that's alright. But most people tend to be blinded by it because if things are repeated too many times, you believe in it and it becomes a habit.

Interviewer: Your father warned you about the bad things in show business. Have you met them too?

Bruce Lee: Of course.

Interviewer: You seem to have come out of it remarkably well.

Bruce Lee: Let's put it this way. To be honest, I am not as bad as some of them, but I am definitely not saying that I am a Saint. (Laughs)

Interviewer: Could we go back to the fighting because this is what you're identified with. Which style - Karate, Judo, Chinese Boxing and so on - do you think is the most effective?

Bruce Lee: My answer to that is this: There is no such thing as an effective segment of a totality. By that, I mean I personally do not believe in the word 'style.' Why? Because, unless there are human beings with three arms and four legs, unless we have another group of beings on earth which are structurally different from us, then there might be a different style of fighting. Why is that? Because we have two hands and two legs. The important thing is how can we use them to the maximum, in terms of path - straight line, curved line, up, round lines, it might be slow, but depending, on the circumstances, it might not be so slow. Physically, how can I be so well co-ordinated? That means you have to be an athlete - jogging and all these basic ingredients. Right, and after all that, then you ask yourself, how can you honestly express yourself at that moment? And being yourself, when you punch, you really want to punch, not trying to punch because you're trying to avoid getting hit, but to really be in with it and express yourself. The most important thing to me is, how in the process of learning how to use my body, come to understand myself? Now the unfortunate thing is, now there's Boxing which uses hands, Judo which is throw-

ing. Now I'm not putting them down mind you, but I'm saying one thing that is a bad thing which is, because of styles, people are separated. They are not united together because styles became law, man. But the original founder of the style started out with hypotheses. But now it has become the gospel truth, and people who go into that became the product of that. It doesn't matter who you are, how you are, how you are structured, how you are built, how you are made; it doesn't matter. You just go in there and be that product, and that to me, is not right.

"The King is Dead - Long Live the King!" that's the cry from the busy studios set on Hong Kong's shoreline. Time must pass, all wounds must heal and now a new star rises in the East to challenge the brilliance of the old! But there are parallels. And in many ways the parallels between the careers of the departed Monarch of the Martial Arts, Bruce Lee, and the Heir Apparent, David Chiang, are close. Amazingly close!

Here we have David Chiang, now an established actor in Kung Fu films. A young man of 26, with the inevitable mop of black hair, an intense expression on his face, a burning ambition driving him onwards. A young man who dedicatedly spends at least two hours every day locked in a private chamber kicking the stuffing out of a heavy punch bag. A man who will spend hours practicing the same balletic, backwards high kick, time and time again, until his leg muscles are screaming for rest and he's mastered it to the point of perfection. To assume the throne of the Little Dragon, nothing else would do.

He's a young man with a taste for speed. He rides a heavy Japanese motorcycle to and from the studio every day through the howling blizzards of Hong Kong traffic. A young man with the performer's drug in his veins, he needs to act, to demonstrate his abilities as an actor and his skills as a martial artist.

It sounds familiar to Western fans. Bruce Lee was all of these things, and the parallels go on. In fact they start right at the beginning, for each of these great Kung Fu stars was a childhood movie actor. David began his movie career, a few years after Bruce's own debut, at the age of four. And like Bruce, he gave it up, and spent his formative years in Hong Kong. Also, he shares with Bruce a family background that ensured a dose of greasepaint and a taste for bright lights in his blood. Bruce's parents were members of a travelling company of actors of the Cantonese Opera. David's parents were film personalities, way back at the beginning Of the Hong Kong movie industry. You could say he never had a chance not to try his hand at Kung Fu stardom!

By the time David was 15, he was running loose on the streets of Hong Kong, just another member of one of the thousands of Hong Kong street gangs. At night, the teenagers square off and try to prove their own mastery of the martial arts, usually something that would bring a smile to the lips of great masters of the art, but deadly enough to keep police and ambulances busy most of the time. To quote David on the subject, "I didn't know what's good for me to do. Then I became a very bad boy."

Again we have a close parallel with Bruce Lee's own career. Bruce was a gang leader in the seamy, teeming streets of Hong Kong in the fifties. He left for San Francisco on his first attempt to get a chance at stardom in 1958. At that time David was still at school, but in the early sixties, when Bruce was getting his first parts in Hollywood (in the Green Hornet series), David Chiang was out fighting on street corners.

There the parallels end, because in the sixties the Kung Fu explosion was already warming up. Whereas Bruce had had to go to California for a new start, David, grew up in in a town where the movie business had suddenly come to life. The reasons for that can be seen most simply in the career of Run Run Shaw, who came to Hong Kong in 1959 and started to put together good quality sword and fist fight films. It's ironic perhaps that Bruce Lee, at that time probably the most charismatic figure in Kung Fu, had already left on a tramp freighter for San Francisco with $100 in his pocket.

David studied at the Chu Hai College and after graduation, he started working as a Kung Fu instructor for the swiftly growing film companies of Hong Kong. The Shaw Brothers' film empire was going full blast by then. Forty films a year were being churned out on their seaside lot and the entire Kung Fu industry was starting to rise to prominence.

David's first real break didn't even come to him! It was his brother, Paul Chin Pei, who was offered a role in a movie called The Sand Pebbles. The company needed a stuntman, and Paul put in a word for his Kung Fu teaching brother; he had the 'fastest fists' on the lot. It was already an accepted tradition in the young Kung Fu film industry that a lot of the stars-to-be started out as stuntmen. David did stunts in twenty or so Kung Fu classics in the years 1967-68. Eventually he got his big break. Run Run Shaw, the genial autocrat who runs the Shaw Brothers' film enterprises with the same sort of direct control that used to be exercised in Hollywood back in the twenties, decided to put two of the best stunt men together in a new film called *Dead End*. It was during the time when Wang Yu, Shaw's

first big Kung Fu star, had broken contract and moved to Taiwan. In a sense, the coast was clear. Director Chang Cheh liked David's style and approach and his career began to go places from that moment.

But it has to be remembered that in those days - seven full years ago - the only image conjured up in the minds of Western audiences by the words Kung Fu were Chinese restaurants and meals with noodles. When the young David Chiang started making movies at the Shaw studios the Mandarin circuit covered the East alright, but that was it. Bruce Lee was a bit part actor in Hollywood TV specials with the occasional movie role and most of the Little Dragon's income was coming from his Jeet Kune Do schools. The explosion had yet to come.

In fact, though, the groundwork had already been laid. Shaw's favourite young executive, Raymond Chow, had got fed up with the old man's 'penny pinching ways' as he put it, and he had left the company; a rift which still causes heartache to Run Run

Shaw. When Bruce Lee revisited Hong Kong, he stimulated interest at Shaw studios in his own career, but they made a mistake in their approach to the young Crown Prince of the growing Kung Fu world. The Shaw studios merely offered the Little Dragon a trainee-actor contract, something he indignantly turned down, and that left Raymond Chow to scoop the world's most instantly successful Kung Fu star.

It was the explosion of interest generated by Lee's big box office smash hits (*The Big Boss*, *Fist of Fury* etc.) that really got the ball rolling for the rest of the Hong Kong industry. Angela Mao was soon headlining at movie theatres all over the world, and following behind these, came an avalanche of new Shaw Brothers movies. Not surprisingly, David Chiang was one of the first stars in their stable to make an impact.

In 1970 David had already taken the Asian 'Movie King' Award in the 16th Asian Film Festival for his performance in *Vengeance*. He also went on to receive the 'Best Actor' award for *Blood Brother*. So when the Kung Fu explosion unleashed by Lee swept around the world, he was in a perfect position for international stardom. Everywhere that Bruce's films went, Run Run Shaw's competing Kung Fu flicks were bound to follow. David's reputation continued to grow as he went through a number of roles in such films as *The Swordsman Trilogy*, *The Boxer from Shantung*, and *The Pirate*. All of these were straightforward Shaw productions with a minimum of expense and acting and plenty of fighting, sword battles and Kung Fu.

In 1973 he was voted the actor with the most 'Modern Personality' at the Asian Film

Festival. Shortly afterwards, he set up in business with director Chang Cheh in an independent production company known as Chang's Scope Co. However they retained Run Run's backing and blessing and their films continued to be distributed through the enormous Shaw Brothers circuit. During this period, he made a series of strongly contrasting films. *Hell Fighters of the East* and *All Men are Brothers* were more traditional Kung Fu movies, with plenty of all-action dynamism. Other films that he directed himself such as *The Drug Addict* and *The Motor Cycle* were more realistic attempts to show a different side of the quality of living in the Far East. They were perhaps the very first 'social comment' films made in Hong Kong.

It was a year later, in 1974, that Run Run Shaw called up David Chiang with news of a film project that he just had to be in. Shaw was even prepared to break his strictly-adhered-to 'non-star system' to give David a chance at it. The film was a first in that it brought together the highly successful Hammer Horror films technique of the West and the Kung Fu action of the East. Released as *The Legend of the Seven Golden Vampires*, it had Peter Cushing teamed with David against the legendary golden vampires of China. Following on the success of other joint efforts, like *Enter the Dragon*, where Hollywood teamed up with Golden Harvest, *The Legend of the Seven Golden Vampires* is guaranteed to be a smash hit in the West, combining as it does, two of the currently most popular screen obsessions.

David is already at work on another co-production with Peter Cushing called *Friends*. Whether he can really occupy the throne of the departed Little Dragon is a matter for Kung Fu film fans everywhere to decide. In the meantime, David Chiang practices every day at the martial arts while living up to his watchword - 'Grace is the word to use in relation to the martial arts.'

BRUCE LEE SPORTS AND SHOULDER BAGS!

Here's a fine new offer from KFM, the world's best selling martial arts mag! We have licensed a reputable bag manufacturer to produce for us these fantastic sports and shoulder bags for all our Bruce Lee fans! Whether you need something to carry your kit to kung-fu class or just to stash your make-up or books and stuff to school and college, these bags are for you! And if you're an older Bruce Lee fan (we know plenty of mums and dads who fight their sons and daughters over who reads KFM first), well, take the load out of shopping with the fun power of the King of Kung-Fu!

The sports bag is the bigger of the two, but both are manufactured to a high standard from durable canvas backed with PVC to keep them showerporff. The zips are metal (not plastic) and the straps are sewn with double stitches to really last. We're proud of these bags and we know that you'd be proud to own one too! The printing is of an exceptionally high standard, four colours on each bag, and you have a choice of red, blue or green canvas.

To order, mail us £1.50 for the shoulder bag and £2.00 for the sports bag (not forgetting to include your name and address and choice of colour) made out to Kung-Fu Monthly. Orders to: **BRUCE LEE BAGS OFFER**, KFM Mail Order, 39 Goodge Street, London W1P 1FD. Price includes all post and packing.

Waterproof! Strongly Made! Metal Zipper!

Hello there... Jenny Lee here again to answer (hopefully) a few of the many thousands of letters which keep pouring in here to *KFM*. Sorry to all those Kung Fu fans whose letters I couldn't fit in this month, but don't let it stop you writing to me in the future. Honestly, I just love hearing your thoughts on Bruce, *KFM* and the Martial Arts each month. Before I get down to business, I'd just like to reply to all the *KFM* readers who inquired about Bruce's as-yet unreleased *Game of Death*. As yet there is no definite release date scheduled for the movie, but if and when it is completed and made ready for release, I will let you know immediately! Also, *KFM*'s Kung Fu comic is as yet not on the stands, but when the launch date approaches, *KFM* will make a special announcement. Enough of that for now and on with the show!

DAVID CHIANG

Dear Jenny,
For the new King of Kung Fu, I am nominating David Chiang. When I saw him in *The Legend of the Seven Golden Vampires*, I thought he was fantastic and just as quick as Bruce Lee. In fact, I read out of a book that Bruce himself recommended him as a good Kung Fu fighter. What really puzzles me is this. Earlier in the year, there was a TV programme called *Taste for Adventure* and it was about Kung Fu and David Chiang. Well, the narrator on the programme said that David Chiang had taken over the title of the King. Can you please tell me what went wrong? Also, please can we have some pictures of David Chiang?
Deborah Davies, Bucknall, Stoke-on-Trent

Dear Deborah,
Well, this is your lucky day! Just turn to our second feature in this month's KFM and you'll see everything you ever wanted to know about David Chiang! All of us here at KFM also think David is pretty fabulous and a very worthy contender for Bruce's title as the King of Kung Fu. It's true that Bruce considered David a pretty good martial artist - in fact, the two superstars were friends as well as fellow actors. As for the TV programme proclaiming David as the King of Kung Fu, well, I'll leave that decision up to the KFM readers. After all, it's the audience who have the final say!

DEVOTED DISCIPLE

Dear Jenny,
I think I have quite a tough question for you to answer. Here it is: My father comes up to me when I buy your *KFM* and says, "Why do you worship a dead man (Bruce Lee) and spend all your money on magazines about him?" I find it very difficult to answer his questions, so please, please answer them for me.
Carl Humpage, Newcastle, Staffs

Dear Carl (I hope I've got your name right),
I know exactly what you mean. The many people I run into who do not know much about Bruce, often ask me why I spend my life working to keep alive the memory of a man who is no longer with us. All I say to them is that they are unlucky not to have felt the magic of the Little Dragon, a magic that, for all those who have experienced it, will never die. Although Bruce Lee was only a man, the inspiration and joy he was able to give to so many people has become something more than mortal, and I for one feel that his example is well worth preserving.

IRON HAND

Dear Jenny,
Please could you tell me more about the Iron Hand and did it really give superhuman strength which I have heard it did? Who first developed it and what technique of Martial Art was it used in? I think your magazine is great and keep up the good work.
Ian Henson, Sevenoaks, Kent

Dear Ian,
Thanks for the kind words and encouragement The Iron Hand technique (also known as the Iron Fist) originated in the ancient Shaolin Temples of China way back in the sixth century. Consequently it became a famous feature of Shaolin Kung Fu - famous and deadly! To an outsider, seeing someone using this technique would have seemed as if some sort of superhuman power was being tapped. Not only was an Iron Fist Disciple's hand able to smash through boards, bricks and solid concrete, but the technique so developed the reflexes that masters were able to slice ripe melons which were thrown into the air! If you're hoping to become a disciple of the Iron Fist, Ian, just remember that it will take many years of punching barrells of hot sand for hours on end every day!

CAMERA STUNTS

Dear Jenny,
My brother and I have got a problem and you are the only person who can solve it. The question is, were there any camera tricks used in any of Bruce Lee's films?
D.S. Bharj, West Croydon, Surrey

Dear D.S.,
A short letter, and the short reply is, no! Before Bruce began making films, the Hong Kong movie industry was built on what were known as 'Sword' movies; exciting tales set many centuries ago depicting the exploits of Chinese and Japanese swordsmen. Unfortunately, these films were riddled with trick camera shots, (such as swordsmen leaping fifty feet into the air and onto a rooftop) and after a while, they began to appear ridiculous. Part of the reason for Bruce's explosive impact on the Hong Kong industry and audiences was that he refused to use trick shots. What he couldn't do, he said, wasn't worth doing. And he was right!

GREEN HORNET

Dear Jenny,
I have been a devoted fan of Bruce Lee for over a year now and I have found out quite a lot about him from what I think is the best Kung Fu magazine in Britain - *KFM* - so I am turning to you for help. I heard a rumour that Bruce's last film *Game of Death* has been released under the title of *The Green Hornet*. Could you please put me right on this? I would also like to mention that I myself am a Karate student of Shotokan style. I don't think that I'll ever become as good as Bruce Lee was, although my ambition is to become a Black belt.
Michael Isaacs, Seacroft, Leeds

Dear Michael,
Sorry to disappoint you, but Game of Death has not yet been released. The film The Green Hornet you mention is in fact several episodes of Bruce's old television programme of the same name which have been strung together. At the moment, The Green Hornet is playing to packed houses in America but as yet, we do not know whether it will be brought to Britain and Europe. One consolation is that, if it is shown over here, it is bound to be given an AA certificate, which means that many young Bruce Let fans will be able to see the Little Dragon in action for the first time.

PEN PALS

Dear Jenny,
Being one of your magazine' devoted fans, I would like to congratulate you and the rest of the *KFM* staff on compiling such an immensely popular magazine. I was wondering if you could help me in finding a Chinese Pen Pal, male or female, preferably the same age as me (16 years), with the same interests - Kung Fu, Jeet Kune Do, Karate, Bruce Lee (I bet you thought I wasn't going to mention him, eh!). Lastly, is it true that that the golden days of the Kung Fu film are over and that we won't hear any more cracks, crunches, crackles and pops?
Adam Pearson, Musselburgh, Scotland

Dear Adam,
Thanks for your congratulations. First of all, your last point: No I don't think that the golden era of Kung Fu films has ended, but perhaps in the future, you will notice a change. Now that the Hong Kong film industry has proved to the world that it can capture audiences of all nationalities, more and more western film companies have caught on to the idea of co-productions along the lines of Bruce Lee's Enter the Dragon; Hammer Films, Shaw Brothers and David Chiang for example. As a result of this, I think you'll find Kung Fu movies will become a lot more polished. Different? Maybe. Dead? Never! I hope that you find a Pen Pal, along with Irene Todd of Co. Durham, N. Ireland and Tony Yeates of Wiltshire, who would both like Pen Pals in China or Hong Kong.

THE POSTER MAGAZINES · VOLUME ONE

1975

EDITORIAL

Hi there, Kung Fu fans...
Welcome to the twelfth issue of *Kung-Fu Monthly*. Yes, we have now had the pleasure of producing a round dozen issues of the World's Best Selling Kung Fu Magazine, and believe me, it was a pleasure! That's not to say number twelve is the end of the martial road for us as we plan to be around a lot longer yet! But to celebrate our dozen, we've pulled out all the stops to make this issue, a *KFM* to remember. The biggest news this month is the *KFM* interview with Bruce Lee's widow, Linda, which we have unearthed in Hong Kong. Any interview with the lady who was married to the Little Dragon for almost nine years must be fantastically interesting, but this one stands out as it was conducted just one short month after the Little Dragon's tragic death. On top of that, we also have a detailed study of Bruce's last gift to the martial arts world - Jeet Kune Do. As with the Linda interview, this article also gives us a true insight into the Little Dragon and his deep-

est thoughts. So there it is; a real Bruce Lee issue to celebrate our first anniversary. We sincerely hope that you've enjoyed the past year as much as we have and all I can say is that I hope to see you all again on our second anniversary!

Well, that's all from me this month,

Felix Yen

Felix Yen
Editor-in-Chief

THE KFM INTERVIEW: LINDA LEE
BRUCE LEE'S WIDOW SPEAKS OUT

This month, *KFM* is proud to present the transcript of an historic interview with the Little Dragon's wife - Linda Lee - recorded in Hong Kong only a month after Bruce's tragic death. In this interview, the first time that it has ever been published anywhere in the world, Linda gives us a rare glimpse of Bruce Lee the martial artist, Bruce Lee the husband, and Bruce Lee the man. Because the interview was taped so soon after Bruce's death, Linda's memories are fresh and clear. The interview also provides a warm picture of Linda; although she is still heartbroken and perhaps a little stunned by her bereavement, she is nonetheless already planning to once again pick up the threads of life for her and her children, as Bruce most surely would have wanted her to do. *KFM*'s interviewer is Hong Kong radio celebrity, Ray Cordeiro.

KFM: Linda, how long were you married for?

Linda Lee: We celebrated our ninth anniversary last month, so we just missed our ninth anniversary.

KFM: During these years, can you recall your happiest moments?

Linda Lee: There's been so many it's very difficult to recall what exactly was the most happy moment. I'd rather not specify one moment. It was more of a growing happiness as the years went by. I can't say the day we got married was the most happiest because as the years went by, happiness became more, love became deeper.

KFM: How did you meet Bruce?

Linda Lee: I had a girlfriend in High School - a Chinese girlfriend - who was taking Kung Fu lessons from Bruce and we all thought it was very funny. We all kidded her about it. Bruce used to come to my High School and give lectures, in Chinese philosophy. My girlfriend was quite struck with him and she took me along one day to her Kung Fu lesson and I thought it was quite a bit of nonsense. Then, some time passed and I started out at the University of Washington where Bruce was also going to school and because my Chinese girlfriend knew him, we became a group which used to meet together between classes. Then the group kind of broke up (Laughs) and Bruce and I sort of just got together.

KFM: You, yourself have taken up Kung Fu?

Linda Lee: Oh yes, from that point on. (Laughs)

KFM: From Bruce?

Linda Lee: Yes, well actually I don't know whether I was more interested in the Kung Fu or the teacher.

KFM: Did it take you long to develop the art?

Linda Lee: Well I can't say I ever developed the art to any degree of proficiency. I've always been very physical and I was a cheerleader in High School so I wasn't completely out of shape. After we got married, he sort of used me as a sparring partner - gently. He'd try new things on me. When the children were coming along and they were young, we didn't continue to practice daily. But he made it very clear that a woman is no match for a man when it comes to fighting. But then again, a man usually doesn't come up to a woman and puts up his fists and says, "We're going to have a fight." He will more likely grab her from behind. In other words, he will be in a very vulnerable position. So the best way he taught me is just to hit the vulnerable spots, scream and run a lot.

KFM: I saw you on television and got the impression you could take care of yourself.

Linda Lee: We sometimes did demonstrations together. But demonstrations are completely different to being proficient in an art; they are a show. As far as my part of a demonstration goes, it is a bunch of tricks.

KFM: After your marriage, what did you do in your spare time?

Linda Lee: He was a very private individual. He didn't like to socialise, didn't like to mix with nightclub people or party a lot, so we spent most of our spare time at home in this room, which is his study. You can live for days here without ever going out. It's supplied with refrigerator, television, books; you could stay in here for days and days.

KFM: Let me describe to the readers what I see here. Two statues; one of Charles Chaplin and one of Stan Laurel.

Linda Lee: There used to be four; W.C. Fields and Laurel and Hardy - but they got broken by my son.

KFM: Also lots of books.

Linda Lee: They cover all kinds of physical training, all kinds of hand to hand combat, any style - Western, Eastern, any kind. Philosophy, worldwide. Many books on improving yourself, knowing more about yourself.

KFM: Over there is a stereo set, more books, more books, a picture of Bruce Lee.

Linda Lee: That was taken about a year ago on top of Ocean Terminal car park.

KFM: What sort of music did you both like?

Linda Lee: Bruce liked modern music. He didn't especially like classical music although we do have a few records of classical music that sometimes we did put on. Some jazz but mostly music with a beat, romantic music, music where the words have a meaning.

KFM: Linda, you have there a list of songs that mean a lot to Bruce and yourself. I see you have *My Way* by Frank Sinatra.

Linda Lee: I love that song very much by myself and every time I hear it, I always think of Bruce because he always did things his way and there were many other ways he could have become successful. He could've, for instance, opened a chain of Kung Fu schools in the United States because it is a fad over there now and he was often advised he should do this, especially after he had done *The Green Hornet* television series. He could have become a millionaire doing that. But he didn't feel that that was the right thing to do because to learn his type of martial art takes very personal instruction. And he could've grabbed hold of several television series which were offered to him over there, but he didn't feel this was the right thing to do. People were always advising him he should do this or he should do that, he should write a book, he could make a mint off of this or that. But he stuck to what he thought was the right way to achieve his goal. He wrote down on a piece of paper in 1969 exactly what his goal was, and that was to become a film star, bringing out the best qualities of Chinese martial arts and showing it to the world.

KFM: What did Bruce think about the Chinese film industry?

Linda Lee: He liked to watch the Cantonese movies on TV mainly because he didn't like so much the movie, as he would be studying the techniques they were using to see what they did good and what they did bad so he could use it. Not only Cantonese but any sort of movie.

KFM: What about the Chinese Boxing movies?

Linda Lee: Yeah, he liked to watch it. He could pick out what he shouldn't do because it didn't look too good. Besides that, he liked to watch those movies because he knows most of the people in those movies and he often worked with them as a child.

KFM: Coming back to the music Linda, I see Bruce liked Sergio Mendes a lot.

Linda Lee: Because of the beat. Bruce could dance really well. In fact, I think it was 1958, he was the Cha-Cha King of Hong Kong. He really liked music he could move by and he used to put music like this on and jump around the room and spar and do movements to get a flow going.

KFM: What about your son Brandon, I believe he is also quite a martial artist?

Linda Lee: Well, he is very, very physical. He's very strong. He can do some elementary things like side-kicks. But Bruce didn't feel it was the right time for him to go into a detailed study of Jeet Kune Do, because it takes some discipline of mind as well as body. So he started Brandon in Judo, not because he believed Judo is a good defensive way of fighting, but more because it involves bodily contact and because you learn to handle your own body.

KFM: Is Brandon able to handle himself?

Linda Lee: Against another eight-year-old? Definitely! He's proved it on more than one occasion. He's very much like Bruce, like if anyone does something wrong. For instance, one time my son and my daughter were playing at another child's house and this other boy pushed my daughter down and Brandon took after him and really beat the dickens out of him. He wouldn't stop. He's very defensive of what belongs to him.

KFM: Linda, Kung Fu is not the name that Bruce used to describe his fighting.

Linda Lee: No. The actual name he used was Jeet Kune Do but he didn't actually like to have a name or a style branded on his way of fighting because he felt that fighting is something that evolves of itself. You react to something not in a way you have been taught or in a stylised way, but in a way that fits the appropriate time, so he hated to be labelled with a certain style.

KFM: What does Jeet Kune Do actually mean?

Linda Lee: The actual translation is 'Intercepting Fist Way'.

KFM: Back to the music again, Linda. I see you have *Impossible Dream* listed there.

What does that mean to you?

Linda Lee: Actually it means, I think, that nothing is impossible. Bruce never said anything was impossible. He always tried harder and reached out for the highest, reached for the stars. He made his dreams come true. He didn't wait for an opportunity to come along; he made his own opportunities.

KFM: Another song - Sergio Mendes and *Look Around*.

Linda Lee: Bruce believed each new day should be a day of discovery, that yesterday has passed by and tomorrow is not yet here; we should live in the present. And that's why every day should be a new day of creation. And this song explains how you should notice the little things that are around you every day that you take for granted, but are really what make up the real world.

KFM: Now a song from Hong Kong - Samuel Hoi, who I know is an old friend of yours, and *The Morning After*.

Linda Lee: There's three ways of saying why I like *The Morning After*. One is because I believe Bruce has passed into a world of a new morning - a new world he has left the

darkness of this world and gone into a brighter world. Another is because now I have to find my new morning; I have to start again. And also, this song should have some meaning to people who are married, or people who have close relationships because I think there's three very important factors in a marriage and I think these were the three most important things Bruce and I were able to give to each other. These things were tolerance, patience and time. Out of these three things grow love, respect and understanding. For married couples, they should always remember, despite differences and stumbling blocks, that there's a morning after.

KFM: *Too Beautiful to Last* by Engelbert Humperdinck.

Linda Lee: Well, I, think that's just it. Our marriage was just perhaps too beautiful to last and Bruce himself was just too beautiful a person. I think probably I'm the only one who really knows how beautiful he was and I guess it just couldn't last forever. I know a lot of things are being said now that make him seem he wasn't always as beautiful as I think he was, but so much of what is being said you cannot believe. You must not believe because it's rumours, absolutely untrue, he was just a human being, he wasn't perfect.

But he was a very, very beautiful person inside. He was always very, very good to me. I could not have a complaint in the world, not wish for a better husband.

KFM: Frank Sinatra and *If You Go Away*.

Linda Lee: There's one line in that song that says, "But if you stay, I'll make you the brightest day," and every time I hear this song, I sorta wish Bruce could come back for even one day and I'd make that day the best day in the world.

KFM: *My World is Empty without You* by Jose Feliciana.

Linda Lee: This expresses a lot of my feelings. My world is not completely empty because I have my two children - Bruce's two children. But a big part of my life is empty now without Bruce. Even though I might go on to live a long, long time, there'll be an empty spot there forever.

KFM: *We've Only Just Begun* by The Carpenters.

Linda Lee: This song had a lot of meaning for Bruce. It seems we were always beginning on a new kind of life, like coming to Hong Kong; beginning in films was a new kind of life for us. Becoming famous and his films breaking records; everything was new all the time and he kept saying this is just the beginning. He had a long way to go, so many more things that he wanted to do. And he also thought of it as sort of a beginning for the Chinese people, what they have to show to the rest of the world. He was very proud of being Chinese and he wanted to show the rest of the world part of the Chinese culture through films, not just the fighting, but he wanted to add in a little bit of philosophy. That was his major in College. He studied all the different ancient philosophies, but then he began to form his own philosophy and he came to the realisation that you just can't borrow another person's philosophy. You have to learn about yourself and create your own

philosophy, your own ways of life. Bruce believed the most important thing in the world is the individual and that each individual must have knowledge of himself before he can relate to other people. He managed to cross the barriers in communicating with people. He could communicate with different people on all different levels. People who were not perhaps as intelligent as he was, or people who perhaps considered themselves intellectuals and thought fighting was something not intellectual, he managed to communicate with all different kinds of people because he didn't believe people belonged to any special class, he crossed the barriers of nationality, race, religion. He believed that if all the people of the world could be one then there would be a great deal more faith and love and brotherhood between people.

KFM: Linda, is there anything else you would like to add?

Linda Lee: Since Bruce has passed away in July, we have received many letters from people in Hong Kong who have not signed their names or who have not given their return addresses. Also I am sure there are many other people who wanted to communicate their feelings to me because so many people loved Bruce. I'd like to thank all those people. It's been a great help to me to know that I have a lot of friends here, even though I am not Chinese, who have welcomed me into your city and into your hearts.

BRUCE LEE'S LEGACY: JEET KUNE DO

When Bruce Lee died, he left behind him many legacies. To film fans, he bequeathed an immortal series of action movies unequalled in excitement, style and charm. To the Chinese race, he left a rediscovered sense of pride and honour. To his friends and relatives, he left the undying memory of greatness tempered by humanity. But perhaps it was to the martial arts world that he left his finest and most important gift - Jeet Kune Do!

Bruce himself was all too aware of the difficulties encountered in trying to set down in cold print the ideals behind a living way of fighting such as Jeet Kune Do. In 1963, he began his own thesis on Jeet Kune Do which took him many years to lick into shape. (Called the *Tao of Jeet Kune Do*, it was unfortunately never published.) The main difficulty about translating Jeet Kune Do into words was that Brute's style was, in fact, no style at all!

Let me explain. It was Bruce's dream to free the body from all restrictions imposed by classical styles. Just stepping into Bruce's Kwoon (school) in Los Angeles' Chinatown was enough to get the point - inside the door was a miniature tombstone covered with flowers. On the gravestone were the words: "In memory of a once fluid man, crammed and distorted by the classical mess."

"There's too much horsing around with unrealistic forms and rituals," Bruce once told a reporter. "It's just too artificial and mechanical and doesn't really prepare a student for actual combat. A guy could get clobbered while getting into his classical mess!"

What Bruce's message to his martial art colleagues was that you must do what comes naturally and don't waste valuable split-seconds pondering how to react when someone attacks. The quickest route to victory was, to Bruce's way of thinking, the best. This he illustrated for an inquirer by throwing his wallet at the man, "That's the way," remarked

Bruce, "You did what was natural. You caught the wallet. Others from the martial world would have squatted or grunted or gone into a horse stance and missed catching the wallet! In other words, when someone grabs you, punch him!"

It's not difficult to see where this line of reasoning came from. It was the tough and vicious streets of one of the world's most crowded cities - Hong Kong! It was as a street fighter, a 'punk' as Bruce would described himself in later years, that the young Bruce Lee drifted into Kung Fu and it was on those same streets, that he learned to always be one jump ahead of his opponent or opponents, or you were dead! It was a lesson Bruce Lee learned off by heart!

Another of the basic elements of Jeet Kune Do is its lack of fancy additions. The idea of practicing Jeet Kune Do is to try and strip it down as far as possible. This was something Bruce learned from his old Wing Chun teacher in Hong Kong - Yip Man. Wing Chun, in fact, had been developed along exactly these lines almost 500 years ago. The school was started by a woman, Yim Wing Chun, who, while studying the martial arts under a Shaolin nun, was dismayed that Kung Fu was beginning to be bogged down by all its classical trappings. She made it her task to cut down all of these impediments and return to the basics.

Bruce fully agreed with Madame Yim's thinking, but soon he discovered that even Wing Chun was still too crowded and cluttered. So was born Jeet Kune Do! "It is basically a sophisticated fighting style stripped to its essentials," Bruce once explained. "In building a statue, a sculptor doesn't keep adding clay to his subject. Actually, he keeps chiselling away at the unessentials until the truth of his creation is revealed without obstructions.

"Thus, contrary to other styles, being wise in Jeet Kune Do doesn't mean adding more. It means to minimise it. It is not a 'daily increase' but a 'daily decrease.'"

But simplicity is not an easy thing to come by. Just a glance at Bruce's superhuman training schedule should convince you of that! Every morning, for instance, Bruce would run a mile and a half accompanied by his faithful Great Dane, Bobo, to unlimber his muscles and build up stamina. Inside his Los Angeles home, gymnasium equipment was scattered all over the place. Much of the equipment was ingeniously original, ordered by Bruce from designs he had made himself. One example was a chrome-plated dummy head which would reel back under the impact of Bruce's lightning finger jabs to the eyes or throat. After the morning run and the workouts in the gym, Bruce would then devote himself to a solid hour and a half of Jeet Kune Do.

"No amount of idealistic land swimming will prepare you for the water," he once observed. "The best exercise for swimming is swimming. The best exercise for Jeet Kune Do is actual sparring."

EXCLUSIVE OFFER!

Another winner from KFM! Just look at these super portrait pillow slips with an almost lifesize picture of the Little Dragon printed over the front! Even Kung-Fu fanatics have to sleep and what better way to exciting dreams than on one of these great portrait slips! Available only through KFM, they are manufactured in good quality cotton and printed in two colours, red or blue. Imagine waking in the morning with your head resting on a lifesize portrait of the Little Dragon! It's a must for all Bruce Lee fans! These portrait pillow slips are £1.10 each or £2.00 for a pair. Mail your cheque or P.O. made out to Kung-Fu Monthly right away to: Little Dragon Pillow Slips Offer, Kung-Fu Monthly, 39 Goodge Street, London W1P 1FD. (We have plenty in stock. Allow three weeks for delivery, state your colour preference and don't forget to include your name and address!)

For Bruce, Jeet Kune Do was much more than just a fighting system; it was a way of life. Some even say it was responsible for his death - that angered by Bruce's scornful attitude towards their styles, a group of classical martial artists had him murdered! Although this theory is stretching belief to an enormous extent, there is no doubt that Bruce did shame some of his martial colleagues with Jeet Kune Do.

But this was no fault of Bruce's. As he once stated, with Jeet Kune Do he was just being himself. "Art is really the expression of the self," he said. "The more complicated and restricted the method, the less the opportunity for the expression of one's original sense of freedom!" In his art - Jeet Kune Do - we see the real Bruce Lee!

KICKBACK: THE LETTERS

Hi there ... it's me again with a really super sackfull of mail to celebrate our twelfth issue of *KFM*! I hope you've enjoyed them all as much I have but I must apologise to all those *KFM* readers whose letters I wasn't able to publish. Even if I had ten times the amount of space, I'd still never be able to fit them all in. Anyway, don't give up if your letter doesn't appear. I read every one and reckon that I have just about the best job going!

ENTER THE KING

Dear Jenny,
Why do people who think of Kung Fu immediately think of David Carradine? For example, I visited Madame Tussaud's in Blackpool and saw a dummy of David representing Kung Fu. Now we all know who should have been there (and those of you who don't - you twits!). It's the Late, Great Bruce Lee. It's a shame that Bruce never, got the part in the Kung Fu series as he would have been a lot better than Mr. Carradine, and just think what it would be like watching the Little Dragon on our screens every week. I would like to know if Bruce Lee's brother Peter has recorded a song dedicated to Bruce and if so, is it released in Britain yet? Thank you for the best Kung Fu magazine in the whole world.
Rosina McArthur, Scotland

Dear Rosina,
Of course you're right; all of us here at KFM know who the only person to represent Kung Fu is. And we agree wholeheartedly that it would be absolutely fantastic to see Bruce on the television every week. But remember, with luck, all of Bruce's fans who are too young to see his movies, will soon be able to see a feature film made up of several Green Hornet episodes starring the Little Dragon himself. I'll keep you posted as to developments. Bruce's brother Peter has not only made a song about the Little Dragon, but in fact, has cut a whole album dedicated to him. Our mail order department is at this very moment chasing up copies of the album in the States, which we hope we will be able to make available to KFM readers in the very near future.

FAN MAIL

Dear Jenny,
We enjoyed *The Book of Kung Fu*. It was worth every penny. By the way, who was the artist who penned the fantastic Legend of Chih Ni'i? The drawings are absolutely incredible. As for your photo, mmmm... Well, anyway, what I wanted to ask you was, would it be possible to make a poster of the picture on Page 59 of *The Book of Kung Fu*?
David & John, Milngavie, Glasgow

Dear David & John,
Thanks for the compliment about my picture (certainly hope it's a compliment!). The artist who penned Legend of Chih Ni'i is our own Paul Simmons, the man who gave you the Beginner's Guide to Kung Fu and who has appeared many times in the pages of KFM. As for the picture, at the moment it doesn't seem as if it is possible for us to turn it into a poster as there are copyright laws involved. Maybe in the future though.

INVINCIBLE BRUCE LEE

Dear Jenny,
Could you please tell me what was Bruce's favourite song and his favourite colours? Last of all, do you know if Bruce ever lost a street fight when he was a kid? Thanks very much for bringing out such a great magazine - I think it's tops!
Trudy Thorose, Tooting

Dear Trudy,
I'll make this short as in our main feature story this month Linda Lee gives us all a look at Bruce's likes and dislikes. All I'll say is that, as far as we know, Bruce never lost a fight!

DRAGON POSTERS

Dear Jenny,
KFM No.10 was great and the photos inside were brilliant. About the photo on Page Three, what film did it come from as I have seen them a lot in *KFM*? The photo on the letter page, couldn't you give us this on a poster because it is brilliant? When are you going to give us posters from *The Way of the Dragon*? I am getting sick of *Enter the Dragon* posters. Also, has Linda Lee made a film?
George Dawson, Sauchie, Scotland

Dear George,
Thanks for your comments on No.10; we here thought it was pretty good too, especially Paul Simmons' front cover. As to your questions, the Page Three shot of Bruce in a blue suit is from Fist of Fury, one of my all-time favourite films. Unfortunately the snap on the kickback page was just that, a snap, and as it is in black and white, it wouldn't be such a good poster. If you just hold on a little bit longer, our Editor has promised a The Way of the Dragon poster. Linda has not made a film. She is, however, involved in plans for a movie to be shot in Los Angeles about Bruce's life.

LEE VS ALI

Dear Jenny,
I like to say that for me, *KFM* is the best magazine in Britain. I have been a devoted Bruce Lee fan for over two years. To me, in my heart, he will never die. Now down to the questions: Was Bruce faster than Ali and could he have knocked down Foreman with his one inch punch? Will Linda Lee be making that film on Bruce? Could you tell me what Game of Death is about? I have written twice already so I hope this is third time lucky!
R. Ginesi, Lordship Park, London

Dear R. Ginesi,
Well you were right, third time is lucky! Was Bruce faster than Ali? I think you'll find - as we have - if you ask the experts, they will all agree that Bruce could run rings around someone as fast on his feet as Muhammad Ali. Quite simply, Bruce Lee was unbeatable. And as far as the one inch punch, it wouldn't have mattered how heavy his target, he still would have been sent flying across the room. As I mentioned above, Linda's film about the life of the Little Dragon is definitely on. And Game of Death? Well, I'm going to be a bit cagey about that and keep my lips closed for now.

EDITORIAL

Hi there, Kung Fu fans...

This time we've really got something for you!! After months of research, *KFM* staff writer Bruce Sawford has come up with the lowdown on the hottest film ever to be produced! Yes, you've guessed it; the legendary *Game of Death*. The news from Hong Kong is that filming has been restarted on Bruce Lee's unfinished swansong. Although we don't as yet have any definite release dates, well let you know as soon as possible - before, in fact! In the very near future we also hope to have a massively detailed follow-up story on this month's *Game of Death* piece which will be fully illustrated.

Before I get too carried away with *Game of Death*, I must just mention our other treats this month. After seeing the preview of *The Man From Hong Kong*, starring the great Jimmy Wang Yu, Don Won Ton raced back to the office and immediately banged out this month's second feature.

Our new mail-order offer this month is the latest best-seller from Don Atyeo and Felix Dennis - the authors who brought you the Kung Fu classic *Bruce Lee: King of Kung Fu*. Their latest work is Muhammad Ali: The Holy Warrior and it too is destined to become a classic. As Bruce Lee himself realised, knowledge of all forms of defence is essential to the martial master. Muhammad Ali is the undoubted king of the Boxing ring, and if ever there was a book to expand your personal combat library, *Muhammad Ali: The Holy Warrior*, is it! Before I finish, I would like to gratefully acknowledge the invaluable inspiration and assistance so freely donated by the staff of the publicity department of Cathay Films Ltd.

Felix Yen

Felix Yen
Editor-in-Chief

GAME OF DEATH EXCLUSIVE

Here it is, the information the whole of the martial arts world has been waiting for ever since that fateful July day in 1973 when Bruce Lee, thee legendary Little Dragon, was no longer. After literally months of painstaking research, *KFM* is proud to announce that filming has resumed on Bruce Lee's unfinished masterpiece - *Game of Death*! So many myths and rumours have sprung up around *Game of Death*, since death itself halted the action back in 1973 that the film has taken on an aura of mystery and intrigue in the minds of fans around the globe. For years now, no-one has ever seemed to know what the movie was actually all about. All anyone could learn was that it starred Bruce's seven-foot friend, American basketball hero Kareem Abdul-Jabbar. Now *KFM*'s Bruce Sawford has at last discovered the truth about what he is sure is destined to become Bruce's martial monument!

For Hong Kong's whizz-kid movie producer Raymond Chow and his smash martial superstar Bruce Lee, 1973 was indeed a year to remember. By the time Christmas had rolled around, business was booming like never before. *Fist of Fury* and *The Big Boss*, after smashing all box office records in Hong Kong, were now, to everybody's amazement, doing the same thing on the Western film circuits. With the USA and Europe going wild, the first of a flood of fantastic offers began pouring in to the Golden Harvest studio, offers that were, to make Bruce Lee the highest paid actor in the world ever! Raymond Chow, recognising the potential of his number one star, agreed to set up a new company - Concord. He and Bruce were to become equal partners in the new venture.

During this time, the Little Dragon, while taking a well earned rest, came up with an idea for a new film. It so happened that an old friend of his, American basketball star 'Big Louis' Kareem Abdul-Jabbar of the Milwaukee Bucks, was staying with him in Hong Kong. Abdul-Jabbar, who stands an amazing seven feet tall, was a recent convert to the martial arts. "Why not join forces for a new film?" thought Bruce. In just one short week, these two unlikely opponents transferred to celluloid, some of the most incredible fight scenes ever filmed and with hardly anything in the way of a script!

But as soon as it had begun, the action ground to an abrupt halt. Big Louis had to get back to the States to rejoin his team and pacify his manager, who had nearly had a heart attack when he heard that his star attraction was fighting Bruce Lee! After all, damaged stars don't make the turnstiles click! Time was also at a premium for Bruce as well. Deals had been struck and work was due to begin on a new Concord/Warner Bros. film to be called *Blood and Steel* - later re-titled *Enter the Dragon*.

Ominously, it was during the final stages of this monster production that there occurred the first suspicious sign that perhaps all wasn't quite as it should have been with the health of the Little Dragon. Maybe it was the heat of the lights, maybe the long working hours or was it the punishment he inflicted on himself in his constant demand for perfection? No one can say for sure, All that is known is that during final voice dubbing sequences, Bruce Lee collapsed into semi-consciousness. His doctors were mystified. They reported that they could find little wrong with him, commenting only on his superb physical fitness. Later another doctor was to exclaim that although over thirty, Bruce had the body of a nineteen year old. Recovery seemed swift, however; and with *Enter the Dragon* completed, the Little Dragon once more turned his attention towards the new film. He decided to call it *Game of Death*.

The plan was appropriately ingenious; a story that weaved its way around the best martial artists available in the world today. The action is focused on an island somewhere near Korea, where there stands a star-shaped pagoda. It reaches up five storeys, containing on the uppermost floor, a priceless treasure. Bruce's quest centres upon retrieving this fortune. In order to do so, however, he has first to overcome various lethal opponents who occupy a level of the building. The island totally shuns the use of weapons such as

guns and, so as to prevent any cheating, the place is littered with metal detectors, ferreting out the hardware. There are also numerous unfriendly guards around to help Bruce limber up prior to his siege of the pagoda, one of whom is described as a gigantic 'hulk-shaped' man.

So to the first floor, where Bruce and four friends are confronted with thirty crack Karate experts. Bruce soon defuses this explosive situation, although he loses two of his side men in the process. Up on the second level, Bruce has to fight in Hapkido style. Here, unfortunately, I am sworn to secrecy about revealing any further information. Suffice to say that the Little Dragon makes out in truly spectacular fashion, and wins his way through to the third floor where he meets the mysterious Gung Fu Men. Sadly, there is little to tell of this no-doubt outstanding battle, for although the fight was certainly filmed, it's also true to say that the plot here, as in other parts of the film, was never finally ironed out. Fortunately, far more information is at hand about the fourth level, subtitled The Temple of the Tiger. It is guarded by the Filipino Escrima, portrayed by Danny Inosanto. Escrima, which is Filipino for 'Skirmish,' is not too well known as a fighting style here in the West. Probably its only other appearance on celluloid was in *The Pacific Connection*, a film which starred Dean Stockwell and Nancy Kwan.

On this level, Danny and Bruce set to with the single - followed by the double - 24" sticks. The Escrima finds he cannot handle the Little Dragon too easily, and so, tossing his stick aside, picks up a 'Chinese Bako' (long stick). Apparently the two of them stage a superb exhibition of Kali (stick fighting) which is only concluded when Danny discards them in favour of a set of nunchakus. Bruce has a pretty hard time of this one and only finally manages to defeat the Filipino Escrima after a thrilling duel in which the nunchakus are used virtually as swords! The defender of the fifth and final floor is none other than - yes, you've guessed it - Big Lew. Subtitled the 'Temple of the Unknown,' this scene is a classic to end all classics! Although Kareem's style is unknown, it is said to transcend all others. He's also ferocious and the story is told that at meal times, chunks of meat are thrown in through the door and only the bones come out! Well, the sight of the Little Dragon taking on all seven feet of Kareem Abdul-Jabbar has to be amazing. David and Goliath have got nothing on this and I'm still waiting to find out how he manages it. But win Bruce does, and later, of course, he successfully recovers the treasure. Further details of the plot are hard to find, for the truth is, that even Bruce himself hadn't decided on the finished story line. In fact he would very much play it from day to day, working out new twists and turns as the ideas came to him.

It's interesting to note, by the way, that Danny Inosanto, playing the Filipino Escrima on the fourth floor, was the man who taught Bruce Lee how to use nunchakus. When he was young he had studied Korean, Okinawan and Japanese Karate and at the age of twenty-eight, had got his Shodan from the legendary martial arts instructor Ed Parker. He first met Bruce at the Long Beach Tournament in 1964 and became one of his black belt instructors. Danny, who is in fact part Filipino and who is now a Jeet Kune Do/Escrima instructor in Los Angeles, soon became the first to admit that at least where nunchakus was concerned, Bruce had become his senior. Another interesting point to remember is that, whereas often only 'fake' weapons are used for filming purposes, in The Temple of the Tiger scene, Bruce and Danny go at it with real nunchakus. Injuries, although not serious ones, did in fact occur!

As far as other parts in the film go, the information available is somewhat sketchy. It seems that Bruce had planned roles for Jhoon Rhee, Chuck Norris, Betty Ting Pei, James Tien and Chi Hon Joi, a seventh degree Korean Hapkido expert. (Sammo) Hung Kam-Po almost certainly makes an appearance, as does Whang In-Sik, whose fight scene with Bruce is believed to have been the last footage shot and remains, at present, sadly incomplete. George Lazenby, currently co-starring in *The Man from Hong Kong*, was signed and had been reportedly studying Bruce's earlier films in preparation for his part. He wasn't to know that only a week later, the martial arts world would lose its number one son.

Finally, just one more name needs to be mentioned; that of Taky Kimura. Taky, who met Bruce back in 1959, is reputed to have been one of the Little Dragon's closest friends and today, he is generally accepted as being the world's number one exponent of Jeet Kune Do. Now an instructor in Seattle, USA, Taky was invited over by Bruce in a rather strange way. One day, out of the blue, a plane ticket to Hong Kong arrived in his post box. Taky rang Bruce asking what it was all about and when it was explained to him, he at first declined, saying that he was no film star. Bruce, however, retorted, "Everybody looks good in my films" and Taky was won over. Twelve hours later, he had a phone call. Someone told him, "Bruce is dead." Without thinking he asked, "Bruce who?" "Lee," came the answer. Taky never replied... he just put down the receiver.

Today, Raymond Chow is faced with an agonising decision. No-one really likes the idea of his using a 'double' to complete *Game of Death*, but the unfortunate fact remains that, for all the brilliant action shots that are thankfully in the can, no work was ever even started on the footage in between the fight scenes and this contributes to over half the

film! So, if he's not to use a double, then just what is Chow going to do? Will he use cuts of Bruce from previous films along with all the continuity problems of clothing and hair style clashes? No, I think not. It seems far more likely that he will take a secondary character and build it up into a more important role, thus providing a credible link between the action sequences. This would overcome the 'now you see the double - now you don't' problem which can be off-putting to say the least. One is left with the feeling that this is the way Bruce would have preferred it; to be present when it really mattered and doing what he loved the best.

Contrary to some opinions, it is absolutely certain that Linda and Raymond Chow want very much to see the film finished. Consider its enormous money earning potential, for instance, and there is no doubt that see it finished they will. The only question is when for another difficulty is currently delaying things still further. Linda, unhappy with the title *Game of Death*, wants an alternative, a title that doesn't include the word 'death.' Chow, however, sees this as being an unwise move that could result in possible confusion amongst the fans.

Despite this, however, sources in Hong Kong bear the glad tidings that shooting on some of the missing footage has begun. This exciting news could mean that the film will be completed before the end of the year. At last there is daylight ahead and our patience is being rewarded. Surely now the day is not far off when you and I, and the whole world shall witness with bated-breath, Bruce Lee's premier production. *Game of Death* will undoubtedly prove to be the martial monument of our time.

THE MAN FROM HONG KONG

Who says the Kung Fu movie industry is on its last legs?! Quite a few so-called 'experts,' that's who! Just how wrong they really are! The critics have been writing off the martial movie boom ever since *The Way of the Dragon* ended its premiere release. "No more Bruce Lee," these misguided pundits pronounced, "No more Kung Fu flicks!" But what the critics have failed to grasp is that the whole industry is in the middle of an enormous period of change. Certainly Bruce has gone (although what *Game of Death* will do to the world's box offices on its release, will be fantastic!). But it is only now that other actors and actresses, once over-shadowed by the Little Dragon's awesome reputation, are coming into their own and showing the way to bigger and greater things.

One recent movie which really highlights this change is the smash Cathay hit *The Man From Hong Kong*. If ever there was a film to breathe fresh life into the industry, this is it! Filmed both in Australia and Hong Kong, *The Man From Hong Kong* is a truly international epic, linking East and West and pioneering new frontiers in universal film production.

There are many reasons why The Man From Hong Kong is such a knock-out success, not the least being its gripping plot. The film opens in Australia with a tourist bus approaching Ayers Rock, a famous Australian landmark. On the bus is Win Chan, a heroin smuggler, who is on his way to unload his deadly cargo of narcotics. Fortunately the police pounce on Win Chan and his Australian contact just as the deal is being made. The Australian attempts to escape, but is killed when his car goes out of control and crashes in a fireball of burning petrol. Win Chan is captured and hauled before Special Branch Agent Chief Inspector Fang Sing-Ling of the Royal Hong Kong Police (who has been brought to Australia to assist in Win Chan's arrest). Inspector Fang forces his prisoner to talk, but on the way to the courthouse, a rooftop sniper kills Win Chan.

Fang chases the sniper and, after a tremendous chase and bloody battle, finally manages to kill him. He searches the body and finds the man was employed as a security guard by Wilton (played by ex-James Bond star George Lazenby), the local Mr. Big and owner of a Martial Arts Academy. Despite the Australian police's displeasure, Fang pays a midnight visit to Wilton's academy. Suddenly he finds himself surrounded by a pack of knife-wielding thugs and is forced to defend himself. The ensuing action is one of the film's greatest martial moments!

Fang, although badly injured, escapes by smashing his way through a plate glass win-

dow, somersaulting onto the pavement and flinging himself into a passing van. Angelica (Rebecca Gilling), one of the van's occupants, takes him to her father, a veterinary surgeon, who looks after him until he recovers. Fang falls in love with Rebecca, but tragedy strikes when Wilton's henchmen try to eliminate the Chinese inspector. Angelica is killed and Fang, incensed with rage, pursues the henchmen in a car until he has evened the score.

Fang devises an ingenious scheme to penetrate Wilton's 17th-floor penthouse ... a hang-glider kite! He bursts into the murderer's apartment and thrusts a grenade into Wilton's mouth, threatening to pull the pin unless he writes a full confession. Wilton attempts to escape and the pin is pulled accidentally from the grenade. Fang escapes by sliding down a rope split seconds before the whole penthouse explodes in a sheet of flames.

As you can see even from this short account of the story, *The Man From Hong Kong* has all the elements of a great Kung Fu movie; action, danger, invention and originality. And the way this script is transformed onto celluloid is superb. Director Brian Trenchard Smith put it in a nutshell when he said, "The film contains 17 different action sequences, spanning a wide range of excitement - explosions, Kung Fu fights, car and helicopter chases, death-defying climbs up buildings and slides down them, plus what we believe are the most breathtaking sequences of kite gliding ever filmed."

Just how dangerous some of these stunts really were can be seen by the number of near disasters which the cast and crew encountered during filming. The Australian crew was dogged by literally scores of injuries - two cameramen suffered broken ankles, the sound man received a broken foot, one stuntman smashed his pelvis and another gashed his leg and had to have twenty stitches. George Lazenby suffered a near-fatal close call when the sleeve of his costume caught fire during filming of the last scene (when Wilton is pushed into an open fireplace). Lazenby had to spend several days in hospital as a result of the near-disaster. It was only quick-thinking by the show's star - the amazing Jimmy Wang Yu - that saved the day.

Which brings me to the real reason behind the film's stunning success - Jimmy Wang Yu himself! The name Jimmy Wang Yu is now legendary amongst Kung Fu and movie fans alike. Born near Shanghai on March 18th 1943, he joined the movie industry in 1964 after graduating from college. After small parts in more than 20 pictures, his big break came in 1967 when he won the starring role in the first Chinese action classic *The One Armed Swordsman*. Wang Yu's performance in *The One-Armed Swordsman* revolutionised the Hong Kong industry and the film opened the door to the whole Kung Fu era. It was Jimmy Wang Yu that inspired Bruce Lee in so many ways, and the two superstars became firm friends. The Chinese Boxer, which has been universally hailed as the first pure Kung Fu movie ever made, once more turned the Hong Kong studios on their head, breaking all box office records in Hong Kong and Taiwan and making Wang Yu the first Chinese actor multi-millionaire!

But when Bruce Lee burst onto the movie scene and began calling all the shots, Wang's glittering career began to fade a little. It was really not until 1970 when Golden Harvest chief Raymond Chow invited him to co-star in *Zatoichi* and *The One Armed Swordsman* that he began to get back into stride. Since that time, he has produced some of the finest films ever to come out of the Orient; *A Man Called Tiger*, *Beach of the War Gods* and *The One Armed Boxer* to name but a few. Now this slight, likeable Karate black belt has set the seal forever on his stardom and secured a lasting position in the Kung Fu Hall of Fame, right next to the Little Dragon himself! The reason that Wang Yu's films stand out from the rest of the bunch is virtually the same reason that made a Bruce Lee movie something different Like Bruce, Wang Yu insists on doing all his own stunt work. Sometimes this can lead to some pretty hair-raising occurrences which is exactly what happened during the filming of *The Man From Hong Kong*! While shooting a hand-gliding sequence, for instance, Jimmy was allowed to soar into the air on the end of a long rope. Suddenly the kite stalled and he plummeted more than a hundred feet to earth. Luckily he landed on some soft sand dunes. Even still, he was rushed to hospital and admitted to the emergency ward. Although there were no broken bones, he did suffer some pretty serious internal bleeding. The next day he was discharged from hospital with strict orders to stay in bed for at least four days. But that evening, he was back at work filming another frightening stunt which involved climing a ten-storey building!

Which is what makes Jimmy Wang Yu the star he is. Other actors may come and go, but in a world of fantasy and make believe, Jimmy Wang Yu is a large slice of reality!

KICKBACK: THE LETTERS

Hi there... Jenny Lee here again with another batch of super letters from you all. I really feel bad that there is only enough space on this page to print half a dozen or so. I know some of you have written in many times and still haven't had anything printed. But please don't give up if you do as I do read them all, I can assure you. If you want me to send you any additional information, do please enclose a self-addressed envelope and I will do my best. Well, I suppose the more I talk, the less space there is for you, so let's get on with it straight away! See you next month...

TRUE FAN

Dear Jenny,
I think *KFM* is the best innovation in Kung Fu magazine tributes to the great Bruce Lee. Also, I think there is some of the best, well-worked-out information that there has ever been put in a Kung Fu magazine of this kind, and this is coming from a true fan who has just read one *KFM* magazine so far. Its well worth every penny! My question is - Is it true that Bruce Lee himself taught the likes of film stars such as Steve McQueen, James Coburn, George Lazenby and Chuck Norris? Also, has Bruce still got some of his Karate schools open in places such as America?
Paul Finnegan, Consett, Co. Durham

Dear Paul,
Thanks for the kind words. I hope you liked your first try with KFM enough to keep on getting us every month. Bruce did teach a number of film stars in his American Jeet Kune Do schools, including Steve McQueen and James Coburn. Chuck Norris - a Karate expert in his own right never learned formally from Bruce, except what he picked up on film location. As for George Lazenby, he knew nothing about Kung Fu until one day on holiday in California, he happened to see a Bruce Lee movie, was completely knocked out, and flew off to Hong Kong to co-star with the Little Dragon. And who could blame him? Yes, Bruce's schools in America still continue, under the direction of his old and trusted friend Taky Kimura.

PEN PAL

Dear Jenny,
I would like to know if there are any Chinese male pen pals buzzing around aged about 14? I am interested in Bruce, all Martial Arts (except Judo) and trying to get in to the flicks when Bruce comes (which I have managed to see two films). Also: 1. What was Bruce's favourite song? 2. Which music did he like best: pop, classical or jazz? 3. Who was his favourite actor and actress?
P.S. Please print this letter as this is the fifth I have written.
A. Briers, St. Helens, Merseyside

Dear A. Briers,
Fifth time lucky! Sorry you have had to wait so long, but if only you could see how much mail I really do get! Hope you get a pen pal, and that those in our Pen Pals Corner also get paired off. As for your questions: 1. And When I Die by Blood Sweat and Tears was played at Bruce's Seattle funeral on his request. 2. Bruce loved all forms of music (see the interview with Linda Lee in KFM No.12) 3. Bruce greatly admired his friend James Coburn.

WANG YU

Dear Jenny,
Congratulations on *KFM*'s first anniversary. No.12 was one of the best issues you have brought out although all the others were brilliant! Please could you tell me if you have found the actor to play Bruce Lee (as if anyone could) in the film of the life of Bruce Lee, and if you have not, I would like to nominate Alex Lung who starred in *King of Kung Fu*. Talking about King of Kung Fu, I would like to say that undoubtedly Wang Yu should be the New King of Kung Fu because he is nearly the same as the Master himself, Bruce Lee. Could you please bring out a poster of Bruce standing in the hall of mirrors as in your issue No.11?
Shakiel Hussain, London

Dear Shakiel,
We must have done something right with issue No.l1 as nearly every letter I have received this month has raved about it and I agree. The poster especially was fantastic. Still no news from the States as to who will play Bruce in the film on his life. I know of a few possibilities who are under close supervision by the producers, but I am sworn to secrecy. As soon as I get the go-ahead, I'll let you know. Watch out for a full-length story on this movie in one of our future issues. I also like Alex Lung and as for Wang Yu, well, just go and see The Man From Hong Kong. Amazing! I am certain you'll be seeing more shots in KFM taken of Bruce standing In the hall of mirrors in the very near future, and you can take that as a hot tip!

SELFISH CENSORS

Dear Jenny,

I am writing to air a grievance that I have carried ever since the Kung Fu movies first hit the British Cinema circuit. I am talking about the censorship of the Martial Arts movies when they cross the ocean to our Island. Sure, I know the films are terrific but they could be that little bit better, if only the censors would keep their grubby little hands off the scenes showing nunchakus etc. Surely all us Chopsocky fans know whether nunchakus and so forth would 'disturb' us without those selfish censors deciding for us. Jenny, do you think someone will have the good taste to show the Kung Fu movies in all their un-interrupted glory? I certainly hope so. By the way, do you have any information on the release date of *Game of Death*? Also is there any way I could get hold of the first three issues of *KFM*? Thanks a lot. Lastly, keep on churning out *KFM* each month; it's great entertainment.
Andrew Lees, Prestwich, Manchester

Dear Andrew,
What else can I say except that we all here at KFM totally agree with you about censorship of martial arts movies. I have seen several of Bruce's movies - as well as scores of other Kung Fu films - before hey have been chopped up by the censors and you just can't imagine how much better they are. The Way of the Dragon was absolutely destroyed in this country by scissor-happy fanatics who wouldn't know a Kata from a cantaloupe! I get so mad when I think about it! If you can get along to a Chinese movie house, you can often see the complete film before it is butchered, though. Ask around in Manchester to see if there is a cinema showing just Chinese films there. As for Game of Death, read all about it in this Issue. Incidentally, the first three KFMs are on their way to you.

EDITORIAL

Hi there Kung Fu fans...

Well, here we are at the end of 1975 - a year, I'm sure you'll agree, which has seen the rise of the martial arts movement continue to grow and prosper without holdup. This year has provided the Western World with a fantastic opportunity to see the very best in martial art film-making, what with titles such as *The Man From Hong Kong*, *Stoner*, *One Armed Boxer* and so on. Also, 1975 has seen the popularity of Bruce Lee I - the late master of modern Kung Fu - leap from strength to strength until, in dozens of countries around the globe, his legend has assumed its correct proportions and his memory has been assured of its place in history. Indeed, it has been a good year!

And 1976 looks like it will be equally as good, as this month's issue of *KFM* readily shows! For our first feature, our correspondent Bruce Sawford continues his investigation into the Little Dragon's unfinished masterpiece *Game of Death*, the film which is almost certain to be bursting onto Western screens in the New Year. In this instalment, we take a long look at the people and personalities the Little Dragon picked to co-star with him in the films he was convinced would rewrite film-making rules.

Secondly, *KFM* provides a round-up of future films on the Little Dragon's life and tragic death. One of these films - *Superstar* - has never been mentioned before in the West and even in Hong Kong, it is a closely guarded secret. The reason is that Superstar stars Bruce's long-term girlfriend Betty Ting Pei and it is reputed that in the film she will reveal just what exactly did happen on the night of his death.

That's all from me this month, so here's to a Kung Fu New Year.

Felix Yen
Editor-in-Chief

GAME OF DEATH EXCLUSIVE – PART II

Last issue, *KFM* took you behind the scenes for a long-awaited look at the myths, legends and realities surrounding Bruce Lee's epic production, *Game of Death*. Exclusively in *KFM*, you read of the people Bruce had chosen to appear with him in the film, how the

plot unfolds scene by scene, and the difficulties which Raymond Chow now faces in his fight to see the film finished. Death may have halted the career of the world's greatest ever martial artist, but the efforts of those who knew and loved him best to see completed Bruce Lee's final triumph are continuing. This month, we move in a little closer to examine the action in more detail and look a little harder at the people who worked with him during those final, fateful months when Bruce Lee played a *Game of Death*.

Hong Kong film boss Raymond Chow once said of Bruce Lee, "He demanded too much from the people who worked with him and was such a perfectionist that sometimes people were scared of him." The words ring true enough, but perhaps he might also have said that the Little Dragon demanded too much of himself, for as Bruce once commented, "I am imprisoned by my own success. I have to keep fighting; the people expect action all the way." Not content with just finishing *Enter the Dragon*, at the

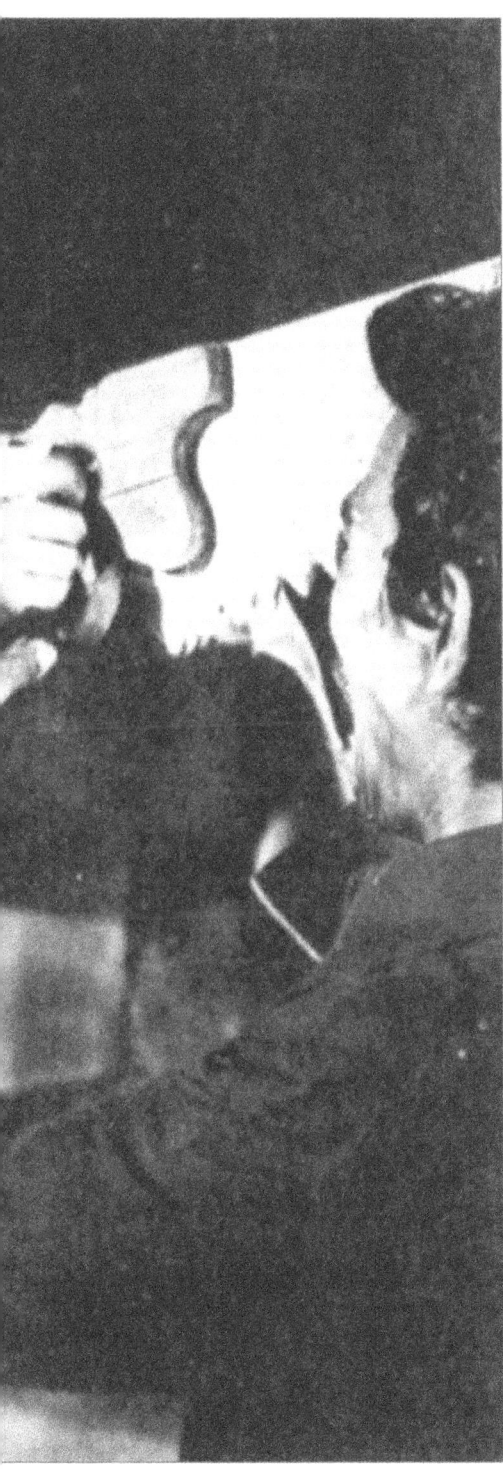

same time he was scripting, producing, acting and fighting the opening sequences of *Game of Death*. Any one of these activities would be enough for you or I, but then, Bruce Lee was no ordinary man.

It's interesting at this point, to go back a while and run through an interview he made just about the time he had started to mull over ideas for a 'new film.' He was adamant that to him, the script was all important, referring to a Golden Harvest offer he has just turned down for that very reason. The script needn't be complete - far from it - but the ideas had to be good. When questioned about his new film, the Little Dragon replied, "At present I am working on the script. I haven't really decided on the title yet, but what I want to show is the necessity to adapt oneself to changing circumstances. The inability to adapt brings destruction". Appropriately, he chose later to call it *Game of Death*.

At this time, Bruce was planning to open the film with a scene that symbolised the need to adapt: "There is a huge tree in the centre of the screen and it is all covered with snow. Suddenly there is a loud snap and a huge branch of the tree falls to the ground. It cannot yield to the force of the snow, so it breaks. Then the camera moves to a willow tree which is bending with the wind. Because it adapts itself to the environment, the willow survives." Whether or not Bruce decided in the end to use this remarkably symbolic opening sequence only time will tell. Who knows, perhaps the Little Dragon was really seeing himself as that huge tree bearing the heavy load! Danny Inosanto, who portrays the Filipino Escrima and guardian of the fourth floor, had mixed feelings towards Bruce prior to their shooting the immortal Temple of the Tiger scene. "A stomach full of iron butterflies" was how he put it. "I was afraid I might foul up Bruce's picture, it's as simple as that".

Fortunately for Danny, Bruce was not only an inspiration to work with, he was also easy to fight. This was the opinion too of Lo Wei, the producer who had seen the Little Dragon shoot to stardom in the short space of two films. Lo and Bruce worked together on both *The Big Boss* and *Fist of Fury* and although their relationship was never, at best, a very happy one, Lo was always ready to admit that "Eighty percent of the credit should go to Bruce Lee. He was a good fighter and actor."

Another vital part of the Little Dragon's make up was his understanding of the feelings of his fellow actors and actresses. Nora Miao, who appeared with Bruce in both *The Big Boss* and *Fist of Fury* remarked that, "He had the ability to put you at ease and make you feel the character you were playing in the film." Bruce Lee ran a one man operation and his movie-making was like his fighting. He just did it. Perhaps now, his friction with Lo Wei becomes more understandable. The films were a part of him and for somebody else to take on the producing was, at the same time, to take away a part of Bruce.

But back to *Game of Death* and I am glad to say I am able to fill you in a little more detail on the Temple of the Tiger scene. Danny Inosanto, the Filipino Escrima, starts the action by felling one of Bruce's aides who is cleared from the floor.

The Escrima then takes to the double sticks and Bruce has a whip. The whip is thin, reedy and known generally as a 'Chinese Jako.'

Inosanto is disarmed and so changes to a set of nunchakus. This prompts Bruce to do the same and what follows must be the classic nunchaku confrontation of all time. Although a 'villain,' Inosanto is deservedly allowed to die an heroic death. Strangely, Danny had never, up to this time, actually been to the Philippines to study his native art of Escrima. Instead, he had picked up most of what he had learnt from such people as John Lacoste of Stockton, Angel Cabales and Leo Giron. As Danny pointed out, "The art is more alive in Hawaii and the United States than in the Philippines. It's like the pilgrims. The better Escrima men were the more adventurous type, always travelling." In fact, this wasn't the first time either that Bruce and Danny Inosanto had worked together. In one episode of *The Green Hornet*, called *The Praying Mantis*, Inosanto fought Bruce in place of the actor Mako Iwamatsu. Interestingly, the two of them worked out all the action for the scene in Bruce's back yard and recorded the fight on video tape. It was from these sessions that the Little Dragon learned the knack of obtaining realism without necessarily making bodily contact.

The idea of using video tape to check out angles and visual effects had proved to be a good one. No sooner had Inosanto arrived at Hong Kong airport than he was whisked away to Bruce's house to buckle down to some tough rehearsals. Commented Danny, "The video was great. Bruce would show me what was good for a movie and what was good for combat. Maybe a technique was too quick, or maybe it wasn't showy enough. And if it was showy enough, was it realistic? So we had to go back and forth and hash it out. He was a genius."

Costumes were important too. Bruce insisted that the film should portray imagination rising above tradition. For this reason, in *Game of Death*, everyone wears native costume of sort or other. Inosanto, for instance, dons a Muslim outfit. The Little Dragon of course uses his famous yellow tracksuit. And so, after three or four days of back-breaking workouts, the scene was finally completed. It opens with the Escrima standing against two of Bruce's side men, one of whom is armed with a heavy staff ("More like a log", laughed Danny later). The Little Dragon runs up the stairs to rescue his defeated compatriots and off they go into the kali, followed by the nunchaku sequence. The last scene is summed up well by Danny. "He (Bruce) comes up with a small stick and I fight him with two. He hits one stick out of my hand, and we keep on fighting. Then, he hits the other one out. I get mad and pull out a set of nunchakus. Then he pulls out his. He defeats me in the end, but lets me die a hero." Inosanto narrowly escaped injury several times, and on one occasion, a badly aimed landing mat nearly brought him to a sticky end. The schedule was extremely rigorous and shooting for the whole scene was completed within two weeks. Bruce would rise early every morning, do his workout, and then get down to business after a quick bite to eat. Right through the day he would keep on going. Complained Danny, "I just couldn't keep up with him. He never stopped! In both rehearsals and

during shooting, he was the most intensive worker I've ever seen." Bruce demanded full attention from all around him and such was his magnetic personality, that was generally what he got. Perfection or nothing!

Someone once said that Bruce Lee made Rudolph Nureyev look like a truck driver. Well, it's easy to see what he meant. To watch the Little Dragon at work was to be aware of pure artistry. Whether battling with the giant Kareem Abdul-Jabbar on the top floor - a man almost two feet higher than himself - or wading through thirty crack Karate men (Karateka) on the first floor, the Little Dragon displayed a unique array of talents, and he set standards that are unlikely ever to be challenged.

Perhaps it's only right that the last words should come from Raymond Chow, the man who probably, more than any other, was responsible for guiding Bruce Lee through his early years and who stuck by his side as business partner and friend right to the end of the road. He felt Bruce's death to be more than a personal loss. Far greater was the loss to the people of Hong Kong, for it was Bruce Lee who finally put Hong Kong on the map. As Chow once put it, "This was only the beginning; there were much bigger things ahead."

SUPERSTAR: THE REAL FACTS? BRUCE LEE'S LAST HOURS!

Bruce Lee Lives! Now, more than at any other time since the Little Dragon's tragic death does that catch-cry of martial arts fans worldwide ring true. Not only does Bruce's memory live on in the hearts and minds of literally millions of people In scores of nations, but his image and legend is now being transferred to celluloid - either for good or ill - in a rash of film studios, both Eastern and Western. *KFM* presents for you, a round-up of Bruce Lee biographical films - including a long look at two recently aired in the West, and three of the more important productions of the future.

First to the future where, obviously, the hot news is that *Game of Death* is back in production. With any luck, we should be able to witness the Little Dragon himself in action before the end of 1976. And as we all know, no matter how good stand-ins and doubles may be, they can never be anywhere near as good as the original! Another exciting piece of news is the production plan by Linda Lee - Bruce's American widow - to film her own story of life with the Little Dragon. After holding auditions in Los Angeles for a Bruce Lee lookalike, the Hollywood production company - which includes Barbra Streisand's boyfriend, Jon Peters - is now well into script preparation and preliminary negotiations. We'll keep you posted as to further news when it arises.

For the last six months, most fans and magazine writers have thought that Linda's was the only major biography of Bruce under production. However, *KFM* has now learned of a second Bruce Lee film biography which is very close to completion. And this one is really interesting! Titled - aptly enough - *Superstar*, it is a Shaw Bros. production filmed entirely in Hong Kong. But what really makes the film interesting is its star, who is none

other than Bruce's long-time girlfriend, the lovely Betty Ting Pei! As you will no doubt remember, it was in Betty's bedroom in the Hong Kong suburb of Kowloon that Bruce died. Complaining of a headache, Bruce had gone to lay down in the beautiful starlet's bedroom, where she gave him a sleeping pill to help ease the pain. It was a fatal mistake: the pill triggered off a seizure and Bruce died in his sleep, never regaining consciousness. Ever since that night, Betty has refused to tell the world's press exactly what took place. Now, Hong Kong rumour has it that she will reveal her side of the whole Bruce Lee/Betty Ting Pei relationship - including those fateful last hours - in *Superstar*! Unknown in the West, the movie has been a closed secret even in Hong Kong. Nobody - apart from those involved in the filming - really knows what it will contain. But by all accounts, it could be extremely explosive. No effort has been spared to make the film authentic. The bedroom set, constructed on the massive Shaw Bros. lot, was built to specifications supplied by Betty, who wanted the set to look exactly like the real thing. It even features her legless, oval bed, the bed in which Bruce passed away. Another indication as to the amount of detail the film provides is Betty's dress bill, which was HK$20,000 for 20 new dresses!

Directed by John Lo Mar, *Superstar* stars Shaw Kung Fu actor Li Hsu-hsien (Bruce Li), who, judging by the stills from the film *KFM* has obtained, bears more than a passing resemblance to Bruce. The fight scenes - directed by Tang Chai - should prove to be well worth watching; already Li has been injured several times during rehearsal! According to the director, there will be two versions of the film - one for Western cinemas and the other for local consumption. He has assured local reporters that the film will stick to the facts about Bruce as closely as possible. All in all, *Superstar* should really be worth holding your breath for, even if it is just to find out what really happened the night the Little Dragon died!

And now, back, to the present. Already the Western world has had the opportunity to see two films about Bruce Lee; *The Bruce Lee Story* and *The Legend of Bruce Lee*. Response to these two movies has been extremely mixed, as here at *KFM*, we've been deluged with letters both complaining and praising the two productions - just take a look at Jenny's Kickback page in this issue. For those of you who haven't seen either film, we've decided to give you some information about them.

Firstly, *The Bruce Lee Story*. Probably the best thing one can say about this Hong Kong-made movie is that the star, Cheung Nik, looks incredibly like the Little Dragon from many angles. In some of the scenes, we literally couldn't believe our eyes, the likeness was so great, especially the long shots and the early fight shots which were meant to depict Bruce rehearsing for *The Big Boss*. Unfortunately Cheung Nik, although he is quite a good actor and often captures Bruce's expressions and actions, is not much of a martial artist. But if you can forget that, the film does contain some quite good moments. The film sets out to tell the 'real' story about Bruce and Betty Ting Pei. As such it is really more of a love story than a life story. Unfortunately, in order to make it into a tragic tale of grand passion, the producers have stretched the facts a little. For example, they turn Linda Lee and Bruce's business associates into villains, out to wreck the Little Dragon's happiness. Poor Linda is treated as a joke the whole way through the film. The only good thing is trying to guess who each character is meant to portray.

The highlight of the film comes at the very end with actual film clips of Bruce's funeral in Hong Kong. In fact, these few short minutes tell more about Bruce and the love he

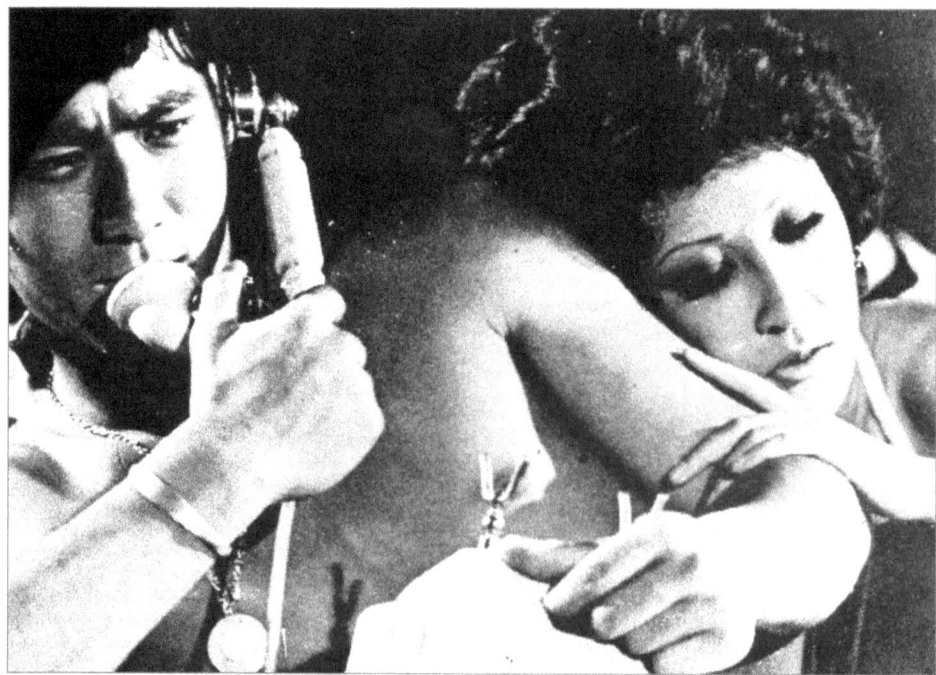

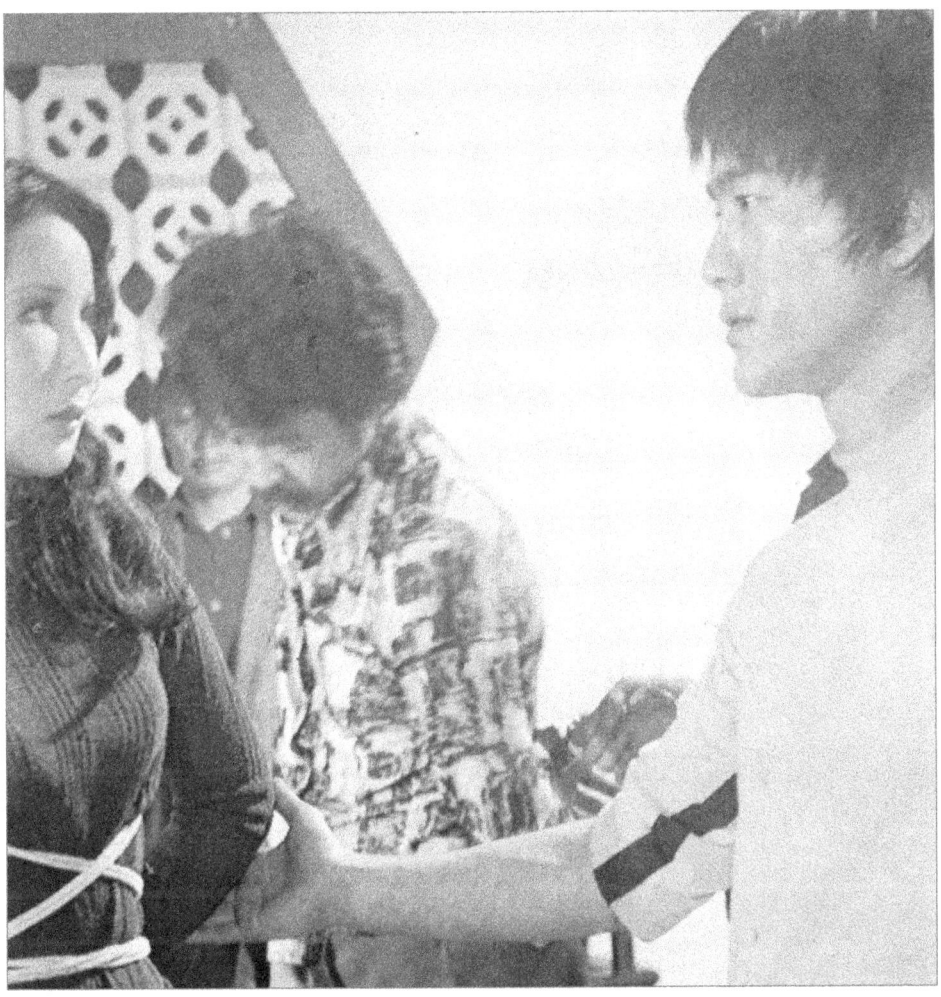

KUNG-FU MONTHLY BOOK OFFERS

THE BEGINNERS' GUIDE TO KUNG-FU
Graphic, easy to understand illustrations by Paul Simmons and carefully conceived step by step instructions make this the perfect book for beginners wishing to take up kung-fu. This book has already introduced thousands of KFM readers to the martial arts and it can do the same for you! It is a serious and carefully planned instructional guide which we claim to be the best of its kind for kung-fu novices in the world. Chapters include: HISTORY AND ORIGINS, EXERCISES, STRIKES, KICKS, BLOCKS, DEFENSE AND COUNTER ATTACK and STANCES.

If you are genuinely interested in kung-fu then you should order your copy today! Mail £2.05 by cheque or postal order made out to Kung-Fu Monthly and enclose your carefully printed name and address.
Kung-Fu Beginners' Book Offer, Kung-Fu Monthly, 39 Goodge Street, London W1P 1FD.

BRUCE LEE: KING OF KUNG-FU
This is the legendary story of Bruce Lee, Yuen Kam, The Little Dragon! Contains scores of exclusive photographs and over 40,000 words covering the entire span of Lee's amazing life story. The authors delve deeply into Lee's early life, his passion for the martial arts, his meteoric rise to world fame and the real cause of his tragic death. Here is a book that will thrill every real fan of Bruce Lee: a book to be kept, to be read and re-read a thousand times. Sales already exceed a quarter of a million copies and Bruce Lee: King of Kung-Fu is sure to become the classic published version of the Little Dragon's life. To obtain your copy mail £1.30 by cheque or P.O. made out to Kung-Fu Monthly, enclosing your name and address, to:
Bruce Lee Book Offer, Kung-Fu Monthly, 39 Goodge Street, London W1P 1FD. You won't be disappointed!

THE BOOK OF KUNG-FU
One hundred pages packed with photographs and articles featuring the superstars of Kung-Fu! This is Kung-Fu Monthly's own special book, with articles on Angela Mao, David Carradine, Bruce Lee's secret training methods, The origins of kung-fu, The power of Ch'i, The wit and wisdom of the Little Dragon and much, much more! Many pages in full colour and absolutely jam-packed with facts, figures, action, comics, illustrations and tremendous photographs. Would you like to speak the language of kung-fu or learn the Ten Commandments of the ancient art? Can you solve the Bruce Lee quiz? Don't miss this book! Rush your cheque or P.O. for only £1.00 made out to Kung-Fu Monthly, to:
The Book of Kung-Fu Offer, Kung-Fu Monthly, 39 Goodge Street, London W1P 1FD.

inspired than the rest of the movie combined! Verdict: Worth a look but don't believe everything you see.

The Legend of Bruce Lee is a little more dishonest that The Bruce Lee Story in that it almost pretends to be Game of Death under another title. The plot is uncannily like the Game of Death plot outlined in *KFM* No.13. Roughly it is this: The film opens with Lung (Lee) being taken to a movie screening room by a man who closely resembles Bruce's real-life producer Raymond Chow. There, on the screen, is another film, which is obviously *Game of Death*. Lung becomes involved with crooks and entrusted with a mysterious bag. After much coming and going (including a scene where Lung is accosted by a black six-foot basketball player - sound familiar?!) Lung's girlfriend is kidnapped. Lung puts on a yellow track-suit (again familiar?) and is told that his girl is being held on the top floor of a pagoda. It is up to him to do battle on every floor to get her back. Lung wades his way through an assortment of weird and wonderful opponents, picks up his lady, and spills the beans to the police. The End.

Although Lung looks like the Little Dragon on the odd occasion, and indeed has captured Bruce's mannerisms extremely well, The Legend of Bruce Lee falls pretty flat. The story is far too confusing, the fighting is more often than not, atrocious, and the action has been cut to pieces by the censor. Verdict: By all means go and see it if it's a cold day and the cinema has central heating. But if its Game of Death you're after, wait until the real thing arrives!

KICKBACK: THE LETTERS

Hi there... Jenny here again to (I hope!) supply some of the answers to a few of your questions. As always, the number of letters I receive is always tons more than the number I can print on this tiny page. But still, even if yours doesn't make it this month, don't whatever you do, give up. Honestly, I do really read every one that comes in here. One reminder before I get on with the job; do please write your letters clearly. You've no idea what a struggle it is to get through a letter which looks like it has been knocked around for a day or so by Bruce Lee himself.

GAME OF DEATH IDEAS

Dear Jenny,
I have read that Bruce Lee wanted to bring the greatest fighters and athletes in the world together to co-star in the film *Game of Death*. Why don't Golden Harvest and Hollywood get together and make another production, but this time, Bruce could be killed at the start of the film. And all the famous fighters could be Bruce Lee's pupils. The piece of film that Bruce made for *Game of Death* could be used as long flash backs like in *Enter the Dragon* and all the fighters could avenge his death. Please let me know if you and the *KFM* staff agree.
Vincent Earimal, Nottingham

Dear Vincent,
What else can I say except that I like it! Perhaps this is just what Raymond Chow has in mind for Game of Death.

THE LEGEND OF BRUCE LEE

Dear Jenny,
I am a very keen Bruce Lee fan but now I am very puzzled. Recently, I went to see a film called *The Legend of Bruce Lee* which starred Lee Roy Lung, who looks fantastically like Bruce Lee. So can you please tell me: 1. Has *The Legend of Bruce Lee* got anything to do with *Game of Death*? 2. Is Lee Roy Lung the new Bruce Lee? 3. Can *KFM* print a picture of Lee Roy Lung so readers can see the likeness? Thanks for the brilliant magazine.
C.A. Morgan, Birmingham

Dear C.A.,
No, The Legend of Bruce Lee unfortunately hasn't got anything to do with Game of Death except that the producers have tried to copy some of Bruce's Game of Death ideas. Read our second feature in this issue and that should clear up the muddle. As to your other question, yes Lee Roy Lung could be the next Bruce Lee, if he spends the next twenty years learning how to fight! Let me hasten to add, that is just my view. How about all you KFM readers out there; what do you think? For pictures of ther man in question, just turn to our second feature in this issue.

THE LEGEND OF BRUCE LEE (AGAIN!)

Dear Jenny,
I have just been to see *The Legend of Bruce Lee* today. The film is an insult to the late great Bruce Lee. The actor Lee Roy Lung, who played the part of Bruce Lee, could not fight his way out of a paper bag. Why make films like this? Linda will be really annoyed when she sees this insulting film. Can you tell me if *Game of Death* is to be completed? I have heard for two years now that it is being completed.
P.S. I have every copy of *Kung-Fu Monthly* since it was first published.
R.L. Chen, Liverpool

Dear R.L.,
You were just one of the many complaints we have had arriving continuously about both The Legend of Bruce Lee and The Bruce Lee Story. If I printed them all, they would take up all the Kickback pages from now until kingdom come! I agree that both films were pretty terrible. However, if you read the second feature in this issue of KFM, you will see that they both have something worthwhile about them. However, I must confess that I would rather they had not been made. Twisting facts after someone has died, especially when that someone is as fine a person as Bruce Lee, is inexcusable! If you have all the back issues of KFM, you will probably know after reading No.13, that Game of Death is well underway. As always, we'll keep you posted.

CHINESE PEN PAL WANTED

Dear Jenny,
Before I start, may I congratulate you on the terrific work you are doing in the letters department. Could you please help me to find a Chinese pen pal, preferably female? Please could you do an article on John Saxon's martial arts career as I saw him fight in *Enter the Dragon*? I am only fourteen but I sneaked into the cinema. I just had to see the King of Kung Fu himself. Well, keep up the good work.
Stuart Westerby, Clapham

Dear Stuart,
Thanks for your good wishes. I certainly hope you find your pen pal. As you know I usually run a Pen Pal Corner in Kickback, but this month, your request is really all I have room for. Next month will be different - I promise! As for John Saxon, KFM's man in Hollywood tells me he is much more an actor than a martial artist. However, there is a hope of an interview with the man himself in the very near future. I can't wait to hear what he has to say about working with Bruce!

DAN INOSANTO AND GAME OF DEATH

Dear Jenny,
I am a big fan of Bruce Lee and I have seen all his films but one, which is *Game of Death*. Is it true that *Game of Death* is to be released this Autumn? Also, is it true that Danny Inosanto, the man who appears with Bruce in *Game of Death*, was as good with the nunchakus as Bruce himself? And last of all, do you think you could print some pictures of Chuck Norris and Bruce in their big screen fight, and some pictures of Danny Inosanto and Bruce in their big screen fight? Keep up the good work.
Pete Carter, Watford

Dear Pete,
Honestly, I think I should get a big sign saying Game Of Death Is Coming, hang it round my neck and walk up and down Oxford Street with it! You just wouldn't believe the number of letters I get asking about the movie! I strongly doubt that it will be released here much before the autumn of 1976, though. Yes, Danny Inosanto was as good with the nunchakus as Bruce was, or so Bruce said and he should know! It was Danny who actually taught Bruce now to use the sticks with devastating results. If you look at KFM No.12 - you will find some great shots of Bruce and Chuck Norris from their Way of the Dragon Coliseum fight

BRUCE LEE FAN CLUB

Rhona McVay, President of the BLFC, requests that members please be patient when waiting for certain mail order items. All the BLFC staff are voluntary and, as they have only weekends to devote to fan club business, so delays will occur from time to time.

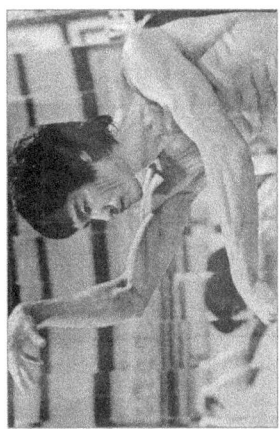

EDITORIAL

Hi there Kung Fu fans...

Well, the New Year certainly seems to have kicked off with a bang for all martial arts and Bruce Lee fans. Not only is *Game of Death* - Bruce's unfinished masterpiece which was cut short by his tragic death - now scheduled for production in the near future, but news has reached us that a young martial artist to play the title role in Linda Lee's Tribute to Bruce Lee has now been found. His name is Alex Kwon, 23-year-old former student born in Hong Kong, and you can read a full biography of him in this month's *KFM*. From all accounts, he sounds an excellent choice to try on Bruce's shoes for size.

Also in this issue, *KFM*'s own Bruce Sawford delves into the early years of the Little Dragon, analysing his childhood films and examining the environment which played so great a part to Bruce's later life. Hong Kong is a fascinating place and Bruce lived his life to the fullest. In the near future, *KFM* will be studying Bruce's early martial arts days, as well as his first years in the United States as a teenager. This month, we are a little puffed up about the photographs we have managed to include in this issue. After literally scouring the world (from Hong Kong, to Europe, to the U.S.A. to Japan), we feel we have obtained some of the finest shots existing of Bruce. We hope you agree. One last reminder before I go. When writing to *KFM*, please mark on the envelope whether your letter concerns one of our monthly mail order offers or whether it is for our Kickback columns. If it is for Kickback, please address it to Jenny Lee, our dedicated and delightful mail girl. How about letting Jenny know which is your favourite Bruce Lee film?

Well, that's all from me this month, so I'll see you next issue.

Felix Yen

Felix Yen
Editor-in-Chief

BRUCE LEE: THE BIRTH OF A LEGEND

Even amongst the greatest leaders of our time, Bruce Lee was unique. The highest paid movie actor in the world, the finest martial artist in modern history, a bridge between the cultures of the East and West, and an inspiration to a whole race of people, Bruce Lee stood alone. How did one man achieve so much in such a short space of time? What did Bruce Lee have that other men have not? *KFM* staff writer Bruce Sawford journeys back into the little Dragon's very earliest years to provide some answers.

The date was November 27, 1940. The country was America. It was the year of the Dragon and also the hour of the Dragon, but to the staff members of San Francisco's Chinese Hospital, it was just another working day. Several of them were aware that one of their patients - a Mrs. Grace Lee - had just given birth to her third son. None could possibly have guessed what the future held in store for this tiny baby boy... not even Mrs. Lee herself.

Actually, by rights, Grace shouldn't have been anywhere near San Francisco. She had been touring America with her husband - a popular and quite-famous Cantonese opera singer/comedian by the name of Lee Hoi Chuen - when her baby became due. She had elected to remain in San Francisco to have the child while her husband travelled three thousand miles away to New York's Chinatown. When the baby boy was born, she named him Jun Fan, which translated means 'Return to San Francisco.' For some reason, Grace felt that way ahead in the future, her son would indeed return to the Golden Gates and the name seemed appropriate.

A further name he picked up at the time, although he wasn't to use it for many years was given him either by a sister or a doctor at the hospital. Stories conflict as to from whom the suggestion actually came; it probably didn't seem too important at the time. Of course, the name was 'Bruce,' but not until later was it to stick. Soon after, his Chinese name, Lee Jun Fan was, for family reasons, changed to Lee Yuen Kam and to heap coals onto the fires of confusion, his mother preferred to call him 'Small Phoenix.' Mrs. Lee had lost her first son, and in true Chinese tradition, she felt it necessary to use the latter name with its feminine overtones in order to baffle evil spirits. It is not too widely known that the Little Dragon made his first screen appearance when only a few months old. Mr. Lee had many friends in the film making business and when somebody expressed the need for a baby to appear in a scene of the American production of *Golden Gate Girl*, he lost no time at all in lining up his son for the part. An alternative source of information names this film as *Tears of San Francisco*, and whether or not these two films are one of the same thing is not, unfortunately, altogether clear. Funnily enough, this humble start to Bruce's film career was, likely as not, looked back on with a certain amount of regret by a father who, in common with many show business artists, had no real desire to see his offspring following in his footsteps. But Bruce was to follow in nobody's footsteps. Soon, the Lee family returned to Hong Kong and the family home, a biggish flat at 218 Nathan Road, Kowloon. Big that is except that in time it was to house no fewer than sixteen people, plus

pets! Be that as it may, the first consequence of the homecoming was near disaster. For the infant Bruce, the change of climate was maybe too drastic. He became weaker and sicker by the day and only the constant love and attention of his family saved him. On his recovery however, the more familiar facets of Bruce's character began slowly to emerge. He developed a positive approach to life, wanting, it seemed, to be everywhere and to do everything at the same time. Bruce's fight for survival on the streets of Kowloon during the Japanese invasion and his arrogant swagger both pointed towards the Little Dragon's ability to look after himself. Later this arrogance was to disappear after it had served its purpose. As Bruce himself once remarked, "Only a humble man can be truly proud." And yet, in those former years lie the elusive clues that help lead us on to a better understanding of this giant among men. Having seen how circumstances forced Bruce to consider urgently a system of survival after being thrown mercilessly into the rough and tumble of Hong Kong at street level, now we leave that side of things for a moment and move to another early influence that helped shape the character of the little Dragon. At the top of Bruce's seemingly bottomless bag of talents came theatrical flair and showmanship. It is often argued that such attributes as these are hereditary, handed down through the ages from father to son. Even if this is not the case, Bruce's father undoubtedly played an enormous part in developing his son's performing talents.

As I mentioned earlier, there were certainly moments when Mr. Lee felt cause to regret his son's dramatic aspirations. Luckily though, it seems that for most of the time he succumbed to the obvious conclusion that the boy was made for the entertainment business and generally he did what he could to help. Though never really what you would call close, Bruce admired and often heeded the advice of his father. He recalled, "My dad used to tell me to save my dough because he knew I wanted to be an actor. He would say, 'When you become an actor, you can earn big money quickly, but when things are down, you may not see any money for months. So save everything you can to stretch your money when you need it.'" Sound advice indeed for the young dragon! Often as a lad, Bruce would hang around backstage while his father was performing and even at that young age, he was fascinated by the excitement of the big occasion. It wasn't long before film parts came his way, again no doubt through his father's influence. At the age of six he appeared in *The Beginning of a Boy* (an alternative translation of the title is *The Birth of Mankind*). The storyline, in keeping with the time-honoured traditions of standardised Cantonese tear-jerkers, went roughly as follows: Boy runs away to climb a fabled magic mountain. He is unsuccessful and winds up back in his home town, completely penniless. Needing money, he takes to picking pockets and all is well until, by pure accident, he picks the pocket of his father. Aware of the theft, but as yet not recognising the thief, the father gives chase. Son, making good his escape, has the bad luck to be run over by a lorry. Father, to his horror and grief, discovers the thief to be his own boy. Film ends! Not surprisingly, even the Eastern film-goers didn't think much of it and the tragedy of this simple tale was matched only by some tragically low box-office receipts. Verdict: a resounding F.L.O.P.

Many an aspiring young actor would have been discouraged by this unfortunate setback, but then, many do not possess the resolute qualities of Bruce Lee. Within two years, he'd touched gold and for the first time, the name 'Little Dragon' swept the Mandarin film circuit. Opportunity certainly crossed his path and did he take it! No fewer than twenty films were to come along during these amazing days in Kowloon and the invaluable experience he gained from this type of work proved to be a powerful factor indeed in the years ahead. Sadly, little physically remains of these remnants of schoolboy glory - save a few yellowed clippings - so it's interesting at this point, to take a slightly longer look at one of Bruce's first attempts, made, in fact, before he was ten years old. The film, entitled *My Son A-Chang*, was made by the 'Elephantine Co' around the late nineteen forties. Probably best described as a comedy with social overtones, it is set in the back streets of Hong Kong. Bruce, starring opposite the great Cantonese comedian E. Chow Shui, takes the part of A-Chang, a small boy being made to work twenty four hours a day by the tyrannical boss of a Hong Kong clothing factory. A-Chang is doing the job to help his out-of-work uncle and it's not long before he sets about righting the wrongs. The young dragon's performance is superlative right down to the inevitable swashbuckling fight (he uses a broom handle) and finally, after joining forces with a certain Dagger Li, he sets out in true Robin Hood style to rob the rich and feed the poor!

Although it seems incredible, even at this early age, the signs were all there. Indeed, on one famous occasion when Mr. Lee was making another of his periodic attempts to bend the Little Dragon's inclinations to a more scholarly direction, the local film directors were nearly down on their knees to get him to relent. They knew talent when they saw it and a resigned Mr. Lee had eventually to admit defeat.

Bruce, however, was becoming steadily more and more disillusioned with the Mandarin film industry. Thankfully though, his slackening of interest was to make way for the next important phase. But before we explore this, mention must be made of Bruce's last film shot during this period, *Orphan Ah Sam*. The plot, perhaps taken in part from his own experiences in wartime Kowloon, centres around a young orphan boy. He takes a 'job' as pickpocket for a street gang but gets caught and is given the choice of either going to school or jail. The lad chooses school and gradually, through the help and encouragement of a friendly master, mends his ways. One day, when urged by the old gang to join in one last raid, he declines. This costs him his ears.

Orphan Ah Sam premiered to a rapturous reception from fans and critics alike on almost the very same day Bruce stepped aboard a boat bound for the U.S.A. It was the end of one era and the start of another.

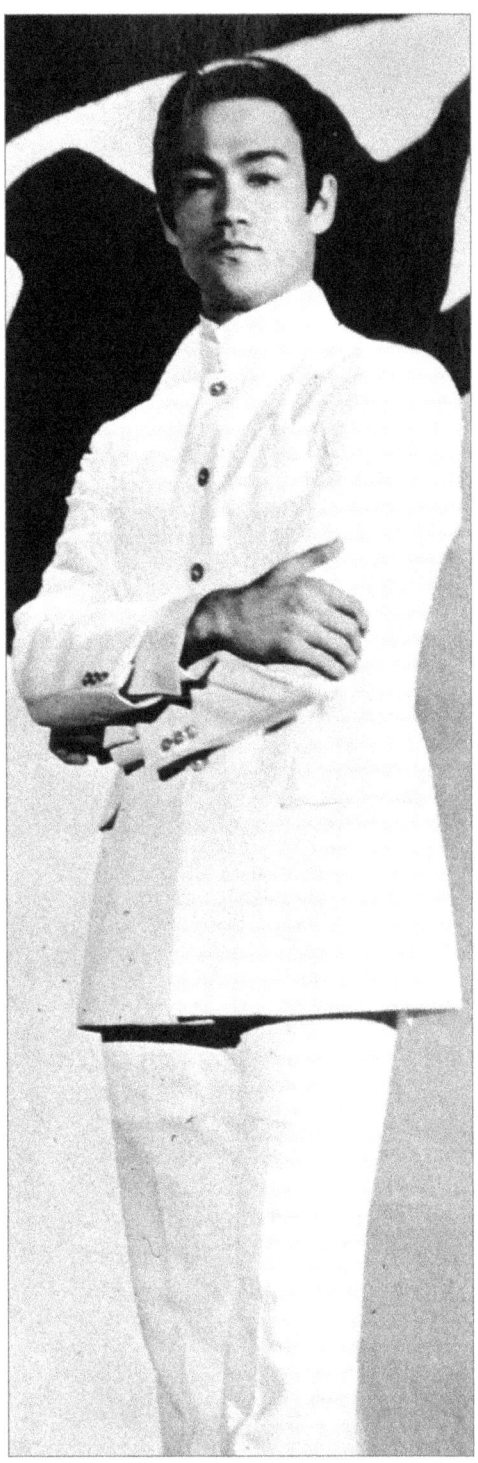

So far we have covered Bruce's early attempts at self defence and the origin of his dramatic abilities. The third and final area to be discussed must be his unique physical condition, coupled with that insatiable urge to improve on perfection. It would be reasonable to assume that the need for fitness arose first during the street fighting days in Kowloon. Then it was a matter of survival and it hadn't taken him long to realise the truth in the saying, God helps he who helps himself. But speed and agility were one thing; his height, however, was another. Bruce began to take the necessity of defending himself more seriously. There had to be some way for him to overcome the bigger and often physically stronger opponents whose challenges he was, frequently to his cost, forced to accept. He's heard a thing or two about a traditional form of combat known generally as 'The Martial Arts.' He broached the subject to his mother and she agreed to pay for him to study under the great master, Yip Man, an old Chinese immigrant from Kwantung Province. The choice was exceedingly fortunate as Yip Man was adept in a particular style known as Wing Chun, based on the ability to overcome superior size and strength by means of speed agility and balance. Yip Man was the beginning: others followed and still there was more to learn. Fitness was essential for a man who was rewriting the history of Kung Fu and later, once he had resolved his differences with the film industry, that same desire for perfection was translated onto the silver screen.

For now though, we leave Bruce on that boat bound for the New World, musing perhaps on his future, for this was a landmark, indeed turning point, in the career of the Little Dragon. The ingredients of success had been fought for and won. From now on the road ahead would gradually become paved with purpose, instincts would become skills and old ideas would be tossed aside like leaves in the wind. Nothing, however, came quickly. Skills take time to learn and genius needs fuel to finally burst into flame, but Bruce had seen the green light and now, at last, he'd found direction.

MEET ALEX KWON: THE NEW BRUCE LEE

Add another name to the growing list of oriental actors stepping into the shoes of the martial master, Bruce Lee. You may recall that back in issue No.14 of *KFM*, we mentioned that Linda Lee and her Hollywood film associates (First Artists) were searching desperately for a Bruce Lee lookalike to handle the title role in the forthcoming *Tribute to Bruce Lee*. Yes? Well that man has now been found, and in a most roundabout fashion at that!

Originally the Hollywood moguls had planned to discover their new *Bruce Lee for Tribute* - based loosely on Linda's recent biography of her late husband - by holding a massive all-day talent audition - something along the lines of a fighting New Faces. Hundreds of hopefuls ranging from small boys to middle-aged men showed up at the studio to test their skills before the cameras. Finally, a short list was prepared of possible candidates. But still, the producers were not entirely happy with the results. It seems none of the candidates really came close to filling the bill, which in itself is no real surprise. After all, how many people do you know who could step into the Little Dragon's shoes, look like him, act like him and fight like him?

Enter Alex Kwok, an up-and-coming young martial artist on the Kung Fu competition circuit. One day Alex arrived at the offices of a leading American martial arts magazine to talk about his recent performances. Although he had read about the Tribute audition, he hadn't paid too much attention to it and certainly hadn't entered. He felt that following Bruce's footsteps would be an overwhelming job, one that could swallow a budding martial artist whole! But as soon as the magazine's publisher set eyes on young Alex, he knew he was perfect for the starring role in *Tribute to Bruce Lee*.

The publisher rushed off some pictures of Alex to the Burbank studio where plans for the film were underway. Executive producer Phil Feldman also liked what he saw and paid Alex's plane fare back to Burbank from Atlantic City, where he was engaged in a martial tournament. In September, Alex presented himself at the studio and underwent a rigorous screen test. Next month a bargain struck and the contract signed. Alex Kwok - now going by the name Alex Kwon - was the new Bruce Lee!

Alex Kwong was born in Hong Kong 23 years ago under the Chinese name Kwok Ki Chung. His father, a physical fitness enthusiast, was the Chinese breast stroke champion before the Second World War. Following his father, young Alex also took up swimming and began capturing titles. But at the age of 10, he became interested in another physical way of life which would soon override his swimming ambitions - Kung Fu!

Alex was schooled in the rather obscure form of Kung Fu known as My Jong Law Horn,

a style hailing from the north of China. It is a very balanced, loose form of martial art which stresses development of both punching and kicking. As with Wing Chun (Bruce's own initial style which he learned from his master Yip Man), it features the famous 'sticking hands' technique which Bruce was to use often during his martial career.

In many ways, Alex is an ideal choice to play Bruce, at least from the martial artist's standpoint. As we all know, after Bruce had mastered Wing Chun, he went on to found and perfect the 'non-style' he called Jeet Kune Do. The basis of his Jeet Kune Do was an antagonism to classical, rigid Kung Fu and Karate styles which he considered to be more of a hindrance than a help during martial combat or tournaments. What Bruce wanted to distil and perfect, was a form of practical, free-flowing street-fighting Kung Fu which would incorporate and draw on all forms of combat technique, be it Western Boxing, Karate, wrestling, Judo or Thai kick Boxing! Fortunately for Alex, My Jong Law Horn, because of its fluidity, is able to allow a proponent to get extremely close to Jeet Kune Do.

"Actually, I have no trouble doing the type of things that he did," Alex told the American Fighting Stars magazine recently. "This is mainly because our styles are versatile and encompass a wide range of techniques. Of course, I will be playing his part and I will be trying to get some of the main points and the actions that he displayed on the screen."

However, although he may attempt to present some of Bruce's actions on screen, Alex

has no plans to pass himself off as a carbon copy of the Little Dragon. He realises that if he tried to copy all of Bruce's finer and subtler actions and mannerisms, he would be risking the wrath of ten million Bruce Lee fans around the globe. What he wants to do is, rather, interpret Bruce Lee and capture the flavour and style of his acting and martial performances. He believes the only way he will succeed in licking the part will be to act naturally and do what his own mind, body and reflexes tell him to do, rather than trying to squeeze himself into someone else's mould.

Now that the starring role has been assigned, it looks as if *Tribute to Bruce Lee* will go into production this spring. Already it looks set to be a monster epic which will enhance the Little Dragon's reputation even more. The Director is to be Robert Clouse, the man who helped Bruce through his paces in the Hollywood box-office smash *Enter the Dragon*. Already, Alex and Clouse have struck up a firm and happy relationship. Bruce's Widow Linda has taken an active part in planning the film, and although she will not be appearing herself, has signed on as an adviser to the production. Bruce's friends in Hollywood have also expressed desires to help. Rumour has it that Steve McQueen - who saw Alex through his screen test and claims he bears an 'uncanny resemblance' to Bruce - will make a brief appearance.

In order to keep pace with the professionals who have now appeared in his life, Alex

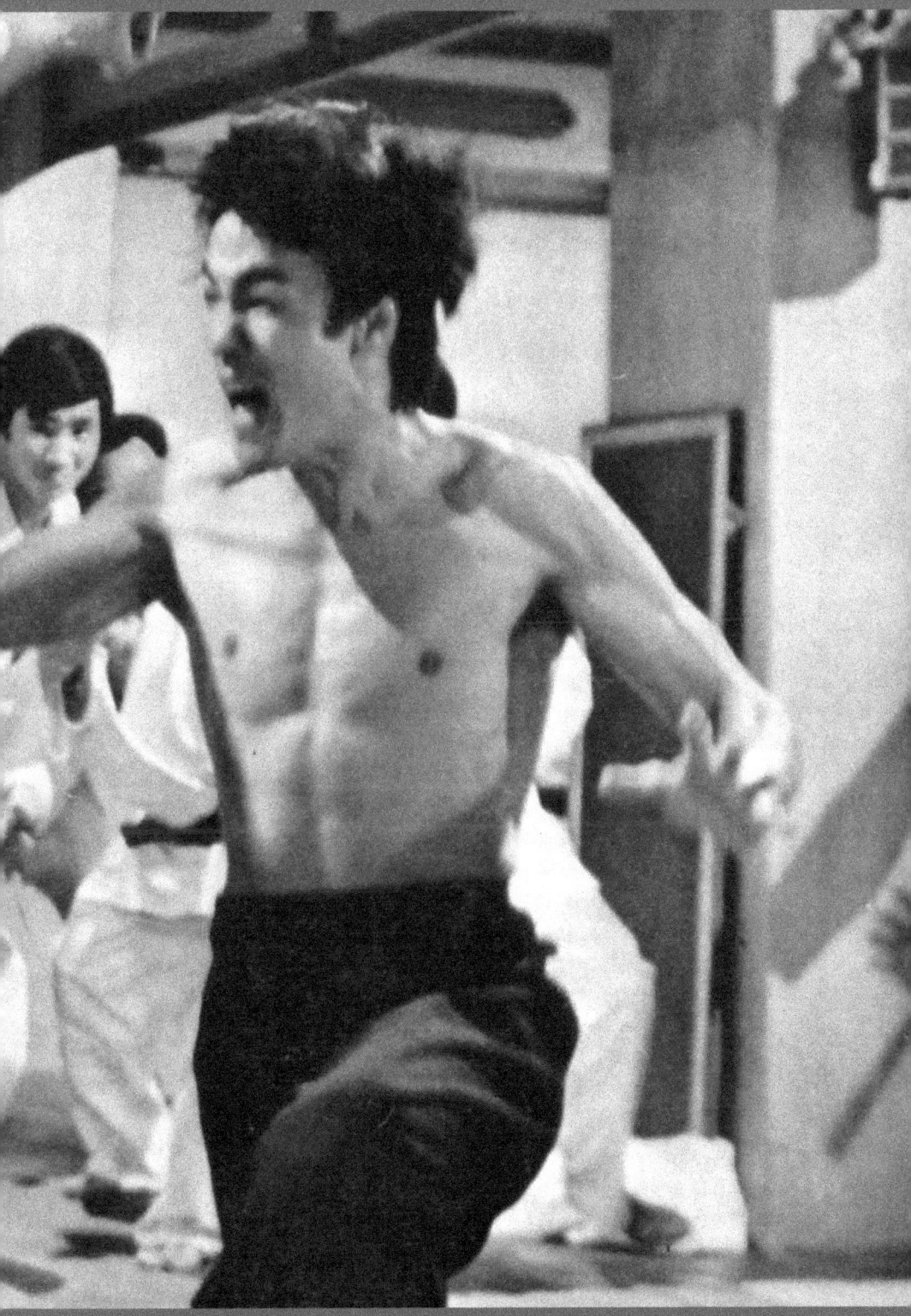

has been enrolled by Warners in a famous Hollywood acting school where he will learn screen techniques, elocution and even take dancing lessons! It's a far cry from his previous life as a student (he holds a degree in mathematics from the University of British Colombia and has also studied computer technology) and his career as a competitive martial artist. However, the change does not seem to have wrought any major changes in his personality. "Many people thought it would," he confessed in a recent interview. "But for myself, I feel just the same."

After all the cheap films which have been released since Bruce's tragic death claiming to portray the 'true' story of the Little Dragon, it is refreshing to see a Bruce Lee biographical movie which is being tackled by reputable people intent on providing the truth. Not the least of those people, it would seem, is Alex Kwon. What with *Tribute to Bruce Lee*, Bruce's own *Game of Death* and Betty Ting Pei's Hong Kong movie about Bruce (re-titled from *Superstar* to *Bruce Lee and I*), Bruce Lee's myriad disciples the world over seem set for a very interesting year!

KICKBACK: THE LETTERS

Hello, Its me here again to answer just a few of the thousands of letters which pour into the *KFM* offices each month. As always, I'd like to thank all the readers who wrote in but did get their letters printed. All I can say is don't give up. I do read everything that comes in. One request, all you readers seeking pen friends, please do remember to include your full name and address. Well, that's all from me, so on with the show!

THE BRUCE LEE STORY

Dear Jenny,
I have written to tell of a new film entitled *The Legend of Bruce Lee*. I want to warn readers that if you think that you can see the King of Kung Fu on the screen (it is an AA certificate), you cannot. At the beginning when the screen titles appear, a lot of Bruce Lee magazines and pictures are shown. The man in the film playing Lee (Lee Roy Lung) dresses in the white costume Lee wore in the graveyard scene in *Fist of Fury*. The plot is pointless, the acting terrible. Lee Roy Lung just doesn't look like Bruce Lee. His copy of Bruce's mannerisms doesn't come off, especially Bruce's famous fighting cry or 'Kiai.' I could not find one good thing to say about the film. It is actually a great laugh and it should be rated as one of the top comedies of the year!
Andrew Couts, Highview, Pinner

Dear Andrew,
Well, I'm afraid I can't help but agree with you and the dozens of other Little Dragon fans who have written in and given The Legend of Bruce Lee a thorough mauling! It does seem such a pity that poor Bruce's memory should be dragged around in such fashion. Still, console yourself with the thought that Game of Death - starring none other than the Great Man himself - is on the way!

THE BRUCE LEE STORY (AGAIN!)

Dear Jenny,
First of all, your magazine is just great - my husband and I both enjoy it. Last night we went to see a movie called *The Bruce Lee Story*. Ugh! It was the most disgusting film we have ever seen. I have read everything there is to read on Lee and we have seen all his films more than once. I just had to write and say that I don't advise any of Lee's fans to see this film - they wouldn't like it al all. He was portrayed as a bully and and a Don Juan which he wasn't. Also, too much of the film wound around Bruce Lee's relationship with Betty Ting Pei which I personally didn't like. Keep up the good work with the magazine.
Carol Buckley, Widnes, Cheshire

Dear Carol,
You wouldn't believe how many letters I have received about The Bruce Lee Story and that other Little Dragon imitation The Legend of Bruce Lee! And it seems that the verdict on the two movies is pretty unanimous - thumbs down. (Have a look at Andrew's letter below!) I agree that especially in Story, facts are spread rather thin on the ground and often, there are downright misrepresentations of truth. However, I think Story gives quite a fascinating glimpse into the Hong Kong movie making scene which makes up for some of the errors. From that point, I was quite glad to have seen it. As for the gossip and falsehood it contains, forget it. No true Bruce Lee fan would ever fall for that rubbish.

A NEW ADDITION TO THE FAMILY

Dear Jenny,
I've been getting *KFM* right from the very first issue and must write and tell you that I think it is the greatest magazine ever to go into print. When *Enter the Dragon* was first screened in Norwich, I went to see it just to see what the fuss was all about and after the scene in the Shaolin Temple, I became an instant fan. Since then, Bruce Lee has been a talking point with my visitors who happen to come around. However on November 8th, my wife had a baby boy and in tribute to the king, we named him Darren Lee. We are hoping that when he is old enough, he will train in martial arts. One thing for certain, the name of Bruce Lee will never be forgotten in our house. Please keep up the good work. Hoping that you print this letter so that I can show it to my son when he is old enough.
Richard Crowe, Norwich

Dear Richard,
Congratulations - what more can I say?

WAS BRUCE LEE MARRIED?

Dear Jenny,
I would be grateful if you could tell me whether Bruce Lee was married? Also, I would like a Chinese male pen pal between 17 and 25, preferably living in Hong Kong.
Carol Mansfield, Preston, Lancashire

Dear Carol,
Yes, Bruce certainly was married - to Seattle-born Linda Lee, whom he met while he was studying in the States.
Also, I'll mention here that 17 year old Mandy Hagley of Ely, Cambridgeshire would also like a 17-year-old (or older) Chinese male pen friend.

GAME OF DEATH

Dear Jenny,
Just what is going on? There are a few major differences I wish you could clear up. Firstly, I read your great review on the 'unfinished' *Game of Death*, which you said remains uncompleted apart from the incredible fight scenes in the multi-level pagoda. Also, you presumed that Raymond Chow and Linda Lee were more in favour of building around the fight scenes involving Bruce rather than playing a double (presumably no-one has equal talents as a martial artist or personality brilliance), but, here comes the confusion. I have read elsewhere that the film has been finished, and been re-titled *The Legend of Bruce Lee*. It seems an almost exact double of Bruce has been found with incredible fighting abilities. I have seen photos of him in action wearing the same yellow tracksuit as Bruce wore in the already filmed *Game of Death* sequences with Big Lew, and the resemblance is uncanny. Thanks for the great magazine. Yours is the only one I can turn to.
Andy Rowson, Harrogate, Yorkshire

Dear Andy,
I haven't yet seen a copy of KFM No.14! In that issue, both the current state of the Game of Death footage and The Legend of Bruce Lee were discussed. Unfortunately you have fallen into a clever publicity trap which tried to confuse the two films in the minds of Bruce's fans. No, Legend definitely doesn't have anything to do with the real Game of Death (which at this present moment has gone back into production) except for a very similar story line, no doubt copied from magazine articles about Game of Death. As for Bruce's new 'double' - Lee Roy Lung - I'm afraid he is rather a long way from the real thing. Keep watching for more news on Game of Death.

THE POSTER MAGAZINES - VOLUME ONE

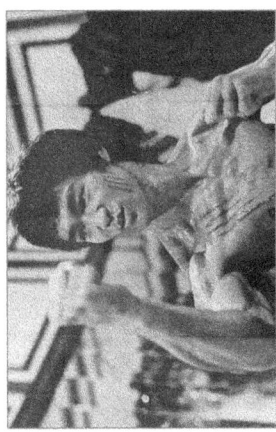

1976

EDITORIAL

Hi there Kung Fu fans...

Have I got news for you! Not only have we produced another unbeatable issue of *KFM*, but we have scooped the pool once again with exclusive information on the life of the late great Bruce Lee! But first, let me say a brief word or two about this month's *KFM*. First up, staff writer Bruce Sawford has obtained a sneak preview of the book the martial arts world has been waiting years for - Bruce Lee's own *Tao of Jeet Kune Do*! As you probably already know, Bruce devoted his life to the study and development of his own brand of Kung Fu, labelled Jeet Kune Do. Now his notes on the martial arts have been compiled and bound into a beautiful manuscript which is, literally, the last word on Jeet Kune Do. Stand by for more news on its availability.

Next we have a special *KFM* profile - Soon Taik Oh, star of the James Bond epic *The Man with the Golden Gun*. Already dubbed as 'The Man with a Golden Touch,' Soon seems set to go a long way in martial arts films. An extremely talented actor and an amazingly versatile martial artist, he makes a very welcome change from Hollywood's usual stock of punch-up men! I'm sure we'll he hearing a lot from him in the very near future.

Now for the big news... the *KFM* Special Issue Bruce Lee's *Game of Death*. If you haven't already seen this fantastic in-depth report on the Little Dragon's last unfinished masterpiece on the news-stands, make sure you put in an order to our mail order department. Whatever you do, don't miss out on this collector's edition. Packed with facts, information and stunning pictures - many unseen in the Western World - of Bruce Lee's *Game of Death* is a martial scoop of truly momentous proportions!

Well, that's about all from me this month, so I'll see you next issue...

Felix Yen

Felix Yen
Editor-in-Chief

THE TAO OF JEET KUNE DO

The death of the late, great master of Kung Fu, Bruce Lee, robbed the world of not only the finest martial artist in modern history, but also two of what would undoubtedly have been among his greatest works. The first of these unfinished masterpieces was, of course, the legendary *Game of Death*, the Kung Fu film that Bruce was working on at the time of his tragic death. The second was the Little Dragon's treatise on his own way of martial arts, Jeet Kune Do.

For years, both these uncompleted projects have lain untouched, the subject of much debate and speculation amongst Bruce Lee's army of fans and followers. Now, in 1976, both have once again burst into the limelight. In the *KFM* Special Issue Bruce Lee's *Game of Death*, you will learn the truth about the Little Dragon's last celluloid adventure. Now, in this issue of *KFM*, staff writer Bruce Sawford reveals the facts about Bruce's legendary *Tao of Jeet Kune Do*.

Right off, let me say that if you're expecting a 'How to be a Kung Fu Expert in Ten Easy Lessons,' then this book is definitely not for you; you'll just be wasting both your time and your money. If, however, you are fed up with life's daily grind and feel that there must be something more to it all than just watching TV, then I cannot recommend *Tao of Jeet Kune Do* too highly.

Jeet Kune Do is a book without beginning or end. Personally, in fact, I would prefer to call it a signpost, pointing along the path of self-knowledge. Again, as in *Game of Death*, Bruce's tragic death prevented completion of this remarkable work, and our gratitude and thanks must therefore go to Gilbert L. Johnson and Linda Lee for their back-breaking efforts in putting it all together. Drawing only from the scattered notes that the Little Dragon left behind, the two of them have brilliantly assembled a lifetime's jottings, diagrams, thoughts and ideas into a definitive book of which Bruce himself would surely have been proud. Nothing, we are assured, has been added, and nothing has been left out.

The first part of this classic work deals with the theories behind Zen and in particular with their application to the martial arts. To be able to control your body and mind, you must first learn to understand them. No amount of exercise and training can make up for this deficiency and Bruce spares no effort in driving home this point. Jeet Kune Do naturally follows from this. It is a style without style, or perhaps, one could say, a game without rules.

If, for example, you are digging the garden, you need the right tools handy, (in that case, a fork or spade). Likewise, in Jeet Kune Do, one learns to be prepared for anything. To this end, the trick is to always have at hand whatever weapons are necessary, be they words, punches, nunchakus or even just a fast pair of legs!

A word of warning though: This chapter, although not an easy one, wasn't put in the pole position without reason. Bruce likened the art to a tree, where kicks, punches and tactics, etc are but the leaves and branches. Its true essence, if you like, is the trunk, without which the leaves and branches cannot exist.

That done, the Little Dragon turn to the first steps, covering in some detail such basic techniques as training, warming up and defence positions. Once again he hastens to emphasise the need for mental as well as physical training. Too often one sees the muscle-bound superman being defeated by the physically less fit but mentally more agile opponent.

Bruce follows this with an urgent plea to dismiss dogma. Distractions are the curse of all men and are themselves opponents to be defeated. Of course, at any stage of learning it is essential not to neglect the importance of checking through all your new-found skills and 'putting them together.' Coming up with the right answer in any particular situation

is not something that can safely be left to chance as luck may not always be on your side. Your instincts, therefore, must without fail, remain in command.

Precision and power, balance and endurance are comprehensively covered, as are timing, rhythm, tempo and speed. To be lacking in any one of these qualities is to be both awkward and vulnerable, and he makes the point that no one exercise can be ignored at the expense of any other. Practicing will only seem tedious to the person who cannot see his goal.

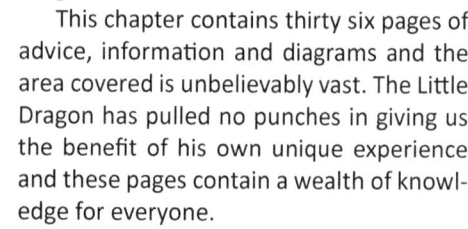

This chapter contains thirty six pages of advice, information and diagrams and the area covered is unbelievably vast. The Little Dragon has pulled no punches in giving us the benefit of his own unique experience and these pages contain a wealth of knowledge for everyone.

In the following chapter, Bruce runs through the tools of his martial trade. To use the right lead and the right counter at the right time is paramount and once again he repeats the need to develop the instinctive response. Getting down to it, he outlines two whole pages of kicks, punches, jabs, swings and butts. Naturally, although the descriptions are for the most part both clear and concise, the finer details he leaves to the imagination. No man can call himself a Jeet Kune Do expert if he hasn't first developed (and can understand) his own techniques. Remember, there are no rules!

Bruce also deals here with specific problems such as a tall man confronting a shorter man and the consequent difficulties of shorter and longer reach. There are also several pages on locks, chokes and foul tactics (hair pulling, foot stomping, etc) and a very handy list of do's and don'ts for dealing with the unexpected attack.

The next section is labelled 'Preparations.' Here Bruce explains when, where and why he uses various feints and parries, taking time to indicate how it can become possible to dictate, and therefore predict, your opponent's moves. A false thrust or a deceiving feint will keep your attacker guessing and, hopefully, fully occupied, while you are working out the true course of the battle to come. Gradually, the full worth of Jeet Kune Do becomes abundantly clear for, as the master points out, the overwhelming advantage given to you by using a style comprising of all styles is that an opponent can never really be sure of what you are going to do next.

So far, Bruce has touched on theory, a little philosophy, and some of the early moves that the newcomer to the world of Jeet Kune Do will need to know. Next the Little Dragon moves on to discuss mobility, stressing first of all the importance of always maintaining the appropriate distance between yourself and your opponent. Experience will tell you that the power behind, say, a punch is dampened (if not completely nullified) by incorrect judgement of distance and Bruce gives some very handy tips on making the right decisions.

Footwork is also given prominence here. One need, of course, look no further than to Muhammad Ali, that supreme master of the Boxing ring, to see the advantage given to a man who can stay on his toes. Bruce also deals with the use of various leg angles and 'step lengths.' Slipping (another Ali technique) is covered in full, plus such tactics as ducking, rolling, swaying and snapping back.

The final chapter in what must be regarded as the Jeet Kune Do practitioner's bible is devoted to attack. Bruce, I suspect, would have agreed with me if I were to say that it really boils down to just two considerations; that is, how to attack and when to attack. Initially, however, he divides the action into primary and secondary offensives.

The preparation of any move is, naturally, of paramount importance and the Little Dragon urges us to follow his own superb example and maintain an 'inner calm.. Nothing, he stresses, will ever be achieved when a martial artist is in an uncontrollable condition of blind anger. The raging attacker will, eventually, more surely arrange his own swift demise than any opponent!

This last section handily summarises most of what has gone before, neatly and eloquently showing each facet in its rightful position. Variety, Bruce notes, is essential in both attack and defence, adding that little will be achieved without the magic ingredient - decisiveness. Having sufficiently mastered a number of moves, he then asserts the need to put together 'combinations.' Nothing is gained at all if, having scored heavily over an opponent, the attacker stands and 'gloats.' The advantage will, as likely as not, be lost.

Those who have studied the Little Dragon's style in any depth will already know the heavy emphasis he put on 'counterattack.' There is an excitement all of its own in a sudden reversal of fortunes and students of Jeet Kune Do will do well to heed Bruce's proven words of wisdom.

By way of illustration, Bruce outlines a series of moves and counter-moves. The choice of retaliation is, of course, dependent upon what form the attack takes. But with practice, your reply to almost any situation will become well nigh instinctive.

Another point the Little Dragon makes is that by supreme manoeuvrability and foot-

work, a master can also make himself extremely difficult, if not impossible, to counter. In other words, what you do immediately after an attack is equally as important as the attack itself. Further, Bruce talks generally about assessing one's opponent's abilities in good time (i.e. before he's defeated you!). Only a fool takes on a fighter knowing that the odds are stacked heavily against him.

Finally in this chapter, Bruce shows us the five ways of attack. These he calls simple angle, progressive indirect, combination, drawing and immobilisation. Sadly, as the editor here comments, these notes constitute almost the last words written by Bruce Lee and the subject remains incomplete.

So there we are. What else is there to say but fantastic! The book is everything anyone ever hoped it would be and in fact, for my money, much more. Not only has the Little Dragon captured the very essence of the art of The Intercepting Fist in such a way as to make it understandable to all, but also has he steered clear of the twin traps of 'over-simplification' and 'over-complication.' Perhaps it would be fair now to add authorship to the Little Dragon's amazing list of accomplishments, for rarely before have I come across such clarity of thought and understanding; Bruce Lee was truly, a man who knew his subject. Need I say that for the aspiring exponent of Jeet Kune Do, Bruce Lee's *Tao of Jeet Kune Do* represents the finest source material available.

In conclusion, just one thing more needs to be mentioned. It's been rumoured for some time that the Little Dragon was very much in two minds whether or not to publish the book. Why, you may well ask, should Bruce not want people to study his treatise on Jeet Kune Do? The answer is simply this. It will be easy, too easy, for readers to misinterpret and misunderstand the ideals behind the art. The book does not constitute a set of rules; recall, there are no rules in Jeet Kune Do. If Bruce had thought for just one minute that a martial artist would become bogged down in the 'classical mess' as a result of reading his words, he would never have wanted to see this work printed. Therefore, may I strongly advise that you take the *Tao of Jeet June Do* for the guide and inspiration it was intended to be. Its fate is in your hands.

MEET SOON TAIK OH: THE MAN WITH THE MIDAS TOUCH

The film: *The Man with the Golden Gun*. The scene: James Bond (alias Roger Moore) trapped inside A Bangkok martial arts academy, and facing his executioner to be. What follows next is Hollywood action at its finest! Rather unsportingly, Bond takes the opportunity of delivering a coup-de-gras kick to the chin of his politely bowing opponent. Waving a fond farewell, he escapes through a window, only to come face to face with dozens of Kung Fu and Tae Kwon Do experts moving in for the kill. Naturally, Bond makes it out OK, but only with the assistance of his trusting police chief Lieutenant Hip, portrayed by Soon Talk Oh, a martial arts expert known now by many as *The Man with the Golden Touch*.

To film director Guy Hamilton, the entire fight sequence worked like a charm. One take and it was in the can! Of course, this sort of perfection only results from hours, days and weeks of back-breaking exertion, but for this movie, the ninth film in the James Bond series, everything had to be right. The plot of the film need not concern us here but suffice to say that James is up against three arch villains - a paid assassin, a corrupt business man named Hai Fat (Richard Loo) who in fact runs the martial arts academy, and Mr. Big himself (Christopher Lee).

For Soon Taik Oh, the film represents a landmark in a career which has by now taken him a very long way indeed from his early days in South Korea. Born there some thirty years ago, Soon, after graduating from High School, turned to studying international relations. Before long, though, his acting ability became obvious and he applied to join New York's Neighborhood Playhouse. These were hard days for the South Korean and after a year, he felt just about ready to quit. At the Playhouse, he was attending twelve hours of instruction each day, at the same time as having to hold down the evening job he needed to make ends meet! Regretfully, he handed in his resignation. But two weeks later he was amazed to learn that he had been chosen to receive one of the Playhouse's rare scholarships! The following year was a gruelling one for Soon Taik Oh, but finally he earned his graduation. Before long, he had also won himself the title of Master of Fine Arts in acting and playwriting. Life, for Soon, was beginning to look interesting. Before long he formed, with a group of Asian actors, the East/West Playhouse and their number one production was Rashomon with Soon handling the role of a samurai. There were many duelling scenes and for these they were fortunate in obtaining the services of Torao Mori (Hachi-Dan) to help with the choreography. Soon was no stranger with the Shinai. When only four

years old and living back in South Korea, he had spent many hours peeking through the window of the Police Station next door, avidly following the afternoon sessions of Kendo and Judo. About this time too he started the fencing lessons that were to be of so much use to him in the years to come. At school, his interest in the martial arts continued in the form of Judo, for which he received the top-ranking brown belt. You can imagine, therefore, Soon's elation at working in the East/West Playhouse along side two such totally dedicated martial artists as Mako and Mori Sensei!

Torao Mori, one of the great kendo swordsmen of our time, had a profound effect on Soon. He recalls, "When I met Mori Sensei, I was really fascinated by him. As he choreographed, he would demonstrate. Of course, there was a tremendous difference in what we could do and what he did. One day, he brought two real swords to rehearsal, to show us how heavy they are and what kind of feel you get with a real one versus theatrical swords. As you know, the Katana is a work of art, not just a weapon. Draw it and it's a different world. From then on begins your love affair with the Japanese sword. It is most beautiful. Again my interest in Japanese fencing grew. I could say that I read almost all the Japanese samurai novels, which leads one to Bushido, which leads to Zen Buddhism."

His affection for the Katana was such that, before too long, he had begun to take lessons in Iaido with Mori Sensei. Iaido is the study of the naked blade and quick draw. Comments Soon, "Iaido is my favourite martial art. When some people stand in a Karate stance, it does something for them, mentally and physically. The sword does something for me."

There are over thirty four types of Katana (swords) but, as Soon indicates, unfortunately the only way to master the weapon is to use the real thing. The mere knowledge that the sword is 'safe' or has a dull blade will lead to carelessness and a sure lack of respect.

He goes on, "Then comes 'Ma,' the timing, the distance, the pause. You don't just blindly draw it. There is tremendous concentration and you execute it. You commit yourself totally, then go back. That's why as an actor and as a human being, I would like to have that personified. Something always moving, but not floundering about. Contained, exploded, then go back. That's my dream." Such words are perhaps almost worthy of Bruce Lee, the great master himself.

Soon moved on to study Shotokan Karate but although he was impressed by the style's

beauty and symmetry of movement, he felt it to be restricting. So he turned to Kung Fu and studied under John Davidson in the Taoist Sanctuary in North Hollywood. Davidson taught a very loose form of Kung Fu known as Choy Lai Fut, which was no doubt something of a relief to Soon after the rigidity of Shotokan Karate. Here, too, he made the' acquaintance of Ki (or Ch'i), the study of inner energy, and he became aware of the many different breathing techniques associated with the martial arts. The young South Korean's training in Kung Fu was to serve him well. Some time after, he played opposite David Carradine in the TV series *Kung Fu*. The two of them engaged in two fights, one in a temple and one in a jail corridor and such was the fantastic success of the programme, that Soon was nominated for an Emmy award.

Right now, the 'Man with a Golden Touch' is involved in the Kenpo style and studying with Bill Ryusaki. The art, is based round defensive moves and counters and is indeed the style used by Soon for the Bond epic. In the interests of accuracy and entertaining action, a Mr. Chen was brought in to supervise the filming under the direction of British stunt co-ordinator Leslie Crawford, who also doubled the stunts for Roger Moore. Chen had worked with Bruce Lee on several occasions and according to Soon, some of the Little Dragon's style had obviously rubbed off. Three weeks' rehearsal took place in Hong Kong prior to the shooting of the scene, plus a couple more in Bangkok. In the South Korean's own words, "It would take a blind man not to see the influence of Bruce Lee!"

During the stay in Hong Kong, Soon spent some time assisting Crawford with the sequence, particularly as regards communicating with the Kung Fu fighters. It became no easy task putting together a fight consisting of Kung Fu, Kenpo and Tae Kwon Do specialists. Some styles, for instance Kenpo, are not so visual, although none the less effective and for a while, Soon was considering going over to Kung Fu for the purposes of the film. Finally, however, he decided that, in the interests of realism, he would stay with Kenpo. As he said to Crawford, "It may be alright to the general audience, but the people who know would say, 'There's no way he could beat those guys with those kind of moves!'"

Getting to Bangkok, Soon and Crawford ran into some problems. They started rehearsals with two Kung Fu men, ten local Tae Kwon Do black belts and of course, Soon using the Kenpo style. Mr. Chen, the Chinese co-ordinator was disturbed because the Tae Kwon Do exponents just couldn't follow the moves of the Kung Fu stylists. The former make use of the feet far more than the southern styles of Kung Fu and the action had to be suitably modified. In praise of the painstaking build-up prior to the shooting of the scene, the

---

KUNG-FU MONTHLY BOOK OFFERS

BRUCE LEE: KING OF KUNG-FU
This is the legendary story of Bruce Lee, Yuen Kam, The Little Dragon! Contains scores of exclusive photographs and over 40,000 words covering the entire span of Lee's amazing life story. The authors delve deeply into Lee's early life, his passion for the martial arts, his meteoric rise to world fame and the real cause of his tragic death. Here is a book that will thrill every real fan of Bruce Lee: a book to be kept, to be read and re-read a thousand times. Sales already exceed a quarter of a million copies and **Bruce Lee: King of Kung-Fu** is sure to become the classic published version of the Little Dragon's life. To obtain your copy mail £1.30 by cheque or P.O. made out to Kung-Fu Monthly, enclosing your name and address, to:
Bruce Lee Book Offer, Kung-Fu Monthly, 39 Goodge Street, London W1P 1FD. You won't be disappointed!

THE BOOK OF KUNG-FU
One hundred pages packed with photographs and articles featuring the superstars of Kung-Fu! This is Kung-Fu Monthly's own special book, with articles on Angela Mao, David Carradine, Bruce Lee's secret training methods, The origins of kung-fu, The power of Ch'i, The wit and wisdom of the Little Dragon and much, much more! Many pages in full colour and absolutely jam-packed with facts, figures, action, comics, illustrations and tremendous photographs. Would you like to speak the language of kung-fu or learn the Ten Commandments of the ancient art? Can you solve the Bruce Lee quiz? Don't miss this book! Rush your cheque or P.O. for only £1.00 made out to Kung-Fu Monthly, to:
The Book of Kung-Fu Offer, Kung-Fu Monthly, 39 Goodge Street, London W1P 1FD.

entire fight was canned in one take, and according to Soon, only four cameras were used.

In a recent *KFM* article on Bruce Lee's *Game of Death*, we mentioned the Little Dragon's preoccupation with getting a fight to took right to the viewer, without actually having to half-kill an opponent. To this end, he made constant use of a small video camera and tape recorder to play back the moves he had just made. Soon, in The Man with the Golden Gun, ran into the same problem. None of the fighters were used to taking (or sucking in) punches. In fact, in Tae Kwon Do, there is very little physical contact, so one can imagine their surprise and distress at being on the receiving end of Soon's deadly reverse kicks and punches. If the fight is to look real, the blows have to land.

The young Korean, realising that he was starting to lose friends, called all the fighters over to explain the problem. To help get his point over, he had Crawford deliver a full-blooded front kick. The blow made contact, Soon survived and the martial artists understood.

When asked how he sees the future of Kung Fu pictures, Soon is optimistic. What started out originally as a blood and thunder exhibition of Kung Fu acrobatics, now shows signs of becoming a more subtle entity in its own right. In much the same way as the gunfight is, as often as not, the high point of a Western, so too should the martial arts scene be used sparingly. "The old premise of any excuse for a fight," he contends, "is now just not good enough. The plot must have substance and any fight scene must stand up in relation to it."

Soon Taik Oh may not be another Bruce Lee but to be quite honest, how could there be another? This young actor from South Korea is simply one of the finest actors/martial artists we see emerging right now, and the chances are that he will make a sizeable name for himself. Soon is a thinking man and is extremely modest about his many accomplishments in the martial arts field. He is drawn to this field perhaps because he sees in it a way of seeing himself. As he says, "When you grow older and become more aware of yourself, you ask what do you depend upon within yourself? Is it religion, gambling? Whatever it is that you depend upon within yourself as a human being. I look for it within my gut.

Your psychological centres are to the gut. When you find them, your hip becomes stable. In martial arts, if your hip is not steady, you're nowhere. In Japanese Noh Dance, if your hip is not to the right place, you're not considered an accomplished actor. If you find it at the gut level, you can be flexible, yet, at the same time, maintain active but intensive quietude. I'm trying to get it there and the day I really do, I'll consider myself an accomplished martial artist."

Here it is, KFM's third Back Issue Bonanza offer. As our permanent readers will be well aware of, our first Back Issue offer (Issues No. 1 2, 3, 4 and 5) sold out almost as soon as we advertised it. Offer number 2 (Issues No. 4, 5, 6, 7 and 8) has now also completely sold out, so please don't write in for it. Now we are offering Back Issue Bonanza No. 3 which includes issues no. 8, 9, 10, 11 and 12 . . . that means FIVE copies of KFM for just £1. Make sure you send in early to avoid disappointment. To complete your collection of KFM send your cheque or P.O. for £1 made out to Kung-Fu Monthly to: **Back Issue Bonanza No. 3, Kung-Fu Monthly, 39 Goodge Street, London W1P 1FD.** *(Please allow three weeks for delivery and make sure you don't forget your name and address!)*

KICKBACK: THE LETTERS

Hi there, it's me again, Jenny Lee, with a whole page of letters from readers around the world. Now that *KFM* had gone 'International,' my mailbag reads like the index of a geography book. America, Canada, Australia, South Africa, Europe - the list is endless! The only things wrong is that now there are so many more letters and really, one page is just no good at all. I do feel really bad when I read through your letters and know that I can only print just a very tiny fraction of them. Still, don't despair if your letter doesn't get printed the first time. Do please keep writing in as I really love to here what is going on out there amongst all you Kung Fu fans. Well, enough from me, so on with the show...

PEN PAL WANTED

Dear Jenny,
I'm almost sure that this is the first letter you have received from South Africa. Nevertheless, I feel that all Bruce Lee fans are one family. After seeing *The Big Boss* and *Enter the Dragon*, I have absolutely become mad about Bruce Lee. For me, he will live forever. I would like to congratulate you and the rest of the *KFM* staff on compiling such a fabulous, wonderful magazine. Could you help me in finding a Chinese male pen pal please? I am a girl and seventeen years of age. I would appreciate letters from Hong Kong especially. Long live the Little Dragon!
Ina Knoetze, Orkney, Republic of South Africa

Dear Ina,
Thanks for your kind words and I hope you find a Pen Pal quickly. Other KFM readers in search of a Pen-Pal are: Cory Wong, Hollywood, California; George Abiona, Ibavan, Nigeria (who is 30 and would like a Chinese or Japanese pen pal of either sex); B.A. Peters, Wrexham, North Wales (preferably Chinese); Anthony John Davies, Caerphilly, Wales (who is 17 and would like a female, oriental pen-pal); Sandra Unsworth, Maesycwmmer, Mid-Glamorgan (who is 25 and would like a male Chinese pen pal); Julie Parry, Anfield, Liverpool (who is 15 and would like a male Chinese pen pal aged between 15 and 18).

THE CENSORS

Dear Jenny,
I have just recently come to stay in this country. As an American, may I congratulate you on your fine magazine. We have nothing like this in the States. I have some questions I would like to ask you: Do you have any Bruce Lee mugs left? How many languages could Bruce speak? I am only 16, but I have seen all Bruce's movies. in the US, we have an 'R' certificate. This means 'restricted' so anyone under 17 can get in if they are accompanied by an adult. Why don't the British censors do the same? I sneaked to see *The Way of the Dragon* and was most disappointed when the part which Bruce uses two sets of nunchakus was extracted. What happened to it? That was one of the best parts of the film!
John Stuart, Tillydrone, Aberdeen

Dear John,
First up, let me wish you a warm welcome to Britain, although, I do wish the weather would do a bit of a warm welcoming as well). As any regular Kickback reader will already know, letters complaining about the ridiculous actions of the British censors take up quite a fair bit of my attention. Honestly, the way they butcher Bruce's films, not to mention a host of less known Kung Fu movies, you would think knew more about the hamburger industry than the film industry! Your 'R' certificate certainly sounds a much better idea than totally banning Bruce's younger fans from the cinema. As for your other questions, Bruce could speak English and Chinese (both Mandarin and Cantonese dialects) fluently, although in his later years, he got pretty much into the habit of speaking in English most of the time. And as for the Bruce Lee mug; Well, I'm afraid they all went a long, long time ago!

MARTIAL ARTS BOOKS

Dear Jenny,
There is one thing that really annoys me. In the shops, there is now available, a good selection of books on the martial arts which weren't in evidence three years ago. These books are clearly being written to cash in on the so-called 'Kung Fu Craze,' yet nearly all of them dismiss the Kung Fu films and Bruce Lee with barely a word. One book does at least say that 'no article on Kung Fu, no matter how brief, is complete without mentioning Bruce Lee,' but it also says that although Lee may been good box office, true martial arts enthusiasts have been less than enthusiastic. Don't the authors of the books realise that Lee was a Martial Arts Master in his own right and not just a film star? Also, if it hadn't been for Lee, they needn't have bothered to write their book because there wouldn't be the people who were interested in reading them.
Diane Webb, Dulwich.
P.S. By the way, my two friends and I had a fantastic holiday in Hong Kong this summer. We visited No.14 Cumberland Road and also walked up Hankow Road (the road that John Saxon rides up in a rickshaw in *Enter the Dragon*). Hong Kong is is a terrific place. There is only one problem - we can't wait to go back.

Dear Diane,
How lucky you are to have been to Hong Kong and seen the true home of the Little Dragon. Both my editors here on KFM have also made the pilgrimage and they agree that Hong Kong is a truly amazing place. One day, I'll get there too,
believe me! I do agree with you that so many people have now jumped on the 'Kung Fu Bandwagon,' that it looks like a travelling circus now. It's unfortunate, but there will always be people around wanting to cash in on other people's talent. That is exactly why Bruce Lee was, for many years, hesitant about publishing The Tao of Jeet Kune Do (see Bruce Sawford's article in this issue). He was scared that it would be seized on by charlatans who would use it to 'teach' Jeet Kune Do. Still, I can certainly say I am glad that The Tao of Jeet Kune Do has now been published. Remember too that there are some really good books on Bruce Lee and Kung Fu around.

SCISSOR HAPPY CENSORS

Dear Jenny,
Thank you for printing such a brilliant magazine and for helping fans like me to find out the truth about the real Bruce Lee! I would also like to thank you for giving me new hope concerning Bruce's film *The Way of the Dragon*, which I have seen 10 times. I will certainly go looking for Chinese film houses that will finally show this incredible film before the scissor-happy censors get their grubby hands on it.
Chris Wenlock, West Bromwich, Warley

Dear Chris,
You win this month's award for having seen a Bruce Lee movie the most times! How about it, Little Dragon fans? Can anyone top ten times? Hope you do find an uncut version, Chris. As John's letter above mentioned, at least one and probably a lot more vital scenes have been lopped by the senseless censors! It really does make my blood boil to think that they can intrude into our life like that!

Kung-Fu Monthly's Inside Story on Bruce Lee's Last Movie!

Although the fame of Bruce Lee has, by now, spread far and wide, much of his life still remains shrouded in mystery and intrigue. Not the least of these mysteries was the film on which Lee was working at the time of his death — the ominously titled *Game of Death*. But until now all requests for information have been met with a wall of silence.

Now KUNG-FU MONTHLY, the world's best selling martial arts publication, has learned the truth about Bruce Lee's unfinished masterpiece.

After travelling to Hong-Kong and visiting Lee's film studios, the editors of KUNG FU MONTHLY have compiled a Special Issue of KFM entitled "BRUCE LEE'S GAME OF DEATH". This Special Issue will be packed with facts and information and stuffed with colour pix from the film itself.

For your collector's edition of the fantastic BRUCE LEE'S GAME OF DEATH just send a cheque or P.O. for 60p (includes post and packing) made out to Kung Fu Monthly and addressed to:

GAME OF DEATH OFFER
Kung Fu Monthly,
39 Goodge Street,
London W1P 1FD.

(Allow three weeks for delivery and don't forget your name and address!)

EDITORIAL

Hi there Kung Fu fans...

First up, *KFM* presents an amazing scoop - an interview with Wu Ngan. In case you've forgotten, Wu was the young servant boy that Mr. Lee brought into the house when Bruce was just a small lad. He and the Little Dragon got along so well together, that Mr. Lee decided to adopt Wu into the family. Wu got about as close to Bruce as anyone, so you can imagine, it's a pretty sensational interview!

Our other story is a special report on an interview featuring the Little Dragon's younger brother, Robert. Now a singing star in his own right, Robert, understandably, has a lot to say about Bruce's early years - the time when they were growing up together - and talks about the influences that finally rocketed to stardom, the world's greatest ever martial artist. As an extra bonus, Chuck Norris comes right in on the action and tells about the time when he first met Bruce and what happened while they were filming *The Way of the*

Dragon.

Finally, for those of you who haven't already bought it, don't whatever you do, miss out on a copy of our *KFM* Special Issue, Bruce Lee's *Game of Death*. Literally packed to the brim with facts, information and superb colour pictures taken straight from the film itself, Bruce Lee's *Game of Death* has already become a collector's item.

That's about all from me for this month, so I'll see you next issue.

Felix Yen

Felix Yen
Editor-in-Chief

AN INTERVIEW WITH ROBERT LEE AND CHUCK NORRIS

There can have been few people closer to the Little Dragon than his younger brother, Robert. Guitarist and singer, Robert Lee was there when it all happened. He saw the struggles, the setbacks and finally, the meteoric rise to fame of a man who was quite simply, without equal. *KFM* discusses a recent interview that featured Robert and world champion martial artist Chuck Norris.

Much has been said in the past about Bruce's fitness, his methods, his films and so on. Less, however, is known about his reasons for turning to Kung Fu and the martial arts. When asked what he thought was the turning point in Bruce's life, the one occasion that perhaps more than any other, set the Little Dragon on the path of the ancient teachings, Robert replied with an interesting tale.

His brother, Robert felt, was always rather a violent child, frequently involved in street fights and brawls. One day, after eating in a Hong Kong restaurant, Bruce and his buddy were set upon by a rival bunch of kids. Fortunately, for the two of them, no sooner had the fight broken out, than a friend's car arrived on the scene and the gang fled. This time he was let off the hook. But once bitten, twice shy. Bruce decided that there had to be a better way to protect himself and, according to Robert, he soon started thinking about Wing Chun, the 'in' martial arts style at that time. The system, Robert went on, concentrates on economy of effort and to Bruce, it seemed the most logical approach for protection. Well, one thing led to another and before long, the Little Dragon was meeting for the first time the man who was to shape his future, Yip Man. Bruce was just fourteen years old when he met Yip Man and he took to Kung Fu like a fish to water. It was as though he'd found his first real interest in life and nothing was going to get in his way.

The conversation then turned to Bruce's film career which, as Robert pointed out, began at the early age of six. Of course, these early films were not in any sense Kung Fu pictures. They were fairly ordinary Chinese romance tales in which Bruce usually took the part of the child hero character. That kind of film was very popular then and there is little

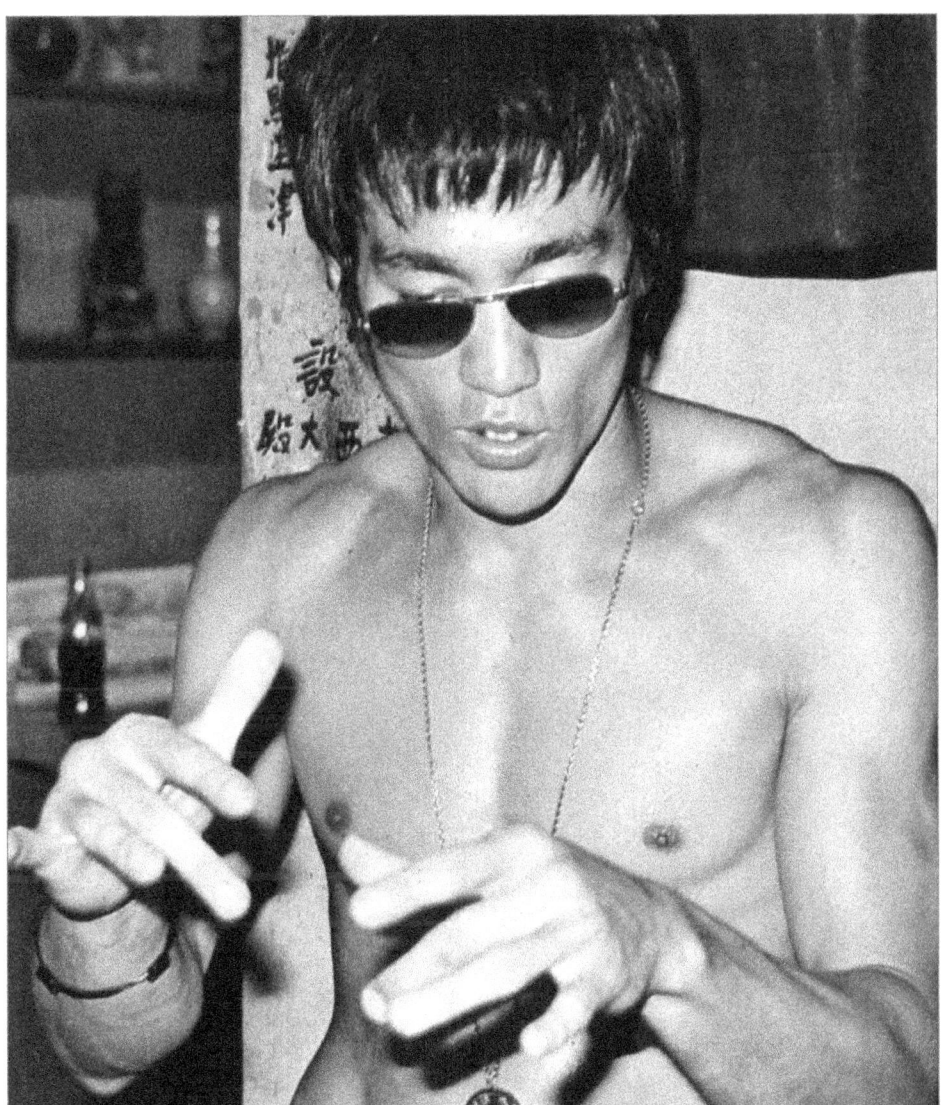

doubt that the young dragon did his best. Unfortunately, some of those films needed a lot of improving.

Robert was asked how he felt about Bruce successfully eliminating the old Oriental/Asian stereotype in the movies and TV and that, through Bruce's efforts, the Chinese actor needed no longer only to portray the insidiously weak Charlie Chan and Fu Man Chu characters.

Robert replied that throughout his life, Bruce had revolted against the dramatic portray of the Chinese stereotype. He had hated it and had always insisted if he ever should get the chance to go into films or TV, he would never allow himself to be used like that. Robert quoted Bruce as saying, "Lord help me bring the Chinese into equality with all the

other races." A noble sentiment, although he was never to have it completely his own way. Old customs die hard and it's easy to imagine the difficulties involved in trying to crack through all those spits of tradition. Bruce, as Robert recalls, felt so strongly about what he considered to be a "disgrace to the Chinese culture." that he never tired in his efforts to redress the situation.

The next question put to Robert was, why did he think Bruce had been so successful? What quality did the Little Dragon possess that enabled him so dramatically and eloquently to portray Chinese people as something other than that portrayed by, in particular, American film makers of the past.

Robert felt there were three aspects to consider. The first was the influence of their father. Mr. Lee's years with the Cantonese Opera, in fact some forty in all, and his subsequent rise to fame, all served to ensure that Bruce was raised in the atmosphere of a show business home. As if this wasn't enough, the Little Dragon had also inherited his father's dynamic personality and, as Robert pointed out, Bruce was able to project that personality in front of a camera or in front of people. The third aspect was Bruce's sincerity. This much abused word must surely fit the bill here as it was the king of the martial arts himself who showed to everyone that Chinese actors can and must be taken seriously.

A number of times during the interview, Robert referred to his brother in the present tense and he was asked why. Robert replied, "I don't know for sure. There's something that's in all of us. Just knowing him or maybe when I'm seeing him in a film, I feel his presence all the time with me. When I'm playing my guitar or singing or walking down the street, whatever, he's always with me." Judging by the many letters that continue to pour through the door of our *KFM* offices, a great number of other people continue to feel just the same way.

It's interesting, too, to ask why people identify so closely with Bruce. Is it because he was just simply a 'nice' person? He was after all well known for helping people and whenever there was any trouble, he would always first of all protect his family. As an old pupil of Bruce's once said, "His character just came out, you know. People see it and they understand it. When a guy's acting, in a way he's got a much harder job on his hands. Bruce was for real... he didn't have to act."

Naturally, Robert was questioned about the Little Dragon's tragic death. Was he satisfied with the official reasons given at the time of the inquest? After some thought, he replied, "Yes and no." Bruce certainly did die of a cerebral oedema, which is a swelling of the brain, brought on by an allergy to a certain medicine he was taking. Robert, however, had reservations, and these seemed to centre around the fact that many people, including a number of Bruce's friends, tended to feel that the whole thing went rather deeper than it seemed. Did he feel that his brother was the victim of a plot? Had he in fact been murdered by the angry 'keepers' of Kung Fu's secrets? This story has, after all, popped up in the press more than once. Robert's reply was short and to the point. "In Hong Kong when he died, there were people really going out to make a buck or two and they didn't really care how they went about it. They made up all kinds of tales about Bruce's death and so on and I guess those stories have just travelled all over the world." These are reassuring words indeed and hopefully they will go some way towards dispelling the ugly rumours that surround that tragic accident Robert was brief and to the point when asked about his brother's style. He summed it up as being a combination of economy of movement, immense speed and power and most important of all, a realisation of the need for complete physical fitness. It would probably in fact be reasonable to say that, without physical fitness, Bruce would have had very little. His dedication to succeed had, at all times, to be matched by a superb body condition and never in his star-studded career did he neglect to remember this.

Robert accounted for his brother's almost mythical success, in life and even more so, after death, by noting that what Bruce did on the screen was something that was new. "Nobody had done it before and he just played what he was - a true, sincere martial artist".

The Little Dragon really did manage to project that image and the public soon cottoned on that it was something quite original. They'd never seen anything like it before and it was pure dynamite. Robert continued, "I believe it myself and I'm his brother!"

Chuck Norris then came in on the action and was asked, first of all, how and where he had met Bruce. He replied, "I met Bruce nine years ago in New York when I was just starting professionally and heading for the world title."

Apparently they were booked into the same hotel and while going up in the lift, they got talking about philosophies and techniques. "As we got to the seventh floor - the one on which Bruce was staying - we were still talking, so we stepped into the hallway. It was eleven o'clock at night and somehow we worked out 'til seven o'clock the next morning." Chuck admitted that it only seemed like an hour had gone by. He was so absorbed with the Little Dragon's knowledge and technique that he described it as, "just a fascinating night."

When asked about the film *The Way of the Dragon*, Chuck related that Bruce had called him from Hong Kong, telling him that he wanted to do a film with a lot of fight scenes. Bruce was convinced it was going to be a classic, right from the start, but to make certain, he and Chuck did a great deal of research and worked solidly until the scenes were really there. "While we were filming the battle in the Coliseum", Chuck went on, "Bruce at one point looked around the arena and said, 'I wonder what it was like fifteen hundred years ago? You know, to be doing this for real gladiators?'".

Chuck had a few interesting things to say about himself. Strangely enough, he was never what you would call an athlete whilst at school, although not apparently for want of trying. He feels strongly that part of the general appeal of Kung Fu rests on the fact that one need not necessary be athletically inclined. Anyone, he feels, can participate, and will be as good as they want to be. He went on, "I always tell people this. I was not an athlete, but I had a strong desire to excel in the martial arts. Through my desire and determination, I've now been world champion for six years. Still, I say if I can do it, anyone can."

The martial arts can obviously be rather violent, but of course it's also about concentration and mental discipline. Chuck felt, in some ways sadly, that most people relate to the arts as strictly a physical application. Naturally, as the Little Dragon himself would often say, equally important is your mental condition, or as Chuck put it, "the increase of your mental concentration span." The Little Dragon's Jeet Kune Do was concerned, not just with physical speed and fitness, but with everything. If the brain acts slow, then so will the rest of you.

So, how long is this renewed interest in the martial arts likely to last? Well, to be honest, it's rather hard to say. Bruce's answer, and probably the right one, would almost certainly have been, "For many years to come." The Little Dragon's contribution to the Kung Fu world was, and still is, so totally immense that even time itself will have difficulty in slowing it down. Bruce unlocked a lid and now everyone can see into the box. Even though the man who opened the box is no longer with us, people can still see in. Bruce, too, lived and died an entertainer and once a film has been recorded on celluloid, it's there once and for all and everyone can see it. So long as people are interested in genius, then so too will they be interested in Bruce Lee, the King of Kung Fu.

WU NGAN SPEAKS OUT ON BRUCE LEE

Lifelong buddy, co-actor, servant, butler, co-company directors... At one time or another, to the Little Dragon, Wu Ngan was all of these, and more. Up to now, meetings with Wu have been rare and of very little consequence. Now, at last, *KFM* has done the impossible. Exclusively for readers of *Kung-Fu Monthly*, we present the first, no punches pulled interview with the man who was there all the way through. From schooldays to stardom, wherever the Little Dragon went, you could be sure that Wu Ngan was not too far behind.

Almost deliberately, one feels, Wu has kept out of the limelight. For a man who has spent a great number of years in the company of the fabulous Bruce Lee, remarkably few people even seem to know his name. More, though, would know his face. He appeared in *Enter the Dragon*, *The Way of the Dragon* and *The Man and the Legend* and although the parts he took were small, his face becomes instantly recognisable. He landed the roles, partly because, with Bruce's teaching, he had become quite a reasonable martial artist. But the Little Dragon also liked to help his friends along, and often that meant finding them bit-parts in his productions.

But in the case of Wu Ngan, it seemed to go further than this. Investigations carried out after Bruce's death by a local newspaper, purported to reveal that Bruce had died almost penniless. They claimed too that Wu was a major beneficiary to Bruce's estate and rumours, naturally, spread like wildfire. But this is going too far ahead. Let's step back now to the time when Wu first appeared in the Lee household. How did he get there and why was he adopted into the family in the first place?

KFM: Wu, when you first came into the Lee household in Nathan Road, you were, I believe, ten years old and at that time, Bruce was five.

Wu: Yes, that's right. When I got there, Bruce was really very small. But I do remember that he was at school and should have been studying rather more than he was. Almost immediately, I just found that we got on very well together. You know how it is. Somehow we seemed to hit it off.

KFM: Can you recollect anything about your life before the time you got to meet Bruce?

Wu: No, unfortunately, I can't remember very much. I was very young then and about the only thing that sticks in my memory is that it was shortly after the Japanese surrender.

KFM: Was Hong Kong a rough place to live in then?

Wu: Conditions at that time were actually quite good. A lot of people think that things were rather worse than that but I really didn't get that feeling. Of course, you have to remember that I was only ten years old at the time!

KFM: What was your impression of Mr. and Mrs. Lee?

Wu: They were very kind people and I had the greatest respect for them. Bruce's father, as you probably know, was Cantonese and his mother, Eurasian. I believe that she was born in Shanghai. To start with, I came into the house just to do work but in the end, things just turned out differently.

KFM: Would you say that at that time Bruce showed any signs of flowering into the supreme martial artist he eventually became?

Wu: I must say I don't recall it crossing my mind, although looking back on it, he was

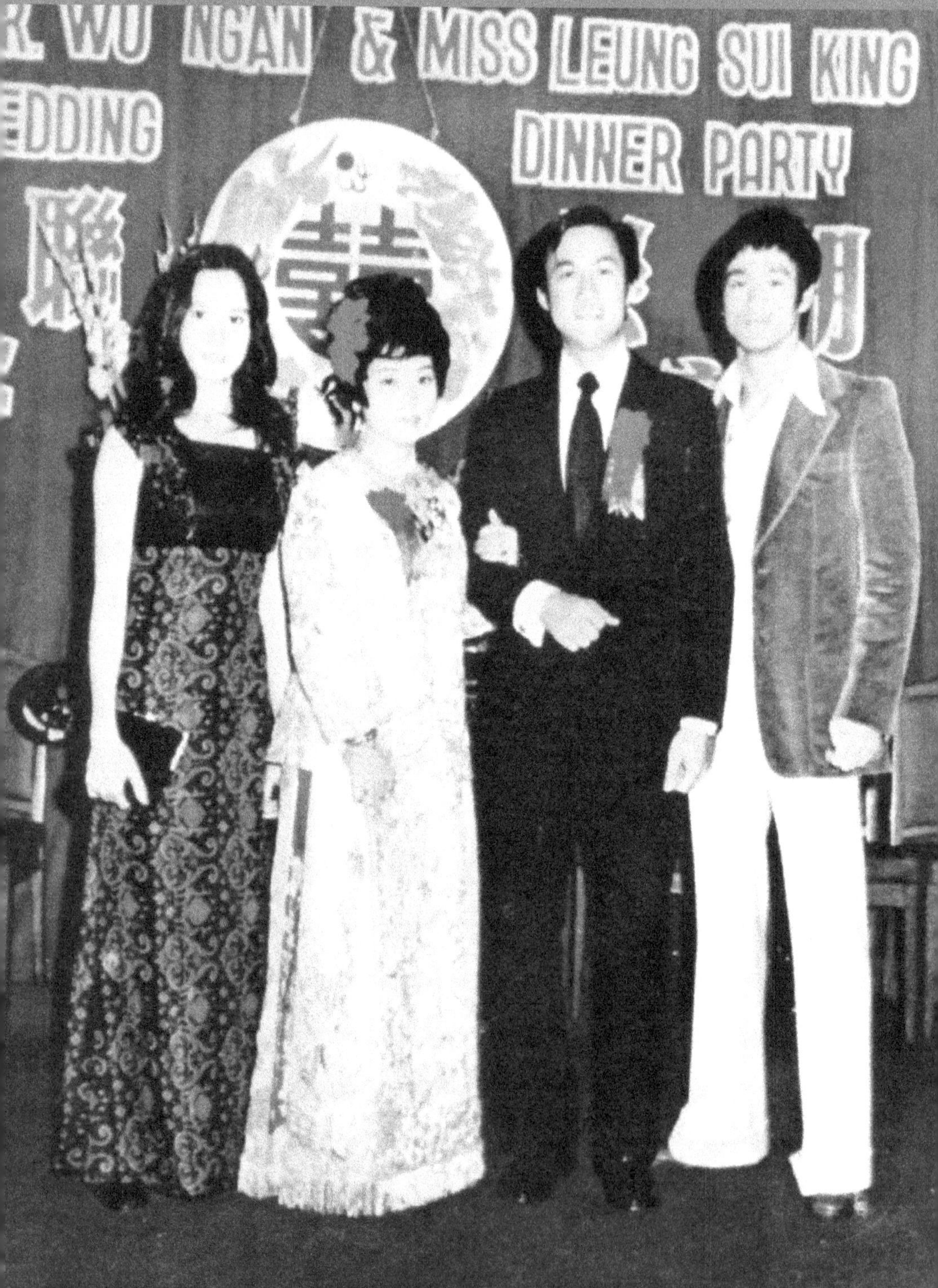
WU NGAN & MISS LEUNG SUI KING
DINNER PARTY

always kinda interested in fighting and weapons and to an extent, in getting his own way. I guess he was what you would call extrovert. Maybe that should have given me a clue. One thing I'll never forget, though. Once, when I hadn't been there long, he and I were playing piggy back rides. Bruce was up on my back and I was bounding along the path, until suddenly, I tripped and fell. My passenger was OK, but in the process I lost two front teeth. That's something you don't forget! Thinking about it, I must say he was pretty naughty. He was often getting into fights over pinching and eating other people's grapes and oranges. That used to happen in school a lot too.

KFM: What was it about him that made him such a good friend?

Wu: Well, above all else, he was a thoughtful person and, of course, always exciting to be with. I don't think anyone could ever ask more of a school buddy.

KFM: You've told us a lot about Bruce, but how did you get along with Peter and Robert?

Wu: My best friend, of course, was Bruce. I found Peter to be a very quiet sort of person. You know, he kept himself to himself a lot, usually he preferred to be alone. Peter in fact keeps telling me that he's coming over here to Great Britain sometime soon, although he's been saying that for so long that I'll believe it when I see it!

KFM: Well, if he does, well be right there waiting for him!

Wu: Anyway, to move on to Robert. He and I got along fine. Strangely, he seemed to fall somewhere in between Bruce and Peter. He wasn't exactly a ball of energy, but then he wasn't really what you'd call quiet. As a matter of interest, I hear he's just signed a contract for Hong Kong television so he's doing very well. I must say I'm very happy to hear it

KFM: Wu, I believe that at one time Bruce and Robert used to stage performances of one sort or another. Can you tell me what went on?

Wu: Well, I don't know if you've heard this already, but Bruce really got into dancing; in fact at one time, he was the Hong Kong Cha Cha Champion! Of course, he had to be pretty agile to do all that and I'm sure It stood him in good stead for the Kung Fu to come. So, anyway, the two of them would get out there, Robert playing his guitar and singing and Bruce dancing away with him. Later on, the Little Dragon got so good at both dancing and Kung Fu, that he charged between fifty and a hundred dollars for a one hour lesson of either.

KFM: How much of an influence would you say Bruce's father had on him?

Wu: Bruce was just generally active when he was a little boy and he spent a lot of time watching his father when he appeared in the Cantonese opera. Perhaps even then, something inside was telling him to make full use of the experience he was getting. Actually, although I myself didn't appear with Bruce in any of the early films, I did in fact make the odd appearance or two with the opera. Yes, Bruce was certainly active and sometimes too much so. He seemed to have a fascination for weapons and he used to play around with, in particular, nunchakus. I still can't honestly say, though, that I ever thought he would become a star.

KFM: Can you tell us anything about those films of Bruce's you appeared in?

Wu: One was with Chuck Norris called *The Way of the Dragon*. I played a waiter in that and I was on Bruce's side. Then there was *Enter the Dragon*. I was supporting John Saxon there, you know, and wearing the yellow suit, I was an enemy that time. Other than those two, there was also The Silent Flute affair. That was supposed to co-star James Coburn

and be filmed in India. Well, I got as far as Los Angeles with Bruce but then somehow, things just didn't work out. I think the trouble was that James wanted to change the script around a little to make it, so he believed, more suitable for Western audiences. Bruce, who had written it all himself, just refused. No way would they agree, so eventually the whole thing got shelved. Interestingly, I believe that Robert maybe has plans to do something with it again. Finally, I made an appearance in *The Man and the Legend*, in the funeral scene.

KFM: Something not generally known is that Bruce actually stayed In Great Britain for a few days during 1971. Do you recall the visit?

Wu: Oh yes. He was here for a short stay before going on to Los Angeles. All I can tell you is that he stayed at a very famous hotel in Park Lane and enjoyed several walks in Hyde Park. Naturally, he paid a visit to Gerrard Street which is London's China Town and while there, had a meal in Lee Ho Fook's, a very famous Chinese restaurant. You're right though, in saying that few people realise he was here. For some reason, it just didn't seem to get around.

KFM: If Bruce hadn't so tragically died in 1973, where do you think he would be by now?

Wu: Things would be so good if he hadn't died. I'm quite certain of that. There were lots of producers waiting for him, although Bruce really had no plans to work for anybody else. The sort of money being offered would probably have made him the richest actor of all time. I know that Sophia Loren's husband, Carlo Ponti, was very keen to do a deal, but at the time, Bruce's plans were to go to Los Angeles for half a year and then back to Hong Kong. That was when he died.

KFM: What can you say about Bruce's last, unfinished film, *Game of Death*?

Wu: To start with, as I expect you've heard, it's only one third complete. All the fight scenes in the pagoda are on film, although what you may not know is that the fight at the door of the tower is missing. I really can't guess what they're going to do about that problem. As far as the linking scenes are concerned, I imagine that they'll be looking for a double but even that will prove difficult. I mean, how do you double for Bruce Lee?

KFM: Then of course, there will be a problem with Bruce's words. As far as I know, all Bruce's films were shot 'wild.' That's to say, without dialogue and it was then added on afterwards in whichever language was needed. Even so, in *Enter the Dragon*, the voice was Bruce's.

Wu: In your particular case, you will indeed miss hearing Bruce's voice. Don't forget, though, that he wasn't able, for instance, to speak Mandarin and another person's voice would have to be dubbed over anyway. At least in the fight sequences, the cries are all from Bruce which, to say the least, must be better than nothing.

KFM: Changing the subject, can you throw any light on Bruce's reported use of cannabis? It's something that we at *KFM* get quite a few letters about.

Wu: Well, to start with, he didn't smoke ordinary cigarettes, which is probably the worst evil of all. Neither did he drink very much. He did claim, however, that occasional use of cannabis helped him think, although I know the amounts he used were very small and the occasions very infrequent.

KFM: Yes, the reports one hears, linking his death with cannabis, are absolutely ridiculous. No doctor in the world would back up such a theory. Can you tell me how Bruce's son, Brandon, is getting on?

Wu: Oh, Brandon is very well and in fact, I hear that he's just got another belt. It looks as though he's really following in Bruce's footsteps, although I believe he had to give up for a year because he broke a leg. Also, I hear he's being trained by Danny Inosanto, who is probably one of the best Jeet Kune Do exponents around.

KFM: Turning to you, personally, for a moment, can you tell me your plans?

Wu: My plans are rather vague right now. I'm really not doing a lot of Kung Fu these days although I do still practice a little. After all, Bruce taught me a great deal and it would be a shame to let it all go. As far as films are concerned, I can't honestly see myself doing any more. My heart's not really in it now Bruce has gone.

KFM: Will you be staying in Great Britain for a while?

Wu: That's hard to say. I really like it here, but on the other hand, I am getting a little homesick.

KFM: Finally Wu, how do you remember Bruce?

Wu: I remember him most as a person, because Bruce himself was a very just man. When he made films, he did it to show the world that the Chinese man is not some sort of pig-tailed buffoon, but a real person with thoughts, feelings and talents. I want the world to remember him for that.

So there it is. Wu Ngan was there at the beginning, he stayed the course and was there right at the end. Such was the high esteem that Bruce appeared to hold in him, it is said that eighty per cent of the Little Dragon's interest in Concord was, in fact, owned by his 'butler,' Wu. Following Bruce's death, rumour had it that Wu also owned a considerable slice of the Little Dragon's Kowloon home. When asked about it at the time, Wu simply replied, "He trusted me." Maybe that just about sums it up.

THE MANY FACES OF BRUCE LEE

A man of many parts - and faces too! Here's just a selection, ranging from the blood-curdling to the comic! Top to bottom, left to right:

a. Bruce in classical style, *b.* Insulted, *c.* Ready for the kill, *d.* In a jocular mood, *e.* Having a good time, *f.* In mid battle, *g.* Poses for the camera, *h.* Relaxed, *i.* The famous look.

KICKBACK: THE LETTERS

Hi there... Jenny Lee here again to answer your sackfulls of letters. It seems like I've really stirred up a hornet's nest by asking readers to write in and tell me how many times they've seen Bruce's movies. You can judge for yourself just how fanatical Bruce's fans can really be by looking at the three letters I've printed below. And these three are just the tip of the iceberg! Keep on writing in, even if your letter doesn't happen to be published. I do read them all! Until next month...

BRUCE LEE LIVES

Dear Jenny,
I have been reading a book entitled *Bruce Lee Lives*? In this book, an American journalist claims he 'broke up' a drug mob with a Chinese crack force. He was attacked by a bunch of martial arts crooks and was rescued by a small martial artist who he claims was Bruce Lee. This little 'agent' was amazingly fast, powerful and beat expert martial artists, a feat that only Bruce Lee could have performed. Also he taped the voice of an agent with whom he arranged to meet one dark night. The journalist compared the voice with the tapes perfectly! When Bruce 'died,' his coffin had to be changed at Seattle which was very strange? Also, there was a scratch mark on the coffin. You see, there is more evidence that Bruce Lee is alive! Do you think that he is alive?
Billy Gibbons, Stanmore, Scotland

Dear Billy,
The short answer to your question is ... no! I too have read the book you mention and it is a load of old rubbish; pure fiction from start to finish. The plot itself is so unlikely that it is laughable. The descriptions of Hong Kong are in many parts extremely inaccurate. I think at one point the author says that 90% of the Hong Kong population live on junks. Ludicrous! Bruce only ever spoke on one of his films - Enter the Dragon - so matching up voices is pretty far fetched. As for changing Bruce's coffin; the reason this was done was because of the scratches and battering it received in transit from Hong Kong to Seattle and not an abnormal occurrence. No, unfortunately Bruce is dead, and although we'd all love him to return, we should get on with the job of living and keeping his memory alive.

HOW MANY TIMES?

Dear Jenny,
In last month's *KFM* No.16, you issued a healthy challenge to *KFM* leaders concerning Bruce Lee's *The Way of the Dragon*. A letter in that issue said the person had seen it 10 times. For the same reasons as that person (i.e. to see a completely uncut version) I have seen *The Way of the Dragon* 39 times! Added to that, I have seen *Enter the Dragon* 67 times, *Fist of Fury* 26 and *The Big Boss* 24 times!
Raymond Tidswell, St. Mary, Essex

Dear Jenny,
After reading this month's *KFM* and reading how many times Chris Wenlock has seen *The Way of the Dragon*, I thought you'd be interested in how many times I have seen Bruce's films: *Enter the Dragon* 52 times, *Fist of Fury* 50, *The Big Boss* 42, *The Way of the Dragon* 21. Perhaps you may think I have exaggerated, but my family and friends can vouch for me. To top it all off, I have met and spoken with Linda Lee when she came to London. She talked to myself and friends for a good 2 ½ hours which was fantastic.
Carole Heister, Colville, Leicester

Dear Jenny,
I have been to see *The Way of the Dragon* 12 times, *Enter the Dragon* 10, *Fist of Fury* and *The Big Boss* 8 times each. I have been a Bruce Lee fan since 1970 and I am now 17. I think it's stupid that Bruce's films should be X certificate and half of them cut to ribbons by the censor. I feel sorry for all people who are fans of Bruce Lee but are under 18. I have had to lie about my age so that I can see the King in action.
Kevin Angell, Chippenham, Wiltshire

Thanks very much to all you Bruce Lee fans who wrote in to tell me how many times you'd seen the Little Dragon in action. You really are all amazing!

GAME OF DEATH MAGAZINE

Dear Jenny,
I would first like to congratulate you and *KFM* for producing a fantastic collectors edition called *Game of Death*. It had excellent photos of Bruce and his last film. I only hope you will do the same for the other great films he made. I would like you to answer a few questions for me. Did George Lazenby learn Jeet Kune Do? Did Bruce Lee learn Judo and/or Tai Chi Chuan? Please print a photo of Bruce Lee from the film *Fist of Fury*?
Carl Humpage, Newcastle

Dear Carl,
Thanks for the kind words about Game of Death. It appears to have been almost a total sell-out, although Bruce our mail order chief has informed me that he has kept a sizeable bundle of copies for KFM readers. Still, I guess you'd better hurry. Now, to your questions... George Lazenby, although a converted martial arts fan, did not, as far as we can discover, learn Jeet Kune Do. Bruce was extremely proficient in Karate and Tai Chi Chuan was, in fact, the very first martial art he learned, taught to him by his father in a Hong Kong park. I'll pass on your Fist of Fury request to our editors.

EDITORIAL

Hi there Kung Fu fans...

Well, it looks like *KFM* has scooped again! First off this time, there's a close look at the man who fought Bruce Lee at the top of that pagoda. Yes, it's a sensational *Game of Death* extra, featuring for the first time ever that giant king of the American basketball circuit, Kareem Abdul-Jabbar. Never one to let the cat out of the bag, Kareem finally climbs down and talks frankly about his relationship with the Little Dragon, where he first met Bruce and how he landed the part in *Game of Death*. Jeet Kune Do gets a mention too and Kareem gives his impressions of how and why the whole system evolved the way it did. Absorbing reading indeed!

Slotting into second place this issue is *KFM*'s own punch by punch account of some of the legendary Chinese fighters of yesterday. Most of them were masters in their own right, but did they ever match up to the genius of Bruce Lee? Some undoubtedly would have become more famous had television and the cinema been around a hundred years ago. *KFM* introduces you to them, one by one, recounting on the way some of the facts, myths and legends surrounding these martial men of old.

Robert Lee, Bruce's guitar-playing brother, has grabbed the headlines again this month. Shock revelations about his possibly deteriorating health came in just a couple of days ago. I'm sure you'll all join us here at *KFM* in wishing him a speedy recovery.

That's all from me - see you next month.

Felix Yen

Felix Yen
Editor-in-Chief

BRUCE LEE VS KAREEM ABDUL JABBAR

It's a *Game of Death*. Bruce Lee's mighty powerhouse of physical talent has seen him safely through four floors of that, by now, famous Korean pagoda. Just one more battle to go and the treasure is his. Suddenly, Bruce's last remaining aide is seized by a seven foot tall opponent and hurled down to the level below. Giving away almost two feet in height, the Little Dragon has to pull everything out of his bag of tricks and more, before finally defeating the giant defender of the fifth and final floor.

Without doubt, the fight, by any standards, was a classic. Yet, strangely, Abdul-Jabbar, Bruce's massive opponent, was and still is by trade, a basketball player and indeed his team's star attraction! What could have induced this mighty man to mix it with the King of the martial arts? *KFM* investigates.

Formally as 'Big Lew' Alcindor, Kareem Abdul-Jabbar was born twenty eight years ago in Manhattan, New York. Right from very early on, the most startling thing about Big Lew was his height. His father, a policeman hailing originally from Trinidad, found it hard indeed to account for the rate at which his son was shooting up. Fortunately though, Kareem was also athletically minded and with the help of his school's physical education instructor, he soon turned his attentions towards basketball. The game suited the young giant in every way. His height and his superb physical condition all combined to raise him to the position of a number one attraction.

That's not to say though that there hadn't been difficulties! His relationship with the sporting press, for instance, was never a particularly happy one. In similar fashion to the Little Dragon, Big Lew was loathed to suffer fools gladly and an icy refusal to answer trivial questions has led in the past to accusations of his being 'unfriendly, uncooperative and un-American!'

BLINDING SKILL

And yet, to see the man in action is to see a real star. Committed and relaxed; childlike yet deadly serious. No rival player is under any illusions as to whom the crowd wants to

see - Kareem is the master! But even so, with all this building up ahead of him, Big Lew felt he needed something more. For all his blinding skill and despite his ever-increasing bank balance, his life, maybe, lacked a little purpose. The martial arts caught his attention and in particular, aikido.

Kareem was put on to Bruce one day after dropping into the offices of *Black Belt* magazine. Already there were whispers of Lee's incredible skill along the Kung Fu corridors of America and Kareem insisted that a meeting be arranged. He could have made no better choice! No sooner had they met, than the action began. Bruce was intrigued at the idea

of working out with a man close on two feet taller than himself and it was a challenge he simply couldn't ignore. They started training together. During that cold Winter of 1967, the time just flew by for the young basketball star. His interest, kindled first of all by a collection of Japanese samurai films, soon erupted into an obsession. In much the same way as the Little Dragon himself had felt the need for some improved form of physical self-defence during his formative years in Kowloon, so Kareem too had seen the probable benefits of an improved survival system; only in his case, the action took place on the streets of New York.

All alone of course, Bruce was edging towards a revolutionary concept of the martial arts that finally crystallised in the form of Jeet Kune Do. Part of this growing awareness was the Little Dragon's insistence on learning the language of the inner self. To break through the physical barriers was one thing; to peep through the door of the spiritual world and to make sense of what you see is quite another. In Kareem, however, Bruce had found a kindred soul. Not only was the amiable giant in tune with the Little Dragon's mystical searches; he was also well versed in the affairs and history of Asia and the Orient. Without doubt, there was plenty in common for them both to chew on. Big Lew's transformation came, as do most things of worth, slowly and surely. It took time for the truths of Jeet Kune Do to sink in, but as he remarked some time later, "After studying for a while, you learn a lot about how easy it is to hurt someone and how easily you can get hurt. That really makes you respect what you're involved in. With violence, you learn to respect it and see how easily you can become victimised by it." Sounding, in a way, almost like the late master himself, Kareem went on, "I think that is something people in the West especially need to learn about violence. I think in the Orient, they accept that violence is counter-productive to anything positive they are trying to do."

DOGS AND CHINESE NOT ALLOWED!

Funnily enough, it was during one of their long and intense discussions that Big Lew mentioned to Bruce something he'd seen in a film called *The Chinese Connection*. Set in southern China during the British occupation, the scene depicted a restaurant in which hung a sign saying 'Dogs and Chinese not allowed.' The sign, in fact, was no Action. Such insults were all too common at that time and Bruce was so taken with the symbolism of the idea that he later adapted it to slot into *Fist of Fury*. As anyone who has ever seen that fantastic film will remember, the dramatic effect was shattering and the scene, one of the Little Dragon's most memorable.

In Bruce Lee's small studio in the Culver City school, Kareem was becoming impatient. Naturally his loyalties lay primarily with basketball and for this reason, time available for the martial arts was strictly limited. Once a week during the basketball season was about it, but fortunately, come the summer of 1968, things got a little better. For a time, Big Lew spent just about all of his waking hours with Bruce, either working out, training or rapping. The days were endless and Kareem's enthusiasm just ran riot.

HELL BENT ON DESTRUCTION

It gradually came home to Kareem that, in the eyes of Bruce, the martial arts most certainly weren't for display purposes only. To a man moderately well versed in the skills of aikido, there was something almost frightening about a fighter hell bent on destruction. Art, to Bruce, had little to do with street fighting and to start with, Kareem found his uncompromising attitude hard to take. Nevertheless they continued to battle it out, Kareem gaining the experience of working alongside the world's finest martial artist and the Little Dragon using his partner largely for experimental purposes. Kareem's height, weight and reach advantages, though enormous in anyone's book, were just the kind of challenge Bruce revelled in. "Somehow, someway," Bruce thought, "any situation, however bad it may seem, can be made to work for you." He was right! Kareem found himself on the end of many a lightning attack.

America influenced the Little Dragon in countless different ways. The country's cosmopolitan atmosphere, its sprinkling of cultures and its opportunities provided Bruce with a solid background on which to weave his own unique pattern. Jeet Kune Do evolved from this mixed input and it's easy to see why. As Kareem put it, "One thing is for sure. Bruce's art was definitely a product of this country. He involved Boxing, wrestling, everything he saw that was classical and efficient. He tried to take it in. It upset some people but he was practical and when he saw something that worked, he used it." To the Little Dragon, fighting was simply fighting and although he was always keen to discuss spiritual matters, he could see no reason to merge the two. Later on, this uncompromising attitude was to soften considerably, matched no doubt by the Little Dragon's growing awareness of himself and of those around him.

But time waits for no man and, though firm friends, the two champions had separate courses to sail. Bruce, of course, soon hit the road to film stardom and rapidly fought his way up the box-office receipts charts while Big Lew, capitalising on his immense physical frame, forged for himself a massive niche in the hall of basketball fame. His popularity was undeniable. A yearly salary of nearly half a million dollars from his current team, the Los Angeles Lakers, will speak for that. But for Kareem and Bruce, fate held something else in store. With success literally hammering on the door, Bruce felt at last, that the time had arrived for him to go for the big one. Many years of experience and training had put him in touch with the very best martial artists and now he wanted to put it all together into one mammoth epic, to be called, *Game of Death*.

"A film to end all films," was how he once put it and indeed it was, or should I say, would have been. Golden Harvest's supreme production was to blend together appropriate quantities of expertise and entertainment and Bruce first of all called upon his old friend Kareem Abdul-Jabbar to provide the opposition in the Temple of the Unknown sequence. "I was a bad guy," remarked Kareem. "I really didn't have a role. I happened to be the last person he fought in the movie." These modest words do little justice to Kareem's fighting abilities. Portraying a martial artist whose style encompasses all other styles, the gentle giant from Manhattan proved to be a natural. Not only was his own technique well up to scratch, he also provided a superb contrast to the compact figure of the Little Dragon.

"HIS DEATH... SENT ME IN A LOOP"

It was some time after the filming of this incredible sequence, that tragedy struck. Kareem heard that his great friend was dead. He went on, "It really sent me in a loop, because I was on my way to see him. I was in Singapore, ready to get on a plane. I was to stop in Hong Kong to see Bruce the morning I left. By the time I got down in Singapore from Kuala Lumpur, it was already in the headlines." Kareem was stupefied. He remembered to send Linda a telegram and then left again. "I figured that was best, with all the confusion. I knew I couldn't do anything."

A chapter was closed. Since then, Kareem has had his ups and downs. On the plus side has been his fantastically successful career and a conversion to the Islamic faith. On the other, threats to his life and the murder of some close friends. Things, however, have now

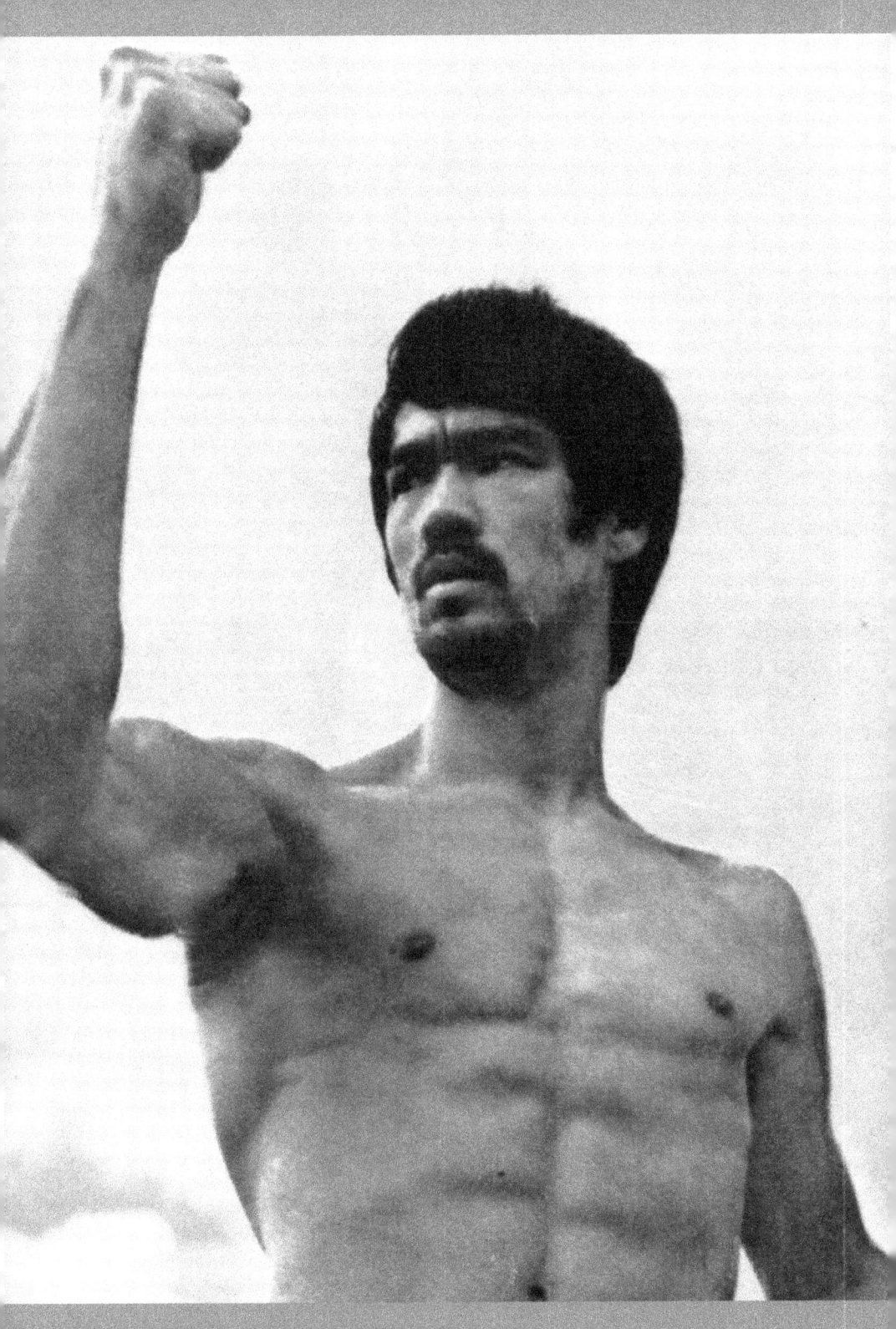

straightened out a little and Big Lew feels he has seen the worst. He no longer practices Jeet Kune Do, but feels instead that he lives it. Put another way, Kareem now attacks life with all the weapons in his armoury and enjoys it to the full. His relationship with the Little Dragon has become a fond memory and one which he will always treasure. Time waits for no man, but memories often stand still. Who, after all, will ever forget Bruce Lee's last fight or for that matter, Kareem Abdul-Jabbar - the man at the top?

LEGENDARY CHINESE FIGHTERS

Bruce Lee would have been quite prepared to admit that he was not the first great Eastern fighter and in all probability, he won't have been the last. Whether there was ever anyone better than the Little Dragon, is certainly an impossible question to answer. After all, how does one make a fair comparison? All that's for sure is that, from time to time, legendary fighters have emerged to stamp their mark in the Kung Fu history books. Some have become well-known, others less so. Remember, they had no television or cinemas in those days to help spread the word and often the popularity and fame was restricted to certain localised areas. Inevitably too, the truth sometimes got mixed up a little as stories travelled from mouth to mouth. But then that's the stuff legends are made of! Let's therefore dive into the Kung Fu archives and take a close look at some of those early masters - the giants of yesterday.

Much of the cherished wisdom and learning, so sought after by the aspiring novice has been lost. Nor likely is it to be re-discovered. Great masters were by nature, secretive and perhaps in a way, they had good reason to be. Why, after all, share your expertise with a man who may later become your enemy? For the pupil, therefore, it was often tough going. Knowledge was imparted slowly and sparingly, that is, if at all! Traditionally, the aspiring novice had to bring gifts to the door of the teacher, sometimes for periods of years. Even then he was by no means guaranteed of the master's attention. Frequently, even when accepted, the pupil had first to train with a senior student. Then again, some legendary figures chose to live an almost hermit-like existence. Shunning the company of their fellow men, they appeared but infrequently. Stories abound of the semi-mythical 'mountain-men' and their shattering, although often totally unorthodox techniques. Many a master met his fate at the hands of just such a lone fighter. Naturally, tales such as these bring to mind the theories of the great Bruce Lee. Jeet Kune Do was, after all, based on the principal of rejecting rigid orthodoxy and knowing the once stupendous range of the Little Dragon's private library, there is no doubt that he drew at times from these sources. The first name to come to mind is that of Sun Lu-t'ang. Sun's early days were not happy ones. His childhood was steeped in appalling poverty and such was his desperation, he narrowly escaped death in a suicide attempt when only thirteen years old. Born in Paoting, Boxing proved to be his saviour and under the wing of Kuo Yun-shen (more of whom later) Sun swiftly rose to prominence. In common with many truly great martial artists, however, he rarely discussed his remarkable skills with his friends. Instead, he preferred, we are told, to contemplate philosophy and astronomy.

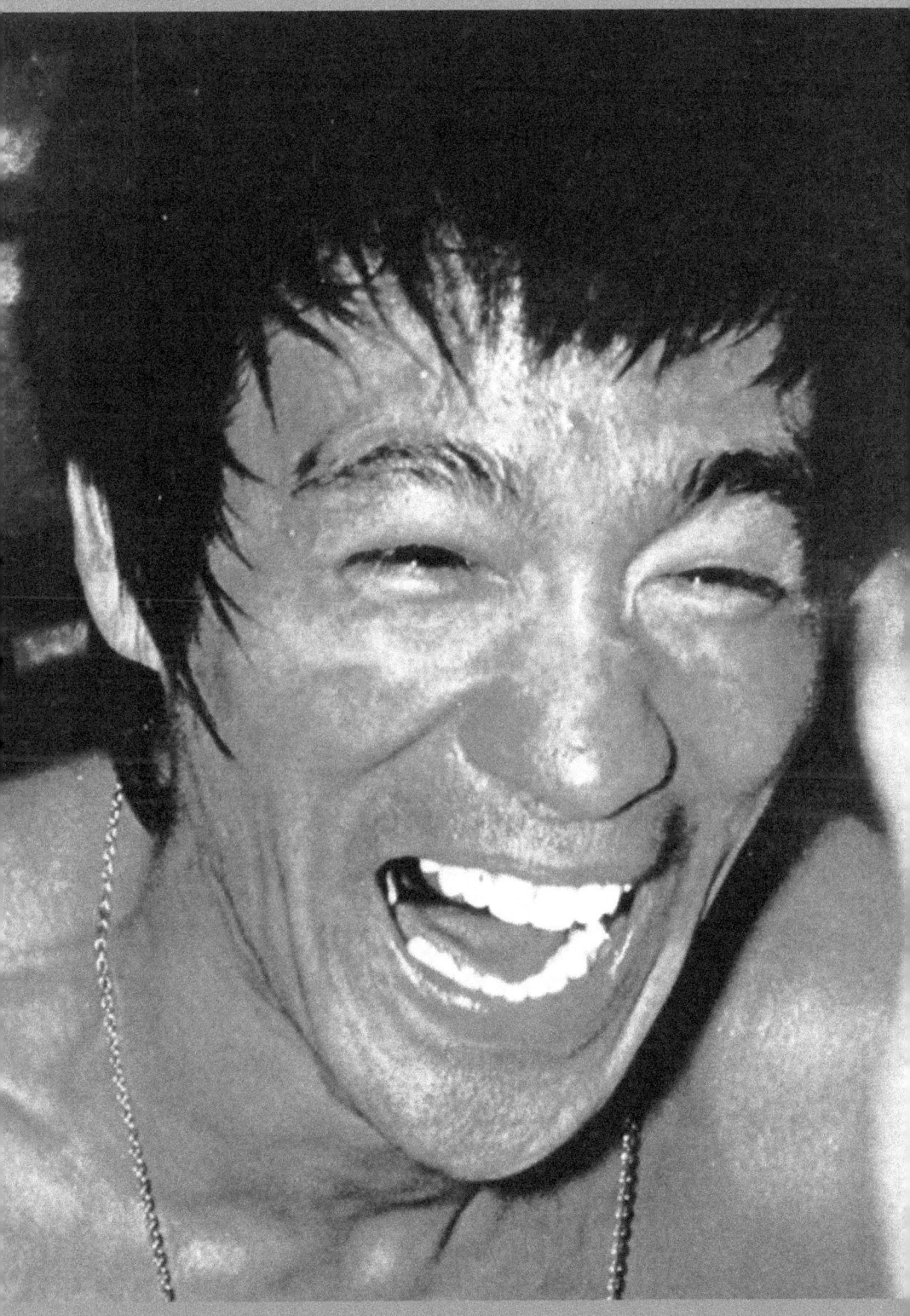

TESTED BY GLORY SEEKERS

Those who recall well the 'restaurant fight' in Bruce Lee's epic *The Way of the Dragon*, will be interested to hear of a similar situation in which Sun one day found himself whilst partaking of an evening meal. He was called out by two wrestlers. One struck with the fist while the other kicked. Eye witnesses report than Sun appeared not to move. His opponents, however, flew several feet through the air! Of course, being 'tested' by glory seekers was and still is part and parcel of the life of a famed martial artist. Some masters, however, not wishing to bother themselves with unworthy opponents, will first of all direct a senior student to take up the challenge.

Another legendary artist was Tu Hsin-Wu. Known chiefly for his extremely free style of Chinese Boxing, Tu fought until into his sixtieth year, at which age he was still able to defeat his most senior student! This was made all the more surprising by virtue of the fact that, in 1928, that same student entered and was subsequently disqualified from a national tournament for reasons of dangerous tactics. In particular, his opponents objected to the use of the deadly 'eye-spear.'

Tu learnt his art from an unknown old gentleman named Hsu. They had met casually at an inn and on being told of Hsu's abilities, Tu insisted on a challenge. The fight was short lived and he was torn apart! Tu, impressed beyond degree, stayed with the aging fighter for over eight years, studying his every move. The effort was worth it and Tu subsequently earned himself a sizable reputation for his ability to repulse an attack from the rear by means of an incredible overhead kick!

THE CRUSHING HAND

Let's move on now to Kuo Yun-shen. Known by some as Divine Crushing Hand (and with good reason) Kuo had travelled early on to Shansi Province to study under the great Li Neng-jan. Before long he'd grasped the finer points of Hsing-i. For quite some time, though, he was hampered by a lack of suitable opposition. Such was his exasperation, it is said that he searched unceasingly and on one occasion, had the misfortune to accidentally kill a combatant by excessive use of the crushing hand technique. For his sins, he received a jail sentence. Kuo, ever after, took the precaution of placing his left hand on the body of an opponent before attacking with the right!

Kuo was only defeated twice in his career. He met his match against Ch'e I-chai. The meeting was a memorable one. Ch'e, a mild man and a protégé of Li Neng-jan, had first of all tried to avoid confrontation. Kuo, however, was ready for action and he prematurely attempted to land the 'crushing hand.'

Ch'e, with a 'Muhammad Ali' side-slip, avoided the punch of destruction with great ease and gently tapping Kuo's shoulder, he murmured, "No hurry." The attacker conceded defeat in an instant. Kuo's only other reported defeat was at the hands of the almost invincible pa-kua boxer, Tung Hai-ch'uan. As the story goes, Kuo attacked and Tung defended for two days continuously. Sadly for Kuo, the Hsing-i attack simply was not able to penetrate the pa-kua defence and on the third day, when almost stumbling in his weariness, Kuo was trounced by Tung's first offensive.

Li Neng-jan, teacher of Kuo and Ch'e was undeniably one of China's finest fighters. It had taken, so he claimed, forty years for him to reach the highest possible level - forty years of patience, perseverance and sheer application. If any legendary fighter can be said to have approached the perfection of Bruce Lee, then surely, it must have been Li, a man of almost magical abilities. This, however, probably cannot be said of Huo Yuan-chia, an ex-stevedore who relied on his enormous brute strength to win him the reputation of 'supreme master.'

THE LABYRINTHINE ART

Huo was invincible at the art of Mi Tsung-i, a form of Kung Fu dating back to the Sung dynasty. Nicknamed the 'Labyrinthine Art,' it surely lives up to its name. The exponent delivers a constantly changing attack, varying in particular between soft and hard postures. Defence against this kind of attack is difficult, to say the least. So great, in fact, was Huo's expertise, it is believed that he never suffered a defeat. Sadly, the giant stevedore died when only forty-eight years old. The circumstances surrounding this tragedy are strangely confused. Many believe he was poisoned by a Japanese doctor who wished to avenge the severe defeat that Huo had handed out to a troupe of his countrymen. Whether the available evidence supports this outlandish theory, we will never know. What is beyond doubt, however, is that Huo Yuan-chia at around the turn of the century, carved out for himself the reputation of being China's number one martial artist.

Although Boxing exhibitions have never been exactly rare in China, masters will seldom attend. Instead, their star pupils usually take the stage, fighting, as it were, for the honour of the school. Besides this, travelling shows have at times been very popular, particularly during the Ch'ing dynasty. These performances were almost entirely non-profit making and the combatants fought solely for the purpose of prestige. Naturally, those taking part therefore had to be pretty well off, especially in view of the fact that expensive forfeits had frequently to be paid out in the course of a fight.

POWER-PACKED PUNCH

Many of these travelling showmen came from the well known Boxing province of Shantung and one, who rose higher than most, was the supreme master of Hsing-i, Shang Yun-hsing. Born in 1863, Shang soon proved himself to be a devoted student. His teacher, the great Li Ts'un-i, considered him to be his finest pupil and certainly there is no denying Shang's early enthusiasm. Although poor and a young man of little learning, he would walk many miles each day to attend his lessons. The routine was gruelling and the rewards few. However, as time went on, Shang built up for himself a sizable reputation, due in no small measure to the immense strength of his famous belly. Challengers even broke wrists on it! Occasionally too, opponents died at his hands.

Shang, though, was not an intentionally cruel man. Rather, his faults lay in a general inability to communicate with others. He was consequently a bad teacher and although some have linked his problem to a low level of intellect, it could, more charitably be attributed to his poor education. An illustration of Shang's sheer cussedness occurred when he was being made to apologise to the legendary Ch'eng T'ing-hua by his teacher Li for stealing some of the great master's pupils. Ch'eng, good-heartedly, attempted to lift the

kneeling Shang from before him, but was resisted by strong opposing forces. Suddenly, Shang arose and suggested to Li that they go outside for a little sport. Hardly the behaviour of a humble man!

And so the list goes on. Many names have come and gone and some have survived better than others. There can be little doubt, however, that to this outstanding list of legendary giants, must be added the name of Bruce Lee. Bruce was a complete artist in every sense of the word. Be it technique, skill, strength, ingenuity, entertainment or whatever, the Little Dragon's genius had the area covered. Of course, few of the great masters we have discussed would ever have had the opportunities to develop in the way that Bruce did. His prowess in the film business somehow managed to add a whole new dimension to his fantastic martial arts abilities. The steps he made have enabled others to follow. Make no mistake, when martial arts history books are being rewritten, one man will surely be added to the list of the great legendary fighters - that of Bruce Lee.

KICKBACK: THE LETTERS

Hi there ... Jenny Lee here again to pull out some more letters from our bulging mail-sack. The big news for me at the moment is the fantastic smash success of our *KFM Game of Death* special. Literally hundreds of you have written in to say how much you liked it and I must admit I agree with you. This month, I'm printing positively the last reply to our 'How many times have you seen Bruce Lee's films?' competition and K. Beardmore seems to be the winner. Congratulations, but where do you find the time? Finally, don't forget to keep writing me those letters. Even if yours doesn't get published, believe me, we read 'em all! See you soon...

TAO OF JEET KUNE DO

Dear Jenny,
First off I'd like to say what a brilliant magazine you produce. I hope you can keep on publishing it for a long time to come. Down to business. In the latest *KFM*, you said that we could stand by for the availability of Bruce Lee's *Tao of Jeet Kune Do*. Presumably that means that you will be selling it in your magazine in the near future? And you can be sure that I will be one of the first to purchase it. By the way, what's the price?
Colin Wilkinson, Falkirk, Scotland

Dear Colin,
Thanks a lot for all your very kind comments. Fingers crossed, KFM will be appearing in your local shop for many years to come! As far as the Tao of Jeet Kune Do is concerned, well, there I have a problem. Until a few weeks ago, everyone was expecting the book to become available just about any minute. News, however, from our friendly import shop has shattered all my dreams. For some reason or other, printing of the book (in America) has suddenly been halted and nobody seems to know why. Of course, we're still battling away to find out what the hitch is and just as soon as any news comes through, be sure well let you know. The price will, I guess, be around the £5.00 mark. That's expensive, but worth it!

KFM SUBSCRIPTION?

Dear Jenny,
I am a soldier in the British army and I would like to know whether or not Bruce Lee poster magazines are on subscription. The reason I ask is that I go to Germany sometime in October and I wouldn't want to miss any copies of *Kung-Fu Monthly* while I am away.
Peter Haynes, Tidworth, Hants

Dear Peter,
Thanks a lot for your letter. The short answer to your question is no. Although we don't carry subscriptions, you can still order current copies direct from us and, of course, if you've got any catching-up to do, there's always our Back Issue Bonanza offers.

HOW MANY TIMES?

Dear Jenny,
First of all thanks for running such a great magazine and the fantastic posters you put in. In *KFM* No.16, I read about the person who won the award for seeing Bruce Lee films the most number of times and you ask if anyone can beat it. Well, I've seen *Fist of Fury* 52 times, *The Way of the Dragon* 56 times, *The Big Boss* 49 times and *Enter the Dragon* 58 times. It may seem hard to believe, but I promise every one of my friends and family could confirm it. I have every *Kung-Fu Monthly* and all the other books on Bruce Lee, including ones imported from Hong Kong.
K.C. Beardmore, Smethwick, West Midlands

Dear K.C.,
Well, as I said at the beginning, where do you find the time. On second thoughts, maybe your father runs the local cinema. Seriously though, thanks again to everyone for writing in and telling me how often you've seen the Little Dragon as it's been a lot of fun reading the letters. I've had another idea. How about telling me which of those films you liked the best and why? Don't make your answers too long and as a tip, it may help to think a while about your reasons before you write. There's a copy of Secrets of Shaolin Temple Boxing going to the KFM reader who sends in the best reply!

ANY MORE *KFM* BOOKS?

Dear Jenny,
I haven't got much to say other than a huge thank you for all the remarkable issues of *KFM* that you've published. I would have asked you some questions, but I can't think of any that you haven't answered already! Oh, there is just one. Are you going to print anymore scrapbooks or *Books of Kung Fu*? I know you must have your work cut out producing such a fine magazine but those two 'specials' were extra fantastic. More please!
Derry O'Malley, Belfast, Northern Ireland

Dear Derry,
Once again, thanks for the words of praise. To be honest, we'd love to do another scrapbook, but my clock tells me there's only 24 hours in the day! The problem is that we now have to look much further afield in order to keep on turning out our monthly articles and that takes time. Actually, we've had hundreds and hundreds of letters asking just the same question so it's something we'll really have to think seriously about.

THE POSTER MAGAZINES - VOLUME ONE

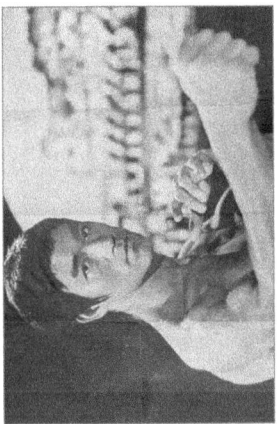

19

1976

EDITORIAL

Hi there Kung Fu fans...

We've really heaped up another plateful of Kung Fu goodies for you this month! Into action and first off, we're paying our respects to *The Wisdom of Bruce Lee*, a really fabulous new book that's to be published in a few months' time. In fact, we like it so much that we've split our review between this issue and the next, so as to give it the works! Also, the fantastic news is that, as usual, we've got there first. The book will be exclusively mail-ordered via the coming issues of *Kung-Fu Monthly*.

This really is an amazing month! Our follow-up feature, too, has just got to have a five star rating. In response to quite literally thousands of readers' requests, *KFM* has managed to get the sensational low-down on film censorship. What are the chances of seeing the Little Dragon's films uncut? And do they all really deserve 'X' ratings? We asked a film man all the questions you asked us, plus a lot more besides, in a unique, no punches pulled interview that rips the lid off the whole business.

Did you notice the number of this issue? That's right, No.19. That means next up is *KFM* No.20 and that's just got to be a great excuse for a celebration. What I'm promising is an extra-special smash issue of truly historic proportions, including our first ever *KFM* competition, with glittering prizes galore! Don't, whatever you do, miss out.

Looking a bit ahead, we're working hard on racking up an exclusive on Chuck Norris' new film that's in the making right now. No promises, but fingers crossed, our correspondent in New York is hopeful that there's some brand new Norris pictures in the pipeline to go with the report. Another *KFM* scoop!

That's all from me for this issue...

Felix Yen
Editor-in-Chief

THE WISDOM OF BRUCE LEE

KFM is delighted to announce a super-sensational book scoop. Penned by Felix Dennis and Roger Hutchinson, *The Wisdom of Bruce Lee*, due to be published in just a few months' time, offers at last, an in-depth look at Bruce Lee the man, and just what it was that made him into a martial arts legend. And what an insight it is! Not since Bruce Lee, King of Kung Fu has there been such a major event on the Bruce Lee book horizon. Once more, *KFM* is proud to tell its readers that this fantastic new publication, as well as arriving soon at your local bookshops, will also be available through our mail-order catalogue, exclusively in *KFM*! Because of the importance of the work, we have decided to split our report into two parts, between this issue and the next (whatever you do, don't miss out on *KFM* No.20!) So without any more ado, let's kick off straight into part one of a review of *The Wisdom of Bruce Lee*.

What really is, or should I say, was a Kung Fu expert? Nowadays, of course, we tend to think of him as being some sort of spectacular martial athlete; someone who is obsessed with physical fitness to the exclusion of just about everything else. Chapter one of the book, headed The Fighting Mind, brings out the fallacy behind this way of thinking. In fact the original Kung Fu expert was rather more a jack of many trades and master of them all. He would probably have been a philosopher and an alchemist, a doctor and maybe a musician. Finally, because of the times in which he lived, he also needed to be able to defend himself, but by no means was this thought to be his prime objective.

As the book indicates, Kung Fu became a pseudonym for the martial arts for two main reasons. Firstly, because of the tyrannical natures of many of the ancient Chinese rulers, thus raising self-defence to a position of sheer necessity and secondly, the power of the film industry. Movie-makers are under no illusion as to what sells films - action! However, as scrap-happy Bruce Lee proved, there's action and there's action. The Little Dragon's kind was a multi-million dollar success story of previously unknown proportions. Many

earlier Kung Fu action films, though, tended to mercifully disappear in the back-street cinemas of Kowloon!

THE PRAYING MANTIS

The book then runs through a broad outline of the history of Kung Fu, in particular, the origins of the 'hard and soft' or 'external and internal' schools. There is an interesting story here of how the Praying Mantis style evolved during the Middle Ages. Wang Lang, a wandering swordsman, finding himself quite unable to defeat the Shaolin Monks in combat, hit on the idea of studying the ways of the insect world, to formulate new and improved methods of attack. That his quest was successful is now part of Kung Fu history and many a school has since adopted his styles and techniques. Several pages are devoted to the way in which the martial arts evolved, including naturally, the concept of Ch'i. China has a long history of sickness and disease with little in the way of genuine medical attention to help alleviate the suffering. Chi, the study of inner strength, was therefore of immense importance to the beleaguered inhabitants.

And yet, Bruce Lee slung the whole thing out of the window. He felt that the time had come for a re-appraisal right across the martial arts board and that he was the man to do it. It goes without saying of course, that to many of the die-hard traditionalists, his actions were little short of sacrilegious. Newfound enemies were forced to knash their teeth as Bruce re-wrote the rules of Kung Fu and made free to all, the 'mysteries' of the East.

His reasons for doing so were techniques of each particular system had become closed books into which initiative was totally excluded. As *The Wisdom of Bruce Lee* reminds us, over the years, instructions that were originally intended to be used as guidelines, somehow always turn into cast iron directives; signposts become the word of the law! The Little Dragon stripped bare the bones of confusion, chiselled away all useless dogma and left us thankfully with a streamlined, yet eminently workable, system of martial arts training. He called it Jeet Kune Do.

SPECIAL OFFER!
BACK ISSUE BONANZA 4
£1.00 ONLY SAVE 60p!

THIS ISSUE ONLY
KFM numbers 13, 14, 15, 16 and 17 for just £1.00 (includes postage and packing).

Catch up on the back numbers of the World's number one martial arts poster magazine. Order NOW while stocks last.

Make out your £1.00 cheque or Postal Order to *Kung Fu Monthly* and post to:
BACK ISSUE BONANZA No.4
KUNG FU MONTHLY
39 GOODGE STREET
LONDON W1P 1FD

Allow three weeks for delivery and don't forget to include your name and address.

(BLOCK CAPITALS PLEASE!)

THE BIG DILEMMA

The book, importantly, raises the issue of Bruce's biggest dilemma - that of religion. As with the martial arts, he was constantly tempted to reject scathingly all mystical and religious learning, seeing it as a blatant sign of man's inherent weakness. He felt it too easy to palm off the unanswerable 'who are we? where are we? why are we?' type questions as being simply the work of a particular God, so that they may then be conveniently ignored. "Was this not," he asked, "a crutch of the worst kind?" On the other hand, Bruce was loathe, too, to dismiss entirely the great visions and 'truths' of religious men, feeling maybe that they should be studied and used selectively in much the same way as Jeet Kune Do accommodated and absorbed the useful parts of many different Kung Fu styles.

The Wisdom of Bruce Lee correctly stresses the little Dragon's supreme position in the world of cinema entertainment. Few stars indeed are able to boast predominance in the field they are portraying. But Bruce was more than just the exception, he was unique! Chapter two of this startling new book explains this and then proceeds to run through in sharp detail, the reasons for this mastery coming about. Right from the early days in Yip Man's Wing Chun School, the Little Dragon showed an inherent knowledge of the direction in which his future would go - an understanding that was almost unhealthy in a boy of his age, plus a total dedication. This deadly duo of talents was to serve him well!

BALONEY!

His philosophies on life in general, however, were never really definitive. A quotation from early on has Bruce as saying, "The world is full of people who are determined to be somebody or give trouble. They want to get ahead, to stand out. Such ambition has no use for a Kung Fu man, who rejects all forms of self-assertiveness and competition." These words ring strangely for a man whose later life was to become dominated by the pressures of ambition. In fact, many a statement that Bruce Lee made in the early days, he later contradicted. Once, on the virtues of Yin and Yang, he snapped, "It's an illusion," and, "Baloney."

If anything, in later years, his condemnation of the 'Classical Mess' and of those who taught it, was to become more and more apparent and The Wisdom of Bruce Lee produces a whole bundle of quotations to support this. For instance, "Too often one of those big belly Chinese masters will tell you that his Ch'i or internal power, has sunk to his stomach. He's not kidding, it has sunk - and gone! To put it bluntly, he is nothing but fat and ugly!" And, "I don't have any belt whatsoever. I think it might be useful to hold up your pants, but that's about all!"

And so we're moved on to consider Jeet Kune Do, Bruce's so-called style without style. The name of the game was, of course, simplicity; the stripping down of the sculpture to the bare necessities. An opponent with a particular style was, to Bruce, a man in bondage and therefore easy meat. As he told *Black Belt* magazine in 1971, "Let it be understood once and for all that I have not invented a new style, composite, or modification. I have in no way set Jeet Kune Do within a distinct form governed by laws that distinguish it from 'this' style or 'that' method. On the contrary, I hope to free my comrades from bondage to styles, patterns and doctrines."

The keynote to the Little Dragon's art was directness. When faced by a man who is about to punch you, you don't waste time going into some elaborate stance or classical position; you make sure you punch him first. Flowery styles are time-wasting and next to useless. "But surely," disbelievers would constantly ask, "there must be some sort of style involved in just delivering a punch"? "Of course", Bruce would often reply, "I've found my way and you've got to find yours." The Little Dragon carried his convictions to almost extreme lengths and with good reason. He was well aware that in the years to come, charlatans would likely appear in the guise of Jeet Kune Do 'experts.' The very idea of these people setting up schools and making a fortune from the ever-gullible public filled him with distaste. Jeet Kune Do had to be strong enough to withstand the onslaught. Chapter four of this sizzling new publication is titled, 'On Training and Keeping Fit,' and what an important section it is. Although Bruce never regarded the development of the body as an end unto itself, he rightly devoted a not inconsiderable amount of time and energy towards his physical condition. Fitness was, he said, "A finger pointing at the moon. Please do not take the finger to be the moon, or fix your gaze so intently on the finger as to miss the beautiful sights of heaven." *The Wisdom of Bruce Lee* describes for us his stupendous gymnasium, a masterpiece of purpose-built apparatus, and also details the Little Dragon's almost 'cranky' eating habits.

BRUCE LEE: "I'VE GOT TO KEEP IN SHAPE."

Running was a strategic point of the Little Dragon's workout. He covered at least a couple of miles a day, often following up with a series of Tai Chi movements, an ancient art that Bruce felt to be ideal for the purposes of keeping in trim, both physically and mentally. Then there were the isometric exercises. These are described as exercises whereby the muscles are improved by pitting them against an immoveable object, such as a wall. We are told that throughout the day, the Little Dragon just never let up. If he was eating, he'd be pushing one hand up against the table. Often, whilst just standing around talking, he'd be pounding a fist into the cupped other hand. Linda tells how she would frequently find him with a book in one hand and a dumbbell in the other. As Bruce once explained to a slightly irritated James Coburn, "Sorry man, I've got to keep in shape."

The Little Dragon's sensational kicks (the Chinese nicknamed him the man with three legs) were the arduous product of high bar gym training and, believe it or not, kicking trees! "When you can kick," he said, "so you aren't jarred, but the tree is jarred, then you will begin to understand a kick." *The Wisdom of Bruce Lee* covers Bruce's approach to a variety of kicks and punches, including his legendary heavy bag training. Nobody will understand more than his old buddy Danny Inosanto, exactly what Bruce meant by 'commitment' to an attack. After trying his hardest for over five minutes to improve his kicking, Bruce still wasn't satisfied. Danny went on, "Finally, he came over and slapped me on the face - at the same time calling out, 'Now kick!' He held up the shield - I was simply blazing with anger and went POW! It was fantastic."

Next month, we dive into the second half of our report, to look at teaching, opponents, Bruce's film career and how he reacted to the fame that was so rapidly heaped around those powerful shoulders. See you then!

KFM RIPS THE LID OFF FILM CENSORSHIP

Dear Jenny,
Please can you tell me why they have to edit Bruce's films...?

Dear Jenny,
Is it possible for you to have the 'X' certificates on Bruce's films changed to 'AA,' otherwise I won't be able to get in to see them for years?

These are just two of the countless thousands of absolutely similar letters that continue to come tumbling in through the *KFM* office door. Though, sad to say, your favourite martial arts magazine can claim to have but little influence over the more unpopular decisions of cinema censors, we do feel at liberty to publish our opinions on the subject. So as to be absolutely fair to all, we decided our appraisal should take the form of a frank interview and we thank the anonymous gentleman concerned for stepping forward to take up the hot seat. He would like to stress though that the opinions expressed are his only and not necessarily those of the Film Censorship Board. Nevertheless, we feel that much good may result from you, the Bruce Lee fans, finding out just what does go on behind the censorship scenes. Who are these faceless film-hackers who decide what we shall and shall not see? - and are they butchers or are they simply protecting us? *KFM* asks in turn, the burning questions you asked us and receives some very surprising answers!

KFM: Can you first of all talk about film censorship in general?
'Mr 'X': Yes, it happens like this. All film companies are obliged to send their products to the British Board of Film Censors. After a viewing and a certain amount of discussion, a number of cuts may be suggested, plus of course, the certificate rating such as 'U,' 'A,' and so on. Sometimes the Board decides that the film is so bad that it can't be censored and that's it - kaput! If the film company were not to abide by the decision, heavy fines could be imposed.
KFM: So you'd say the control they have, is total?
Mr 'X': Oh yes and you've got to remember too that these days most local areas have their own 'watchdog' committees, so it's not unknown for a film that has been passed by the Board to need cutting a second time. These local bodies have power to bring legal action and the Board is obliged to take notice of their findings.
KFM: Who are the members of the British Board of Film Censors?
Mr 'X': They are people appointed by the government and also, believe it or not, by the film industry itself! The idea is that the industry sets them up and then actually pays them to censor the films. Of course, if a film isn't given to them for approval, the company concerned could find itself in serious trouble. Also, any cinema manager who showed that film would very likely find himself banned from screening the products of other companies.
KFM: Do you think the whole business is carried further than strictly necessary?
Mr 'X': I'd say sometimes, yes! Occasionally, rather over-zealous editors go a lot fur-

ther than is strictly necessary. In other words, the censors might ask for the cutting of a particularly gruesome shot from a martial arts battle and the editor, just to make certain, then removes the whole scene! It really does happen. Then I'd say that many editors take the opposite approach and cut the least possible.

KFM: Do you believe that all films are treated with the same degree of fairness?

Mr 'X': Now you're asking! I think I'd have to say no. The members of the Board are only human beings and when they've had to sit, for instance, through ten Kung Fu films in one day, I'd put my money on the last one really getting knocked! Of course, it is possible to appeal against the decisions, but there need to be very good reasons. Then it goes off

to a higher Board, although nine times out often, nothing is changed.

KFM: If all you say is true, how is it that uncut Bruce Lee films used to get showings in private cinemas?

Mr 'X': There used to be these Chinese cinema clubs where, on payment of a membership fee - you could be six years old - you could see uncut martial arts films. Now, however, proper distribution companies have been set up in this country to handle the imported films and there are no uncut showings.

KFM: Where is the Kung Fu censorship line drawn?

Mr 'X': To be honest, it depends on what the current trend is. Right now, violence is getting the chop. Bruce Lee fans I suppose, worry, in particular about cuts in *The Way of the Dragon* and that's the one that gets talked about most. First of all, let me say that it most certainly was not mutilated in the way many people have suggested. In fact, only the nunchakus scene was edited, on the insistence of the censors. At that time, the popular press was full of tales of people damaging themselves with home-made weapons, after purportedly being influenced by the Bruce Lee *The Way of the Dragon* scene. The newspapers were making such a meal of it that the censorship board just had to take action.

KFM: Do you think it was a particularly violent scene?

Mr 'X': No. In fact it was quite funny! He fights an Italian who uses a similar weapon. Unfortunately, the Italian isn't very good and he knocks himself out by mistake! That just goes to prove that you don't mess with nunchakus unless you know what you're doing.

However, the censors decided in view of the media reactions, the scene had to go. It was a shame. To drift from the subject for just a moment, I must say I've always been impressed by Bruce Lee's sense of humour. I'm told he devised many of his comic sketches after studying his young son, Brandon. He'd take note of the expressions and then adapt them to use himself. The other thing I really admired about Bruce, was his demand for perfection. It's obvious that every movement, kick, punch and so on was worked out in fine detail. I wasn't at all happy cutting the Little Dragon's films.

KFM: We weren't if too happy about it either! Do you believe that censors take a particularly vicious attitude towards Kung Fu films?

Mr 'X': I think they have an attitude in general against Chinese pictures! I'll explain why. You could have, say, an American martial arts picture, an Australian martial arts picture and a Hong Kong martial arts picture. You will find that the American one will come through almost intact, the Australian one will have a few cuts and the Hong Kong film will be butchered! Why? I suppose the way of thinking is that the American companies have put up more money and devoted more time and effort and so they deserve better rewards.

KFM: Are all Chinese films treated in this disgraceful manner?

Mr 'X': No. I can remember one Asian film in particular that got away with hardly any cuts. The reason was that it had a high technical merit. This is, however, unusual and generally, they are put through the mincer. That film, by the way, was *Skyhawk*. The only film to better this score was *Fist of Fury*. That had absolutely no cuts in Britain at all, probably because it came on the scene early, before the anti-violence lobby had really got going.

KFM: How about *The Big Boss*?

Mr 'X': Most of the cuts in that were for the co-star, James Tien. Bruce was hardly touched at all. The censors took objection to the 'blood-spurting' and to the 'hatchet attacks,' feeling it to be violence for its own sake. You've got to remember, though, that Bruce would probably have understood their reasoning. He always maintained that the film was made for Eastern audiences and he was never too keen on it being shown in the West. Out East, audiences lap up any amount of blood; it's just part and parcel of the film business. You might see, for instance, a man with a hundred arrows in him, just get up and keep on fighting! In China, they like everything to be exaggerated. To use the corny old phrase, "Life is cheap out there and violence is just part of the norm."

KFM: Do you feel that in the future, Bruce Lee films are likely to be shown in less edited forms than they are at present?

Mr 'X': I hope so. I think that everybody ought to see them at least once in their entirety. Whether or not a special showing for club members can be arranged, I don't know. I'm sure there are enough of them! To get round the censorship business, you'd have to make it a private showing. I believe all the uncut films are still available, although only in Chinese. Then again, possibly the BBC will decide to buy a Bruce Lee film. Because they have their own form of censorship which doesn't abide by the same rules as the cinema, it is on the cards that you'd see a more complete version.

KFM: How many of the Bruce Lee film cuts were made for reasons of violence and how many for reasons of keeping to time schedules?

Mr 'X': One at least was cut to fit schedules. I recall going to watch a Little Dragon film at the London Rialto and seeing a fairly long love scene. The next night when I went again, the scene had gone! But other than that, it was mostly violence that got the chop. Funnily enough, the extra cutting tended to be needed for the more sensitive local areas where, although the manager himself would sometimes complain of the brutality, he'd often too be the first to ask for a re-run. Something about having your cake and eating it, I believe!

The press, too, has much to answer for. You'll probably remember when interest in martial arts films was just getting off the ground; a time when every case of assault was reported as a Kung Fu attack! It sells lots of papers, but doesn't do much for the martial arts image. I even recall seeing in a newspaper a picture of some prime minister who was just plain falling over, with a caption that jokingly read that he was delivering a Kung Fu kick! Probably this all had more effect on public feeling and therefore censorship, than anything.

KFM: How do you feel about that other form of censorship - age limitation? Would you say that the censors have been harsh in the handing out of the 'X' ratings?

Mr 'X': In a word, yes! I'm not at all convinced that age should be criteria for judging whether or not fans should be able to see Bruce Lee films. I think the customers are there primarily to appreciate the Little Dragon's enormous skill and personality and I believe the 'X' rating to be quite unnecessary.

KFM: In that case, do you feel that censorship is useful at all?

Mr 'X': Yes, I do because otherwise we'd have an awful lot of rubbish around. I mean, where would it all stop? Technical merit and expertise would be forgotten. The keyword would just be sensation and that's not good for the customers or the film industry. I'd say that the system we have at the moment is fair enough, except that it is, I feel, overly sensitive to trends in public opinion. What it comes down to I suppose, is a clash between East and West cultural opinion. And then, no two people are ever going to agree on what is fair censorship and what is not. There are those who would like to ban Tom and Jerry!

KICKBACK: THE LETTERS

Hello, it's Jenny here again, with another page of letters picked straight out of the *KFM* postbag. I'm sure we've got a really interesting batch this week - you wouldn't believe how hard it is to choose! A lot of you have been writing in about the closing of the Bruce Lee Fan Club and I know just how badly you all feel about it. I'm hoping, fingers and toes crossed, that someone else will soon be taking up the reins, but as yet there's nothing definite. Now would be a very good time to thank Rhona McVay and her team of workers for all the hours of unpaid work they've been putting in over the years. If you could just have seen the mountain of mail that piled through her door each and every day, then you'd have a good idea why she's having to step down. That said, it's on with the letters!

THE POWER OF CH'I

Dear Jenny,
After reading through your magazines, I am amazed to hear about the hidden powers of Ch'i. I have just begun Karate lessons with a local club, but I would so much like to find out more about Ch'i. Please Jenny, can you help me find how to achieve this power?
Christopher Cox, Newbridge, Gwent

Dear Christopher,
Thanks for your letter. Very briefly, in ancient China, the word Ch'i described an ancient and mysterious force that was, and still is, thought to be inside everyone. The mother who manages to lift a car to free a trapped child - the man who sleeps on a bed of nails - these are both thought to be examples of Chi. Without getting involved too deeply here, the best I can say is that its release appears to have a great deal to do with breathing techniques. If you want to pursue the matter, I suggest you write to: Oriental World, 18 Swan Street, Manchester 4. They carry a very comprehensive selection of books dealing with martial arts matters, including Ch'i.

DANGER!

Dear Jenny,
Firstly let me congratulate you and *KFM* on a very good magazine. Secondly, let me give you a warning to all Kung Fu fans. You will have no doubt heard of the nunchakus (clubs or sticks held together by a chain). Well, I have a friend who made a pair at school. That night, he must have been practicing with them, because he never reappeared the next morning. I heard later that he'd broken his jaw and wrist while showing off.
Shaun Welburn, Selby, North Yorkshire

Hello Shaun,
Thank you indeed for your praise of KFM and thank you also for a timely warning about the dangers of Kung-Ku and in particular, nunchakus. I wish I could tell you how mad I get when I hear of accidents like this. I'll keep on shouting til I'm blue in the face that the martial arts CAN be dangerous and it MUST be taken seriously! No one, and I mean no one, should ever even consider playing around with nunchakus without the attendance of a trained instructor. Please don't do it!

GAME OF DEATH AGAIN

Dear Jenny,
After reading about the problems of completing the unfinished *Game of Death* in your fantastic collector's edition, I have come up with a very rough outline of one way they could go about it.
1. Treasure stolen. As scripted, villains swipe a priceless Korean treasure.
2. Agents. Special agents would be brought in to regain the treasure. They decide the only man for the job is Bruce. Information tells them that the treasure is stashed at the top of a pagoda on an island in the Pacific which is guarded by metal detectors. A briefing, possibly using cuts from the *Enter the Dragon* briefing scene would take place.

3. Action. Bruce arrives at the pagoda. It is night and a stand-in may be used. The ground floor is in darkness as Bruce and his aides enter. Suddenly a blazing light fills the room and a large Judo expert jumps out on Bruce. Bruce is still dazzled by the light and the Judoka starts throwing him about. The Little Dragon's aides are busy with four or five other Judoka. After a two-way battle, Bruce, with the aides just polishing off the Judokas, bursts into life with a flying kick that finishes the expert. A take that went wrong from a later scene could perhaps be used.
4. Finale. Fight scenes already shot by Bruce on his way up the pagoda would be used to complete the film. The film could run something like this and have a 'AA' certificate.
Stephen Leigh, Pattingham, Staffordshire

Hi Stephen,
You must have had your thinking cap on! Really, it sounds fine to me, but whether or not Raymond Chow has something different in mind, I don't know. Actually, I have a great idea! How about all of you sending in your ideas on how to finish off the film? Well print the best of them here in KFM and send them off to the Golden Harvest studios. I'm pretty sure they'd be interested in what you've got to say!

THE FAN CLUB

Dear Jenny,
I find it hard to understand why Bruce Lee, the most popular man on earth, should lose his fan club. As a member, I would gladly pay more to see it stay open and I think any real fan of Bruce would agree with me. I would like to congratulate you on *KFM* No.16. They get better all the time. *Kung-Fu Monthly* comes second in my world of Kung Fu. Bruce Lee comes before all.
Eileen O'Connell, Bally Coolin, Ireland

Dear Eileen,
As I said at the start this month, I'm as upset as everyone else about the closure of the club. Let's just keep hoping that better news is around the corner. Thanks a lot for your very kind words - how could we begrudge coming second to the fabulous Bruce Lee!

KFM PEN PAL CORNER

Miss D Davies, Bucknall, Staffs wants a Chinese male 17 to 20 years old. Lynn Humphrey, Selly Oak, Birmingham want Chinese male living in Hong Kong - 18 to 20 years. Rick Edwards, Coventry wants girl, any nationality, around 20 years. Miss Marie Hampton, Erdington, Birmingham wants Chinese - 17 to 25 years. Michelle McKenzie, Deptford, London wants Chinese male, 15 to 16 years, send photo. Christine Hamer & Lesley Berry, Bolton, Lancashire wants two Chinese males, 16 to 18 years. Colin Mason, Castleford, Yorkshire wants girl, about 20 years.

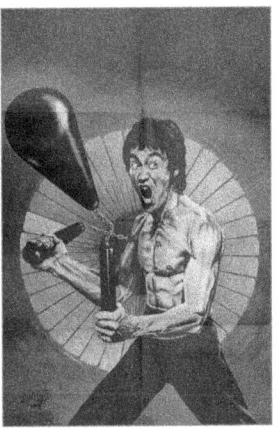

EDITORIAL

Hi there Kung Fu fans...

As I'm sure you've guessed by now, we've really knuckled down to it this month and sorted out a top notch issue for you. For starters, there's our first ever *KFM* Competition and five fabulous prizes to be won! If this one goes as well as I suspect it's going to, then we'll make a regular feature of it.

First up we have our *KFM* Flashback article entitled Bruce Lee - Kung Fu Conqueror. Sadly, having now exhausted our supply of early issues, we've lately been unable to help all the thousands of *KFM* fans who write in requesting valuable back issues. In fact, many are now collector's items! To make amends therefore, we bring you a potted history of *KFM*, including snippets from all the really sensational features of yesteryear. Who could ever forget Don Won Ton's incredible 'Bruce Lee's Last Hours' article in *KFM* No.3? Or come to that, the amazing 'Bruce Lee's Last Interview,' exclusive in *KFM* No.11? We haven't, and it's all there in our salute to the Kung Fu Conqueror!

Still more to come! Part two of the review of Felix Dennis & Roger Hutchinson's *The Wisdom of Bruce Lee* fills our second feature spot and to be honest, I hardly know how to tell you what a great book this is. I've read it from cover to cover twice now and still the depth of their investigation astounds me. I don't just recommend you go get yourself a copy - for the true Bruce Lee fanatic, it's a martial must! Sorry, I still can't give you a UK publication date, but hang on though as it won't be long.

That's it from me - I'll be with you all again next month! 'Til then...

Felix Yen

Felix Yen
Editor-in-Chief

BRUCE LEE: THE KUNG FU CONQUEROR

Would you believe that during the last two years, *KFM* has had over half a million letters to open!

In order that we were able to achieve this martial arts' success story of the century, we have to thank firstly, you the dedicated *KFM* reader and secondly, Bruce Lee, the Little Dragon, for having made the whole thing possible. History seldom repeats itself. Probably never again shall we see the likes of Bruce Lee. He was a phenomenon - unique and a man without measure. Right back in issue one we promised, in the words of the master, to bring you a magazine that was 'real and natural' and we hope you agree we've done just that. It's hard to believe that *KFM* started over two years ago, and boy have we travelled a long road since then! For those of you who have stuck with us all the way - thanks. I hope you enjoyed the ride, so far, as much as we did. But please, may we have your indulgence? *KFM*, on behalf of the many fans who missed early issues is for this month only, going to kick-back through the early issues, pulling out some of the fantastic scoops and revelations that Lady Luck brought our way. It's not every day that we do a bit of trumpet blowing, but then it's not every day that we reach issue number twenty!

KFM **No.1**, naturally enough, featured a brief run through of the life and death of Bruce Lee. Nothing sensational about it now, but to the fans then, thirsting-after information about the 'late, great' Little Dragon, the article was a godsend. At last, someone was taking the trouble to dig 'straight and true' and *KFM* hammered home its future intentions by following up with a brief explanation of the world of Kung Fu. Already we were starting to see some of the stupendous pictures that were to set the martial arts world alight. Suddenly every-body was talking about Bruce Lee!

And so to *KFM* **No.2** and here we featured the 'grasshopper rebel,' David Carradine.

Although not an accomplished Kung Fu expert in his own right, David surely was instrumental in bringing the 'word' to the people. His fantastically successful TV series, *Kung Fu* though not in many ways "genuine,' mustn't be underestimated. Many a martial arts fan found his way to Bruce Lee via the exploits of the Wandering Monk, Kwai Chang Caine. An important 'first' for this issue was the appearance of the Paul Simmons martial arts page. The acclamation to this and to his later efforts - a tribute to the superb clarity of his diagrams - was soon to lead to the publishing of a collection of his work. It hardly needs me to remind you that his book was the best-selling *The Beginner's Guide to Kung Fu*.

    KFM **No.3** and the letters were coming in by the ton! Our own Jenny Lee arrived to join the team and the sigh of relief was heard all the way from London's West End through to Clearwater Bay! The feature story was an important one. *KFM*'s own Don Won Ton jetted over to Kowloon to find out the real story behind the untimely death of China's number one son. The investigation unearthed a full chain of stranger-than-fiction events. Somehow, the reasons for his death seemed conclusive, but were they? The rumours flooded on. Many of his fans indeed refused to believe in their hero's demise - could it be a publicity stunt? Sadly, time has confirmed that it wasn't. We have to accept that the death of the world's fittest man came about because of an accident.

    KFM **No.4** featured the sayings of Bruce Lee. Containing his thoughts on philosophy, the film world, the martial arts, acting and fame, the introduction ended with the sentence, "Someday somebody will undoubtedly collect together in a book the sayings of Bruce Lee." Little did we know that just a year and a half later, the task would be accomplished. We are of course currently reviewing *The Wisdom of Bruce Lee*. Don Won Ton's selection of some of the Little Dragon's wittiest and most profound statements were included in *KFM* number four. The world was beginning to take note of the extent of Bruce Lee's genius ... the Kung Fu king had something more than superb skill and fitness to offer - he also proved himself to be both intelligent and perceptive!

Angela Mao took the honours for the second feature. The First Lady of Kung Fu we called her and time hasn't proved us wrong. Even at the tender age of twenty-four she could reel off a list of film parts as long as your arm, culminating of course in the never-to-be-forgotten flashback scene in *Enter the Dragon*. Born in September 20th 1950, Angela enrolled at the age of five in Taiwan's Fu Shing Academy and like the Little Dragon, much of her earlier experience was gleaned from the roles she handled in the Peking style opera. Her acting and singing talents had never been in doubt but, as *KFM* emphasised at the time, she was no slouch either when it came to Kung Fu, Angela Mao showed just how deadly the female of the species can become!

Next up came *KFM No.5*, containing Don Won Ton's famous article entitled, 'How the Little Dragon sparked off the Kung Fu Revolution.' Don ignited the action at around two thousand years BC, about the time of the Yellow Emperor and then painstakingly followed the history of the martial arts right through to the present day. He contended that as far as Bruce Lee fans were concerned, the turning point centred around a Madam Yim Wing Chun. It was she who formalised the style that became known simply as Wing Chun. Her conviction that Kung Fu as it was then was far too formal and stylised would surely, he felt have won her the approval of the great master himself. How that style was eventually adopted by the legendary Yip Man and how he in turn passed on his convictions to the then young tear-away, Bruce Lee, was lovingly recounted. You could almost have 'climbed inside' the Little Dragon's mind as Don described in fine detail exactly how Bruce found his way through to Jeet Kune Do.

That moves us up to *KFM No.6* and the fantastic feature article, 'How Bruce Lee tamed Hollywood'. Really we pulled out all the stops on this one. To quote, "For every 'star' in Hollywood, there are a hundred others struggling to break into the big time, and for them, Hollywood is not a paradise but a nightmare cruelly driving them to desperation and defeat. And such is the power of Hollywood that it almost crushed the finest martial artist the world has ever seen - Bruce 'Little Dragon' Lee!" Bruce, however, rose to the challenge until finally he had clawed his way up to the top of the tree. It's a story of courage and determination against all the odds and a battle against every kind of discrimination. Singlehanded, Bruce grabbed the Hollywood movie-moguls by the throat... and won!

"Like any genius, Bruce Lee made his art look easy. It is only when you try to imitate it that you realise how difficult it is." Thus begins The Deadly Art of Bruce Lee, the feature story to *KFM No.7*. The Little Dragon's prowess in the world of Kung Fu was no accident. His training routines, his techniques, his attitude towards opponents and his unquestioned skill with the various Asian weapons of war... all are fully described and explained. Co-starring in this issue is Jimmy Wang Yu, the man who, but for Bruce Lee, would probably have been acclaimed the crown-king of the Kung Fu film circuit. His story is one of martial mastery and box-office bonanzas and such films as *Zatoichi* and the *One-Armed Swordsman*, *The Man from Hong Kong* and The One-Armed Boxer bear testimony to the success of China's first ever actor-millionaire.

KFM No.8 and *KFM No.9* keep the *KFM* ball rolling in fine fashion. First off, we get the low-down on all the various styles that fall under the general heading of the martial arts. Our writer gives you a punch by punch and a kick by kick analysis of many of the Little Dragon's fight sequences and tells why he believes that Jeet Kune Do must always succeed if only because of its superior flexibility. Meanwhile in *KFM* nine we ask the question,

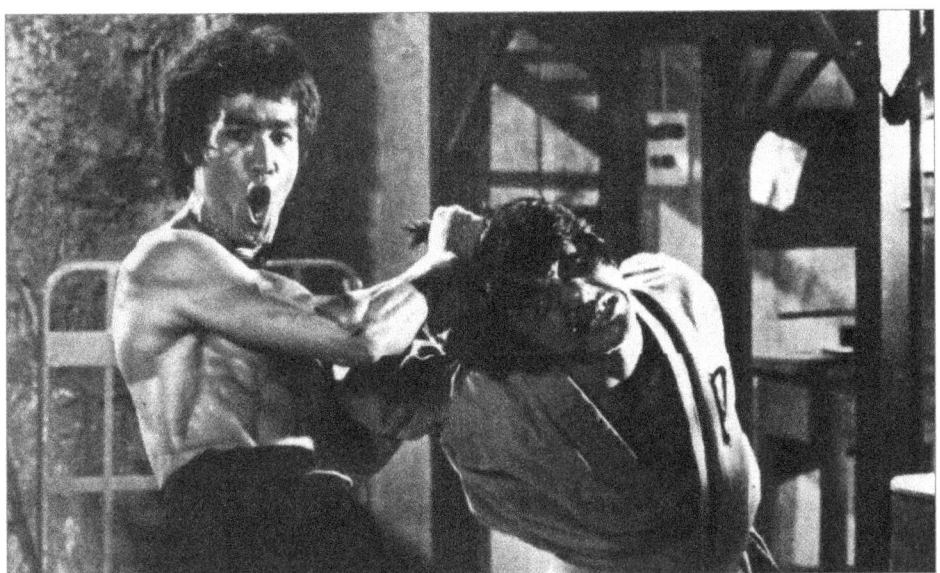

'Who's Knocking Kung Fu?' In the face of much adverse press comment, we decided to answer the questions that many people were asking; Do Kung Fu films turn their audiences into vicious psychopaths? Should people be encouraged to teach or learn Kung Fu? Does Kung Fu encourage racial violence? It was necessary that these questions were answered and hopefully some of the martial art's more misinformed opponents had a lot of their misconceptions set right.

On to *KFM **No.10*** and two winners here! Firstly we took a glimpse behind the Bamboo Curtain at some of the deadly Chinese Secret Societies. Most of them get a mention, from the White Lotus to the infamous Triads. Naturally too, reference was made to the accusation that the Little Dragon was in fact murdered by one of these shadowy sects. Following up, came a definitive feature on the King of the Hong Kong film industry, Raymond Chow. He recounted his side of the Bruce Lee story and told us too of his hopes and ambitions for the future. Whether or not the Mandarin film industry takes the next dramatic step towards world acceptance is a question probably only Mr Chow and a few others can answer.

*KFM **No.11***'s premiere feature must rate as a real scoop. For the first time ever, readers were able to read verbatim the transcript of Bruce Lee's last ever interview, taped at Radio Hong Kong shortly before his death. It's all there, the wit, the charm and the wisdom and the depth in which he replied to many of the seemingly trivial questions, is indicative of a man who stood alone. He took little but gave all!

*KFM **No.12*** presented a transcript of another interview that took place on Radio Hong Kong, this time with Linda Lee. With Bruce having tragically died only a short month earlier, Linda's courage in facing such an ordeal was all the more outstanding. It would be pointless here to reprint quotations from either of the interviews, Suffice to say that for the true follower of Bruce Lee, both make imperative reading.

There's no need, I feel, to itemise particular issues of *KFM* any further. Probably many of you have all the issues concerned anyway. However, one further milestone in the success story of *Kung-Fu Monthly* deserves attention. That, as you may have guessed, is our research into Bruce Lee's final martial epic, *Game of Death*. Only by battering away at the solid wall of silence did we finally manage to bring you the truth of the situation. Just what were the chances of the film being finished? Who were the stars? How far had Bruce Lee got before he died? All these questions and many more besides were answered in two no-punches-pulled features, plus, of course, the spectacular *Game of Death* Special.

Once again, *KFM* got there ahead of them all!

COMPETITION

Jenny Lee has locked away in a very safe place, five complete sets of *Kung-Fu Monthly* and five complete sets of Bruce Lee Film Posters. For this month's competition, five winners will each get an autographed collection of *KFM* Nos.1 to 20, plus the film posters from *The Big Boss*, *Fist of Fury*, *The Way of the Dragon* and *Enter the Dragon* (with special thanks to Cathay Films Ltd Warner Brothers Ltd.) Talk about a collector's dream!

Now, all you've got to do is to look closely at the following six Bruce Lee pictures and tell us which films hey are from. Sounds easy doesn't it? But take care, there are a couple of tricky ones! When you've made your decisions, just write them on a postcard and post it off straight away to: *KFM* Competition, 39 Goodge Street, London, W1D 1FD.

The five lucky postcards will be plucked from the hat by an executive of Cathay Films Ltd and announced in *KFM* No.22. Finally, last entries must be in by July 31st, please and don't forget to include on the card your name and address!

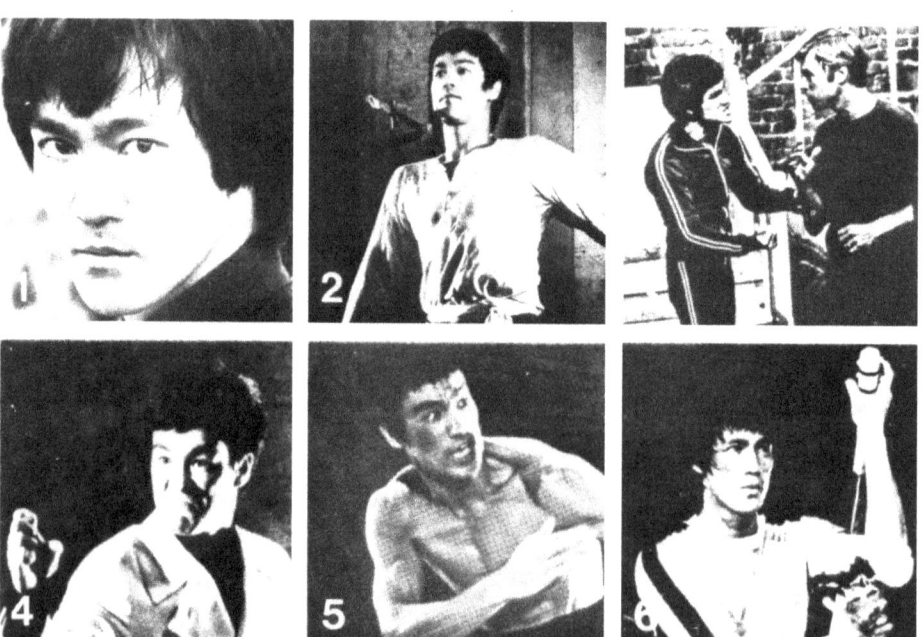

THE WISDOM OF BRUCE LEE

Last month, *KFM* took you through the first four chapters of that soon-to-be published and truly sensational new book, *The Wisdom of Bruce Lee*. We glanced briefly at how the martial arts came about, who were the original practitioners and how finally Bruce Lee untied the regimented reins of Kung Fu and turned loose the 'mysteries of the East.' This superb publication pulls out quote after quote to help illustrate the Little Dragon's philosophy of the martial arts, his reaction to the 'classical mess' and covers in fine detail the path leading ultimately to his concept of Jeet Kune Do. Finally last month, we took in the chapter dealing with Bruce's very individual style of training and just how he persuaded his old buddy Danny Inosanto to pull out the biggest kick of his life! Great reading indeed. But that's enough of last issue. We have to attend to the final power-packed chapters of Messrs. Dennis and Hutchinson's dynamic tribute to the Little Dragon - *The Wisdom of Bruce Lee*.

Bruce Lee started teaching Kung Fu from a car park in Seattle. He was studying at the University of Washington at the time and was pretty broke. He needed a job of some sort and teaching the martial arts "... sure beat washing dishes." The classes caught on. Within a few months, Bruce had quit the University and opened up shop. He charged just twenty-two dollars a month!

Headed 'On Teaching,' chapter five of *The Wisdom of Bruce Lee* digs deep down to uncover background details never revealed, the need for the pupil's emotional involvement was stressed right from the start and to this end, Bruce would never take on more than six students at any one session. He felt that the real aim of the school was not so much to teach, as to help the pupils find out for themselves. Although certainly cut out for the job, he obviously too found it tough going. Many of the students, for one reason or another, were quite literally hopeless; five minute wonders and so on. However, he persevered and before long was opening a new in Los Angeles. Importantly, the book summarises the Little Dragon's famous three stages of learning, which I quote in full.

THE THREE STAGES OF CULTIVATION

1) The primitive stage of total ignorance, in which a man or woman knows nothing about the art. Instinct alone prevails in deciding whether to block or attack in combat during this stage.

2) The mechanical, or sophisticated stage, when a pupil has begun his training. In this stage, the pupil has certainly improved in techniques of blocking, striking, breathing, etc., but there is usually a tendency to lose the instinctive fluidity the pupil possessed in the previous stage. Many martial artists, Lee realised, remained in this stage all of their lives, which is why he introduced the revolutionary third stage.

3) Which is that of alertness and spontaneous action. It can only come after years of serious and hard practice, and is the sign of the real master. Without having lost any of the abilities developed in the second stage, the fighter throws his rule book out of the window. That is, he reverts to the fluidity of the untrained man, ready for any combat

situation, Karate, Boxing, whatever, and in Lee's own words, "He adjusts himself to his opponent like water pressing on an earthen wall. It flows through the slightest crack."

Before long, the Little Dragon was making a good deal of money. The school had caught on and James Coburn, Steve McQueen and James Garner headed a long list of movie superstars that came under the practiced eye of Bruce Lee. Despite charging up to a thousand dollars for a ten hour course, still they came along and still the Little Dragon refused to let up on his principles. Everybody, whether they were famous or not, got the same attention. No one was in for an easy ride! *The Wisdom of Bruce Lee* recounts many of the reactions to the Little Dragon's fireball energy from those same early pupils. Ed Parker explained, "He was one in two billion. If God could give a man all the natural talents, he had them. His problem as a teacher was that he could pass on his ideas, but not his talent."

Dennis and Hutchinson, however, assert that there is plenty of reason to suspect that Bruce was only too aware of the limited potential of many of his students. A pupil was more than a number, he was a real, living person and wherever possible, that man's syllabus became tailor-made for him. Judge for yourself as you read the many personal tributes paid to Bruce at the time; there are some gems!

LOSER SHALL DIE

From thugs to stuntmen, from school kids to Kung Fu masters, the Little Dragon at one time or another, fought them all. *The Wisdom of Bruce Lee*, turning its attention to opponents, traces out a tale of sheer skill and total superiority. Egged on to fight during his formative years in the streets of Kowloon, the Little Dragon took in the early message well. Probably his most celebrated Hong Kong tussle was the 'loser shall die' confrontation which took place atop a five story apartment block. Bruce, however, after breaking both his opponent's arms, instead called an ambulance.

Times weren't easy either when he first set up school in California. Martial arts academies were already in abundance and several of the 'opposition' decided that Bruce's made it one too many! Their deputation was headed by a Wong Jack Man who issued the challenge that should the Little Dragon be defeated, he should either close down his school or at least stop passing on their 'secrets' to Westerners. To learn the full details of exactly how Bruce pulled Wong Jack Man apart, you will have to read the book. Suffice to say that the school stayed open and the Little Dragon continued to teach Westerners.

From schools to film sets and still the challenges came along. In fact, throughout his turbulent career, Bruce was dogged by prospective opponents who either hoped to topple the king of Kung Fu or in many cases, simply wished to prove that his apparent abilities were just a sham. They all learnt to their cost! One of the more memorable of these occasions was the time when the Little Dragon was helping out his old friend and former pupil, Stirling Silliphant. Two stuntmen who had been hired to do some fight scenes were sceptical that the 135-pound Chinese could handle the choreography for the battle to come. Within minutes, both of them had landed up in the swimming pool!

The Wisdom of Bruce Lee takes us through many of these instances, as well as recounting the answer to a question put to him one time on Hong Kong radio. He was asked how he felt about the pressure of being constantly challenged, and the way the Little Dragon handled his reply was both illuminating and superb. "But can you take care of yourself?"

the interviewer persisted. "I will answer first of all with a joke, if you don't mind. All the time, people come up and say, 'Bruce - are you really that good?' I say, 'Well if I tell you I'm good, probably you will say that I'm boasting. But if I tell you I'm no good, you'll know I'm lying.'" Bruce Lee once commented to his wife, Linda, that movies were not an art. "They are," he explained, "a combination of commercial creativity and creative commerce." As *The Wisdom of Bruce Lee* argues, he probably knew better than Sir Laurence Olivier exactly why people go to the cinema. Certainly the days spent during his childhood touring with his father and the Cantonese Opera House stood him in good stead. The experience he gained then and during his early childhood films and of course the filming of the TV series *Longstreet* saw him well primed to then explode into his first full-length Mandarin movie, *The Big Boss*.

BRUCE LEE - A BLOODY, VIOLENT MAN?

It was an important film and in fact, Bruce saw it as vital to the Chinese film world. In retrospect, it's obvious that the cinematic mind of Bruce Lee was developing faster than the local cinema industry. The book explains that at the time of *The Big Boss*, he frequently gave interviews to the press expressing discontent with the state of things and reaffirming his intention to do something about it. He started by drawing the line between violence and action. "An action film borders somewhere between reality and fantasy. If it were completely realistic, you would call me a bloody violent man!" The combination of Bruce Lee and Golden Harvest boss, Raymond Chow, the Run Run Shaw renegade, proved to be unbeatable.

The Wisdom of Bruce Lee takes us entertainingly through the making of all the Little Dragon's films with the quotations, anecdotes and revelations literally piled mountain high. His struggles with himself and with those around him are fully highlighted and his fight to produce the "Best goddam films ever" makes compelling reading. Perhaps the most understandable comment to come out of this long chapter on the Little Dragon's cinema career, is where he is attempting to compromise living the somewhat ambiguous life of a martial artist cum film star. He said, "As an actor, I am frustrated between business and art, with the hope that through harmonious reconciliations of these I can then come out expressing myself and truthfully communicating."

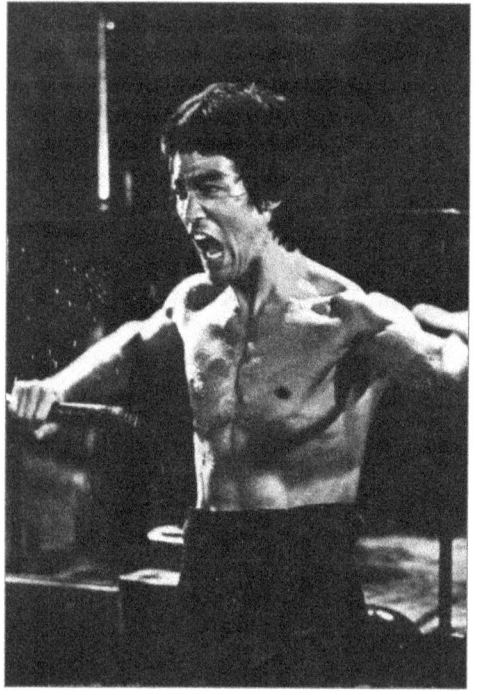

And how did the Little Dragon react to the fame that was heaped around those willing shoulders? How did he take to the constant adulation and intrusion into private life that is the luck of most great movie stars? *The Wisdom of Bruce Lee* tells us that he adapted to it as well as could be expected. Remember though that Bruce surely had his hands fuller than most. How many other film actors are obliged to spend precious time each day maintaining fantastic fitness? It would not after all be unreasonable to expect the world's greatest ever martial artist to spend most of his day just holding on to that supreme position, let alone having to live the life of a Hollywood film star at the self-same time!

His frequent brushes with astrology are well documented. For all his western ways, Bruce could not finally bring himself to reject the trappings of Chinese superstition. Strangely though, a number of the predictions seem to have been deadly right! One of the seer's saw financial success coming the Little Dragon's way in 1971 and he was correct, although as Bruce later remarked to Fighting Stars magazine, "Having money doesn't solve all your problems but it sure beats not having money." He soon discovered that the film industry was then, in many ways, crooked and corrupt. Bribery seemed to be the norm and there were times when he had good cause to regret his new found fame and fortune. Probably the most irksome thing about it all was the lack of privacy. As he one day said to Linda, in despair, "It's like I'm in jail. I'm like a monkey in a zoo."

The book, *The Wisdom of Bruce Lee* is at pains to point out that the Little Dragon was

not a 'perfect man.' Come to that, who is? And what exactly constitutes a 'perfect man' anyway? To quote, "He was a man of deep and complex nature, whose explorations of himself make a fascinating, truthful study of a remarkable personality'. His great points were his charm, his wit, his brilliance in conversation and his dynamic energy. Many people too would bear witness to his kindness and generosity." As Linda told Radio Hong Kong, "He was always very good to me. I could not have a complaint in the world. I could not wish for a better husband, ever."

The final, unforgettable chapter of this remarkable new book contains a collection of Bruce Lee's thoughts and sayings on the broader themes of life and truth. We have room here but for a few quotations to whet your appetite:

"Self-education makes great men."

"Showing off is a fool's idea of glory."

"Real living is living for others."

"To change with change is the changeless state."

And that brings us to the end of the review of *The Wisdom of Bruce Lee* and what a fabulous book it is! There's literally something here for everybody and many biting anecdotes that I have certainly never come across before. Really, Felix Dennis and Roger Hutchinson deserve a martial medal for the thoroughness of their investigations and without doubt, they will soon be receiving the thanks they so richly deserve for producing such an extraordinary publication. As I said last issue, we plan to be selling the book through our mail-order service in the very near future, so keep a close watch on the pages of *KFM*. I promise you that you'll not want to miss getting your copy of *The Wisdom of Bruce Lee*.

KICKBACK: THE LETTERS

Well, we've really made it. Issue twenty and you can bet your life there'll be some corks popping in the *KFM* offices tonight. First of all, it's congratulations to Zafar Jybal (I hope the spelling's right) whose letter is printed first. To my mind, he sent in the best reply to my little 'Talk about your favourite Bruce Lee film' contest. Thanks, of course, to everyone who took part. You have no idea how hard it is to judge when there are so many fine entries. I've also had several letters in lately from readers who have been having difficulty in getting their copies of *KFM*. Goodness knows why that should be, but I have been advised in cases like that, the best thing to do is to order it from your nearest WH Smiths; I'm sure that'll soon sort things out. Let's move on to the letters!

NUNCHAKUS AGAIN

Dear Jenny,
After watching *Fist of Fury* recently and seeing Bruce handle the nunchakus perfectly, I thought it would be a brilliant idea to print a 'front-on' poster of Bruce with the nunchakus whirling round him. If you did this I think it would be the best poster you ever printed, so how about it? Also where can I get *KFM* No.3 and Robert Lee's *Ballad of Bruce Lee* album?
Allan Briers, Peasley Cross, Merseyside

Dear Allan,
We read your letter and thought it really was a great idea. Unfortunately, there simply aren't any suitable pictures available, so we've done the next best thing and commissioned Jeff Cummins to paint another of his superb portraits - I hope everybody likes it! As far as your other two questions go, I don't think the Robert Lee album is available over here. Finally, KFM No.1 is in the post!

THE WINNER

Dear Jenny,
The projector starts rolling in the cinema as you perceive Bruce Lee in shorts and Kung Fu Boxing gloves. He slowly, but surely, walks towards his opponent, they bow to each other as your heart suddenly starts beating faster. A minute later the opponent is seen sprawled out on the floor. This exciting scene was, of course, from *Enter the Dragon*. *Enter the Dragon* was Bruce Lee's best film because it showed the attributes of Kung Fu. That Kung Fu must be honoured and not misused, is demonstrated by Shih Kien as the evil, scheming Han and also aboard the ship when Bruce was challenged by another fighter. And it also shows that avenging a loved one's death is not a bad thing if done in a trained manner. All these aspects put together with the fight scenes (especially at the end Shih Kien v Bruce Lee) make it Bruce's most exciting film.
Zafar Jybal, Blackwood, South Wales

Hi Zafar,
Thanks for the entry, and as I said earlier on, you win! A copy of Shaolin Temple Secrets is coming your way soon.

DAVID CHIANG / WANG YU / ANGELA MAO

Dear Jenny,
Having been an avid reader of *KFM* since issue four, I feel it's about time I dropped you a line to express my appreciation of the painstaking work and detailed investigation that goes into each issue of *KFM*. The magazine is so thorough and complete that I can't think of any questions to ask except maybe one. *KFM* is a martial arts magazine, right? Well, with no disrespect to the King, how about having pin-ups of other leading martial artists, like crown prince David Chiang, or Wang Yu, or Kung Fu's heroine, Angela Mao? Finally, can you tell me where I might be able to get hold of *KFM* No. 1, 2 and 3?
Sue Myers, Clitheroe, Lancashire

Dear Sue,
Compliments, compliments; still they're always very acceptable! About your question, I must say the same idea has crossed my mind a few times. The trouble is that it's one of those things where you don't know whether you've made a right or a wrong move until you've actually done it. I have the feeling though that the majority of our readers still want to see Bruce on the big poster. How about some of you fans writing in and telling me what you think! Bye the bye Sue, copies of KFM No. 1, 2 and 3 coming your way in the post.

BRUCE LEE ... SKINNY LITTLE MAN!

Dear Jenny,
I am studying at college and one of our main subjects is film study. Just recently, *Enter the Dragon* came to our little screen and I was shocked to see and hear the jokes that the other students made about the film and about the Little Dragon himself. There were words used like 'skinny little man,' 'the film is far fetched, it's like the old time movies,' 'it's too funny to laugh at and the sound effects are ridiculous.' All I can say is that I feel sorry for these people because they are too ignorant to see the talent and feel the magnetism of this one unique person. Sometimes I wish Bruce would reach the hearts of a lot more people in my area as it could be a much happier place to live in. Thanks for producing a great magazine and keep up the good work.
Ian Grant, North Shields, Tyne and Wear

Dear Ian,
How I really do sympathise with you. The trouble is there are Philistines in every walk of life and you just have to learn to live with them. Funnily enough, you would probably find if you were watching the film with just ONE of the 'scoffers,' I guarantee he'd almost certainly not make a sound and in fact, he'd thoroughly enjoy it. Perfectly reasonable people sometimes do the most strange things when they're in a crowd. They think passing 'clever' comments makes them look big!

THE KFM PEN PAL CORNER

Michelle Crews, Irvine, Scotland wants Chinese female, aged 13-14.
Violet McDonald, Irvine, Scotland wants Chinese male, aged 16-17.

DRAMATIC NEWS!

KFM is planning to start its own Bruce Lee fan club! Hold on though; don't write in yet. Full details in will be revealed in *Kung-Fu Monthly* No.21.

EDITORIAL

Hi there Kung Fu fans.

Great heavens, what an amazing issue we've got for you! Right away, let me say that although by the time you've finished reading this issue, you're sure to have found out about the sensational Bruce Lee Secret Society. What you won't know is that Shiela Boardman of Manchester has just formed the Official David Chiang Fan Club. I'm sure that David has got a whole heap of fans out there in crazy Kung Fu land, so how about dropping a line to Shiela (include a stamped addressed envelope please) to find out more details. Oh, and Cathay Films ask me to remind you that any letters addressed to them without SAEs will not get answered! Now, let's take a look at this month's stunning line-up...

The *KFM* research team have been at it again and to tie in with a long overdue re-release,, we present in this issue, an in-depth look at the *The Way of the Dragon*. After reading this article, you'll see *The Way of the Dragon* as you've never seen it before! Did you know that Bruce played percussion on the soundtrack or that the film was the first ever Chinese film to be shot on location? The team have really turned on the taps this time to bring you two whole pages, jam-packed with up-to-date information on what was arguably Bruce Lee's most significant film.

Nunchakus grab the headlines for this month's other feature. After a very great deal of thought, *KFM* has decided to break two and a half years of silence on the subject. The result is a searching and definitive account of what is possibly the most evocative family of weapons in the martial arts world.

That's all from me for this month, but watch out for the next issue as we've got a surprise in store for you!

Felix Yen

Felix Yen
Editor-in-Chief

SECRETS OF THE DEADLY NUNCHAKU, BRUCE LEE'S WONDER WEAPON!

In issue 19 of *Kung-Fu Monthly*, we published a simple and direct letter from a *KFM* reader, concerning the dangers of using the nunchaku. Wisely, Jenny replied saying that it was stupid and dangerous to 'play' with nunchakus, emphasising that expert tuition was essential. Since then, another letter has come through our door, one that we consider so sensible as to publish it here in its entirety. There could be no better front-piece to this unique feature.

> *Dear Jenny Lee,*
> *Having read of someone recently receiving some nasty injuries and your very sincere words of warning about fooling around with nunchakus, I must say this is very good advice. You suggested being taught by an expert and that is certainly the best way but they do tend to be expensive. I am now fairly proficient with the flails and I am also self-taught, so please don't think KFM fans, that because your pocket money doesn't stretch that far, you are going to have to give up all hope of learning the art. But I followed a few simple and common sense guidelines.*
> *Firstly, I purchased a professionally made pair of nunchakus and borrowed several good books on the art (your local library will help) and I made absolutely certain nobody could enter my training area unnoticed by myself. Then, I did every move slowly and with deliberation for some weeks. Only then did I try for speed and finally co-ordination and power, learn how to make my own nunchakus to suit my individual needs, although that also requires certain skills.*
> *I have found that other self-taught people I've met, because of the dedication and time spent on learning the art, have lost the desire to show off or act stupidly. So KFM fans, be dedicated, but not foolish.*

You may have noticed that up until now, *KFM* has followed a deliberate policy of avoiding any feature articles on nunchakus. For two reasons, however, we feel that the time has come to revise that policy. To begin with, in order to defuse a subject, it's best to demystify it and secondly, we feel confident that our readership now represents a responsible group of people who will not abuse the possession of such information. Let me, however, point out in the strongest possible terms that the nunchaku is considered to be an offensive weapon and as such, should not be handled in public places.

THE HISTORY

The present day nunchaku comes to us from the Philippines and its basic layout consists of two cudgels of equal length, connected by a chain or nylon cord. Legend has it that the original nunchaku or 'big sweeper' was invented around the time of the first Emperor of the Sung Dynasty. Then, its design was somewhat different; in particular, one of the cudgels was made longer than the other. The short length was fourteen inches and the longer, forty. A hybrid of the 'big sweeper' became the very popular three section staff. The design of this variation is interesting. The cudgels are approximately one inch in diameter and their lengths should each equal the arm length of the user. This is important in order to facilitate correct use of the weapon.

DANGER!

It has been calculated that when Bruce Lee was moving at his fastest, his nunchakus collided with a force of over 1,600 pounds at the point of contact. Believe it or not, a human bone can snap when subjected to a force of only 10 pounds Take great care and remember, for practicing purposes, a special rubber version is available which on impact does far less damage. Even they though can cause considerable pain if misused. Remember too to take great care of your nunchaku. Check frequently for any damage or worn cord links. In a moment of carelessness, it's you the user who is most likely to get hurt. Finally, when it comes to ease of practice, long cudgels are simpler to use than short and hard surface 'grips' are easier than soft.

GETTING STARTED

Take a look at the Little Dragon in action. Immediately you are aware of a man of lightning responses, hair-breadth timing and a superb sense of balance. These are what you must strive for, but have patience; nothing of worth comes quickly or easily. As a tip it's useful, when starting, to move around on your feet, while slowly building up the arm swinging techniques. This helps no end with the development of bodily balance. Check constantly from whatever guide book or information sheet you are using that you are not learning any of the steps incorrectly. It may only take a week to learn a wrong action but it could take a lifetime to lose it again! Once you are satisfied that you have mastered the first basic moves, it's time to start using a target and for that, we would suggest a static sandbag. Later, when your confidence has become more assured, have a companion take the target around while you chase.

EXERCISES - BRUCE LEE'S WARMING-UP ROUTINE

The following exercises represent excellent limbering-up routines, prior to any nunchaku practice session.

- Fold the two cudgels of the nunchaku together and grip in the right hand approximately midway down the length. Hold them out in front of you and twist them to and fro like the sails of a windmill. Repeat with the other hand. This action produces a two-fold effect. Firstly, the gripping power of the fingers is improved and secondly, the wrist and arm joints become more flexible.
- Separate the cudgels and hold them in a horizontal line above the head, keeping the feet wide apart. Then, without flexing the knees, bend to the left as far as you can, straighten up and then bend similarly to the right. Do this a number of times. It's invaluable for toning up the spine and developing the waist muscles.
- Assume a similar position to that of number two, but this time form a horizontal line with the nunchakus at roughly shoulder height and in front of you. Without flexing either the legs or arms, rotate the body first one way and then the other.
- Sit down on the floor with your legs positioned straight out and wide apart. Holding one cudgel in each hand, hook them around the left foot. Pull the torso forward and down until the head makes contact with the knee (or comes as close as is possible). The leg must be kept straight. Repeat with the other leg. This exercise is marvellous for limbering-up the leg muscles.

Editor No.2 Bruce Sawyer outside the office on Goodge Street showing off a pair of Bruce Lee's actual nunchakus from the 1972 film Fist of Fury.

Here would be a good moment to discuss your approach to warming up exercises. Far too many people attack them like a bull in a china shop. Not only is that not necessary, it can also be positively dangerous. A muscle that has been forgotten for many years needs to be treated gently. Like anything which is in a weakened state, it will break down if misused. Don't worry if your head doesn't quite reach your knee in the last exercise as it probably will in time, if you don't force it! Even Bruce Lee, the great master himself, once strained a muscle in his back so badly that he was virtually immobile for many months. Finally in this section, for those of you who do not have and perhaps cannot afford a pair of nunchakus, don't despair. These early exercises can easily be carried out with a home-made substitute but I will leave that to your ingenuity. I need hardly repeat though, that these should NEVER be used in the manner of true nunchakus.

Bruce Lee not only became deadly adept at using the nunchaku and the three pole staff, he also learned to handle two nunchakus at once, with a skill never before seen. Although it would be wrong to infer that the Little Dragon invented the twin cudgels, it would certainly be true to say that he invented its current popularity. His control over the wonder weapon was unique and the power he consequently had laying at his finger tips was immense. His winding up routine (see, for instance, Enter the Dragon) where he whirls them around his head and shoulders while changing from one hand to the other is positively mesmeric. In fact every time I've seen that slice of action on film, the sequence never fails to bring a gasp of amazement from a stunned audience.

I've lost count of the number of letters we've received from readers asking if Bruce really did do all the stunts in his films and were some of them camera tricks. Let me tell you this. I have it on the highest possible authority that the Little Dragon's nunchaku scenes were in actual fact slowed down so as to let the people see what he was doing. He really was that fast, and more! Bruce's old friend Danny Inosanto was partly responsible for the Little Dragon's early inspiration. Dan, at the time an acknowledged club swinging expert, surprised Bruce with his sheer dexterity. He could switch it from left to right hand three or four times in the space of a second and the Little Dragon soon  grew to realise the great potentialities as yet unrealised in the twin cudgels.

Dan, a professor of sports and histology, is quick to refute the common idea that Bruce 'picked his brains' when learning to master the nunchaku. He comments, "No, not at all! My club playing only motivated Bruce to play with the nunchaku. After watching me at work, he created the nunchaku of Jeet Kune Do." The Little Dragon, however, would often argue otherwise. He felt that no one could match his old friend when it came to using the 'magic rod.' Whichever way the argument swings, there can be no doubt that both mas-

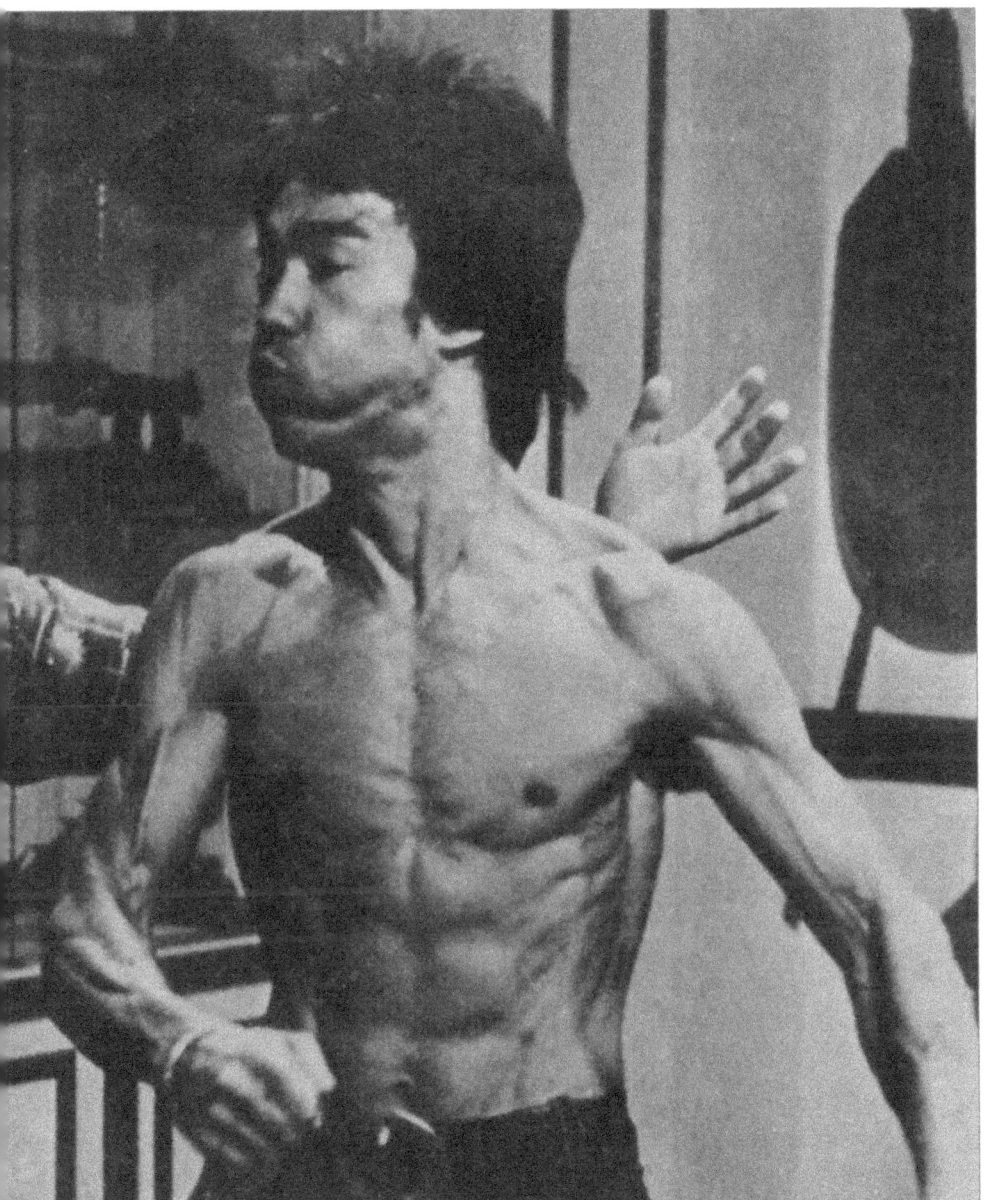

tered the art to a point of total refinement.

Looking at *Fist of Fury*, it is apparent that Bruce's flails axe uncommonly short. In fact, each measures approximately thirteen inches with a connecting chain length of seven inches. This makes it a difficult instrument to handle but remember, the shorter the cudgel length, the greater the skill required. The Little Dragon however, saw it as a defensive weapon and therefore decided there was a need for it to be small enough to be carried around unnoticed. Perhaps in *Fist of Fury*, we see the master of the nunchakus at his best.

Chen Chen (Bruce) is encircled by members of the opposing Japanese school. Quickly he pulls out his nunchaku and attacks.

His weapon flies around the room like an aeroplane propeller, thrusting, blocking, spearing and wrenching away knives, swords and sticks from his opponents, while the audience sit watching in numb disbelief! And to heighten the final effect, Bruce also developed a technique he called 'put out' and 'take in.' He told a reporter, "That is to intensify the dramatic effect. After chopping, side-hit and pointing, if I continue to fight on fiercely, the audience will not have time to absorb its flavour. If I put it out, and then take it in, it helps to build up the atmosphere, and secondly, the people have a chance to rest."

For the Little Dragon, film sales are assured for many years to come. Who, after all, would ever want to miss out on a chance to see in full flight Bruce Lee, the King of the Kung Fu Cudgels?

HOW BRUCE LEE MADE WAY OF THE DRAGON

Much has recently been said about Bruce Lee's crowning cinematic creation, the *Game of Death*. It is understandable that this tantalising cliff-hanger of a film should grab the throats of the legions of Little Dragon fans. After all, it is unfinished and unseen. However, *KFM* intends to put aside this exciting prospect for a short while so as to bring readers up to date on some of Bruce Lee's earlier triumphs. The net has been cast far and wide in our search for new information and this month, to tie in with a sensational UK re-release, *Kung-Fu Monthly* is turning its attention towards Bruce's classic film, *The Way of the Dragon*.

Linda Lee said of the film, "I've seen the picture over and over. It's a funny thing that this film, more than the other films he made, is the one I never get tired of looking at." As far as the Mandarin cinema industry was concerned, *The Way of the Dragon* pulled in a whole bundle of firsts. To start with, never before had a Chinese actor directed, co-produced and starred in the same film. Bruce went several steps further as he wrote the screenplay, devised and designed the sets, chose the costumes and handled the editing too! An almost unbelievable feat for a man with only two other major productions to his name. To round off this stupendous success story, *The Way of the Dragon* was also the first Mandarin film to be shot in part, on location in Rome. We hope that the extra insight gained from reading this powerful article will help fans of the Little Dragon everywhere enjoy even more what must be one of the Kung Fu King's greatest ever achievements as it kicks its way back on to the UK film circuits.

Before going any further, it would probably be a good idea to backtrack on the story. Tang Lung (Bruce) goes to Rome to lend assistance to a friend of the family, a girl named Chen Ching-Hua (Nora Miao). She tells him that local thugs are threatening to take over her restaurant. Chen, however, feels that Tang is of no use as he resembles a country bumpkin. Tang starts work in the restaurant and one evening while the waiters are practicing Boxing, the gangsters appear with a demand that Chen sign over the deeds to the restaurant. Tang, seeing the thugs laughing at the waiter's style of Boxing challenges them and wins. Everyone is impressed with Tang's performance, although Uncle Wang, the cashier, warns them against having false hopes.

The gang tries to kill Tang, but fails. Even the offer of a free air ticket home does not sway him. Unfortunately, while Tang is busy pursuing the gunmen, Chen is kidnapped and taken to the gang's headquarters. Tang, with the help of the waiters, storms the stronghold and rescues Chen. In a last desperate attempt to do away with Tang, the gangsters hire the services of a top international Karate champion (Chuck Norris). He and Tang meet in the Coliseum to fight it out, where after a nail-biting contest, the champion is thrashed. Surprisingly, Uncle Wang too turns out to be a traitor and he traps Tang. The police, however, arrive to save the day.

GRUNTING NOISES

Bruce liked to play the country bumpkin. It suited his style of humour for one thing and for another, it gave him a perfect opportunity to make good use of his vast range of facial expressions. The film shifts into gear with Tang arriving at Rome Airport. Immediately, Bruce can't resist the temptation to introduce a little humour. Not only is Tang hungry after his long flight, he also can't speak a word of the language! A small boy walks by eating an ice-cream and Tang, seizing his opportunity, runs up to try and find out where he got it. Unfortunately, the sight of Tang pointing into a wide open mouth and emitting grunting noises fails to produce the desired effect. The boy obviously thinks he is a lunatic! Now, the amazing thing about this sequence is that it was almost certainly shot live. In other words, Bruce just happened to have the cameras set up and running and the small boy actually did just happen to walk by eating his ice-cream! Of course the classic restaurant scene takes place at the airport.

Tang, still hungry, enters a buffet and naturally enough, finds he can't read the menu. Not wishing to look stupid, he points at a number of dishes and keeps his mouth shut. Every item turns out to be a different kind of soup! Again, the expression he pulls on seeing the bad news is superb. The Hong Kong audiences had no difficulty at all in associating themselves with that embarrassing situation. It's worth mentioning here the criticism that's been levelled at whoever was responsible for allowing the film to be totally translated into English. Were Bruce Lee not playing the part, it would have been easy for the entire scene to fall flat on its face. On one hand, the plot is saying that Tang cannot speak the language and therefore cannot read the menu. On the other, the voice dubbing for the entire cast is in English! It's only the Little Dragon's personality and magnetism that holds it all together. All the European actors in the famous Coliseum sequence, in fact, were never in Rome. Their parts were all shot back in the studios. Jon Benn, for instance, who handled the role of the gang leader was a very prominent Hong Kong businessman and the rest of the 'heavies' came from the same area. But if the airport scenes were in part unrehearsed, the Lee/Norris Coliseum battle was quite the opposite. It was the climax of the film and we hear that Bruce wrote out no fewer than twenty pages of fighting instructions. Every punch and kick had to be tried and tested and then filmed from the correct angles. The Little Dragon studied the film 'rushes' for hours on end and anything that wasn't perfect, was re-shot, re-shot and re-shot until it met his exacting requirements.

One of the finest sequences in the film has, outrageously, been chopped out of the British version. It's the alleyway scene where Tang confronts the gang and they try to persuade him to accept an airline ticket home. Bruce takes on the mob, countering their sticks and knives with just two pairs of nunchakus. The comedy ending where the final gangster, an Italian, seizes a pair of Bruce's nunchakus and then knocks himself out, has to be seen to be believed. At least it should be seen to be believed. Our uninspiring censorship laws dictate that we shall not. This of course doesn't bode too well for future *Game*

of Death nunchaku scenes! Surely the Little Dragon's superb handling of his weapons and his precision timing deserve a better fate!

It's worth emphasising here that Bruce himself had no intention of putting *The Way of the Dragon* onto the western film circuits, lie regarded the film very much as a testing ground for Asian audiences in the same way as he looked on *Enter the Dragon* as an opening door to international productions. Observant *KFM* readers will probably have noticed that many of the fight scenes in *Enter the Dragon*, in fact derive from *The Way of the Dragon*, for example the stave lighting in the cells. Having experienced the artistic freedom of *The Way of the Dragon* and then his polished, but restricted role in Enter the Dragon, it's not surprising the combined experience of the two should lead to a major step forward. That step was *Game of Death*.

If the Little Dragon learnt just one thing during his tragically short lifetime, it was how to combine commercialism with art. He was helped no end in this by an incredibly wide circle of friends. Whatever type of person he was looking for at any one time, he could always put his finger on the perfect candidate. It was his infectious enthusiasm that kept friends close to him and although he just couldn't stop poking his nose into everyone's business, in general, nobody minded. To take one instance, Bruce decided to commission a specially composed soundtrack for *The Way of the Dragon*. In the Mandarin film industry, this was virtually unheard of. Most pictures were backed musically with just about whatever was handy, with James Bond themes and the Shaft soundtrack being common favourites! The Little Dragon had to be different and not only did he get his own theme music, he also played on part of it. When the titles are going through and the Dragon flies across the green sea, listen out for the drum. That's Bruce handling the percussion!

Laying on soundtracks wasn't easy. In Hong Kong, it's almost impossible to record during the day because of outside noises and poor soundproofing. Generally it's done at night and therefore Bruce found himself filming and directing all day and then arranging the sound dubbing most of the night! And why, you may ask, didn't he use his own voice? The answer is simple - he just hadn't got the time. The Little Dragon did, however, go to some lengths to find someone whose voice resembled his own as closely as possible. Naturally though, the 'fighting noises' are all Bruce. He never found anyone who could duplicate those!

The Way of the Dragon represented to Bruce, an escape from the strangulating bonds of the Hong Kong film industry. His decision to quit the Mandarin machine came soon after Fist of Fury. He'd gone ahead with a third film entitled *Yellow Faced Tiger* under the direction of Lo Wei. It was about a Chinese cop in New York whose partner got murdered. The cop sets out to avenge the death. Bruce, who was working on the script just couldn't see eye to eye with Lo Wei and so he pulled out. Later the film was completed with Don Wong taking over Bruce's part and Chuck Norris as the co-star. It turned out pretty well although most say that Don could no way match up to the Little Dragon. His style of fighting simply wasn't developed enough and anyhow, the company made the mistake of trying to find someone who resembled Bruce.

THE BRUCE LEE SECRET SOCIETY. FULL DETAILS NEXT MONTH! GET READY TO JOIN

It's all very well to go hunting for lookalikes and maybe one who even fights in the same dynamic style as the Little Dragon. The problem is that no matter how well they perform, nobody will possess the Bruce Lee charisma. Bruce Li, who is currently appearing in many 'bandwagon' Bruce Lee pictures, is a classic case in point. Of course, superficially, you associate him with the Little Dragon. Nobody, however, is under any illusions. They know only too well that this isn't the real McCoy and the result can only be third rate.

Perhaps in *The Way of the Dragon*, Bruce came as close as he ever came to resolving his great conflict. He wanted to be the best in the martial arts field and also he felt the need to give people something to remember him by. Not particularly for reasons of money or commercialism, but simply to satisfy himself that he'd used his many talents to the full. Certainly that's why the fans fell for him so quickly and although some experts in the Kung Fu world still try to reject Bruce for, as they see it, debasing the arts, perhaps they ought to think for a while of all the enthusiasts in the western world who are practicing some form of Kung Fu just basically because of this one man. Obviously, to capture on celluloid, a production like *The Way of the Dragon* involves taking certain 'martial liberties' or poetic licence if you like. But what price is that to pay for the sheer enjoyment of watching an expert at work - Bruce Lee, the supreme master.

KICKBACK: THE LETTERS

Hello, it's Jenny here again, picking my way through the June letters. First of all, oh dear, oh dear what have I started? I seem to have collected enough film plots to finish *Game of Death* a hundred times over and so many of them are good. And the trouble also is that my two favourites are both too long to print! Anyway, thanks to A.I. Briers of St. Helens, Merseyside for his solution featuring the evil drug-pushing Mr. Wai-Shu (an infamous martial artist) and thanks too to Nicola Simpson of Ruislip, Middlesex for her version of the story (microfilms, gems and chemical warfare in this one!). Those two will be on top of the pile to be sent on to Golden Harvest. Time is short so I won't go on too long about the fabulous new club and besides, there'll be lots more about that in our next issue. And now, the letters!

BRUCE LI

Dear Jenny,
I have recently read that the star of two previous Bruce Lee rip off films is planning more on the same lines. He now calls himself Bruce Li and his latest films will include *Bruce Lee We Miss You*, *Fist of Fury Part 2* and worst of all, *Bruce Lee and the Supermen*. If *The Legend of Bruce Lee* and *The Bruce Lee Story* are anything to go by, this man is simply cashing in on Lee's name and fame. As they may receive AA certificates, I hope that none of your younger readers (who have never seen the King in action) will be taken in by these films. If there is to be a new King (though for me, Lee will always be the Sifu), let's make sure it is a worthy one; someone with his own identity and not this poor imitator.
Diane Dulwich, SE21

Dear Diane,
I'm afraid that I have to say that I couldn't agree more. I know that imitation is supposed to be the sincerest form of flattery, but somehow, seeing all these Bruce Lee travesty films (as I call them) making money out of the Little Dragon's fans fust makes my blood boil. I wish there was something I could do about it! All I can suggest is that you make your feelings known to as many people as possible. Of course, the other half of the problem is that so many of our younger readers have still not been able to see Bruce on film. It's understandable that they grab at anything which has the remotest connection.

ENTER THE DRAGON SOUNDTRACK

Dear Jenny,
In past letter columns, I have noticed that people have been asking you where they might buy the soundtrack of *Enter the Dragon*. To console those who have not been able to obtain it, this is my offer. In exchange for one item on Bruce Lee, no matter what it is - magazines, posters, etc - I will tape the soundtrack for them, providing they send me a cassette tape which must be at least half an hour long.
Paul Taylor, Dundonald, Belfast

Dear Paul,
Thanks a lot for sending in the offer but I'm sorry to have to say no, don't do it! Such a swap is quite illegal because it goes against our very strict copyright laws and you could find yourself in trouble. I'm afraid anyone who wants to hear the Enter the Dragon soundtrack will have to buy it for themselves.

WAY OF THE DRAGON

Dear Jenny,
I would like to know what has happened to *The Way of the Dragon*? It was last screened in this area two years ago and I've even heard rumours that it has been taken off the film circuit. I would also be pleased if you could tell me of any possible way of getting *KFM* No.4, as it is the only one I have not got. Finally, congratulations on producing a magazine that no other martial arts magazine can compare with.
Robert Bewick, Middlesbrough, Cleveland

Dear Robert,
Well, if you've read through our features this issue, then your question is pretty well answered. I can't give you exact dates yet unfortunately because they haven't been finalised, but rest assured it will be soon. Lastly, thanks a lot for the words of praise! Oh, and KFM No.4 is on the way.

BRUCE LEE'S DIET

Dear Jenny,
I think that *KFM* is the best magazine out and even though I cannot buy it over here, my relatives in England send it to me every month. Anyhow, my question is, did Bruce Lee have a special planned out diet, and if he did, could you please send it to me?
Garry Lamb, Garofali Village, New South Wales, Australia

Dear Garry,
First may I say 'good on ye' to your relatives in England for posting the KFMs all the way over to you in Australia - that's great news! All I've ever read is that he at one time was living on fresh meat and vitamin pills... which I find a little hard to believe! One point I will make, though, is this. Whatever his diet was, it'll almost certainly not be the right one for you. Remember, everyone is built a little bit differently and one man's pleasure is another man's poison. The secret is to experiment a bit to find out what suits you.

KFM PEN PALS CORNER

Colin Lee of Romford, Essex wants Chinese pen pal 15 years old.
Ian May of Plymouth, wants Chinese female pen pal 15-16 years old.
John Holmes of Dublin, Ireland was female pen pal.

22

1976

EDITORIAL

    Hi there Kung Fu fans, Without a shadow of doubt, we've really pulled out all the stops on this one. Just take a look at the run down for this superb issue. For starters there's all the information you need to know about our unique new club. Yes, the Bruce Lee Secret Society is finally stood on the starting block ready for dynamite action and with an annual subscription of only £2.95, you've just got to admit it's fantastic value for money. Pam and Carmella will be making their introductions from the Society News column and they'll be telling you exactly how to go about joining.
    We're always proud of the great pictures we go on unearthing for you month after month, but in this issue, we've totally surpassed ourselves. I promised you last time that we had a surprise in store for you and if you want to know what it is, take a look at our new poster - just amazing! So as far as I know, it's the premier time of publishing for this fantastic studio shot of the Little Dragon and as usual, *KFM* got there first! Historically it

dates back to Bruce's *Green Hornet* days and next month we'll be showing you another from the same set! Continuing our in-depth scrutiny of the Little Dragon's film triumphs, we present this month the facts, figures and information surrounding *The Big Boss*. For Bruce, this was the one that started the legend and naturally it's always occupied a very special place in the hearts of the fans. Traditionally there's been something of an air of mystery surrounding this martial masterpiece and *KFM* is pleased indeed to have slotted in a few more pieces of the jigsaw. Our other feature, in response to enormous popular demand, involves that undisputed king of Karate, Chuck Norris. The pictures again are brand new - we commissioned them especially for *KFM* - and the low-down surrounding this likely contender for the Kung Fu throne is there for all to see.

Felix Yen
Felix Yen
Editor-in-Chief

BRUCE LEE STARS IN THE BIG BOSS... UPROAR ON OPENING NIGHT!

May of 1970 was a month to remember for the movie moguls of the Mandarin film industry. Raymond Chow, who had recently quit the Run Run Shaw organisation, had formed Golden Harvest, a picture company with a difference. Not content with the shambolic state of affairs prevailing at just about every level of the Chinese film business, Chow had his sights raised higher. Proper scripts, better studio equipment, original scenarios and above all, a more professional outlook spearheaded the attack of the new boys at Hammerhill Road. Perhaps it's only right that in the forefront of this Oriental renaissance should appear a man more qualified than any other to carry the banner of this great new step forward. Bruce Lee, then of *The Green Hornet* fame, was chosen to star in what turned out to be Golden Harvest's first tantalising taste of success. The picture, symbolic in many ways of Chow's inspired thinking, was called *The Big Boss*.

The Big Boss, starring Bruce Lee, Maria Yi and James Tien, and directed by Lo Wei, opened at a special midnight preview in a Hong Kong cinema, boasting not a spare seat in the house. Ninety-two minutes later, the place was in uproar! Raymond Chow knew, Bruce Lee knew and very soon the world was to know that this was no flash in the pan. A take of one and a half million dollars from just two weeks of public screening told its own story. The opposition film companies, victims of their own lack of inventiveness, were literally caught with their pants down and for a while at least, the magic duo of Chow and the Little Dragon were to have things pretty much as they liked.

In a number of ways, *The Big Boss* provided unique entertainment to the delighted cinema-goers of Hong Kong. To begin with, it possessed an interesting story line, an ingredient largely ignored by rival film outfits. This went as follows: Cheng Chao-an (Bruce

Lee) arrives in Bangkok and begins work in an ice factory. Cheng, who has promised his mother that he'd not get into fights, is looking to start a new life and at first, all goes well. The owner of the factory, Hsa Mi is a prominent member of the overseas Chinese society and apparently a perfectly respectable businessman.

What Cheng doesn't know is that the company is just a cover for Hsa Mi's underground vice racket. One day several of the workers notice something unusual in the ice blocks. After taking a closer look they are quickly summoned away by the management and are never seen again. Bad feeling spreads round the factory and Cheng, ignoring the promise he made to his mother, is quick to spring to the worker's defence when the action begins. Hsa Mi, however, is nothing if not clever. Seeing the young man's fighting abilities, he promotes him to foreman, while at the same time persuading Cheng of the goodness of his intentions.

Cheng hears of a fellow worker being cheated and beaten up at a local casino and quickly goes to the rescue. When he gets there, he is bewildered to find that the owner of the place is none other than Hsa Mi. In an effort to try and sort things out, Cheng sends the other workers home. This move, however, only has the effect of alienating all his friends against him and in particular, his girl friend, Lin Hau-mei. A desolate Cheng comes to know a prostitute by the name of Wu Meng and she spells out to him in capital letters the full extent of Hsa Mi's evil operations.

Cheng needs no further convincing. He soon discovers the ice factory to be a cover for drugs manufacture and inside some ice blocks he comes across the bodies of the missing workers. Systematically, Cheng sets about eliminating the villains, but with his task nearly done, his sweetheart Lin is abducted. Cheng, guessing that she is being held by Hsa, soon arrives at the Big Boss' villa for the final confrontation. Naturally our hero wins the battle and all ends happily with the rescue of his girlfriend.

Bruce sealed the deal with Golden Harvest while on a return visit to Hong Kong. He had been greeted home like the prodigal son and although the original intention of the journey was to promote *The Green Hornet* TV series (in which he was co-starring), in fact it turned out to be hardly necessary! His fame had arrived before him and when Chow proposed a deal, the Little Dragon was delighted to accept. The prospect of making it big in front of his own people proved to be irresistible. Bruce, sensing that his acting had improved immensely from the old *Longstreet* days, felt ready, willing and able to take on his first starring role in a feature film.

July 1971 and it was a tough first time round for the Kung Fu King. Much of *The Big Boss* was shot in Thailand where meat (Bruce's staple diet) was almost completely unavailable. He lost ten pounds in weight through just eating rice and his physical condition suffered badly. To make things worse, he sustained a badly cut finger on the right hand quite early on in the shooting but because of the tight schedules, he just had to carry on - even with ten stitches in his hand! He wrote many letters to Linda who was waiting back home and complained bitterly of the conditions he was working under.

A little known fact is that Lo Wei was not Chow's original choice for director. That honour goes to an unknown gentleman who left the production after three or four abortive shots. Bruce then rewrote most of the script and Lo was hired for the job. Their relation-

Kung-Fu Monthly's Inside Story on Bruce Lee's Last Movie!

Although the fame of Bruce Lee has, by now, spread far and wide, much of his life still remains shrouded in mystery and intrigue. Not the least of these mysteries was the film on which Lee was working at the time of his death – the ominously titled *Game of Death*. But until now all requests for information have been met with a wall of silence.

Now KUNG-FU MONTHLY, the world's best selling martial arts publication, has learned the truth about Bruce Lee's unfinished masterpiece.

After travelling to Hong-Kong and visiting Lee's film studios, the editors of KUNG FU MONTHLY have compiled a Special Issue of KFM entitled "BRUCE LEE'S GAME OF DEATH". This Special Issue will be packed with facts and information and stuffed with colour pix from the film itself.

For your collector's edition of the fantastic BRUCE LEE'S GAME OF DEATH just send a cheque or P.O. for 60p (includes post and packing) made out to Kung Fu Monthly and addressed to:

GAME OF DEATH OFFER
Kung Fu Monthly,
39 Goodge Street,
London W1P 1FD.

(Allow three weeks for delivery and don't forget your name and address!)

ship, as regular readers of *KFM* will know already, was never what you might call amiable. Both liked to run things their own way and it was hardly surprising that after *Fist of Fury*, the two never again successfully worked together. A third film was planned by Chow, entitled *Man Called Tiger* but Bruce refused to do it. The role was filled by Wang Yu.

Compared to many western productions, *The Big Boss* was a 'quickie.' The whole film only took around six months to make, including the location work in Thailand. However, by comparison with most other Mandarin cinema productions, the budget was almost lavish. Chow used three or four cameras most of the time (often Chinese films are shot with only one) and it had its own especially composed theme tune (played on the UK version by a German brass band). Studio equipment was still, by western terms, rather primitive and the results were all the more amazing when you consider that much of the picture was filmed by agile cameramen climbing up and down, wooden boxes to achieve the right shooting angles!

To Bruce, the character he played in *The Big Boss* was, "A simple straightforward guy. If you told this guy something he'd believe you, and then, when he figures he's been had, he goes animal." He liked the role because, "It's better to play someone of a little more depth," and there is little doubt that overall Bruce was pleased with the results he achieved. There's little doubt either that the public too were pleased. It broke every box-office record going in Hong Kong including that champion of them all, The Ten Commandments which had been running since 1958! *The Big Boss* played 875 performances at the Hong Kong Majestic, the Odeon, the Katong and the Ruby and when it hit the western world, much to Bruce's surprise, it still took the same kind of money.

And so, for the man who previously could boast only a few bit parts under his belt plus the *Longstreet* and *The Green Hornet* series, the offers were soon rolling in. A rival Hong Kong company, probably Shaw Brothers, offered him double anything Golden Harvest would pay, plus the cost of all legal fees. Bruce replied, "I have already signed a contract and for ten times the fee, I won't break my promise. Furthermore I'll sign up for a third picture because of the goodwill between Golden Harvest and me." The Little Dragon had good reason to dislike Shaw Brothers. Once, as an unknown, he had gone to see them for work and all they offered him was a trainee actor's fee.

Warner Brothers came into the act with the offer of a TV role for ten thousand dollars a week which Bruce promptly turned down! Sometime before, another series had taken his fancy. Called *The Warrior*, it was about a Chinese who fled to America in the 1860s after a killing. Bruce did a pilot episode and for a while, was convinced he'd got the part. Then he heard one day that he'd lost out to an actor named David Carradine. The series of course became known later as simply *Kung Fu*. The reason for Warner's change of heart was probably 'cold feet.' It's one sort of risk having an unknown for your starring role. Having a Chinese unknown is quite another and *The Big Boss* still hadn't made it across to the States to spread the word!

Bruce always said of *The Big Boss*, that he knew it was going to be a success from the start. One good reason, he felt, why it should have made more money than any other Chinese production was that so many of the Mandarin films were, "Just awful." He went on, "Everybody fought all the time and what really bothered me was that everybody fought exactly the same way. When you get in a fight, everybody reacts differently and it is possible to fight and act at the same time. What I hope is that *The Big Boss* will represent a new trend in Mandarin cinema. People like films that are more than just one long fight. Most of the Mandarin films have been very superficial and very one dimensional. With any luck, I hope to make multi-level films in Hong Kong - the kind of films that you can sit and just watch the surface story or you can get in deeper if you feel like it."

And there I feel we should leave the Little Dragon for this time. Satisfied beyond doubt with his first throw of the dice and raring to head off into his next major production, which of course, was *Fist of Fury*. The kind of lessons he'd learnt from *The Big Boss* were visual ones, that were to strike home with a vengeance in *The Way of the Dragon* and *Enter the Dragon*. Good, exciting camera angles, short, sharp doses of action, plus of course that very special Bruce Lee sense of humour. *The Big Boss*, however, was more than just a launching pad. It's very rawness lent to the film, a quality of high originality and as an example of original Bruce Lee, it stands alone.

Next month in part three of our Bruce Lee film round-up, *KFM* digs deep down into the cinema vaults to bring you the real facts and figures behind *Enter the Dragon*. See you all then!

CHUCK NORRIS: WORLD KARATE CHAMPION!

When it came to choosing the right man for the part, Bruce Lee was a master of decision. To achieve complete realism in any particular action sequence, he never had any doubt that his opponent needed to be a professional Karateka. No film actor or stunt man could possibly do the job to the Little Dragon's satisfaction and wherever he could, he attempted to hire the services of experts in their field, coaxing them along the way with the persuasion that acting was 'just a piece of cake!' Dan Inosanto, Jhoon Rhee and Bob Wall are just three that spring to mind. People of their calibre were hired explicitly to add 'backbone' to the fight sequences of the battling Bruce Lee. Perhaps the most famous Kung Fu collision of them all (as I'm sure you'd agree from reading last month's *KFM*) is the Little Dragon's clash in the Coliseum with a 'top Karate man.' Many would say it was the fight of Bruce's life - certainly it comes over that way - and none I'm sure would begrudge a cheer, and in fact a feature article in *KFM*, to the loser - that self made king of the American Karate circuit, Chuck Norris.

No one could say that early on Chuck had experienced an average upbringing. There were years when the family was unsettled, such as the move from Wilson in Oklahoma to California in the early fifties. Young Chuck was only eleven at the time and then sometime later when his father decided to walk out, it came upon the shoulders of Norris junior to handle many of the headaches of running the family home. With his two younger brothers to take into the reckoning too, life wasn't easy and money at times was hard to come by. It's likely, though, that through these experiences, Chuck developed strength of mind and purpose - adversity can be the keenest of opponents - and possibly his character was given the 'shot in the arm' it needed.

Post-war Korea intervened. Chuck, whilst serving his turn in the American Air Force, was directed to serve in that battle scarred land during the aftermath of one of the world's

most tragic wars. He had to make up his mind. Either like most he could 'mess around' for a time, or else he could do something constructive. Thankfully, he chose the latter. No visitor to Korea could possibly be unaware for long of that land's great cultural/physical pursuit - Karate. Its popularity was unbounded and Chuck soon latched on. He decided first of all to study a type of martial arts known as Tang Soo Do, and such was his innate expertise, within a year he had gained the prized black belt. Bruce Lee, on returning to the USA from Hong Kong for the first time, had quickly realised the best way to make a living was by teaching what he knew most - naturally, Kung Fu. Hence that famous class he once held in a Los Angeles car park. Arriving back in the States, it hadn't taken Chuck long to conclude likewise.

Chuck Norris, however, had a problem. He lacked the extrovert streak that so typified the actions of the Little Dragon and he'd never admit to being at his happiest when standing up in front of a class. But if nothing else, he had guts and after all, in the end, practice can at least make sufficient, it not perfect. His speaking improved and by 1963 he had opened up the first historic Chuck Norris school of Karate. It was in Torrance, California and the rent for the building was crippling.

He worked hard and long to improve both himself and the business but unfortunately in so doing, he very nearly went broke!

Chuck, high on Karate skill as he was, could claim then only to be a C minus when it came to the commercial world. He brought in partners to help run things and initially at least, the Norris Empire of schools boomed. Then suddenly, the bottom fell out. The partners were experts in business, not Karate and the result was a near catastrophe. Picking up the pieces, he started again, but this time with the help of better advice. The offshoots are back in action again, only this time with a sense of co-ordination and purpose. Despite his insistence of apparently not caring whether he has money or not, Chuck just has to be proud of his superb new Virginia Beach studio - an impressive monument to his unending work and enthusiasm.

Meanwhile, in every land, the name of Norris continues to strike fear and admiration in the hearts of all who oppose him. No tournament is complete without the handsome American master present. (As a measure of the skill of the man, he has now been proclaimed champion of the Karate world no fewer than seven times!) Hobnobbing as he does with the stars that have come knocking at his door has naturally turned his mind towards acting and when the Little Dragon approached him one day about a part in *The Way of the Dragon*, Chuck wasn't slow to take the bait. The role was ideal for the now famous Karate champion. As a starter film for him, it was good in that he needed only to produce the goods in terms of blinding action rather than routine acting ability.

BRUCE LEE'S TAO OF JEET KUNE DO

We said we'd get it for you...and we have!

For a short time only, KFM is delighted to have on offer to its readers the book that every true Little Dragon fan has been waiting for. Indeed, what kung-fu collection could be complete without a copy of BRUCE LEE'S TAO OF JEET KUNE DO.

Now, at last, you yourself can analyse at first hand Bruce's recipe for success. Containing as it does page after page of detailed instruction, figure drawings, hints and tips, this Tao stands as the ONLY complete treatise on Jeet Kune Do in existence *that was actually written and drawn by the Little Dragon himself*. It will probably only be in print for a limited period of time so don't lose your chance! Send £6.00 plus 85p p&p as soon as possible to:

Tao of Jeet Kune Do Offer
Kung-Fu Monthly
39 Goodge Street
London W1P 1FD

Bruce chose wisely and Chuck was set along the road to film stardom. Thinking back now, it's difficult indeed to conceive of anyone else who could have handled that role in quite the same dynamic way as Chuck. Following Bruce's choreography instructions to the letter, he attacked and defended with such intense realism, it was hard to believe he hadn't forgotten about the script three pages before! As a fitting climax to Bruce's third major film, none could have been better. The champion of all styles fighting it out with the Karate Sensei - a veritable battle of the giants. After the Little Dragon's sad farewell, Chuck soon realised where his particular path led. Without Bruce to point the way, he rightly foresaw that the Kung Fu film empire would likely flounder for a while at least and so he decided to concentrate on cultivating his own market. Acting lessons helped a lot plus numerous small parts in TV shows such as FBI to pile on the experience. An early break with Dean Martin in the world famous Matt Helm serial helped secure for

Chuck a new kind of audience and since then, after biding his time waiting for the right film to show up, at last his patience has been rewarded. The movie is entitled *Good Guys Wear Black* and Chuck plays an assassin sent out to smash a narcotics ring. The plot has a decidedly American sound about it although of course the champ gets plenty of opportunity to exercise martial superiority over the villains.

That's not to say though that Chuck has forsaken TV for the tinselled world of film stardom. On the contrary, a very close relationship with the up and coming producer, Robert Plone, should soon be reaping its own rewards. Plone had met up with the Karate master while engaged in compiling a documentary of the martial arts called *The Warrior Within*. The idea was to feature the top artists around and in anyone's language, that just had to include Chuck Norris. Shooting began and within a very short space of time, it had become obvious to Plone that Chuck was more than just a two bit fighter. For a man of little experience, his camera presence proved to be way above average and the producer's thinking started to switch tracks.

Maybe Norris could handle his own show? The two of them chewed over ideas and finally came up with something called *Black Belt with Chuck Norris*. The concept was certainly original. Part one of the programme was to highlight systems of self defence, not for experts or enthusiasts in particular, rather just plain good advice for the family. The next chunk of the show was to be a personality interview. The guests needed to be celebrities who, probably unknown to all but the closest of their fans, had some sort of connection with the martial arts. A little investigation proved there was no shortage of takers for that spot! The final part of the programme was to lend itself to the origins and history of it all.

In the words of Chuck, the concept was 'fantastic' although, as of yet, the American TV networks have shown little sign of interest. It will be tragic but perhaps predictable if the pilot show bites the dust. Television companies are notoriously disinclined to play around with new ideas and *Black Belt with Chuck Norris* could in no way be described as fitting into a formula. However, it's not the only card up the Karate King's sleeve and doubtless he won't be too disheartened if all the work turns out to be of no avail. A second film has now been lined up entitled *Chocolate and Vanilla* and this, Chuck senses, could be the big one.

Again the film could be described as being martial arts 'plus,' with a zippy but fairly lightweight plot. Chuck and a friend decide to leave New York and head for Montreal where they intend to establish a new night club. Getting there, all manner of disasters befall the pair, not the least of which is when they walk into a bank robbery that's just getting into full swing. Naturally in a display of martial mastery, the dynamic pair manage to snuff out the hoodlums and lo and behold, they've saved the day. Permission for their club is then readily granted and all ends happily. Chuck, who has no stomach for blood and gore movies, is more titan happy with the combination of light relief and action that this production should provide and it'll be interesting to see whether or not the final result lives up to his full expectations.

It's hard of course not to draw a comparison between Chuck's philosophy and that of the Little Dragon. Even before making *The Big Boss*, Bruce was readily putting down the outrageously violent Mandarin film epics that had long since ceased to retain any connection with reality, emphasising strongly his wish to bring a little 'quality' into the product. Having had Bruce in front of him to clear the ground, Chuck will maybe find the going a little easier. There is no doubt too that he is in a ready made position to continue where Bruce left off. He has the looks, the acting ability and the martial arts skill to carry it through in a big way and certainly it's all to his credit that Norris has no pretensions about trying to be the 'new' Bruce Lee. Whichever way his finger of fate should point, Chuck can always content himself with the satisfying thought that his perseverance has paid off. The franchise for the *Chuck Norris Karate Schools* has removed any financial worries that he might have had and he is free at last to choose his direction. That his chosen path should be films can surely come as no surprise. Bruce himself quickly understood the speed at which posterity forgets even the legendary performer and movies surely are the only way of overcoming this. To be able to transfer the fruits of one's talents on to celluloid is to be able to entertain quite literally millions of people. Chuck Norris has seized this rosy apple and we wish him luck!

THE BRUCE LEE SECRET SOCIETY

Hi - it's Jenny Lee here and am I happy to be writing these few words? Thanks largely to a lot of persuasion from you, the *KFM* readers, I am delighted to announce the grand opening of the Bruce Lee Secret Society. Yes, your own *Kung-Fu Monthly* is taking up the reins along with Pam Hadden and Carmella Rapa (who will be joint presidents of the club). They'll handle all the letter writing and day-to-day running of things. Good luck Pam and Carmella, I know you're going to need it! OK, I've said my piece so it's back to the mail for me. Over to you ...

Thanks for the intro Jenny - we couldn't have done it better ourselves! Because we've got so much to tell you, I hope you'll forgive us if we itemise everything - that way well be able to squeeze more in.

- On application you'll receive your membership card and a number, plus the fabulous Society Kit, containing your very own official certificate of membership (for framing), a Bruce Lee Secret Society badge and sticker, an autographed Bruce Lee picture and four incredible photos of the Little Dragon in action that we promise have never been published in the world before! All this plus news, views, facts and info - what a great package!
- Then, once every three months, we'll post to you the quarterly Society news sheet - brim full of the latest chit-chat, letters, pen-pals, club offers and much more.
- In every single issue of KFM you'll find your very own Bruce Lee Secret Society corner and we'll be handling that!
- All members will soon be able to get a discount on most KFM mail order offers.
- On top of all that, there'll be lots of special Bruce Lee mail order products exclusively on offer to club members.

- We are very sorry, but we have to point out that there is NO connection whatsoever between this and the previous Bruce Lee Fan Club. Regretfully therefore, we shall not be able to enter into any correspondence in regard to problems arising from its closure.
- Sorry again! ... but we do really have to restrict membership to the UK only.
- Finally, may we say here and now that we shall not be replying to letters that come without stamped addressed envelopes - you have been warned!

So there it is - what a great line-up and all for an subscription of only £2.95 - not bad eh?
Judging by the deluge of mail that comes in through Jenny's door, we think we have a fair idea of what we are letting ourselves in for - it's a good thing we're gluttons for punishment! But remember, if you've got any bright ideas on what you'd like to see in your club, don't hesitate to write... we promise you ALL letters will be answered. And by the way, don't forget that's exactly what it is - your club. After all, what's a club without members?
The old Bruce Lee Fan Club apparently had around five thousand members when it closed, so let's see if we can double it - and keep open! DON'T DELAY! Just send your £2.95 to: The Bruce Lee Secret Society, *Kung-Fu Monthly*, 39 Goodge Street, London W1P 1FD. (Cheques/Postal orders made out to *Kung-Fu Monthly* please.) We'll get your Society Kit and membership card off to you as quickly as possibly. See you soon - **Pam and Carmella**

KICKBACK: THE LETTERS

Hello, its Jenny here again with another huge pile of fantastic letters. To start with, it's apology time. Apparently in many copies of the last issue, it wasn't possible to read the caption to the Kickback page nunchaku picture, so here once more are the details. Each cudgel measures 13 inches in length and is 1.5 inches in diameter at the widest point. The chain has eleven links and is eight inches long. They are black and weigh in at 530 grams. OK, that's my good deed for the day; the next problem is back issues. You just wouldn't believe the number of letters the Mail Order Department get in asking for early back numbers and as I said some time ago, we just can't help any more. But, good news - there's going to he a Society 'Swop Shop.' Pam and Carmella will be telling you more about it when you join the club, but the idea is that anyone wanting to buy, sell or swap *KFM* magazines should write in with all the details. These will then be included in the quarterly Newsletter to be sent out to all club members. With any luck, everyone will end up with what they're after! Finally, may I say here and now that the result of the 'Should we or should we not keep Bruce on the big poster' debate: By a letters margin of nearly fifty to one, the answer is yes, we should. Sorry Sue Myers, but there's your answer. Now, the letters!

KFM FILM CLUB

Dear Jenny,
Firstly let me congratulate you on a simply magnificent magazine. I have every issue from No.1 and look forward to each new edition. Secondly, after reading the marvellous article on film censorship in *KFM* No.19, I too hope we will be able to see uncut Bruce Lee movies soon. Would it be possible for *KFM* to start a film club with this view in mind? You could have life or yearly membership with a sensible age limit. I am sure that there are enough fans to make this work.
Willie Nixon, Carlisle, Cumbria

Dear Willie,
Thanks a lot for the ever welcome praise - I must say I thought the censorship article was particularly good myself. As far as a film club is concerned - well, I'm not really supposed to talk about this yet but we have had a little idea up our sleeves for a while now. I won't go into details but just to say that for all you fans of Bruce Lee films, there could be a very pleasant surprise coming!

SECRET FIGHTING ARTS OF THE WORLD

Dear Jenny,
Congratulations on reaching your 20th issue and I can say that I'm not surprised this excellent magazine has reached this number of issues. I have been avidly reading the world's best selling martial arts magazine since I was able to get my eager hands on issue 2, and was happy to see the feature in issue 8 about the other martial arts besides Kung Fu. Being interested in the other arts, I was glad to be able to get hold of *Secret Fighting Arts of the World* by John Gilbey and was wondering if the ever resourceful *Kung-Fu Monthly* know, or could find out about any other secret fighting arts and possibly produce a feature on them. Also, I must congratulate Jeff Cummins on his great artwork.
Lee Percy, Hainault, Essex

Dear Lee,
On behalf of Jeff and the staff of KFM, I thank you for the congratulations! I agree with you that Fighting Arts certainly does make a good read and I only wish I had knew more books of that sort to recommend. Unfortunately, nothing else immediately springs to mind. Someone I would suggest you contact for more up-to-date information is Cimac in Birmingham. Apart from selling a fine range of martial arts equipment, they also stock just about every Kung Fu book worth having and are a mine of information besides!

THE BIG BOSS

Dear Jenny,
Each time I go and see *The Big Boss*, I see grown-up people genuinely cheering when Bruce starts to fight. He put so much into this film; great acting, beautiful fighting and a superb sense of humour, that it makes me proud to be a fan when I watch it.
John Burnett, Halifax, Yorkshire

Dear John,
What a lovely short, yet concise letter - a pleasure to receive! I have a hunch you're going to be extra happy with this issue of KFM - we've given The Big Boss the full KFM treatment and for my money, that's no more than it richly deserves.

POSTER REQUEST

Dear Jenny,
As a Bruce Lee fan, I agree with you totally. I should think that a large majority of your readers of *KFM* magazine because it deals mostly with Bruce Lee articles and has giant posters of him in the centre. I believe that as soon as the articles and posters of Bruce go into decline, so will your sales. After all, who is greater than the Little Dragon - no one! Finally, in *KFM* No.4, there is on page three, a photo of Bruce with his nunchakus around his neck. This would make a great centre poster.
Maureen Binks, Rotherham, Yorkshire

Dear Mrs. Binks,
Thanks for confirming my own feelings exactly So long as the majority of readers want to see Bruce featured, then so he will be. We kicked off over two years ago in memory of the Little Dragon and that's the way we aim to carry on! About the photo in KFM No.4 - we beat you to it. Around issue 16, we thought about it but found the quality just wasn't good enough for blowing-up the poster.

CHINESE CONNECTION?

Dear Jenny,
What can I say but well done on having the greatest martial arts magazine. I started reading *KFM* with issue No.1 and what I like best are the letters in Kickback, because some of them are very interesting. As a matter of fact, in issue 20, you mentioned that many readers have had issues in getting back copies and you said to try WH Smith & Son. Well, I used to work for Smiths and the number of people who came in asking for back issues of *KFM* was unbelievable. It was really great seeing the fans walk out with a copy they had ordered from us. Finally, I have a question to ask. Was Bruce Lee the star co-star in the film *Chinese Connection*? I've not seen the film and the few books I've read off Bruce Lee hardly mentioned it at all.
David Simmonds, Reading, Berkshire

Dear David,

Glad to hear my faith in Smiths wasn't misplaced! I must say I've heard from other readers just how good the shop is for bringing KFM to the fans. By the way, I bet you have seen the Chinese Connection. That's the American title for Fist of Fury and Bruce Lee most certainly did star in it! Actually, I've just had another of my ideas. I'd urge everyone to drop me a line and tell me which part of KFM they like the most and why. There's a free year's subscription to be going to the writer of the most interesting reply!

Thanks to you, the KFM readers, the entry figure for our first competition has been absolutely staggering. Over six thousand people sent in post cards and the saddest part of it all, is that only five can be winners. Next time we'll see if we can't increase the number of prizes!

COMPETITION RESULTS

The winners, picked from the hat, are: Jacqueline Beazant of Leigh in Lancs, David Gibbs of High Wycombe in Bucks, Miss A. Slade of Wednesfield in Wolverhampton, Mr N. Whitfield of Maidstone in Kent and Stephen Greenhalgh of Bootle near Liverpool.

These five (along with several thousand others!) correctly identified the pictures as coming from: 1. *Enter the Dragon*. 2. *The Big Boss*. 3. *Longstreet*. 4. *Marlowe*. 5. *The Way of the Dragon*. 6. *Game of Death*.

The *KFM* Nos.1-20 sets and the film posters are on the way!

AT LAST YOU CAN SUBSCRIBE TO KUNG-FU MONTHLY!

Ever since Kung-Fu Monthly started we've literally been deluged with requests for subscriptions. Now here's your chance to make sure you never miss out on a single issue of the world's greatest martial arts magazine!

For only £4.00 you can subscribe to the next 12 monthly editions of Kung-Fu Monthly. As a service to our readers, KFM is actually making a substantial loss on the postage, packing and handling which is all included within this price.

Remember, the only way that you can be absolutely certain of receiving each and every copy of Kung-Fu Monthly is by taking up our fantastic subscription offer.

Keep your KFM collection up to date! Just send a cheque or postal order (made out to Kung-Fu Monthly) to:
KFM Subscriptions
39 Goodge Street
London W1P 1FD
Finally, please print your name and address clearly!

THE POSTER MAGAZINES - VOLUME ONE

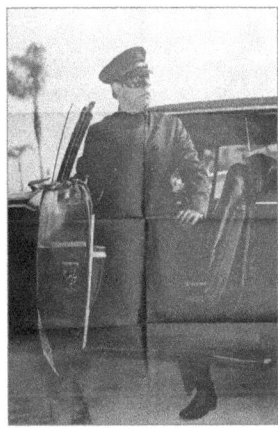

EDITORIAL

Hi there Kung Fu fans...

Come rain, come shine there's one thing you can always rely on. Once a month, *Kung-Fu Monthly* is going to come leaping into your favourite local newspaper shop and to prove it, here we are again! Let me say first off, how great it is to hear that the level of mail from you the *KFM* readers is still growing higher and higher every month - now that's the kind of news I like! I don't think there can be any other magazine in Britain that gets the same kind of loyal response from the fans that we do.

Continuing our run through the Little Dragon's list of epic feature films, this month we come up against a real biggie. Right, for starters, we've slid *Enter the Dragon* under the searching eye of the *KFM* microscope and boy have we dug out a few surprises! There's no doubt that despite some fierce opposition from *The Big Boss*, *Fist of Fury* and *The Way of the Dragon*, this film just 'nods it' in the popularity stakes and after reading our feature article, perhaps you'll have a better idea why.

Following on, we step back into the days gone by to look at the incredible world of the Ninja. Spies, assassins, Kung Fu experts, magicians - who exactly were these supermen of yesterday and how much of the story is actually true? *KFM* examines the evidence behind the legend and comes up with some shattering information on the weapons and death tactics of the greatest undercover agents the world has ever known. I've had word from Cathay Films of two double features opening soon in selected towns. Firstly there's *The Spoilers* and *Devil's Men* which will be appearing in the Plymouth, Bristol, Ipswich and Nottingham areas during October and secondly, *Stoner* and *Seven Magnificent Fights* - sorry no locations yet on these two. That's about all from me for this month, so I'll see you next issue...

Felix Yen
Editor-in-Chief

ENTER THE DRAGON: THE FILM THAT SPLIT THE BAMBOO!

Lee always steadfastly maintained that *The Big Boss*, *Fist of Fury* and *The Way of the Dragon* were never made for the Western market. The success of these Asian epics on this side of the Bamboo Curtain came as a complete surprise to him and in fact it wasn't until 1973 that he consciously made any attempt at capturing the cinemas of Europe and the USA. The invasion was well planned - a million dollar budget, a Bond style story line and a sprinkling of genuine martial arts experts to give the whole thing an air of authenticity. But somehow Warner Brothers seemed unconvinced that a Chinese martial arts maestro should be given the full star treatment - he had to share it with John Saxon and Jim Kelly - and for many fans, this lack of 'believing' (remember, Warners rejected Bruce for a part in TV's *Kung Fu* and instead hired David Carradine) underlies a basic weakness in the film. And yet, so far as the Western fans were concerned it was the Little Dragon's most popular picture, possibly because of the more familiar Hollywood-style treatment. Out East, however, acceptance was longer in coming. They felt not so much that Bruce had betrayed them but that he had been betrayed by the West - their star was suddenly now only a third of a star and they were upset. After his tragic death of course, all such nit-picking was, soon forgotten. Anyway, the spots are coming on and the cameras are warming up so pick up the threads of the action with us now as *KFM* takes you behind the scenes of Bruce's most lavish and controversial cinema production, *Enter the Dragon*.

An early promotional sheet for the film kicks off in fine style with the comment that Bruce Lee, Asia's reigning superstar, has been a major factor in the international success earned by martial arts motion pictures. His uncommon combination of great physical strength, fine looks and acting style has made him the top martial arts film star. Funnily enough, the name *Enter the Dragon* was originally the title for *The Way of the Dragon*. At the risk of confusing just about everyone, apparently Warners liked the *Enter the Dragon* name so much, they persuaded Bruce to swap the two around. The Little Dragon agreed to the idea mainly because he saw *Enter the Dragon* as a toe-hold in the West and therefore of extra importance. But this is stepping too far ahead. First things first and for anyone who has not yet seen this Bruce Lee spectacular, let's first have a synopsis of the plot.

Lee (Bruce Lee), the outstanding martial arts student at the Shaolin Temple, is approached by Braithwaite (Geoffrey Weeks), an agent for an international intelligence organisation. He wants Bruce to head for a sinister island fortress and take part in a rather unusual martial arts tournament. The agent's intention is that Bruce should gain evidence of drug peddling and vice, sufficient that Han (Shih Kien) a former Shaolin Temple student and the boss of the fortress can be arrested and imprisoned. Lee remembers that three years ago at the time of the last island tournament, five of Han's men led by Oharra (Bob Wall) had attacked his sister Su Lin (Angela Mao Ying). Su had stabbed herself to death with a piece of broken glass rather than let them take her. Bruce loses no time in deciding to go and he boards a Chinese junk along with some other selected martial arts experts. These include Roper (John Saxon), Williams (Jim Kelly) and Parsons (Peter Archer). The festivities start that evening with a lavish banquet where Han greets the martial artists who have come to try their luck. The winners are offered top jobs in the island's security system and the losers often die! While the entertainment is continuing, Bruce

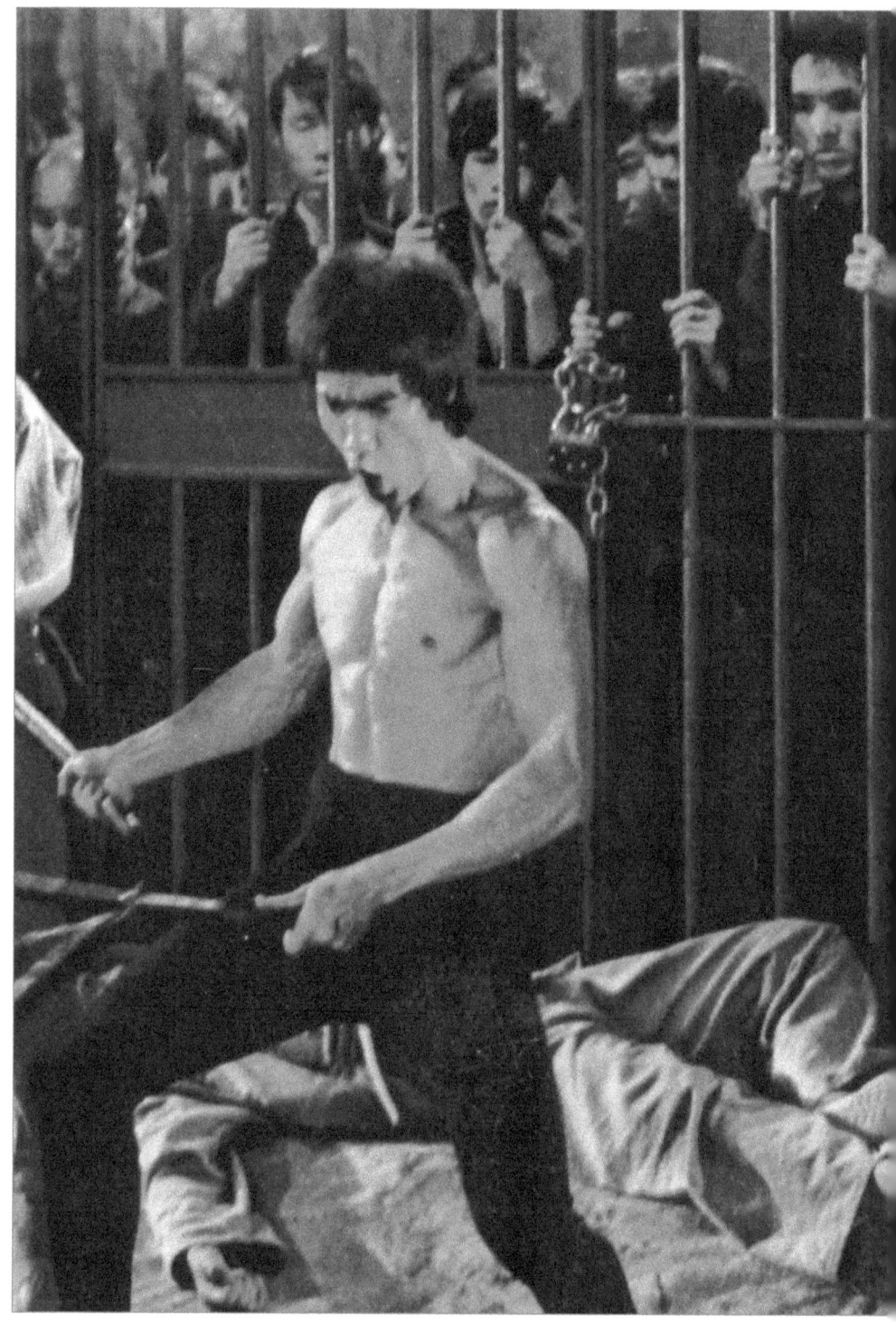

takes a walk around the grounds and discovers a vast opium processing plant. Han finds out and the next day he has his bodyguard Bolo (Yang Sze) kill the guards who allowed this to happen. In his first contest, revenge is sweet as Bruce kills Oharra with a flying kick. Han, who suspects Williams of attacking some guards, engages him in fierce combat and dispatches him with his deadly artificial hand.

That night, after capturing a venomous guardian cobra snake, Bruce re-enters the underground cavern where Han conducts his evil business and succeeds in sending a radio message to Braithwaite before being captured. The following day, Bolo is killed in combat by Roper, who in turn is matched against Lee. Han hopes they will fight to the death. However, Roper and Bruce join forces and at that moment, Mei Ling (Betty Chung), another of Braithwaite's contacts, releases hundreds of Han's prisoners from the underground cells. They flood onto the tournament ground and a great battle ensues. Bruce pursues Han into a mirrored maze where, after a ferocious confrontation, Han is left impaled on a spear. The evil man's army has been defeated by the released prisoners and Bruce and Roper stand surveying the rout as helicopters filled with troops descend upon the island.

Enter the Dragon was filmed in Hong Kong and only took around thirteen weeks to shoot. There was time enough for plenty of accidents! Bob Wall recounts, "I grabbed a bottle in each hand, smashed off the bottoms and got set. I looked down at the jagged ends - they were lethal weapons alright. It surprised me even more when I found out they were real glass. All Bruce said was, "Come on at me." It went perfectly, but unfortunately the scene had to be done again from another angle. This time, however, Bruce moved a fraction of a second too early and his fist crunched straight into the glass. Spurts of blood flew into the camera and over the floor." That was certainly a piece of realism that the Little Dragon hadn't bargained for!

Another time, Bruce was supposed to walk past the cobra, grab it and shove it in a sack. As luck would have it, it bit him and although the snake had previously had most of its venom taken out, the Little Dragon still needed medical treatment. Mind you, Bruce wasn't on the receiving end of all the upsets that Dame Fortune handed their way. One sequence, where Bruce pushes the bully over the side of the boat, nearly resulted in a tragic real-life drowning and the actor only managed to escape death by the skin of his teeth. The bully idea was a typical one for the Little Dragon. In all his films you'll see one scene or another where he defends the underdog and ends up righting the wrongs.

Enter the Dragon was billed as the first American martial arts picture. It was certainly the first Hong Kong made picture to receive American backing and so far as can be seen, the tag is correct. Many other films, like *Goldfinger* for instance, had martial arts sequences but none were what you could call Kung Fu pictures. Often when you read the credits for *Enter the Dragon*, part of the copyright is missed out. In fact, it should be designated as a Concord/Sequoia/Warner Brothers production. Concord was the company owned by Bruce and Raymond Chow and Sequoia, the company of Fred Weintraub and Paul Heller, the producers of the film. Chow in fact frequently called the film a Golden Harvest production (probably due to habit as much as anything) and Bruce admonished him for it on several occasions!

A little known fact is that the film was originally going to be a Concord/Sequoia production only, but money started to get scarce and so Warner Brothers came in on the deal. It seems the original idea for the film came from Weintraub and Heller. They approached Bruce with the concept of an independent picture and he liked it. It's by no means unusual for producers to link up with a major company like Warners for distribution - the pair did exactly the same thing again with *Black Belt Jones*. Fred's brother Sy of TVs *Tarzan* fame also came along on this one, as did *Enter the Dragon* director Robert Clouse. *Black Belt Jones* was to be Jim Kelly cast in the Bruce Lee mould and boy did he try, all unfortunately, to no avail. He struck the same poses - tried to fight in the same sort of way - and even had himself advertised as *Enter Jim Dragon* Kelly! The by-lines read "From the team that brought you *Enter the Dragon*," which was a bit silly too. After all, Bruce had produced all the fight scenes in *Enter the Dragon*, so without Bruce there, how could it be the same team?

Enter the Dragon actually went over its allotted budget to the tune of around five thousand dollars. It caused some consternation because the production, intended to be a cheap one, finally ended up costing somewhere around the million dollar mark (Bruce's first and only million dollar film). Most of the excess five thousand dollars was spent commissioning a musical score from Lalo Schifrin. Lalo was, by then, famous as the writer of the theme tune to *Bullitt*, the film starring Bruce Lee's former pupil, Steve McQueen. His new score was excellent to the extent that part of it (from the mirror sequence with Han) is being used now in an American TV advertisement for cigarettes! Bruce too was happy with the final overall result.

It's well known that during the final dubbing stages, the Little Dragon became very ill. Later, when he felt better, he went to the States to promote the film. He appeared on various programmes, such as the Johnny Carson show with a great deal of success, but sadly he died before *Enter the Dragon* was released and he was never able to taste the respect and adulation it later brought him. A piece of news that may not yet have come the way of all you collectors of off-beat information relates to the suit that he actually wore in the film. There always seems to be a lot of interest amongst the fans in what happened to Bruce Lee's famous suits and the one from *Enter the Dragon* is probably equal favourite with the one from *Fist of Fury*. Well, I can tell you - he was buried in it.

It's been said that Bruce eventually decided to play to the West rather than the East. That, however, was simply not true. Basically, he was an idealist - money didn't bother him much - and his main aim was simply to improve Chinese pictures. If he could make a little money too and also further the martial arts in the process, then all well and good. He made *Enter the Dragon* so as to raise the level of Asian films in the USA and Europe from fleapit features up to something approaching box-office bonanzas and that he succeeded is obvious.

And so we leave Bruce's last complete film. Next month we link up with the dynamite Fist of Fury to complete our survey of the Little Dragon's smash successes. See you then!

BRUCE LEE: VICTIM OF NINJA DEATH SQUAD?

Throughout the turbulent pages of Japanese history, there has seldom, if ever, been an espionage system as feared or as successful as that of the Ninja. Information on these people and their tactics is even now scarce and difficult to locate; secrecy after all was the name of the game and most practitioners went to great length to keep their identities to themselves. Surprisingly, their true abilities often outstripped supposed accomplishments. He (or she) was Japanese, adept at using many weapons, a master of disguise, superb in the art of psychology, had the endurance of a present day world-class athlete, possessed great animal cunning and to top it all, often ran two or more families and homes at the same time (without either knowing the existence of the other). Unless in disguise, he dressed from head to foot in black and carried a veritable arsenal of lethal devices with which to assail the unfortunate and unsuspecting victim. These legendary men, who had the ability it is said to fly, become invisible, walked on water, flowed through brick walls or even transformed themselves into animals based their creed to a large extent on the Spartan traditions of almost total self-denial in their endless quest for practically superhuman perfection. Few who challenged them lived to tell the tale and from the 13th to the 17th

Centuries, the people of Japan lived in terror of the deadly shadows of the night.

It is said that the art of Ninjutsu originated during the reign of Empress Suiko around the year 600 AD and that it owed its origins to the then highly developed Chinese espionage techniques. A soldier by the name of Otomo-no-Saijin who had assisted the winning of a war in the land of Omi by the use of devious spying tactics was given the title Shinobi (literally, to steal in) and gradually the name Ninjutsu derived from this. They hailed to a great extent from just two major parts of Japan, Iga and Koga, both being wild, inaccessible areas and both ideal for the protection of identify. Naturally therefore the secrets tended to pass along from father to son and it is said that even today in some Japanese households, the art is still practiced.

The young Ninja started his training at an early age. As soon as he was five, the toughening-up procedure began. A regular diet of back-breaking exercises plus balancing and endurance routines became his daily meat. The emphasis of course was not merely on the physical. Apart from the obvious skills of running, jumping, swimming and so on, he needed to develop strength of mind and purpose, the ability to resist pain and a general immunity to fatigue. When he reached his early teens, weaponry skills were added to the agenda, including the now famous Shuriken (a deadly, multi-pointed throwing star). On top of all this, he needed to learn thoroughly various cultural pursuits to aid him in his future need for disguises. We are told that there were essentially seven popular disguises, they being a travelling actor, an itinerant priest, a strolling magician, a monk, a travelling entertainer, a farmer and a merchant.

Nothing was neglected in the young man's education. He became virtually a walking survival kit and even carried pills around with him which had the apparent effect of delaying thirst for nearly a week. He learnt to read and draw maps and he studied nature and the tactics of infiltration. Walking too became a speciality and there were up to ten variations to choose from to suit any particular situation. Some were to ensure silence, some were to make tracking impossible while others were simply to ensure great speed. All Ninja needed too, to be well versed in Shinso Toho No Jutsu, an acrobatic technique which involved walking on the hands.

The true Ninja was a master of versatility. Not only had he to carry round with him an almost absurd personal cache of weapons (including sword, daggers, darts, sticks, bow, arrows, explosives, guns and poisons) he would also be a master of unarmed combat. Often too, the weapons would be of his own making so that by means of cunning design, a particular lethal instrument could be made to double for two or three other purposes as well! For instance, his sword would serve as a hook, his spear maybe as a vaulting pole and his scabbard an underwater breathing device. When disguised for instance as a priest, the staff he carried could, in a second, be transformed into a spear and if all else failed and he was being hotly pursued, the Ninja would draw from his bag of tricks, a handful

of spiked metal caltrops or Tetsubishi, to ensure his getaway. Derived from the naturally growing plant caltrops, these were vicious, multi-pointed metal stars that whichever way they landed had sharp metal ends sticking upwards - the bare or sandal-footed pursuer hardly stood a chance!

Poison sprays were another of the Ninja's specialities. He devised a primitive sort of water pistol out of bamboo cane and then ejected home-made poison into the eyes of the enemy. It was indeed a formidable weapon with a reputed range of over fifty feet. Unfortunately, there isn't time here to go through the entire range of Ninja weaponry. Suffice it to say that incendiaries, bombs, guns, flaming arrows, poison darts, fire-crackers and grenades all at one time or another came into the willing hands of the elusive Japanese espionage squad.

Behind every fantastic Ninja tale that you hear, there is an element of truth. Sheer ingenuity rather than magic sums it up I suppose, but to the terrified people of Japan, some of their escapades must indeed have seemed magical. It's said for instance that he could walk on water. Well, almost true - history tells us that he developed watertight pots that when tied to his feet enabled him to appear to stroll across rivers. The Ninja could walk up vertical walls. Again, nearly true - by attaching metal spikes to his hands and feet, he could indeed scale perpendicular walls. How about staying underwater? Yes, again the Ninja developed what could only be described as a primitive version of the aqualung and for shorter distances, he'd use a bamboo tube or reed which just penetrated the surface, thus allowing him to breathe freely.

Smoke bombs were another speciality of the Japanese super-spy. Having manufactured a temporary screen, the Ninja would make good his escape, giving rise in the process to his reputed ability to disappear literally in a puff of smoke. The art of flying has also frequently been attributed to him and indeed it seems likely that he was able to drop considerable heights by using his carefully designed billowing cape! Signalling by means of rockets was another 'ahead of its time' part of the Ninja armoury. All in all the early Japanese spy could only have been described as superbly equipped for the job. Chain mail protective clothing was frequently worn so when you consider in addition the weight of all the weapons, tools of the trade and so on, the still mobile Ninja must indeed have been a fantastically fit man.

Naturally, with his need for curatives, poisons, gunpowder and what else, the Ninja had to be well versed in chemistry. In his case of course, the only ingredients available were the wild flowers, trees and animals he had around him but the results were none the less effective. Noxious gas fumes were a favourite for disabling guards. A mixture of newt, mole and snake blood was impregnated into paper and tossed onto fires. Astonishingly, the victims did indeed become drowsy after inhaling the fumes. Another strange concoction which it is claimed will achieve the same purpose is the powder of three male rats, several leaves of the paulownia tree, a fat centipede, a few cotton seeds and some yellow cattle dung. When thoroughly dried and tossed onto glowing charcoal, the fumes are claimed to induce instant light-headedness! The Ninja didn't miss a trick. He had itching powders and drugs which reduced his victims to helpless laughter or even temporary insanity.

To add to his list of accomplishments, the Ninja wasn't adverse either to a little strategic hypnotism. There are, the record states, eighty-one ways of twisting the fingers together so as to capture the attention of an opponent and numb his speed of reaction. This early form of mesmerising, accompanied by mutterings and incantations and surrounded by Buddist esoteric dogma proved itself to be supremely effective. Another outstanding claim of the Ninja was his supposed ability to achieve instant dislocation of certain bone joints whenever the occasion required. Houdini himself would have admired such formidable escape tactics.

It goes without saying that there have been some truly spectacular moments in the history of the Ninja. One of the supreme examples was the attempted assassination of Samurai General Oda Nobunaga. As the general lay sleeping one night, he was unaware that on the floor above him sat Ishikawa Goemon - a renowned Ninja. Through a small hole in the ceiling came a light thread which ended just above the general's lips. Then, little by little, Goemon fed small drops of deadly poison down the thread towards Oda's mouth. Fortunately, the General was a light sleeper and he awoke in the nick of time. Goemon was not so lucky. He was captured some time later and for punishment, was thrown into boiling water!

A further story which needs to be investigated is of course the alleged Ninja involvement in the death of Bruce Lee. The medical explanation of the Little Dragon's tragic passing is clear and has been discussed before in the pages of *KFM*. But be that as it may, there's no doubt that many people had strong motives for seeing Bruce out of the way. His fabulous success provoked much jealousy

and his frequent disclosures to the public in general of many of the 'Mysteries of the East' stirred up more antagonism amongst fellow Kung Fu experts than was healthy. Ever since that fateful day, the dreaded name of the Ninja has been on the questioning lips of those who were closest to him. Proof, there is none but suspicions, there are many. Any self-respecting Ninja would be able to commit a murder in such a way as to make it look entirely natural and Bruce himself was well aware of this. Threats on his life were almost commonplace and he took every one of them seriously.

The Ninja of course belongs to the past. No more than one or two could possibly survive in today's world and preserving anonymity would be almost impossible. Their strength of purpose, however, should not be forgotten. The great Bruce Lee proved he could do what most people would have considered impossible and it is to that kind of dedication we should turn (although not of course with the Ninja's often criminal intent!). The fruits of life are all around us - if we can but reach high enough to take them!

THE BRUCE LEE SECRET SOCIETY

Hi - and it's a big hello to you all from Pam and Carmella! We thought it wouldn't take long for the ball to start rolling and how right we were. Welcome therefore, to all the first month's members. Judging by some of the letters we've already had back, there's no doubt that our choice of pictures, facts and info for the Society Kit has struck a happy note amongst the fans - we've really got a good thing going! Not only that, you'll see if you look at the *KFM* mail order section that the new reduced prices for Society members are now in operation. Please remember though to quote your membership number when ordering - otherwise you may miss the reduction.

The first tasty item of news is that we've just established very firm links with Dragon Club of Hollywood, USA. Gary Kohatsu who runs it has written us a very long and interesting letter about how things are Bruce Lee-wise in the States and that letter, plus our reply, will be published in full in the next Society News Sheet. One point he did bring out though was this. Apparently someone over there is organising a Bruce Lee Memorial Exhibition and the exciting news is we are invited to send something along from Great Britain. We don't think there is all that much time to go, so how about all you Society members write in as quickly as possible with your ideas on what form the entry should take. Remember it has to be practical - six foot high statues of the Little Dragon are definitely out! The second Bruce Lee Secret Society News Sheet will be out around Christmas time so we reckon we just have to include an extra something for the Christmas stocking! Because the idea is still a bit in the planning stage we're not going to tell you what it's going to be until next month - you'll have to put your guessing caps on - all we will say is if you still haven't joined the Society, you'd better get your skates on, otherwise you'll be missing out!

Finally may we once again say a great big thank you to all the new members who have written back to us so quickly, offering everything from congratulations, advice and ideas to even the occasional criticism . You've no idea how much fun we have picking our way through the daily stack of mail - that is what makes it all worthwhile.

Sorry for running over it all again, but for all the *KFM* readers who missed the last issue - it's time to join the Bruce Lee Secret Society! You'll get a whole pile of goodies when you join, plus a regular New Sheet sent directly to your home.

Don't delay - just send £2.95 to: The Bruce Lee Secret Society, *Kung-Fu Monthly*, 39 Goodge Street, London, W1P 1FD. See you all again next month! **Pam and Carmella**

KICKBACK: THE LETTERS

Hi there - it's Jenny Lee here again and what a surprise I've got for you this month! As Felix Yen said in the editorial, there really are more and more letters coming in and although I'd be the last to complain about that, it doesn't exactly increase the chances of you seeing your letter in print. So, crafty old *KFM* has come up with not one but two solutions. Firstly, we've reduced the size of the words just a little bit (alright, no jokes about magnifying glasses please) and secondly, starting this issue, you'll see there's now a Quickies Corner. That's where I'm going to be dealing with all the many letters I get in which but for space problems would have merited a full reply in Kickback. As you'll see when you look in Quickies Corner, I'm not going to be printing the letters you send to me - simply the name and the part of the country you come from, along with a quick reply to the questions you ask. I really hope everyone likes the idea. I think it's a great way of squeezing more in, so, deep breath and here we go - the letters!

LASSITUDE ANYONE?

Dear Jenny,
May I congratulate you on producing such a marvellous magazine? It seems that you and the team are the only people in the magazine field who get their facts straight and true. Anyway, down to the questions. As I have studied the arts for a long time, it worries me that I am occasionally bugged by a feeling that makes me lose all interest - I think it is called lassitude. Could you please tell me more about it - my martial life is at stake? Also is The Way of the Dragon soundtrack out yet?
Graham Harrison, Stockport, Cheshire

Dear Graham,
First of all may I say that your congratulations are, as always, very gratefully received! As far as your lassitude is concerned, well now that's a difficult one. I don't really fancy myself as a long-range doctor so I'm hard put to give you concrete advice. Have you asked yourself whether you are still really that interested? Maybe you've got into a kind of rut and you're getting bored? Then again, perhaps your health is not what it should he? The only real recommendation I can give, is for you to set yourself targets, then go on out and meet them. I'd stress though that if you really feel it's a physical thing, then please go have a check-up with the doctor. Finally, The Way of the Dragon soundtrack. Hmmm, well, I've been trying to get one myself without any luck so far. Maybe someone can help the two of us!

NUNCHAKU GRADING SYSTEM

Dear Jenny Lee,
Recent correspondence on the subject of nunchakus particularly interested me as a 3rd year student of this weapon. For well over two years now, I have practiced daily - missing only two days through illness - and can now speedily perform basic Katas - even blind-folded or in a darkened room. If I am an advanced student at this stage, then I consider that I am just scratching the surface and that there are years to go yet. Being self-taught, I found that the elbows took most of the punishment in the early stages, though this is rarely so now. Nunchaku Kata fascinates me as a discipline and martial art form and I make a point of practicing with both Japanese and Chinese weapons, my interest being triggered, you will have guessed, by the late Bruce Lee. It was with surprise and disappointment, though, that I recently learnt there is apparently no grading system for Kata prowess with this weapon, which seems a pity, and I wonder if you can throw any light on this aspect please. If the reader who wrote to you about nunchakus in the last issue would care to write to me, then perhaps something could be done between us - perhaps start a martial arts school specifically for students of Kobu-Jitsu? Finally, my compliments indeed on a well edited and responsible publication. As an editorial wallah myself (for Thomson Regional Newspapers) I know a good thing when I see it and *KFM* is in a class of its own. In the 2 1/2 years of publishing *KFM*, you have kept faith with what must surely be a rapidly growing readership and your continuing loyalty to Bruce Lee has never been shaken. It's good to see consistency in uncertain and troubled times. By the way, I have to ask; could the nunchakus shown by your staff member in the last issue possibly be for sale? I would give almost anything to own them.
Keith D.J. Manning, Hockley, Essex

Dear Keith,
Very many thanks for such an absolutely delightful letter. It's not often that I'd print such a long one in its entirety but yours just has to be an exception! Firstly regarding your comments about the nunchaku grading system; so far as I can make out, you're right (if I'm wrong there'll be a thousand letters to prove it!) I suspect in this country that the idea has always tended to be swept under the carpet. You ask about the actual Bruce Lee nunchakus? Well, I'm sorry to say the only way you're going to lay your hands on them is by using dynamite! They are locked away permanently in the film company's safe.

KICKBACK QUICKIES

Yuk Chiu Lam, Liverpool, Lancs - *Tao of Jeet Kune Do* is now on sale and *KFM* most certainly is still available for 30p + 10p p&p.
Kieran Donnelly, Carrickmacross, Eire - So far as I can discover, *The Silent Flute* was never made. Plans are, however, afoot at this very moment.
Clifford Aitkenhead, Preston, Lancs - Something on Jim Kelly? I've passed your idea straight on to the editor.
Kenneth Walters, Gateshead, Tyne & Wear - No measure was ever taken of Bruce's flying kicks. Rumour has it however that it certainly exceeded seven feet. In answer to the second question, Bruce studied and could handle most styles.

Wendy Kasabian with a pile of mail order correspondence at the Kung-Fu Monthly offices. Wendy would go on to become Felix Dennis' secretary, then his personal assistant - a role she would fill for the rest of his life.

Inderjeet Saini, Birmingham - Thanks for telling us that the *Enter the Dragon* theme is available right now from most local record dealers.

C. Dreyer, Reading, Berks - Thanks for telling us that less censored versions of the Little Dragon's films can be seen at the Hollywood Boulevard Cinema, outside Montmartre metro Station, Paris, France - Holidaymakers take note!

H. Chonk, Hounslow, Middlesex - You're right, there was an error, Bruce was born under the sign of Sagittarius.

Gary Chedgzoy, Liverpool, Lancs - Thanks for reminding us about the single *In Memory of Bruce Lee* (Warners K163S4) recorded by John and Rosalind. It may be deleted now, but it's worth a try.

Terry Schuler, Poplar, London - So far as I know, there's no age limit for buying nunchakus. They are, however, only sold at the discretion of the shop owner concerned.

Patrick Smith, Liverpool, Lancs - Sorry I can't answer all your questions, but: 1. there may soon be a book out dealing with Bruce's films and 2. *The Book of Kung Fu* is still available for £1.05 (inc p&p).

Lorraine Atherton, Wigan, Lancs - Should have news of the Robert Lee album soon, sorry no mugs or treasure kits available right now.

Gary Elliott, Beechdale, Nottinghamshire - The Bruce Lee Classical film never got beyond the costume stage.

KFM PEN PAL CORNER

Jill Symonds of Kirkby in Ashfield is looking for a male/female Chinese pen pal, aged 17-20.
Mr. D. Josper, Kavensmead, South Africa wants American girl pen pal, aged 15-18.
Miss Carol Kallend, Caistor, Lincs wants male penpal, aged 16-18.
Julius A. Fernande, Nigeria wants male/female pen pal, any age.

THE POSTER MAGAZINES - VOLUME ONE

24

1976

EDITORIAL

Hi there Kung Fu fans...
Welcome aboard the *Kung-Fu Monthly* ship as we get ready to set sail once more on the Bruce Lee sea of discovery. And if you think that sounds good, just wait until you've turned on to part four of our Little Dragon film round-up. This month, we scrutinise *Fist of Fury*, Bruce Lee's second major picture and for many people, the most enjoyable in terms of raw martial arts expertise. Once again, *KFM* digs deep down to bring you the sensational details surrounding this monster martial epic - the facts and figures, the people and the places. Some you will maybe know already but much will be completely new to you! Next up, we take a look at George Lazenby and in particular, his new film, *Stoner*. As most of you will know, Bruce selected George for a starring role in *Game of Death* but the Little Dragon died before any footage could be put in the can. Since then, George has been working hard at developing his own particular style and technique - seen to great effect in

his latest smash, *The Man from Hong Kong* - and his linkup with martial master, Wang Yu, really looks like taking him places.

I hardly know how to say how pleased we are here at *KFM* with the response you've given to the new club. The astounding news is that within one month of opening, we topped the five hundred mark and the presidents reckon it's only a matter of weeks before we reach a thousand members. We intend therefore, to celebrate that occasion by presenting a rare set of *Kung-Fu Monthly* back issues to the 1000th application we receive to join the Bruce Lee Secret Society. It could be any moment now and it could be YOU!

That's all from me for the moment.

Felix Yen

Felix Yen
Editor-in-Chief

FIST OF FURY: THE FACT AND THE FICTION

Many people do not realise that the storyline of *Fist of Fury* is based firmly upon fact. Golden Harvest boss, Raymond Chow, being something of an advocate for history in the cinema, picked on the true life tale of Huo Yuan-chia as the setting for Bruce Lee's follow-up to *The Big Boss*. The choice was bold, imaginative and unquestionably successful and for most connoisseurs of the Asian movie market, nothing has ever matched the supremacy of Fist of Fury. This was real Chinese cinema at its greatest and Bruce seized upon his extra length of acting rope with glee. His comedy routines, for example the Japanese telephone engineer sequence, contained a degree of humour that at times became lost on the western movie-goer. It's truthfully been said that only a Chinese could properly understand the hilarity of the situations. Well, we aim to do something about that! After many months of painstaking research, we've come up with a whole bundle of special points to look out for - revelations that will make your next visit to *Fist of Fury* seem like it's the premiere time all over again! But first, as usual, let's take a look at the plot.

Set in 1908, Chen (Bruce Lee) arrives in Shanghai to attend the funeral of his teacher, the founder of a Chinese Kung Fu school. While he is there, members of the rival Japanese club across the road deliver a formal 'insult' to Chen and his club. He returns the insult by entering the Japanese school and defeating everybody there single-handed. They in turn decide to return the compliment and in Chen's absence, enter the Chinese school and eliminate many of his friends. Before long, Chen discovers that his teacher had in fact been murdered - poisoned by two Japanese who were masquerading as Chinese servants. Chen exacts the necessary vengeance but in so doing, he incurs the wrath of the police. He goes into hiding to plan revenge on the Japanese school. Secretly he breaks in and defeats the Chief Instructor and a famed Russian Kung Fu expert employed there. Chen then faces the Principal, winning a violent duel. Revenge is complete, but sensing that his violent actions must be called to task and not wishing to answer the charges brought by the Japanese-controlled police force, he dies in a hail of bullets while executing a final glorious leap.

Fist of Fury was set in the time of the Japanese occupation, thus accounting for much of the anti-Japanese feeling in the film. Regular readers of *Kung-Fu Monthly* will have seen our feature on legendary Chinese fighters (*KFM* No.18) and will have read the story of Huo Yuan-chia, an ex-stevedore of enormous strength and ability. Huo specialised in Mi Tsung-i (or the Labyrinthine Art), a style dating back to the Sung dynasty and tradition has it that he was poisoned by a Japanese doctor. Apparently a troupe of Japanese fighters had come to Shanghai to challenge him and Huo had routed them. The doctor's action was to exact revenge. There are many variations to this tale, yet there is little doubt that such a man did exist and there were many mysteries surrounding his sudden and early death. It is said that Huo's senior student (Chen?) sought revenge for the killing of his teacher. A further incidental twist in the story handed down to us is that Huo is said to have once frightened a Russian in Tientsin into leaving China!

The film was shot in 1972, mostly in the Golden Harvest studios, but some of it in the park outside. In the course of shooting, there were several title changes and at one time, it was to be called *The School of Chivalry*. More confusion set in when Chow decided to name it *Fist of Fury*. That title could not be used in the USA because the Little Dragon's first major film (called *The Big Boss* in Great Britain) had already been re-titled *Fists of Fury* for the American market! So for the USA, *Fist of Fury* became *The Chinese Connection*. It opened in Hong Kong and within 29 days, shattered the record set by *The Big Boss*, grossing HK$4.3million in less than a month!

The pressures on Bruce were enormous. People would come up to him in the street and press money into his hand saying, "Remember me, I'm your friend." Right then, anyone friendly with Bruce could get whatever he wanted. The Little Dragon, however, was a whole lot brighter than they thought and he let the bribes just fly over his head. It's estimated that he tore up over six million pounds worth of cheques - an incredible sum of money to just throw away! If any single action of Bruce could be said to have typified his iron will and resolve, this must surely have been it.

Things were going just as crazy elsewhere. In the Philippines, *Fist of Fury* held its run for over six months and was only pulled off when the government decided it was an unhealthy situation for the home film market. The production went on to win the prized Asian Oscar known as the Golden Horse Award. It hadn't been an expensive package. The total outlay was in the region of HK$700,000 and from start to finish, the entire film took just six weeks to make - using only three cameras. Lo Wei, the producer, borrowed just one out of those six weeks to 'can' the location shots in the local park. That in itself wasn't always easy; to begin with there were the ever-present street gangs to contend with. The leader of the nearest bunch would arrive to demand payment for using 'his' bit of road and if the protection wasn't handed over, the consequences could be very unpleasant. Rumours have it that sometimes the film companies paid up, much to the annoyance of Bruce who had to be physically restrained at times from attacking the hoodlums concerned. It's said in fact by some that it was the leader of one of these gangs who applied to the Little Dragon the 'vibrating palm,' leading several years later to Bruce's tragic death.

The supporting cast in *Fist of Fury* was impressive. To begin with, James Tien was brought in to follow up his successful appearance in *The Big Boss*. James can honestly claim to be one of the few genuine Chinese actors to have made the transition to martial

arts films. Generally speaking, the stars of Hong Kong Kung Fu films tend to be ex-stunt men whose acting ability sometimes borders on the negligible. James Tien, however, came the other way. He switched first from straight acting to sword fighting and then decided to take his chances with Kung Fu. Little Dragon fans have of course one more date with Mr. Tien - he appears in *Game of Death*! Outside of the Bruce Lee films, probably his biggest success was a lead role in *Shaolin Boxing*.

Another prominent name to appear was fighting actress, Nora Miao. She already had under her belt *The Blade Spares None* and *Invincible Eight* with Angela Mao. In that, they'd used eight different kinds of people who had eight different kinds of weapon and in true Hong Kong style, they'd taken on literally thousands of opponents and won! Which makes it all the more strange that in *Fist of Fury*, she had accepted a role amounting to little more than a bit part. Another anomaly about the film was the almost 'under-playing' of Robert Baker (the Russian). His name wasn't even on the original film poster, despite the fact that next to Bruce, he was probably the most competent person there! The Little Dragon had chosen him specially for the part (Robert was an ex-pupil of Bruce's) and 'the Russian' didn't let anyone down! His performance was superb, matching that of Chuck Norris in *The Way of the Dragon*. Possibly the reason for Robert not being credited on the poster was simply political. At that time, it was thought better to publicise Chinese names only as the Asian audiences preferred it that way.

Naturally the plot of *Fist of Fury* bore only a superficial resemblance to the legendary story of Huo Yuan-chia. Whereas Bruce walks right into the enemy camp to wipe out large numbers of Japanese pupils single-handed, it's pretty certain that Huo's revenge seeking student took on only one or two opponents at a time and then over a period of years. In the film, after the Japanese have retaliated and Bruce has gone into hiding, he then discovers the truth about the two Japanese who are masquerading as Chinese servants. It's not obvious to western audiences how exactly he goes about this, although really the explanation is quite simple. There is a difference in the under-clothing protection worn by Chinese and Japanese and Bruce spotted the mistake!

The Little Dragon disposes of the murderers and proceeds to suspend them from a pole in the road outside. It's not often realised that the place chosen for the hanging is significant - it's by the house of the Japanese Consul! The highlight of the entire film for many people is where Bruce sneaks into the 'Nippon' club disguised as a Japanese telephone engineer. While there of course he finds out all the details of the plot to destroy the Chinese club. Western audiences again probably fail to appreciate the sheer absurdity of a Chinese posing as a Japanese telephone man. Out East, however, the fans went berserk. The idea was not only totally original, it also struck deep into the hearts of people who could well recall the times of Japanese oppression.

Fist of Fury does have its 'love' aspect as well, although the relationship (between Chen and the daughter of the School's Principal) is seldom treated with any sort of seriousness. In fact, it hardly really gets off the ground. The idea no doubt was to make 'Chen' look a bit more human, but by the end of the picture you've just about forgotten that the girl ever existed! The accent is definitely on revenge and after Chen's discovery that his teacher is dead, Bruce comes over as some sort of revenge-seeking maniac. After wiping out most of the Japanese school, he comes back to find they have returned the compliment. Bruce, after completing his personal vendetta, discovers that unless he hands himself in, his club will be closed. In the finale when he shakes his fist to the people, he is not simply gesticulating to the stupid Chinese policeman; he is shaking it in contempt towards the Japanese officials and the gesture is completed with a classic flying leap. Although he'd certainly never have hit anyone, the policemen's instinctive action was to shoot him. Michael Pai, the man in charge of dubbing the film into English was a worried man! His previous work with Chinese pictures had simply required him to have such lines as 'OK' and 'I think it's time for you to leave' placed into the required positions. Generally the words were spoken more or less in a monotone voice that sported a John Wayne accent! In the case of *Fist of Fury*, however, the performances actually called for acting ability and this really made his job tough! Bruce wasn't prepared to put up with any bad work either. He said, "If you have to dub my films into English because people can't understand me, then at least you can do it well." Around this time of course, his English was rather below par - he wouldn't be trusting himself to speak that language in a film for some years to come. In fact, to be honest, if the Little Dragon had had his way, neither *Fist of Fury*, *The Big Boss* nor *The Way of the Dragon* would ever have found their way onto the western market at all.

Bruce couldn't have asked for a better partner than Raymond Chow. This famed producer started the Kung Fu ball rolling when working with Shaw Brothers as their production manager. The martial arts pattern was set with the making of *Chinese Boxer* and from then on, he never looked back. The Brothers were heartbroken when Chow left the fold as they knew what they were losing! Chow, however, still maintains to this day, that he would never have gone in the first place had Shaws shown more foresight and imagination. Kung Fu films were by no means a new idea and Chow partially got his inspiration from watching Chan Kee Ka in the *Sky Hawk* series. Chan became a major Cantonese star around the early fifties and the 19 or 20 films he made became bombshells. Chow in fact

was so taken with Chan, he persuaded the star to make just one more film, this time in colour. The result was another classic!

After the success of *Fist of Fury*, Bruce was in a bit of a quandary as to what to attempt next. Money and offers were coming in from all directions and deciding on the best move was a problem in itself. Golden Harvest executive, Andre Morgan, remarked at the time that Bruce knew what the people wanted to see and what they didn't but he also knew what HE wanted to do. The Little Dragon was suddenly confronted with mountains of conflicting advice and he just didn't know who to take notice of. As Bruce said, "I didn't know who to trust and I even suspected my old pals. I didn't know who was trying to take advantage of me."

Fortunately, his relationship with Chow provided a cornerstone to his life and career. Such was the honesty of Golden Harvest's dynamic boss that shortly after finishing *Fist of Fury*, Chow approached Bruce and told him flatly he could in no way match the huge and tempting offers that were coming in thick and fast for the services of the Little Dragon. Not wanting in any way to hold back Bruce's chances, he suggested terminating their contract (which still had three films to run). The Little Dragon was stunned by the character and politeness of the man who had brought him to stardom and the result of that conversation was the formation of Concord, the joint film production company of Bruce Lee and Raymond Chow.

So the curtain begins to close on *Fist of Fury*. One role so far not mentioned, is that of lovable old Mr. Wu, the Japanese translator. His superb comic acting provided a wonderful foil to the anger of Chen and if for no other reason, he will always be remembered for the worst unintentional dubbing pun in the history of Chinese movies. Who else, while hitting Chen on the face, could have remarked "What's the matter - you yellow or something?" The Chinese subtitled version of the film too is not without its humour. As Chen finally kills Mr. Wu, the translation flashes up, "Why is everyone always picking on me?" There is more we could have delved into; for instance, the sequence where Bruce hurls a bowl of rice at the face of the Japanese Sensei (remember, even pouring out rice in front of an Oriental is a terrible insult!) but there we must leave it.

For the Chinese people, Bruce had done more than anyone could every have expected of him. *Fist of Fury* had everything the once oppressed Chinese people could ever have asked for. There was superb action, marvellous comic relief, a higher standard of acting than from most films of the time and finally, plenty of digs at their arch-enemies of old, the Japanese. After all, that sign reading 'No Dogs or Chinese Allowed' did actually exist, in Shanghai. Revenge, if only of the film variety, is sweet.

FIST OF FURY CREDIT TITLE LIST

Starring: Bruce Lee and Nora Miao.
With: Maria Yi, James Tien, Tien Feng, Hwong Chung Hsin, Han Ying Chieh, Lo Wei, Lee Quin, Feng Yi, Tony Liu, Chin San, Robert Baker, Arimura Jun and Hashimoto Riki.
Producer: Raymong Chow. **Executive Producer:** Liu Liang Hua. **Director:** Lo Wei.
Scriptwriter: Lo Wei. **Assistant Director:** Chih Yao Chang. **Dubbing:** Wang Ping.
Martial Art Instructor: Han Ying Chieh. **Recording:** Kao Vang.
Music: Ku Chia Hui Joseph. **Editing:** Chang Yao Chung.

GEORGE LAZENBY: FROM BOND TO STONER

Having landed the most sought after role in the history of the cinema - 007 in the Bond thriller, *On Her Majesty's Secret Service* - George Lazenby will be the first to admit that he blew it! Put it down to wrong decisions, inexperience or sheer bad luck - whichever way you look at it, Dame Fortune turned her back on the 6'2" tall actor from Goulburn in Australia. Yet George is by nature, a sticker and from whatever high ledge he may fall, you can be sure he's going to land back on his feet. In a future *KFM*, we'll cover how Lazenby took the hard route in his climb through the movie jungle. Right now though, we're going to concern ourselves with reviewing his brush with the world of Kung Fu and in particular, his great new film, *Stoner*.

From car salesmen to friend of Bruce Lee seems a strange transition in anyone's book, but for George Lazenby, it's just a case of business as usual. After the fall of the Bond days, nothing really happened for well over a year. He lost money on *Universal Soldier* (an Italian gun-running thriller) and then proceeded to turn down a part in *Last Tango in Paris*! George, pretty broke by now, returned to England for no particular reason other than that he knew London. One night, more out of boredom than anything else, he went to see *The Big Boss* and immediately, he got excited. This just had to be the new thing and he wanted to be there when it happened.

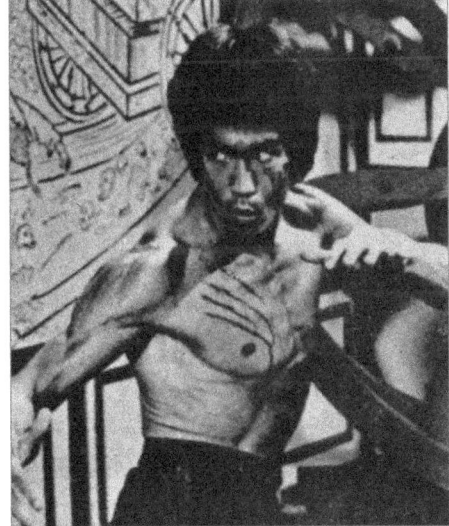

After one false move to Singapore, Lazenby soon found out that Hong Kong was the place to head for, so scraping together virtually all the money he had left in the world, he bummed his way over to the offices of Raymond Chow. George's luck was in as Secret Service had just opened there and he was a popular man! Chow telephoned the Little Dragon to see if he could arrange a meeting between the two biggest names in Hong Kong but but Bruce wasn't impressed. Later that day though, the Little Dragon turned up anyway and the three of them went to lunch. The conversation centred around *Game of Death*. Bruce explained to George that the film was still only half finished - he'd had to hold back production in order to finish *Enter the Dragon* for Warner Brothers, but now that was done, he was raring to get going again.

Bruce then offered George a part in the unfinished film, suggesting for him, the role of a western counterpart. This is interesting and in some ways, surprising news. It was thought by many that Bruce had intended *Game of Death* to be again, directly aimed towards the Asian market and yet, here he was, lining up Lazenby to play a western role! It also indicates just how loosely the Little Dragon preferred to make his films. It's by no means usual and not normally at all easy to just 'slip' another starring role into a half-fin-

ished film. You could say, in fact, that it takes a genius like Bruce Lee to be able to handle a situation like that.

As they drove back to Bruce's place there was a bad storm blowing and when they got there, the Gods had a bad omen in store. A tree had snapped in the gale and fallen in the yard - the little Dragon was not one to ignore such a portent of ill luck. Still, George settled down cosily in Bruce's superbly equipped library. The Little Dragon, as Lazenby remembers, proved to be a stickler for attention. Whenever Bruce said something, he'd check that George had really taken it in. Contracts for the film were signed on the fourth day and in the evening, Chow and Lazenby waited at a restaurant for Bruce to arrive for the 'celebration supper.' The Little Dragon never got there and George had lost another opportunity, plus this time, a 'real good friend.'

He stayed in Hong Kong though, despite it looking for a time as if that old bad luck had stuck for good. Then came *The Man From Hong Kong*, with George handling the 'baddie' role against martial wizard number two, Wang Yu. It was a tough production, but a rewarding one. During shooting, George managed to land himself in hospital with a nasty case of second degree burns - something went wrong with the insulation during the fire sequence! Still, at last he'd made another commercial success and the next step up the ladder was to be Stoner. As if playing opposite Wang Yu wasn't enough, he was now linking up with China's own Kung Fu princess, Angela Mao.

Stoner, for George Lazenby, looks destined to be the big one and the story outline runs as follows:

In Hong Kong, the evil Mr. Sinn possesses the formula for a new Superdrug - in this

case, an aphrodisiac! Sydney detective, Stoner, decides to fly over and try his hand at smashing the racket. Meanwhile, unknown to Stoner, attractive agent Li Shou-Hua (Angela Mao) has also been assigned to the case and she poses as a villager to pick up clues. Sinn has heard about Stoner and he quickly sends out henchmen to arrange for the detective's downfall. Stoner, however, manages to overcome the attackers. Pretty Li continues her vigil and eventually succeeds in obtaining some of the drug. She makes one abortive attempt at entering Mr. Sinn's 'temple' headquarters (foiled by the automatic alarm system) and returns later that night for another go. Stoner and the girl (disguised as a boy) meet up and, not realising their common purpose, they start fighting. This trips Sinn's alarm again with the result they are both captured. The evil boss administers the wonder-drug to the two of them and then leaves them handcuffed inside a cage.

So how do they get out and finally right all the wrongs? Well, it wouldn't be fair to give it all away! You're just going to have to see *Stoner* for yourself. Betty Ting Pei and Whang In-Sik are in the film too, so take my tip - it's well worth a visit.

As for the George Lazenby of right now - well the future seems to have picked up a bright spot or two. He's back in Hollywood at the moment, trying his luck with a new production. If *Stoner* grosses the way it should, George, with all that Kung Fu training under his belt, should be well in line for some bigger and better martial arts pictures. Let's just hope that nothing goes wrong for him this time. I'd hate to have to write once again that George Lazenby blew it!

THE BRUCE LEE SECRET SOCIETY

Hello, it's Pam and Carmella here again...

Firstly - apology time! Due entirely to circumstances beyond our control, up to the time of writing we haven't been able to include the sticker in the Society Kit. To put no finer point to it, the manufacturer let us down badly and we've had to take the job elsewhere - it's disgraceful, but there it is. Hopefully the delay should only be for a few weeks and I'm sure you'll be happy to bear with us.

Now the good news! The Bruce Lee Secret Society is proud to announce that three people have accepted honorary membership. They are: 1. Mr Tony Love of Cathay Films, 2. Mr Roy Byrne of Cathay Films and 3. Mr Eddy Pumer of Capital Radio (in London).

We're delighted to welcome all three to the fold and look forward to a long and happy relationship. By the way, we'd love you to write and tell us of anyone you think should become an honorary member of the BLSS. We'll add the name(s) to the short list that we ourselves have already drawn up and as people accept we'll be letting you know who they are.

Thank you for all the marvellous letters you've sent (and are still sending!) wishing us luck in running the club. As so often happens, not everything has gone as smoothly as we would have liked and there have been some delays in getting membership kits out. However, all that's in the past and now we've slipped into top gear, problems should be few and far between (we hope). Something that does help is clear writing. It's awful having to guess at names and addresses - have we got it right or haven't we? - so please use capital letters if you think your writing may not be completely legible. Also try not to forget to include your first name. It's horribly formal to have to write to I. Smith or E. Jones and we don't even know if you're male or female!

Don't forget in the next news sheet we'll be including our first Swop Shop - so if there's anything you want to buy, swap or sell, write in quickly. There's a pen pals section too and of course both these columns are completely free to all Society members.

We've had so many enquiries about the Bruce Lee film soundtrack cassettes, we've decided to investigate the situation. So far, we've discovered that of the Little Dragon's four major films, only the *Enter the Dragon* soundtrack has ever been released in the UK (and that itself is now deleted). Any other Bruce Lee film tracks you may have seen will be imported ones - probably from USA, Hong Kong or Tokyo.

Anyway, these are the three places we intend to start our search, so keep your fingers crossed for us! (Of course if any of you members have 'inside information,' please let us know.)

Finally as a special gift to all Bruce Lee Secret Society members, with the next news sheet, we will be including a Society Christmas Card, either for yourself to keep, or for you to send to someone else (further copies will be available at a reasonable price). We also expect to have one or two other mail order items available in time for December 25th, including (due to your enormous demand) club badges and stickers. On top of all that, of course, in the next News Sheet you'll find a competition, the swop shop and pen pals corner, plus all the usual news/views info and pictures. We both look forward to seeing you all again then! **Pam and Carmella**

KICKBACK: THE LETTERS

Hi... It's your old friend Jenny here once again, ready, willing and able to sort through the last four weeks' mail! Firstly may I say thank you a million times to all the many hundreds of people who wrote in saying that Kickback was the best part of *KFM*. Well - what do I say? I think I'll fire the staff and write the whole thing myself! Seriously, though, your response was really tremendous and to be absolutely honest, just about every section of the magazine got a fair crack of the whip. My good turn for this issue is to pass on a message from Pam and Carmella. They've had over ten Society applications come in without names and addresses, so if you think yours may have been one of these, please write in as soon as possible giving the postal order numbers. OK - that done, it's letters time!

CHINESE GUNG FU BOOK

Dear Jenny,
May I say what a splendid magazine you all produce each month on Bruce Lee. I think it's a great outlet for the thousands of fans, including myself and several other people up at Capital Radio. I agree about the poster in No.22 - it's undoubtedly the best so far. Also in No.22, why did you print a picture from *Fist of Fury* when the film in question was *The Big Boss*? Another query I have is a picture of a book I have called *Chinese Gung Fu - The Philosophical Art of Self Defense* by Bruce Lee. I've been searching for this book for over a year now. Have you any ideas where I might obtain a copy?
Eddy Pumer Capital Radio, London

Dear Eddy,
Marvellous to hear we've got Capital Radio on our side! As far as the Fist of Fury picture is concerned, well, new pictures aren't always that easy to come by these days and The Big Boss ones are the rarest. Generally though, we do try to fit the picture to the article. As for that book, thereby hangs a tale. Bruce assembled it when he was just starting his American school and so far as I know, only about 5,000 were ever printed. It's VERY rare! You could have come to our office to see a copy; that is until a visiting KFM reader decided to put it in his pocket. What a mean and callous person like that can hope to gain from reading a Bruce Lee book, is open to question. I certainly don't ever want to see him again!

KFM SUBSCRIPTION

Dear Jenny,
I would like to become a subscriber. In issue No.21 in the advert for subscription, you state that *KFM* will lose on it. Well, I think *KFM* is much too good a magazine to lose. Therefore please accept my subscription fee as £5.00 - no less. *KFM* is a winner for sure and it won't lose a penny on my account - it will gain if I can help it.
John Solagbade, Temple Fortune, London NW11

Dear John,
Believe me, with loyal readers like you around, KFM won't ever lose. Your letter just made my day!

GAME OF DEATH

Dear Jenny,
I think I have got the greatest idea of all for finishing *Game of Death*. How about leaving the film exactly as the master left it and then completing the duration with a documentary on Bruce's life?
Philip James, Kendal

Dear Philip,
I just couldn't resist answering this one. They say that often the simplest ideas are the best and here is a really prime example. Good thinking, Philip!

BRUCE LEE THE GREATEST

Dear Jenny,
It's difficult to say which is the best part of *KFM* - it's all breathtaking, but I think the best things are the stories and interviews on the ultimate Kung Fu master, Bruce Lee. They give one a better and truer insight into the life of the world's greatest martial artist and actor, and the stories let you know how he worked and the things he liked. And the interviews tell you what kind of person he was and how warm and loving he could be whether off the screen or on. They also let you know how he fought for his title and what superb a fighter he really was. I'd like to say more but for the real Bruce Lee fan, this should be enough. To explain fully what I feel for Bruce Lee, the ultimate Kung Fu master, would take more than a sheet of paper.
Richard Green, Smethwick, West Midlands

Dear Richard,
You win the 'What I Like Best in KFM' prize - a free year's subscription is yours!

Mike Devereux of Warrington in Cheshire has come up with another great idea for a competition. So far as I know, no one has yet designed a poster for *Game of Death*. Now I'm not promising anything, but the film company might just be interested in your ideas, so how about it? Don't send in full size works of art - just a small sketch will do. Another free year's subscription to the best entry!

KICKBACK QUICKIES

Jerry Desmond, Welwyn Garden City, Herts - well spotted Jerry! Yes, Bruce did sometimes use rubber nunchakus when there was a danger of other actors getting injured.

Norman Dawson, Belfast, Northern Ireland - *Game of Death* Tracksuit? We're trying to arrange something for all the people who've written in.

Billy Cain, Widnes, Cheshire - Full marks for observation - the *KFM* trademark was changed for legal reasons.

Brendan Toner, HMS Rhyl, London - Sorry to say that it's quite illegal to sell 8mm copies of most films.

Bruce Whale, S. Africa - Sorry, the film company insists that Secret Society membership be UK only - perhaps you have a club over there already?

Roger Egerton, Wilmslow, Cheshire & Jonathan McNalley, Nunsthorpe, Middlesbrough - 1. Bruce sometimes did wear a ring when offset. 2. He was 5'7" tall. 3. I believe he wore approximately size 9 shoes.

Sheila Boardman of the Official David Chiang Fan Club tells me that things are going great guns - but she still needs more members.

Terry Shorten, North End; Hants - *KFM* once a week? - Help!!

James Rudely, Greenock, Scotland - We're checking out the latest on Brandon right now. Yes, Scrapbooks are just about available still - 45p.

Billy Goodey, Hay Mills, Birmingham - Try Cimac in Birmingham for a good nunchaku book.

Nigel Kersey, Purley, Surrey - Count Dante? - Don't know much about him. Anyone help?

Stewart, Rochester, Kent - Glad you're not a street show-off when it comes to Kung Fu. I always look the other way when I see them!

Dieter Crockett, Immingham, S. Humberside - Yes, we knew DeMile was coming over soon, but so far we have found no proof of his claim to have been a pupil of Bruce's.

Mike Johnson, Huyton, Liverpool - Bruce did continue with *Game of Death* after *Enter the Dragon* was completed.

Michael McDonnell, Kilmarnock, Ayears oldhire - Thanks for the drawing. Yes, Bruce could use the three sectioned staff. Sorry, no Kick posters at present.

Stuart Lawrie & James Campbell, Alness, Rossshire - The best training manual for Jeet Kune Do for my money, is Bruce's *Tao of Jeet Kune Do* - check it out.

KFM PEN PAL CORNER

Martina Attracta Flanagan of Dublin wants Chinese/Cantonese pen pal about 5'8", 23-30 years old (female).

Ian May of Plymouth wants Japanese or Chinese pen pal, aged 15-16 (female).

Maxine Haycock of Cannock, Staffs wants Chinese pen pal, aged 18-19.

Barbara Whitton of Menzieehill, Dundee wants Chinese pen pal, aged 17-25 years old, preferably male, interested in Bruce Lee, Judo, Karate.

Niranka Nonis (male Sinhalese) of Colombi, Sri Lanka seeks pen friend.

25

1976

EDITORIAL

Hi there Kung Fu fans...

What a cracker of an issue we've put together for you this month! To start with, although as you can imagine, Bruce Lee pictures are getting harder to find all the time, the *KFM* research team have pulled off another major coup. Yup, a batch of great colour pictures has come our way and you'll be seeing some of them right here in these pages. There's soon to be a sensational new book out on the Little Dragon, but one with a very big difference. OK, I'll admit it - we've been keeping a secret from you! Some months ago, that same *KFM* research team stumbled across the find of the century - a collection of over a thousand Bruce Lee pictures that have never been seen before! Sounds incredible, but it's true. Paul Simmons (co-author and illustrator of *The Beginner's Guide to Kung Fu*) helped us select the best sequences and then added descriptive captions. It just has to be essential companion reading to Bruce's *Tao of Jeet Kune Do* and *KFM* is going to be reviewing it next month! Whew, with not much space left, we've made it to this month's features! First off, against all the odds, we've managed to do a special on The *Green Hornet*. Information on this, Bruce's first big foray into the dog eat dog world of American TV has always been difficult to find. Now, after months of spade work, we've made it and you'll agree it's a startling report. Second in line is a discussion of the Bruce Lee type 'killer instinct.' No kid's stuff here - just a close-up investigation into what makes powerful people tick. I'd say everybody had that sort of drive inside them somewhere - read the feature and maybe you'll get just a little closer to finding your own kilter instinct.

Good News Part Three, and how about this! Special *Game of Death* tracksuits may become available early next year, manufactured by the same people that made Bruce's! Now, as you can imagine, they aren't exactly going to be cheap - in fact, the figure looks to be around the £17-£18 mark at present. Is it worth us bringing them in at that price? If enough of you say yes, we'll go ahead.

That must be quite enough for now - so see you next month.

Felix Yen

Felix Yen
Editor-in-Chief

BRUCE LEE AND THE GREEN HORNET

Just about everyone must be pretty well acquainted by now with Bruce Lee's four major film epics plus of course, the unfinished *Game of Death*. Far less though, is known about the Little Dragon's early brush with American television. In a confused world of high speed filming, sponsors and TV ratings, the young Bruce learnt his lessons well and took to the routines like a duck to water. Though he was probably only too well aware of the failings of some aspects of the show, at least he wasn't going to let anyone down. To set the calendar right, the year was 1964/65 and he'd already quit the University. His martial arts school was coming along well although, as it turned out, his success on TV was to add several noughts on to the fees charged! Long Beach had been and gone and already his fame was spreading. It was not just by chance that Bruce Lee was chosen for the part of Kato by the television team. He'd earned his opportunity and was glad to stand alongside Van Williams in the new Fox production of *The Green Hornet* - to start with at least!

Probably many people don't realise that The *Green Hornet* was based on a very popular 1930's radio serial that featured the same major characters and basic story line (somewhat akin to the English Dick Tracy series). The gist of the idea was that it concerned the exploits of one Britt Reed, a newspaper publisher with a difference. Instead of just writing about crimes, he actually went out and solved them as well! He was an extreme example of what perhaps is better known in the business as a 'campaigning newspaper man' - he'd be knocking the villains over the head one moment and sticking them on the front page of his paper the next! By day he'd be attending to his chosen trade and by night he would put on his special costume and with the aid of Kato, his man servant, he'd drive out to do battle with the baddies.

When it came to choosing somebody for the part of Kato, the producer had a serious problem. Not only had they to find a Chinese performer who was suitable for the part, looks-wise and acting-wise, he also had to be able to pronounce the name Britt Reed! Strange as it sounds, this is no easy task for a Chinese speaking person - the letter 'R' and its western pronunciation is virtually unknown In the eastern world. A reporter once asked Bruce why he got the job and Bruce answered him, "The only reason I got it was because I was the only Chinese man in the whole of California who could pronounce the name Britt Reed." The reporter was later said to be somewhat taken aback by this now famous reply, as after all, it's not particularly usual for actors to get TV parts for reasons of that sort. It's only fair to add though that undoubtedly the Little Dragon was being a little tongue in cheek when he made the comment. After all, his good looks, acting ability and superb skill in the martial arts must have counted for something!

The series itself ran for about thirty episodes, which by American standards, is not too long. Of course it was by no means a disaster as was, for instance, a certain well-known Jerry Lewis show that was put on one day and immediately removed the next. The sponsors naturally are all important and considering the general low level of ratings that *The Green Hornet* notched up, they showed a remarkable leniency, it was televised during the 1966/67 season and although in the U.S.A. it was a flop, Bruce Lee came out of it all pretty well. In fact he succeeded in building up quite a following in that short time and if anyone can be said to have emerged with any credit at all, it must have been the Little Dragon and

possibly William Dozier, the executive producer.

The show's time allocation was tight. They had just half an hour each week to make something interesting happen and that's asking quite a lot of anybody. Simplicity of plot was the only way around it and probably that tended to make the stories rather predictable. To try and get over the problem, they experimented with two-part programmes; in other words, episodes carrying on from the one before. This can and often does work well, but unfortunately, it's better suited to shows that are fairly popular to start with. To a low-rating series like *The Green Hornet*, it didn't really help at all and in fact, the move probably helped sound the eventual death knell.

After seeing some of the shows, a disbeliever once asked Bruce if he was really as fast as he tried to make out. He replied, "At first it was ridiculous. All you could see were people falling down in front of me. All the camera showed was a blur!" In fact of course, Bruce really was that fast and to get over the speed problems in his later films, he actually slowed down sequences, particularly when using the nunchakus. Anyway, many viewers became convinced that the Little Dragon was merely a sham and it wasn't until some

years later that the world was to be finally convinced of his immense skill and unique ability.

Others used to get angered by Bruce and thought he was simply a show-off who'd do just about anything to get on the shot. Well, the Little Dragon was certainly nobody's fool but to some extent they were right! No way was he going to let this chance go by. At the least excuse, if they said "Bruce," he'd rip off his shirt and start flexing his muscles, whether they were filming at the time or not. But then, who could deny Bruce the right to show off his superb physique? He used any occasion he could to get into the public eye. He'd attend charity shows, being quite a celebrity by that time, and dutifully he'd display a muscle or two and often follow up the routine with some one-finger push-ups. Before long, he became quite the rage of the charity show circuit.

When filming of the series began, Bruce was earning only around $400 a week which was good money as far as he was concerned, but by no means a fortune considering his position in the show. Fortunately, as his popularity soared, so to (to an extent) did his wage. Of course to start with, Van Williams as Britt Reed got the star billing, but later on, when several episodes were strung together to make a movie film, the situation was amended. The title changed to Bruce Lee as Kato in *The Green Hornet* with the Little Dragon naturally getting top billing this time around. Even so, the TV Company must have been kicking themselves in later years for not giving Bruce a more prominent role,

AT LAST YOU CAN SUBSCRIBE TO KUNG-FU MONTHLY

Ever since Kung-Fu Monthly started we've literally been deluged with requests for subscriptions. *Now here's your chance to make sure you never miss out on a single issue of the world's greatest martial arts magazine!*

For only £4.00 you can subscribe to the next 12 monthly editions of Kung-Fu Monthly. As a service to our readers, KFM is actually making a substantial loss on the postage, packing and handling which is *all* included within this price.

Remember, the only way that you can be absolutely certain of receiving each and every copy of Kung-Fu Monthly is by taking up our fantastic subscription offer.

Keep your KFM collection up to date! Just send a cheque or postal order (made out to Kung-Fu Monthly) to:
KFM Subscriptions
39 Goodge Street
London W1P 1FD
Finally, please print your name and address clearly!
PLEASE ALLOW 3 WEEKS FOR DELIVERY
CLUB MEMBERS' PRICE, £3.75 ONLY

rather than just second stringing him to Williams.

At the time of filming, Van Williams was a little-known 'B' actor who had made it pretty big at one time only to fade into relative TV obscurity like so many others before. The producers of the show were Richard Bluel and Stanley Sheptner and the executive producer was of course William Dozier. Scripts were written by Jerry Thomas, music by Al Hurt and the director was Norman Foster. Dozier was the originator of the idea. Up to that time, one of his biggest productions had been the fabulously successful *Batman* series. He saw that, however, as 'mainly for the kids' and he yearned to try his hand at what amounted to an adult version of the same sort of thing. *The Green Hornet* idea sprang to mind - an updated version might just fit the bill! The stars for the show were quickly rounded up with just one exception, that of Kato.

For Bruce Lee, Lady Luck gave him a winning card in the shape of one Jay Sebring (a society hairdresser whose only other claim to fame was his subsequent murder in the outrageous Sharon Tate/ Charles Manson carnage). An old friend of Sebring's was *The Green Hornet* assistant producer, Charles Fitzsimmon. Well, it's one of those complicated chains of people, but what happened was Ed Parker took some pictures of Bruce performing at the renowned Long Beach Tournament, he showed them to Sebring who was most impressed - so much so that he took them to Charles Fitzsimmon. As you can guess, it hardly took Charles a second to realise what he was holding in his hand and immediately he called in top man, William Dozier. Straight away, they knew they had struck gold.

In fact, *The Green Hornet* wasn't the only production they had lined up for the Little Dragon. Their first thought was to cast him as, yes, you've guessed it, Charlie Chan's *Number One Son*! Anyway, Charles and Bruce struck up a good relationship and a handy tip he gave the Little Dragon was one regarding the running of his Jeet Kune Do classes. Charles was adamant that the Little Dragon ought to be charging higher rates for his tuition services - he was convinced the stars would be willing to pay far more for it. Bruce soon discovered just how right his friend was! Not only were Steve McQueen and James Coburn eager pupils and constant visitors to the school of training, what is certainly less known is that Roman Polanski once flew Bruce Lee over to Switzerland for private lessons. Anyway, the link between Bruce and the man who had made it all possible, Charles Fitzsimmon,

soon started to pay dividends in the shape of *The Green Hornet*.

During the filming of the series, Bruce was repeatedly asked to take on various franchise agreements - in other words, to advertise such things as 'Kato's Self-Defence School' and 'Kato gets his strength from so and so's vitamin enriched breakfast food'. Typically, however, the Little Dragon always turned down these sort of proposals because he, "Just didn't think it was right." Interestingly, it's a moot point whether or not the serial would have lasted longer and been more successful had Bruce not stuck so strongly to his principals. He was after all very popular in the part and a little free advertising might have worked wonders for the show. For a man in such an enviable position, it's always tempting to sell-out and take what money you can. The Little Dragon, however, was wise enough to think of the possible later recriminations to his good name and in general, he always avoided such business arrangements.

Before long *The Green Hornet* began to be shown in other countries. It was offered to the UK but rejected on the grounds of excessive violence! (It's nice to know that our welfare is being so well protected). Hong Kong, Singapore and the Philippines were a little more bold, however, and instantly it became an overnight smash hit - much to the surprise of the makers of the series. It proceeded to break all known television rating records in the Far East, proving beyond doubt that one man's meat is so often another man's poison. That's not to say of course that falling to the vagaries of the U.S.A. sponsoring system is anything to be ashamed of. As Jerry Lewis once remarked after the collapse of his own short-lived series, "If they televised World War Three and the ratings fell anything short of what the sponsors expected, they'd immediately pull it off."

It goes without saying that for Bruce, probably the happiest consequence of the whole business was his promotional trip to Hong Kong. It turned out that he didn't really need to promote anything as the series was already huge and the Little Dragon had become a national hero in his own absence! Everywhere he went, he was surrounded by praise and adulation, very much a sign of the times to come. It was during that Hong Kong visit that he was first approached by Raymond Chow, boss of Golden Harvest films. The eventual upshot of that fortuitous meeting in the late 1960's was destined to change the face of the film world, although neither of them knew it at that moment.

The Green Hornet gave Bruce his first opportunity to use the nunchakus on film. His earlier meetings with that expert of the 'magic rods' Danny Inosanto, soon started to bear fruit and there is little doubt that The Green Hornet film subsequently constructed from several of the TV episodes contains some of these rare sequences. (You'll be glad to hear by the way that *KFM* has succeeded in locating the company who bought the rights for *The Green Hornet* film and we are hoping soon to have some news of when we might expect to see it screened here). It has in fact already been out in France (or so we are told) under the title of *Return of the Dragon*. In the U.K. unfortunately, a little known film company then proceeded to release something completely different under the same title! Perhaps they were hoping to fool people into thinking they were seeing some early Bruce Lee fighting material so beware of fakes!

The making of the series finally ground to a halt in the U.S.A. sometime around 1967. It hadn't been a particularly happy show at any time. Many of the actors were rather upset and despondent about the way everything was being handled and of course, the low ratings finally put the lid on it. The sponsors lost heart and the series was dropped. Actually this is a very common occurrence in the annals of American TV and nobody at the time thought much about it. For Bruce, however, it was something more than that. He knew the show wasn't right and he knew it couldn't last that long. In fact, he probably didn't want it to. The important thing for him was that at last he had been accepted by the movie making establishment and it was an important step in the right direction.

We've discovered that this hasn't been the first time that *The Green Hornet* has hit the cinema screens, or even in the TV form in which it was shot. Ten or more years ago,

there was a Universal fifteen part series which was called *The Green Hornet Strikes Again*. Obviously this itself was a remake of an even earlier effort, though as yet, we've been unable to trace it. Anyway, the Universal version starred Warren Hull as Britt Reed and Keye Luke as Kato. Now, the strange news is that Keye, who was born in 1904, was very popular in the early days as Charlie Chan's Number Two Son!! Perhaps the Little Dragon was absolutely correct when he once sarcastically remarked that, "The only way to get on in Hollywood is to play one of Charlie Chan's sons." It's good to hear that Keye Luke still does a lot of TV work and the chances are that he was in and around the Universal studios when Bruce was making *The Green Hornet* series for Fox.

It must have been interesting for him to see somebody acting out a role that he himself had once played some years ago - but handling it in such a different way to the original. Remember, prior to modern times, realism generally just went by the board. In the old days, you simply waved your fist at someone and he fell over. Until recently, that same accusation could have been aimed at Asian films. So often you'd see the hero with a hundred arrows in his back just get up and carry on fighting! Thankfully, Bruce stopped a lot of that with his own brand of Kung Fu perfection. *KFM* has it in mind to try to arrange an interview with Keye Luke. His experience of the early years in Asian films would make an extremely interesting feature.

Looking back, the thought occurs that, had Bruce really made his big break in *The Green Hornet*, rather than having to wait for the impact of *The Big Boss* in the early 70's, the chances are he would have been as 'big as Bond' several years earlier. It's sad in a way to think that, had be made his first smash in 1968, we'd almost certainly have been treated to two or three more Little Dragon films before his untimely death. Had he perhaps taken up those franchises and sold out a little, maybe the world would have found out just that bit sooner about Bruce Lee. The same of course could be said of his strong relationship with James Coburn around the time of *The Green Hornet*. There's little doubt their *Silent Flute* enterprise would have been enormous. After all, the script was written by their mutual buddy, Stirling Silliphant (who wrote, among many 'biggies', *The Poseidon Adventure*). The possibilities were simply enormous and yet it was to be some time on before fame and fortune really came the way of Bruce Lee. He'd made his first break, but as he was soon to find out, that was only the start of the battle.

THE KILLER INSTINCT OF BRUCE LEE

No, don't stop reading right here thinking 'this is just one for the kids' - it isn't! It's easy in a way to be a fan of a superstar like Bruce, to collect all the magazines, books, pictures and so on. It's much harder for many people to understand what the ideas and philosophies of Bruce Lee were really about. To dream of the Little Dragon carving his way through countless numbers of villains using punches, kicks and nunchaku blows is to see everything from only a one sided point of view. Bruce, as he himself once remarked, wanted things to be 'multi-dimensional' and to a large extent, his life, his films and the wisdom of his Jeet Kune Do mirrored a much deeper search within himself. Often those ideas become cloaked in mystique and confusion. In this article, we aim to try to unlock some of those closed doors - to make it just a little plainer exactly what Bruce Lee stood for and how and why he made such great use of the killer instinct.

The Little Dragon began his life with roughly the same advantages and disadvantages facing him as face you and I. As a child, he wasn't particularly strong physically and at times he found it difficult to defend himself from the bigger and stronger children around him. OK, stop right there. We reach the first crossroads in Bruce's short life. Faced with this problem, he could have done roughly one of three things. Firstly he could have carried on exactly as before, worrying a lot but doing nothing about anything. Secondly he could have retreated within himself to hide away from the big bad world (and isn't it easy to do that!) or thirdly he could come up with a positive solution. Bruce chose the third option and he decided to face the problem in his own (at that time) elementary way.

After all, problems are only there to be solved! The Little Dragon proved to himself and to us that the physical strength of those around him could be conquered by using the right skills. He had to ask people, be taught by them and to read books to discover those skills but he had to find the dedication to do it within himself. In other words, strength of character is hidden away there inside all of us and can be called upon any time provided we feel badly enough about our particular problem. So how do we make sure that when we feel badly about something, we remain calm enough to think about possible solutions? Simple - we keep physically and mentally fit!

Now that's strange you may say, "Bruce used to do just that." You're right, he did and it's no coincidence either! It's true to say that the unwise man who neglects his body's fitness will not be able to think well and the athlete who neglects the health of his mind will not win races.

So where does that leave us? Well to get back to the Little Dragon, after overcoming that first problem with the use of a few elementary skills, the thought occured to him that maybe the physical skills could be several steps further. Stop right there again! Why, you may ask, did the Little Dragon wish to carry on the learning process even after his early Kung Fu skills had achieved their desired effect? The answer is an interesting one. Bruce was by now fit, both physically and mentally and therefore in a position to reason things out very clearly. His brush with the martial arts world had taught him very many things about the world around him, about people, about history, about keeping the body and mind healthy and also the fact that, as far as Kung Fu was concerned, there was much that could

be improved and clarified after all its many years of misuse. Principally that misuse came about through money-making charlatans and ignorance.

So Bruce at this point, is faced with another problem and who better to solve it than he? He quickly realised that major change, to be effective and permanent, must come slowly. Of course, with his theatrical background, what better vehicle to use than films to get his message over to the people. As he soon discovered, that area of entertainment is a jealously guarded castle and time and cunning is needed to break through the wall. He attacked from his home base - the Jun Fan Gung Fu Institute in Oakland, California. Soon, the stars in his eyes were being matched by the stars who came knocking at his door. To gain their confidence, he knew that he had simply to be the best. Once again, his clarity of thought had served quickly and accurately to pin-point the nub of the problem.

So, what constitutes the killer instinct? Well, to begin with, it's tied up closely with strength of purpose. Experience in life generally, is needed to fuel the flame and thirdly, the motives for that instinct must be strong and clearly thought out. Once any person has achieved these necessary conditions, the effort associated with, for instance, physical training or self-education, ceases to be a chore. They become but signposts leading to the destination and the killer instinct is simply the ability to see and understand the path to that destination as if it were clear as day. So you could say that Bruce developed the ability to see a problem - to think carefully and clearly enough to arrive at a solution to it - and he had enough belief in himself to see whatever he had decided, through to the bitter end. That is the true killer instinct.

Many people say, as Bruce died in his early thirties, then surely something went wrong; he must have miscalculated somewhere along the line. It simply isn't true! For most of his adult life, the Little Dragon was a super-fit, super-healthy and successful human being. That he died early because of a bodily failure is nothing more or less than a case of terrible luck. It could have happened to anyone and unfortunately, in this case, it happened to Bruce.

THE BRUCE LEE SECRET SOCIETY

Hello there everyone... Pam and Carmella here again! There's lots of news about the fantastic Bruce Lee Secret Society for you this month.

First off, we're delighted to say that the final problem has been solved. Yes, the stickers have at last arrived and they'll be sent off to you along with the next News Sheet. December 25th is drawing closer, so included in that package there'll be a special Christmas card signed by both of us PLUS a mail order sheet for ordering those late Xmas goodies.

The Swop Shop has really gone a bomb and between you and the two of us, there's at least one complete set of *KFM*s for sale at a very reasonable price. Jenny tells us that the demand for issues 1 to 3 of *KFM* seems to be increasing by the month so who is going to be the lucky Society member to get those? Other than that, there are lots of rare books and posters waiting to be swapped or sold around so the best of luck to everyone concerned. Of course, if YOU have something in mind you'd like to swap, sell or buy, please don't hesitate to let us know - we can put you in touch with the people who matter!

The pen pals section has been given a big boost in a very unexpected sort of way. Our old friend, Gary Kohatsu, of the Dragon Club in Hollywood, USA, reckons it's a good idea - and we agree with him - to start a little transatlantic communication between the faithful followers of Bruce Lee. So, what he's done is to round up the name and addresses of some of the hottest Little Dragon fans in America and sent them over to us. We simply can't let him down after a gesture like that, so how about it? All details of where to write are in the next News Sheet, so as soon as it pops through your door, get cracking with those pens!

What else have we got for you? Well, there are full details of the first ever Secret Society Competition with copies of *The Wisdom of Bruce Lee* to be given to the first five correct entries out of the hat. The questions (we hope) will make you think a little so stand by for a bit of brushing up in your Bruce Lee history books - it should be fun.

During a sudden brainstorm, we came up with the idea for a new sort of Society magazine. Without giving too much away here, the suggestion is that it be made up of contributions from Society members. Exactly what goes into it is largely a matter for you to decide - the only stipulation is that entries be connected in some way with Bruce so on with the thinking caps!

Finally, we are attempting on your behalf something which I think could make us pretty popular. Dotted around the country are many small Chinese cinema clubs. They show all sorts of Asian - and in particular - Kung Fu films and no doubt, many of you would love to have the chance to go along to one. Well, we're negotiating with someone right now to try and arrange just that - something special for Society members only Nothing has been agreed yet, but keep your fingers crossed ... you never know.

See you all again next month - **Pam and Carmella**

KICKBACK: THE LETTERS

Hi, it's Jenny here, on my marks and ready to go jumping head first into this month's mountain of mail! I'm glad to say, I've had nothing but praise for the new Quickies column. It's marvellous to be able to get so many more of the interesting comments and questions you raise into print - after all, that's what Kickback is all about. Right now, I've got two special points to raise. Firstly, there's a couple of letters here to pass on to Keith Manning of Hockley in Essex, who wrote in to *KFM* about the lack of a nunchaku grading system. Sad to say, Keith, your address has been, 'cleared up' by mistake (my fault!) but if you write again (enclosing a big SAE) you'll get them in a day or two. The other little tit-bit is, as they say, completely different. Over the last few months, I've had several letters in from readers claiming to be spiritually in touch with Bruce Lee and in all honesty, I haven't known quite how to approach the subject. Therefore, to help me over this problem, perhaps you, the readers, could let me know your feelings (and of course personal experiences, if any) on this unusual subject. That said, it's letters time!

BRUCE LEE'S INSPIRATION

Dear Jenny,
I am taking the liberty to write to you particularly as you appear to be the most articulate connection amid the elements of your very commendable magazine. The penmanship on my behalf is not great, due to my chronic handicap, which means I execute life from the unenviable position of a wheelchair. I am the victim of a progressive ailment, robbing me of my muscle power and the philosophy and inimitable mystique of Bruce Lee has been an inexplicable inspiration in my fight for fitness. Since I first saw the incredible domination of life itself by this man, not to mention his eclipse of the comprehensive fighting techniques, I set myself a goal to keep fit - which I still am from head to waist - ridiculing the medical probability of total invalidity expected years ago. I have striven desperately to strengthen physically (with success) and mentally I have consolidated my outlook via the mental and physical character of 'one in a million' Bruce Lee.
Patrick Hennessy, Dublin

Dear Patrick,
Very many thanks for this and the other letter you recently sent to KFM. May I say firstly that all good wishes of the Staff of KFM go to you in your fight against this illness. It's marvellous to know that the spirit of the master is still able to give strength to those who have need of it most - and your battle is an inspiration to us all. Please keep in touch and let me know how you're progressing.

KUNG FU PHOTOS

Dear Jenny,
I have an idea for your already magnificent magazine. My suggestion is for readers to send in photographs of themselves in typical Kung Fu positions. You could choose the best of these and print one each month on the Kickback page.
David King, Waterloo, Liverpool

Dear David,
I like it! But wait a minute, before you start sending in all those amazing pictures, let me give you a few guidelines. For us to be able to use them they should be as clear as possible, not too small and preferably taken against a plain background (e.g. wall). Colour or black and white is OK and if you want your picture sent back, you must enclose a stamped addressed envelope.

BRUCE LEE DOCUMENTARY?

Dear Jenny,
I think it might be a good idea to make a film documentary of Bruce Lee. This could feature clips from his films showing his fighting abilities and also pre-recorded interviews with Bruce before his death. Many of his friends in the film industry, namely producers and directors from Golden Harvest and Warner Brothers would gladly assist in interviews and production of this fascinating documentary. Maybe even clips of the unfinished epic *Game of Death* could be included. Given an 'A' certificate, this would enable younger followers to see their idol.
Kevin Crummey, Ordsall, Notts

Dear Kevin,
Sounds like another one for the 'good ideas' department! Firstly, I have to say that I'm surprised it hasn't been done already. I suspect actually, that Golden Harvest will be thinking very much along these lines just as soon as Game of Death has done the rounds.

REAL KUNG FU MAGAZINE

Dear Jenny,
I am writing to tell you about a Kung Fu magazine called *Real Kung Fu*. I bought it because it had an article on Bruce's Jeet Kune Do. When I got home and read the article, I was disgusted by it. The magazine implied that Bruce's Jeet Kune Do was just a mock up of Wing Chun, the style Bruce first learnt. A few pictures were shown of Bruce doing the style in question, making it seem as if Bruce was lying about his Jeet Kune Do. Since then, I have looked at Bruce's *Tao of Jeet Kune Do* and there are only a few illustrations of Wing Chun (which just happen to be in examples shown in the *Real Kung Fu* magazine). Some misguided Kung Fu fans might get the impression that Bruce Lee was a phoney and a liar, which is what this crumby magazine is trying to do. It also gives no thanks to Bruce Lee for making their magazine popular.
Phil Cook, Leicester

Jenny didn't answer this letter.

KICKBACK QUICKIES

Ray Cain, London - 1. I know how you feel about censors. How indeed do Peckinpah and Kubrick get away with it? 2. You're right, the *KFM* No.21 picture was printed back to front!
John Stuart, Tillydrone, Aberdeen - *KFM* binders? - A great idea and we'll work on it. *The Wisdom of Bruce Lee* is late, but coming soon.
John Kemp, Patchway, Bristol - Glad you got the soundtracks OK - *Green Hornet*? - Your wish is our command - Drawing competition is coming up in the New Year.
S. Fairclough, Essex & M. Gooderham, Ipswich - Like anything else, it's best to use a book like the *Tao of Jeet Kune Do* in conjunction with lessons. It's not easy to learn exercises just from a set of instructions.
Robert Smith, Romford, Essex - A good Ninja book? Try Cimac.
Colm Quinn, Limerick, Eire - I hope you're right and that Bruce is still alive - Sadly, I think you're wrong!
Kevin Foster, Chopwell, Newcastle - 1. Bruce evolved his Jeet Kune Do over many years. 2. I doubt we will see his films on TV within two years. 3. Both *KFM* No.14 and the book *Bruce Lee King of Kung Fu* are essentially correct in describing Bruce's death.
Ivan Sewall, Swallownest - *KFM* No. 1-3 are right out I'm afraid - The censorship of Bruce's films makes no sense to me either.
Mr. E. Canham, Worksop, Notts - Glad you like our pictures so much - I hope the

editors can find the 'phone engineer' one for you.
R. Mainwaring, Abertillery, Gwent - Hello, binders again - I shall have to look into this.
Miss Patricia Chadwick, Ashton under Lyne, Lancs - Bruce Lee tracksuits? From what I hear, your luck may be in.
Steven Dore, Gosport - Bruce really did use the nunchakus just as you see it - only faster!
Colin Wood, Consett, Durham - Bruce was developing Jeet Kune Do throughout his life. His final concept will probably best be seen in *Game of Death*.
Bruce Ali, Causeway, Coventry - Bruce's favourite colour? Well I don't know for sure but he did seem to prefer mauves and blues.
Dale Loughridge, Carrick Fergus, Northern Ireland - Yes, we hope soon to have a book out on Bruce's films.
M. Holmes, Rhondda, Glamorgan - So far as I know, Fu Shen has no fan club in the UK at present.
Marios S., Palmers Green, London - Glad to hear *KFM* makes it out to Spain - Picture of me? Sorry, I'm camera shy.
Paul Collins, Rochdale - *The Way of the Dragon* remains as censored as it ever was. No firm *Game of Death* release date yet.
Mick Parker, Accrington, Lancs - The Linda Lee book the UK has a different cover to the USA version.
Antony Kelly, Worlsey, Manchester - We didn't rate Jim Kelly's performance in *Black Belt Jones* either. He could do better.

KFM PEN PAL CORNER

Pius Erhunmwunsee, Nigeria seeks male or female, Chinese or Japanese.
Carol Myatt, Willenhall, West Midlands, seeks male or female, Chinese 15-16 years old - must be Bruce Lee mad.
Jane Hammond, Leigh on Sea, Essex seeks female, Chinese, 16-18 years old. (Interested in Chinese costume).
Grace Gegwint, South Africa seeks male or female, Japan or Hawaii, 16-18 years old.
Caroline, Cape Town, South Africa seeks male, New Zealand, 18-21 years old.
Rhoda, Cape Town, South Africa seeks female, France, 15-16 years old.
Elizabeth West, Cape Town S. Africa seeks male/female, any country, 16-17 years old. Send photos with letters.

THE POSTER MAGAZINES - VOLUME ONE

EDITORIAL

Hi there Kung Fu fans...
"Follow that!" I've heard some people say after our last stupendous issue. Well, believe it or not we aim to do just that - and more - in this month's power-packed edition of *Kung-Fu Monthly*. Last time, I said we'd be reviewing *The Secret Art of Bruce Lee* - you know, the smash new book containing those sensational never-before-seen action pictures of Bruce Lee - but we've changed our minds. We're going one better! After negotiations with the author, I'm delighted to say he has given his permission for us to reproduce right here in *KFM* No.26, the entire first chapter! Yup, it looks like your favourite magazine has scooped the opposition yet again and what a way to kick off the New Year. The book is a real gem. Not only does it fill many of the gaps in our knowledge of the Little Dragon's early years Stateside, it also features the world's only comprehensive photographic record of Bruce Lee demonstrating his own unique form of Kung Fu. For the serious student

of Jeet Kune Do, *The Secret Art of Bruce Lee* is essential companion reading to Bruce's own Tao of Jeet Kune Do. For the faithful followers of China's number one son, the new pictures and information are an indispensible addition to any bookshelf. And watch out as it'll be in our mail order list soon! Phew, what next you may say? Well, many a *KFM* reader has written in over the years asking if we could do a feature on the Shaolin Temple and its particular form of boxing - and we reckon it's time we did just that! After all, the Shaolin style is without doubt the 'daddy of them all' and what could be more appropriate at his time than to move back through the pages of history to the days of ancient China when much of what we know of as Kung Fu really began.

That's all from me for this month. Keep in touch.

Felix Yen

Felix Yen
Editor-in-Chief

THE SECRET ART OF BRUCE LEE

The book you are holding represents a milestone in the history of the martial arts. It is the sole surviving photographic record of Bruce Lee's Jeet Kune Do as demonstrated by Lee himself. Forgotten for more than a decade, the photographs shown here - for the first time ever - have now come to be recognised as probably the finest illustration of his martial arts, they are invaluable.

Although, at the time of his death, Bruce Lee had reached the pinnacle of success in two spheres of achievement - films and the martial arts - he left little in the way of a tangible legacy. Unfortunately, most of Lee's fame and exposure came with the release of his films in the Western world after his death. All that is left of his extraordinary acting career are four films of varying quality, twenty minutes or so of a fifth, uncompleted film, and a handful of taped or written interviews.

From his martial art career, even less survives. At the time of his death, Lee was working on a book setting out his thoughts on the martial arts 'style' he had created - Jeet Kune Do. To be called the *Tao of Jeet Kune Do*, this book was to have been a distillation of seven volumes of notes and writings that Lee had compiled in his last years. Since his death, Lee's widow, Linda, has overseen the cataloguing of these volumes and the *Tao of Jeet Kune Do* has now been published. As a written record of the processes of Jeet Kune Do, it is excellent. Nevertheless it is, unfortunately, far from the definitive work one would have expected if Lee had lived to finish his work.

Besides the *Tao of Jeet Kune Do*, Lee also left a few brief interviews - notably with Black Belt Magazine - in which he discussed Jeet Kune Do. These, together with the instructions he gave his pupils, are all that remain to guide the student along Lee's path to martial mastery. No films of Lee in action except, of course, the obviously stagey and exaggerated feature movies were ever taken, and still photographs have hitherto been of little value, concentrating in the main on Lee's movie star face and features, rather than on his art.

It is therefore a stroke of unbelievable good fortune that the photographs in this book have been rediscovered. That they would have in obscurity for so many years, considering the worldwide demand for any Lee material since his death in 1973, is nothing short of incredible.

The history of the photographs dates back to California, 1966. They were taken by a freelance Hollywood photographer named Chester Maydole during four shooting sessions at three separate locations - Portuguese Bend in South Los Angeles, Lee's apartment in West Los Angeles, and the famous Malibu Beach. At that time, Maydole was working as a 'photographer to the stars,' taking assignments from major film and television studios in Hollywood who needed publicity shots of their actors and actresses. He first met Bruce Lee on the latter's arrival in Hollywood to make his television debut as Kato in the ill-fated *The Green Hornet* series.

"I'd done some shots of Batman, which were very successful at that time," remembers Maydole, who now lives in New Mexico, "and I was asked by the company to take pictures of Bruce and Van Williams. They were for the fan magazines as I recall."

Maydole found Lee extremely easy to work with. Lee was bubbling over with excitement about his new career and was eager to help in any way. "He'd done pictures in Hong Kong before, but I suppose he was making a lot money now and it must have been quite a thing, a half-hour show which might run for a long time. It didn't, of course, but he wasn't to know that." During the course of the session the two men struck up a happy working relationship which quickly turned to friendship.

"He was a terrific guy," recalls Maydole. "I liked him very much. He was smart but not Hollywood smart, but he really knew his stuff. He was a very natural and down-to-earth sort of person. He didn't take much part in the usual Hollywood goings on; he was more interested in his martial arts. He was a very spiritual person and I know he meditated a lot. After all, Kung Fu is a very heavy thing, especially if you are Chinese and you have all that tradition behind you. It sort of becomes a religion. Yet it's a funny thing that, although Bruce went in for the whole thing, he taught just the opposite. He taught that people don't have to follow ritual. He taught you shouldn't be bound; you should be free." Which, as we shall see later, was the very essence of Jeet Kune Do.

Maydole remembers Lee as being obsessed with the martial arts, living Kung-Fu twenty-four hours a day. He was always exercising, constantly performing impromptu movements. The only time he was still was when he was engrossed in a book from his enor-

mous martial arts library.

"I can't say enough about his Kung-Fu and his teachings," says Maydole. "I had great respect for him. He had probably the most perfect body I have ever seen. He was small - perhaps 140 pounds - but his physique was most unusual, especially for a Chinese. He worked on it all the time. He was very particular about what he ate. He ate a lot of Chinese food, naturally enough, cooked specially for him by one or two of the Chinese restaurants in Chinatown. I remember how he would sit there eating this special food with all his students around him, holding court."

With his television career established - at least for the moment - it wasn't long after his arrival in Los Angeles that Lee's thoughts turned to seriously resuming his martial arts career. After looking around the city for a suitable place, he opened a Kung Fu school in Chinatown. His arrival, according to Maydole, caused quite an uproar. "Nobody had every taught Kung Fu here before. Several top Karate black belts such as Danny Inosanto went over to Bruce and there was a lot of jealousy among the Karate people who said that Kung Fu didn't mean anything. Bruce challenged them on several occasions, but nothing ever came of it. I suppose they knew in their hearts how good he was." As their friendship developed, Maydole made a point of dropping in to Lee's new school where he picked up a few fragments of instruction. However, the photographer was sceptical as to the possible violent practical potential of Kung Fu. Although he had studied judo in the Army, he was reluctant to commit himself too deeply to Kung Fu. Judo was designed to ward off an attacker, he felt, but to him Kung Fu seemed designed primarily to kill people or cripple them for life. Lee's expertise in particular unnerved him. "Bruce had this big wooden dummy which he would use, and once he showed me 52 ways of kicking it. By kicking on a certain place you could blind a person, cripple him, kill him - whatever you chose. And Bruce, with his big toe, he could kick in any one of those 52 places. He was always wearing bare feet or ballet shoes so he could use his toe more freely. His big toe was a lethal weapon. He could kick you with it on the chin from any direction without warning."

Although he never took up Kung Fu, Maydole was immensely impressed by Lee's many deadly skills. He decided these movements would look good on film, and the photographs in this book are the result. They were taken, recalls Maydole, "Just for the hell of it." He thought that with a little pushing, he could sell some of them to a Karate magazine, and so the first of four sessions was set up. On Malibu Beach, Lee and his pupil, Danny Inosanto ran through a series of attacks and defences for Chester Maydole's camera.

These shots of Lee and Inosanto sparring together are the finest photographs ever to be taken of Bruce Lee in action. Dressed in his black uniform with the Yin Yang symbol he adopted as his school's emblem, he demonstrates a wealth of techniques for stance through defence movements to attack. Together with their respective captions, these photographs should illuminate much of Lee's martial wisdom which has hitherto been limited to mere words.

The photographs taken in Lee's 20th-floor luxury Los Angeles apartment are, of course, less valuable to the martial arts student, although they do depict some of Lee's training methods and equipment, plus a section of his martial arts library and weapons collection. However, as a record of Lee the man, they offer a touching glimpse into a little-known private life.

"Bruce was very proud of his wife and young son Brandon," remembers Maydole. "His other child was born after we lost contact with each other. Linda was very quiet. She never said a word which made her rather hard to get to know. Maybe she had decided to take

a backseat to Bruce because he was the star. She was a martial artist herself though. And Brandon should be very good at Kung Fu when he grows up, too. Even at that age he was learning."

As it turned out, Chester Maydole never did sell the photographs. Suddenly he found himself working flat out, and he simply never got around to it. His heavy business schedule not only forced him to forget about the pictures, but it also brought about the end of his friendship with Lee. Bruce kept pressing Maydole to meet with him to plan a book on Jeet Kune Do, using Chester's pictures as illustrations. Maydole, with assignments as far

away as India, had to keep postponing the meeting. Eventually, Lee stopped phoning. "It was just circumstances," recalls Maydole sadly, "Both of us trying to make a living. And, of course, I'm really sorry I didn't do the book."

As for the photographs, they just lay there gathering dust. "I stuck them in my dead picture file and forgot about them," says Maydole. "Then recently, my agent mentioned he was after pictures of Bruce Lee. I said I had lots of shots of Bruce doing Kung Fu. And that was that."

So, a decade after they were taken, Chester Maydole's remarkable collection of photographs has finally been published. In order for the reader to fully understand and realise the value of these historic records, they are divided into twenty-five numbered sequences accompanied by detailed captions and a comprehensive text. The first part of the text charts Lee's life and martial career, providing a record of his achievements and the influences that he incorporated into Jeet Kune Do. The second and final part of the text is a detailed analysis of Lee's own martial creation, Jeet Kune Do, culled from the written and taped source material that he left behind.

It was always Lee's great fear that his art would be twisted and distorted by imitators. Here, then, for the first time since his death, is Bruce Lee performing his own art for that art's sake. If Chester Maydole's photographic portraits in any way provide a clearer, less distorted view of Bruce Lee's revolutionary legacy, they will have been well worth the wait.

THE TRUTH BEHIND THE SHAOLIN TEMPLE

For over a thousand years, Chinese boxing has dominated the fighting instincts of an entire race. Naturally over such a period of time, much confusion and inaccuracy has tended to come about. Tales of truth become twisted in the telling. Even so, with close investigation, fact can be separated from fable and after many years of research, world famous historians have recently found themselves able to recount, with some accuracy, the tale of the Shaolin Temple. It's a story of secrecy, intrigue and spiritual revolution. Of hardships, endurance and total physical fulfilment. Our part of the world has no such history. Brute strength and ignorance would perhaps aptly describe many of the fighting techniques of the West - with of course some notable exceptions. However, it's never too late to learn and what better path to retread than that leading back to the origins of organised Chinese boxing. The road is stony and criss-crossed with cul-de-sacs. Above all, few people are prepared to divulge what to them represents a lifetime's work. They know only too well that truth lies in the finding - a few words cannot sum up thirty years of dedication and study. Well they would have understood these words at that home of Chinese boxing, the Shaolin Temple.

Often the question is heard: What exactly is meant by Shaolin Boxing'? Unfortunately, the answer is none too simple.

To begin with, many orthodox teachers ascribe all forms of Chinese boxing to the name Shaolin, with the exception of just three - T'ai-chi, Hsing-i and Pa-kua, the so called 'soft' or 'internal' systems. This sweeping generalisation leaves us sadly wide of the mark. In truth, Shaolin boxing represents only a few styles, among several hundreds (although it would be correct to say that most of the others owe more than a little to Shaolin origins). Neither are the Shaolin forms necessarily all 'hard' or 'external.' Many styles began their existence with almost assault course savagery, only to become mellowed and extended in the years to come. One good example of this is the famous Tzu Jan Men style. After its ferocious childhood, the form took a more spiritual course and gradually, like Jeet Kune Do, it became a symbol of freedom of action.

So why therefore, did Chinese boxing evolve in that famous Asian Temple? Well, the answer seems to be that the monks decided they needed to develop more physically demanding exercise routines. Of course, the sacred ground was well guarded, so the intricate systems that came about were to remain confidential to non-Buddhists for many years to come. It's not exactly clear when or why exercise gave way to self defence, but legend lends us a fairly plausible explanation.

To begin with, anyone with any knowledge of the Buddhist faith will confirm that principal to their creed is a policy of non-violence. It seems likely therefore that many of the fighting monks of Shaolin were not in fact monks at all. Certainly the easy going men of the Temple frequently gave offer of sanctuary to many an 'on-the-run' rebel and indeed probably it was these very rebels who transformed the monk's superbly efficient exercise routines into equally efficient fighting formulae. That's not to say, of course, that the real monks remained entirely passive. Their creed simply stated that such skills should be used defensively and then only as a last resort!

Remember by the way, that Chinese boxing has little in common with what we in the West know of as boxing. To us, the term implies a tough game with many a rule and regulation to take heed of. To the Asian man, however, boxing simply means combat - battles with no holds barred! In fact, as an indication of the toughness of the rigorous training at the Shaolin Temple, many have it that the dreaded White Lotus organisation began its days within those walls.

The famous set of eighteen training routines was evolved originally by the monk Ta Mo. He was a much respected student of both boxing and Zen, living in China around the time 500 AD. Legend has it that this wise and venerable man came to the Shaolin Temple at Honan and proceeded to sit staring at the wall, 'listening to the ants scream' day in and day out for nine years! Once, to his extreme self-reproach, he allowed himself to fall asleep. So furious was he, that he cut off his eye lids and tossed them away. It was said that where they fell, shortly afterwards grew a tea shrub (a rare plant around those parts at the time). The monks, since then, have traditionally made use of tea to help prevent sleep interfering with their meditation.

Ta Mo is also given the credit for introducing the monks to the rigours of exercise in the first place. It's said that he introduced the eighteen forms so as to improve their physical and mental fitness. It disturbed him that his brothers would continually keep dozing off during meditation - a sure sign, he thought, of a sadly deteriorated condition. This point is in fact one which the master himself, Bruce Lee, understood only too well. Little can be achieved without effort and in many ways, each step forward can be likened to a chain. Each link can only move forward from the one behind to the one in front. The rearmost link can but look in awe at the topmost - it can never reach it! Ta Mo saw to it that the five intrinsic styles he formulated were well supported by the eighteen exercises (which had such fascinating names as 'Pushing the Mountain' and 'Golden Leopard Reveals Claws'). Nothing was ignored and the basis of Kung Fu as we know it now could be seen in the kicking and sweeping exercises he instructed.

As so often happens, after the death of Ta, disaster almost struck. There was nobody immediately around to follow in his footsteps and so the system he so carefully evolved very nearly got forgotten. An enormous debt of gratitude is owed therefore to the priest

Cheuh Yuan. A man of tremendous foresight, he realised the danger and the worth of what the world was about to lose! After a good deal of thought, he re-formulated the styles and expanded their scope by increasing the number of methods from eighteen to seventy two. That he got his sums right is now a matter of history, but never was it easy! Backwards and forwards across the length and breadth of China he travelled, seeking out the best fighting men of the day and testing them as nobody had ever tested them before.

Once during his wandering, he saw a display of energy control he found almost beyond belief. An old man, on being assaulted, dispatched his attacker with a simple two-finger touch! Cheuh questioned the master and discovered that he had learnt the art from one Pai Yu-feng of Shanoi. Pai was a very unusual man and his unique character made a great impression on the travelling monk. The two of them joined forces on working out the final revision on Ta Mo's original concept of Shaolin Temple boxing. The outcome was that the seventy forms expanded into one hundred and seventy and from those humble beginnings was born Chinese boxing as we now know it.

It would be useful at this point to discuss the meaning of Ch'i - the intrinsic energy and a very important consideration on the Shaolin schedule. The concept is not an easy one to follow, but the importance of understanding it is paramount. In brief, it consists of two stages. Firstly Ch'i has to evolve within the body - then it must be made to move to the right place at the right time. No amount of physical effort will help the novice to achieve Ch'i, meditation and the understanding of the concept alone contain the secret. Putting it into practice is a rather different matter - here, breathing exercises hold the key.

Although a student yet to achieve Ch'i may find the idea quite baffling, in fact evidence of its existence can be seen all around us. Two men may throw similar punches at each other. One might fall as light as a drop of summer rain, the other blow as heavy as a mountain. The latter has Ch'i! Many an ordinary person has been seen to have Ch'i without knowing it. The mother lifting the car from a trapped child is an absolutely classic example. And of course Ch'i need not only be manifested in terms of sheer weight and strength. 'Walking Light' - the ability to effectively make the body as light as a feather was a trick of the Ninja and again, Ch'i holds the secret.

A second Shaolin Temple reportedly stood in Fukien Province - erected over one thousand years ago by the priest Ta Tsun-shen. The stories surrounding this Temple are legion, running from monks (forbidden from using axes) cutting down wood with their hands, to the statement of the chief monk which went as follows: "We may not have knives, so make each finger a dagger. Without spears, every arm must be a spear, and every open hand, a sword." A lot of nonsense has been said about the training routines - from fighting strange monsters to having to defeat many ingeniously designed wooden dummies. It certainly wasn't difficult to leave though and many a boxer, unequal to the task, did just that!

Both Temples appear to have been razed to the ground on several occasions, but both survived long enough to ensure the survival of Chinese boxing. They weren't the only centres of martial learning, but like Bruce Lee, they were the most important. A glance at the Little Dragon's library list will convince anyone of the esteem in which he held these pioneers of old. He knew just how much he owed his art to the men who had the strength to follow through their visions and inspirations - and such men were the founders of Shaolin Temple Boxing.

THE BRUCE LEE SECRET SOCIETY

Hello again, and a special welcome to all the many new members who have just joined our Society!

Firstly, a couple of people have written in to enrol without including an address. Their names are Mr C. Cooper and Mr M. Gray, so if both these gentlemen would quickly write back, we'll make sure their kits and News Sheets are rushed off as soon as possible. (By the way, no cheating anybody - we do know what areas they come from!) Finally for the problems section, we'd like Mr L. Cumming who has recently left his address in Larkhall, Lanarkshire to contact us. His membership kit came back to us marked 'moved away".

Arthur Stone (member No. 1150) has been keeping his eyes well peeled! Apparently Midlands TV screened *The Wrecking Crew* on the 27th October, starring Dean Martin as Matt Helm. At the end of the show when the titles came up, surprise surprise, who should be credited with arranging the fight scenes but Bruce Lee! Arthur wants to know if the Little Dragon worked on any other films in a similar capacity - does anyone have any ideas? Let us know if you have. It just goes to prove that the final few frames of a TV programme are definitely not the time to go putting the kettle on!

Lots of members have written in asking if there are any new posters available of Bruce. We must agree that, other than the great ones we get month by month in *KFM*, there's little else of interest around at the moment. Actually, some time ahead (when we get a bit richer!) we'd dearly love to bring out a special new poster for club members only. The trouble is, unless they're printed in absolutely enormous quantities, the price of each one can be very high indeed. Anyway, any members coming across something new, be sure to let us know where you got it and we'll make sure everyone has the address.

Late News - Very shortly, the membership subscription to the Bruce Lee Secret Society will have to rise. We're sorry about this but hopefully everyone will understand that this has been simply forced upon us by rising prices. The moral is, if you're going to join, join now and save yourself money!

Finally, for all those who've written asking for a picture of the two of us, we're trying to arrange something around the time of the next News Sheet. We hope you know what you're letting yourselves in for! **Pam and Carmella**

KICKBACK: THE LETTERS

Jenny here again, raring to get stuck into yet another great stack of *KFM* reader's letters! Right away, let me say how amazed I was at the fantastic pile of entries for the *Game of Death* poster competition. Really, the level of artistry amongst our readership surprised everyone here in the *KFM* offices, including our very knowledgeable art director. In all fairness therefore, being one of those people who can barely recognise one end of a paintbrush from the other, I decided to ask somebody more qualified than I to judge the entries. Who better, I thought, than the publicity department of *Game of Death*'s own Cathay Films. Well, they were delighted to take on the task, so stand by for the results next issue! A special word of thanks to all the kind people who put me out of my ignorance re the mysterious Count Dante. Although some of the snippets sent in by no means endeared the man to me, he certainly, as Andrew Couts of Pinner put it, seems to have been 'one of the more colourful figures of modem day martial arts.' In fact I've passed on all the tit-bits of information to our editor - sounds to be worth a feature to me. And now, it must be time for the letters!

MUHAMMAD ALI IN GAME OF DEATH?

Dear Jenny,

I recently read that the film company which produced *The Game of Death*, are contemplating using Mister Bigmouth himself, Muhammad Ali, to finish this potentially brilliant film. How could such a thing be allowed to happen? I'm sure most *KFM* readers will agree with me when I say that no one can take the place of the late great master, especially Ali, who hasn't even a basic knowledge of Jeet Kune Do. To replace the Little Dragon with Ali would be like palming Maggie Thatcher off as Marilyn Monroe! Finally, where can I get hold of a decent sized transfer of Bruce, suitable for a t-shirt?
Brian Langston, The Scotlands, Wolverhampton

Dear Brian,
What an astounding letter! Nobody has mentioned to me the possibility of Muhammad Ali taking over Bruce's part in Game of Death and to be honest, I somehow doubt whether anyone's mentioned it to Ali either. As you say, it's a pretty absurd suggestion and much as I admire 'The Champ' for what he is, really I don't see him transforming himself into a martial artist! You ask about a t-shirt transfer of Bruce. I wave my magic wand and just take a look at the mail order section - how do we do it?

CLUBS AND SHOPS

Dear Jenny Lee,
I've been receiving your magazine now for some time and I think it's very good. One thing though, couldn't you list some clubs and martial arts shops because where I live I can't find any of these places?
Kevin Sands, Heathfield, Sussex

Dear Kevin,
One more for the 'good ideas' file! After discussions here around the office, we reckon the best thing to do is this. All clubs and martial arts shops, please write to us straight away giving details of your activities, stock lists, etc. Using this information we will then make up some special 'where to go in your area' sheets, to be given away free to anybody interested. Don't start writing in for the sheet yet though - we need the information first! I'll give you the word when it's all sorted out and ready to go.

ENTER THE DRAGON - UNCUT

Dear Jenny,
My friends and I recently had an envious experience. While visiting the Cinema section of a country club, we had a very pleasant surprise - we saw *Enter the Dragon* - UNCUT! One of the parts that was cut from the public film is the best scene of the film. When Bruce rights Oharra and kicks him to the floor, the film usually cuts to one of Han's men claiming Oharra dead. In fact, what happens is Oharra smashes two nearby bottles and lunges at Bruce. Bruce kicks the bottles away and roundhouse kicks Oharra to the floor. Then Bruce leaps high in the air and crushes Oharra to death. There is a close up on Lee's face and the expression has to be seen to be believed. I wonder if the censors can explain why that was cut out?
Les Bedminster, Bristol

Dear Les,
Do you mind telling me the whereabouts of this club? So far as I knew, it was impossible to see uncut versions of Bruce's films in this country, so this comes as a total revelation! Your description of the 'usually censored' scene sounds just about as dynamic as the film itself - well done.

KICKBACK QUICKIES

Michael McDonnell, Kilmarnock - Great idea, collecting signatures to demand the de-censorship of Bruce's films - you've got mine for starters.

William Geddes, Buckinghamshire - 1. *Game of Death* is not finished right now. 2. *When Kung Fu Strikes* was never made it I'm afraid.

Dean Sample, Cheltenham, Glos - I'll do my best to connect you with the man planning the nunchaku grading system.

Alistair Twigg, Curruck, Carlisle - Bruce hardly ever smoked or drank at all.

Mr A. Veo, Durban, South Africa. - No Kung Fu schools in South Africa? Disgraceful, must be an opening there for somebody.

Hazel Broome, Bulwell, Nottingham - Great to hear you've named your new son after The King - when does he start training?

Anto Timbrell, Yate, Bristol - Bruce's grave we believe has been moved by his wife from Seattle to Los Angeles.

Damian Sullivan, Tyseley, Birmingham - The Chinese magazines you mention are all on special sale to Society members via the new News Sheet.

Derrick Johns, Wednesfield, Wolverhampton - Sorry, any 8mm versions of Bruce's films would be quite illegal.

Mrs C. Hurn, King's Lynn, Norfolk - I suspect the rickshaw in *Fist of Fury* was a special light one!

Paul Corrigan, Eccleshill, Bradford - Thanks for the really good poems - I've passed them to Pam & Carmella who are compiling a members magazine (I hope you've joined the Society!)

Adrian Jeffery, Kent - My means of self-defence is called running fast!

Andrew White, Bewdley, Worcs - More Cummins paintings? - Sounds a good idea. Hiring Bruce's films via your Karate club is interesting - I wonder how many others have done it?

James Billings, Middleton, Manchester - When I saw *The Way of the Dragon* recently, it topped over *Thunderbolt*. If your cinema reversed it, they must have rotten taste.

Jeff Worthing, Shrewsbury - Thanks for an interesting letter - As far as specials go, well, look out - there's some coming up.

KUNG-FU MONTHLY

THE ARCHIVE SERIES
PUBLICATION DATES

THE POSTER MAGAZINES - VOLUME ONE

It is extremely difficult to put together a definitive list of publication dates for Kung-Fu Monthly. In the early days, the magazine was probably expected to fold in a very short space of time and therefore not many records were kept. That, combined with an ever-changing merry-go-round of staff and writers plus focus on newer publications does not help matters. It also does not help that the magazine was not a strict monthly publication despite its name suggesting so.

This list of publication dates has been compiled from several information sources including The History of Kung-Fu Monthly by Felix Dennis and the Kung-Fu Monthly magazines themselves, by utilising key dates of book releases, film releases, advertisement and conventions.

This list is not completely accurate and should only be viewed as a rough guide.

No. 1	Apr 1974	No. 34	Sep 1977	No. 67	May-Jun 1982
No. 2	May 1974	No. 35	Oct 1977	No. 68	Jul-Aug 1982
No. 3	Jun 1974	No. 36	Nov 1977	No. 69	Sep-Oct 1982
No. 4	Jul-Aug 1974	No. 37	Dec 1977	No. 70	Nov-Dec 1982
No. 5	Sep-Oct 1974	No. 38	Jan 1978	No. 71	Jan-Feb 1983
No. 6	Nov-Dec 1974	No. 39	Feb 1978	No. 72	Mar-Apr 1983
No. 7	Jan-Feb 1975	No. 40	Mar-Apr 1978	No. 73	May 1983
No. 8	Mar-Apr 1975	No. 41	May 1978	No. 74	Jun 1983
No. 9	May-Jun 1975	No. 42	Jun 1978	No. 75	Jul-Aug 1983
No. 10	July-Aug 1975	No. 43	Jul 1978	No. 76	Sep-Oct 1983
No. 11	Sep 1975	No. 44	Augt-Sep 1978	No. 77	Nov-Dec 1983
No. 12	Oct 1975	No. 45	Oct-Nov 1978	No. 78	Jan-Feb 1984
No. 13	Nov 1975	No. 46	Dec 1978-Jan 1979	No. 79	Mar-Apr 1984
No. 14	Dec 1975	No. 47	Feb-Mar 1979		
No. 15	Jan 1976	No. 48	Apr-May 1979		
No. 16	Feb 1976	No. 49	Jun-Jul 1979		
No. 17	Mar 1976	No. 50	Aug-Sep 1979		
No. 18	Apr 1976	No. 51	Oct-Nov 1979		
No. 19	May 1976	No. 52	Dec 1979-Jan 1980		
No. 20	Jun-Jul 1976	No. 53	Feb-Mar 1980		
No. 21	Aug 1976	No. 54	Apr-May 1980		
No. 22	Sep 1976	No. 55	Jun 1980		
No. 23	Oct 1976	No. 56	Jul-Aug 1980		
No. 24	Nov 1976	No. 57	Sep-Oct 1980		
No. 25	Dec 1976	No. 58	Nov-Dec 1980		
No. 26	Jan 1977	No. 59	Jan-Feb 1981		
No. 27	Feb 1977	No. 60	Mar-Apr 1981		
No. 28	Mar 1977	No. 61	May-Jun 1981		
No. 29	Apr 1977	No. 62	Jul-Aug 1981		
No. 30	May 1977	No. 63	Sep-Oct 1981		
No. 31	Jun 1977	No. 64	Nov-Dec 1981		
No. 32	Jul 1977	No. 65	Jan-Feb 1982		
No. 33	Aug 1977	No. 66	Mar-Apr 1982		

To view detailed information as to how this list was compiled, please scan the QR code below to go to the Kung-Fu Monthly Archive Series website where an updated version of this list will be displayed as more information becomes available.

KUNG-FU
MONTHLY

THE ARCHIVE SERIES
MAGAZINE CREDITS

KUNG-FU MONTHLY TRADE DUMMY / COPYRIGHT 1974

Editor: Don Won Ton
Design: Rik Kemo Sabi

KUNG-FU MONTHLY NO.1 / COPYRIGHT 1974

Editor: Don Won Ton
Design: Rik Kemo Sabi
Photo Credits: Warner Bros., South China Morning Post,
Inside Kung-Fu, Cathay Films Ltd

KUNG-FU MONTHLY NO.2 / COPYRIGHT 1974

Editor: Don Won Ton
Design: Rik Kemo Sabi
Features: Jo Nat Hon
Photo Credits: Warner Bros., Ron Mesaros, Cathay Films Ltd,
Hong Kong Star, Chang Vung Dijh

KUNG-FU MONTHLY NO.3 / COPYRIGHT 1974

Editor: Don Won Ton
Design: Rik Kemo Sabi
Features: Jo Nat Hon
Photo Credits: Warner Bros., Cathay Films Ltd, Hong Kong Star,
Chang Vung Dijh, Paul Chang

KUNG-FU MONTHLY NO.4 / COPYRIGHT 1974

Editor: Don Won Ton
Design: Rik Kemo Sabi
Features: Jo Nat Hon
Photo Credits: Cathay Films Ltd, Paul Chang, George Snow

THE KUNG-FU MONTHLY ARCHIVE SERIES

KUNG-FU MONTHLY NO.5 / COPYRIGHT 1974

Editor: Don Won Ton
Design: Rik Kemo Sabi
Features: Jo Nat Hon
Photo Credits: Check

KUNG-FU MONTHLY NO.6 / COPYRIGHT 1974

Editor: Don Won Ton
Editor-in-Chief: Felix Yen
Design: Rik Kemo Sabi
Features: Jo Nat Hon, Tong Inch-iek
Administration: Bruce Sawford, Judy Love, Shirley Divers
Photo Credits: Warner Bros., Concord, Golden Harvest Films, Cathay Films, Paul Chang

KUNG-FU MONTHLY NO.7 / COPYRIGHT 1974

Editor: Don Won Ton
Editor-in-Chief: Felix Yen
Design: Rik Kemo Sabi
Features: Jo Nat Hon, Tong Inch-iek
Administration: Bruce Sawford
Photo Credits: Warner Bros., Concord, Golden Harvest Films, Cathay Films, Paul Chang, Paul Simmons

KUNG-FU MONTHLY NO.8 / COPYRIGHT 1974

Editor: Don Won Ton
Editor-in-Chief: Felix Yen
Design: Rik Kemo Sabi
Features: Jo Nat Hon, Tong Inch-iek
Administration: Bruce Sawford
Photo Credits: Warner Bros., Concord, Golden Harvest Films, Cathay Films, Paul Simmons

KUNG-FU MONTHLY NO.9 / COPYRIGHT 1975

Editor: Don Won Ton
Editor-in-Chief: Felix Yen
Design: Rik Kemo Sabi
Features: Jo Nat Hon, Tong Inch-iek
Administration: Bruce Sawford, Judy Garnham
Photo Credits: Warner Bros., Golden Harvest Films, Paul Chang, Jeff Cummins, Richard Adams, Shaw Bros.

KUNG-FU MONTHLY NO.10 / COPYRIGHT 1975

Editor: Don Won Ton
Editor-in-Chief: Felix Yen
Design: Rik Kemo Sabi
Features: Jo Nat Hon, Tong Inch-iek
Administration: Bruce Sawford, Judy Garnham
Photo Credits: Warner Bros., Golden Harvest Films, Paul Simmons, Paul Chiang, Chang Vung Dijh, Concord

KUNG-FU MONTHLY NO.11 / COPYRIGHT 1975

Editor: Don Won Ton
Editor-in-Chief: Felix Yen
Design: Rik Kemo Sabi
Features: Jo Nat Hon, Tong Inch-iek
Administration: Bruce Sawford, Judy Garnham
Photo Credits: Warner Bros., Cathay Films, Paul Chang, Shaw Bros.

KUNG-FU MONTHLY NO.12 / COPYRIGHT 1975

Editor: Don Won Ton
Editor-in-Chief: Felix Yen
Design: Rik Kemo Sabi
Features: Jo Nat Hon, Tong Inch-iek
Administration: Bruce Sawford, Judy Garnham
Photo Credits: Golden Harvest Films, Cathay Films, Chang Vung Dijh

THE KUNG-FU MONTHLY ARCHIVE SERIES

KUNG-FU MONTHLY NO.13 / COPYRIGHT 1975

Photo Credits: Cathay Films Ltd

KUNG-FU MONTHLY NO.14 / COPYRIGHT 1975

Photo Credits: Chang Vung Dijh, Warner Bros., Shaw Bros., Variety Films

KUNG-FU MONTHLY NO.15 / COPYRIGHT 1975

Photo Credits: Golden Harvest Films, Cathay Films

KUNG-FU MONTHLY NO.16 / COPYRIGHT 1975

Photo Credits: Golden Harvest Films, Cathay Films

KUNG-FU MONTHLY NO.17 / COPYRIGHT 1975

Photo Credits: Golden Harvest Films, Cathay Films
Special Thanks: Wu Ngan, Rhona McVay and the Bruce Lee Fan Club

KUNG-FU MONTHLY NO.18 / COPYRIGHT 1975

Photo Credits: Golden Harvest Films, Peter Bennett, Dijk, Peter Li, Peter Jones

KUNG-FU MONTHLY NO.19 / COPYRIGHT 1975

Photo Credits: Golden Harvest Films, Cathay Films

THE POSTER MAGAZINES - VOLUME ONE

KUNG-FU MONTHLY NO.20 / COPYRIGHT 1975

Photo Credits: Golden Harvest Films, Cathay Films, Warner Bros., Peter Bennett

KUNG-FU MONTHLY NO.21 / COPYRIGHT 1975

No Credits Given

KUNG-FU MONTHLY NO.22 / COPYRIGHT 1975

Photo Credits: Golden Harvest Films, Cathay Films, Warner Bros., Peter Bennett, Rex Features, Fred Cook of Keystone

KUNG-FU MONTHLY NO.23 / COPYRIGHT 1975

Photo Credits: Golden Harvest Films, Cathay Films, Warner Bros., Peter Bennett, Rex Features, Fred Cook of Keystone

KUNG-FU MONTHLY NO.24 / COPYRIGHT 1975

No Credits Given

KUNG-FU MONTHLY NO.25 / COPYRIGHT 1975

Photo Credits: Golden Harvest Films, Cathay Films, Warner Bros., Peter Bennett, Rex Features

KUNG-FU MONTHLY NO.26 / COPYRIGHT 1975

Photo Credits: Golden Harvest Films, Cathay Films, Warner Bros., Peter Bennett, Rex Features, Chester Maydole

**ALL ISSUES PUBLISHED BY
H. BUNCH ASSOCIATES LTD**

THE KUNG-FU MONTHLY ARCHIVE SERIES

A HISTORY OF KUNG-FU MONTHLY

Writer & Primary Researcher
Carl Fox

BIBLIOGRAPHY

More Lives Than One: The Extraordinary Life of Felix Dennis
by Fergus Byrne (2015)

Felix Dennis Interview for Martial Arts Illustrated
by Peter Jagger (December 2011)

A Short History of Kung-Fu Monthly and The Bruce Lee Society
by Felix Dennis (1979)

The Secret Art of Bruce Lee
by the editors of Kung-Fu Monthly (1978)

The Wisdom of Bruce Lee
by Roger Hutchinson & Felix Dennis (2021)

The KFM Bruce Lee Society: A Retrospective Look at Bruce Lee Mania & The Kung Fu Craze of the 1970s
by Carl Fox (2021)

The Kung Fu Years
by BBC TV (1997)

Conversation with Dick Pountain
Conversation with Jeff Cummins
Conversation with Jonathon Green
Conversation with David Jenkins
Conversation with Bey Logan
Conversation with Colin James
Conversation with Don Atyeo
Conversation with Richards Adams
all by Carl Fox (2021/22)

SPECIAL THANKS

Richard Adams, Don Atyeo, Fergus Byrne, Jeff Cummins, Jonathon Green,
Peter Jagger, Colin James, David Jenkins, Bey Logan, Tony Lundberg,
Michael Nesbitt, John Overall, Dick Pountain, Matthew Robins,
Bruce Sawford and Andrew Staton.

THE K.F.M. BRUCE LEE SOCIETY

"BEAUTIFULLY CAPTURES THE HEART, SOUL, AND SPIRIT OF THE UNITED KINGDOM'S FLEDGLING BRUCE LEE FANBASE. UNDENIABLY COLLECTIBLE."

— BRUCE LEE REVIEW

"NOT JUST A COMPILATION OF NOSTALGIC NEWSLETTERS, BUT A BRITISH HISTORY GUIDE TO A PERIOD TIME WHEN WESTERN PEOPLE DISCOVERED THE UNIQUE TALENTS OF THE UNDISPUTED KING OF KUNG FU - BRUCE LEE."

— ANDREW J. STATON, BRITISH JUN FAN JOURNAL

"THANK YOU VERY MUCH FOR YOUR TIME AND EFFORT TO HONOUR PAM FOR HER GREAT WORK AND DEDICATION. I, TOGETHER WITH THE BRUCE LEE FANS WHO KNEW PAM SALUTE YOU!"

— ROBERT LEE

THE **KUNG-FU MONTHLY** BRUCE LEE SECRET SOCIETY BEGAN IN SEPTEMBER 1976, RUNNING FOR 30 ISSUES BEFORE IT'S FINAL ISSUE IN SEPTEMBER 1983. RUN BY THE FORMIDABLE PAM HADDEN, THE BRUCE LEE SECRET SOCIETY FUNCTIONED AS THE SOURCE OF INFORMATION FOR BRUCE LEE FANS IN THE UK AND LATER, THE REST OF THE WORLD. FOR THE FIRST TIME EVER, ALL 30 ISSUES HAVE BEEN PAINSTAKINGLY RE-EDITED AND RE-PRINTED IN THIS BOOK, ALONG WITH UPDATED NOTES AND RETROSPECTIVE STORIES BY THE PEOPLE MOST RESPONSIBLE FOR KEEPING BRUCE LEE'S MEMORY ALIVE - THE FANS.

AVAILABLE FROM **WWW.KUNGFUMONTHLY.UK & AMAZON**

THE WORLD FAMOUS
MARKETPLACE

DON'T FORGET TO VISIT OUR WEBSITE FOR OTHER FANTASTIC ITEMS INCLUDING CLOTHING AND LIMITED EDITION SETS!

◄ BRUCE LEE
KING OF KUNG FU

Written by Felix Dennis & Don Atyeo, Bruce Lee King of Kung Fu is the original and still one of the greatest books on Bruce Lee ever written. Packed with photos and essential information from the immediate year after Lee's tragic death, Bruce Lee King of Kung Fu provides the best of rock-solid backgrounds to the story of the man we all know and love.
170 PAGES

BUY ONLINE NOW!

amazon
WHSmith
Waterstones

OR VISIT OUR WEBSITE AT
WWW.KUNGFUMONTHLY.UK

KUNG-FU MONTHLY ►
THE POSTER MAGAZINES

Volume One - No. 1 to 25, trade dummy plus an in-depth article on The History of Kung-Fu Monthly 1973 to 1979.
Volume Two - No. 26 to 55 plus interviews with former KFM staff.
Volume Three - No. 56 to 79, double-poster special edition issue plus an in-depth article on The History of Kung-Fu Monthly 1980 to 1984.
540-670 PAGES

THE BOOK OF ►
KUNG FU

The Book of Kung Fu was to be Kung-Fu Monthly's special annual issue, but was only published in 1974. Over one-hundred pages, many of them in colour, with a durable soft cover and scores of photographs, illustrations and articles. Don't miss this book! Bruce Lee, Angela Mao, David Carradine, Kung Fu Quiz, Comic Book and more - an incredible publication!
144 PAGES

THE SECRET ART OF ►
BRUCE LEE

In 1976, the world took its first look at the now legendary Chester Maydole photographs. Arranged where possible, in 'fast-frame' action sequences, The Secret Art of Bruce Lee shows the founder of Jeet Kune Do, assisted by his friend and student Dan Inosanto, demonstrating the early development state of his art Jeet Kune Do during early days in Los Angeles.
110 PAGES

THE LOST KFM BOOK
FIRST TIME EVER IN THE UK!

◀ THE WISDOM OF BRUCE LEE

The Wisdom of Bruce Lee was to be one of the first books in the world to look at Bruce Lee's philosophy on life and martial arts. Mysteriously never released in the UK, The Wisdom of Bruce Lee is finally available to UK Bruce Lee fans after a wait of over forty years.
The full-length version includes a new introduction and interview with author Roger Hutchinson by Jun Fan Journal writer Andrew Staton, while the shorter abridged version is formatted in the style of the original Kung-Fu Monthly books.
70 PAGES / 170 PAGES

◀ THE UNBEATABLE BRUCE LEE

The Unbeatable Bruce Lee presents readers with a fighter's view of Bruce Lee the man and Bruce Lee the martial arts master. Beneath the sheer weight of known facts and figures that surround the tragically short life of Hong Kong's number one son, lies a strata of truth that only now is beginning to be picked.
112 PAGES

◀ BRUCE LEE IN ACTION

With Bruce Lee in Action, the Editors of Kung-Fu Monthly had compiled another fine addition to their library of Bruce Lee publications. Lavishly illustrated throughout with many previously unseen photographs at the time, this informative book investigates clearly and concisely, the birth and subsequent development of Lee's fighting style Jeet Kune Do, both on and off the screen.
106 PAGES

THE POWER OF ▶ BRUCE LEE

Bruce Lee was possibly the greatest exponent of the martial arts ever produced. The fact that he was a movie star often clouds his enormous contribution to the field. The Power of Bruce Lee explores many of his revolutionary methods of attack and defence, especially those relating to Jeet Kune Do, Lee's name for his own fighting system
110 PAGES

WHO KILLED ▶ BRUCE LEE?

Who Killed Bruce Lee? is a study of the pressures and the forces that, on the one hand were to elevate him to the highest plains of stardom and on the other, were to so tragically strike him down before his final fulfilment.
Who Killed Bruce Lee? was one of the first books to delve deep into the newspaper stories of Lee's early death.
108 PAGES

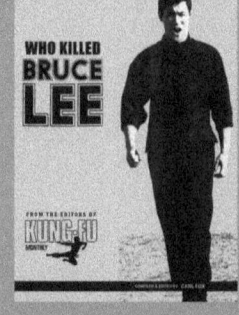

THE GAME OF DEATH

This book combines two Kung-Fu Monthly special edition magazines released prior to Golden Harvest's 1978 film. Researched exclusively in Hong Kong, Kung-Fu Monthly reports on Lee's plot for Game of Death, the cast he intended to appear in the film, the scenes already filmed and Lee's hopes and expectations for the success of the project. Incredibly accurate for the time, this publication represents an important part of Bruce Lee fandom in the UK.
XXX PAGES

THE BEGINNER'S GUIDE TO KUNG FU

Originally released in 1974, The Beginner's Guide to Kung Fu was the first martial arts book aimed primarily at the Kung Fu Craze generation. The graphic, easy to understand illustrations by Paul Simmons and the carefully conceived step by step instructions made this the perfect book for beginners who wished to take up Kung Fu.
XXX PAGES

THE BRUCE LEE SCRAPBOOK

In 1974, Kung-Fu Monthly issued a Bruce Lee scrapbook in the form of a large A3 magazine, followed by a smaller A4 sized book in 1979. As part of the KFM Archive Series, both scrapbooks have been combined in a new chronological layout with brand new captions, location information and dates by Carl Fox and Jun Fan Journal writer Andrew Staton.
150 PAGES

THE KFM BRUCE LEE SOCIETY

Long before the internet communities we know today, The Bruce Lee Society was the source of information in the United Kingdom for all things Bruce Lee. Now the history of the Bruce Lee Society is finally told in The Bruce Lee Society: A Retrospective Look at Bruce Lee Mania and the Kung Fu Craze of the 1970s. For the first time ever, all thirty issues of The Bruce Lee Society newsletters have been painstakingly re-edited and re-printed in this book, along with updated notes and retrospective stories by the people most responsible for keeping Bruce Lee's memory alive - the fans.
544 PAGES

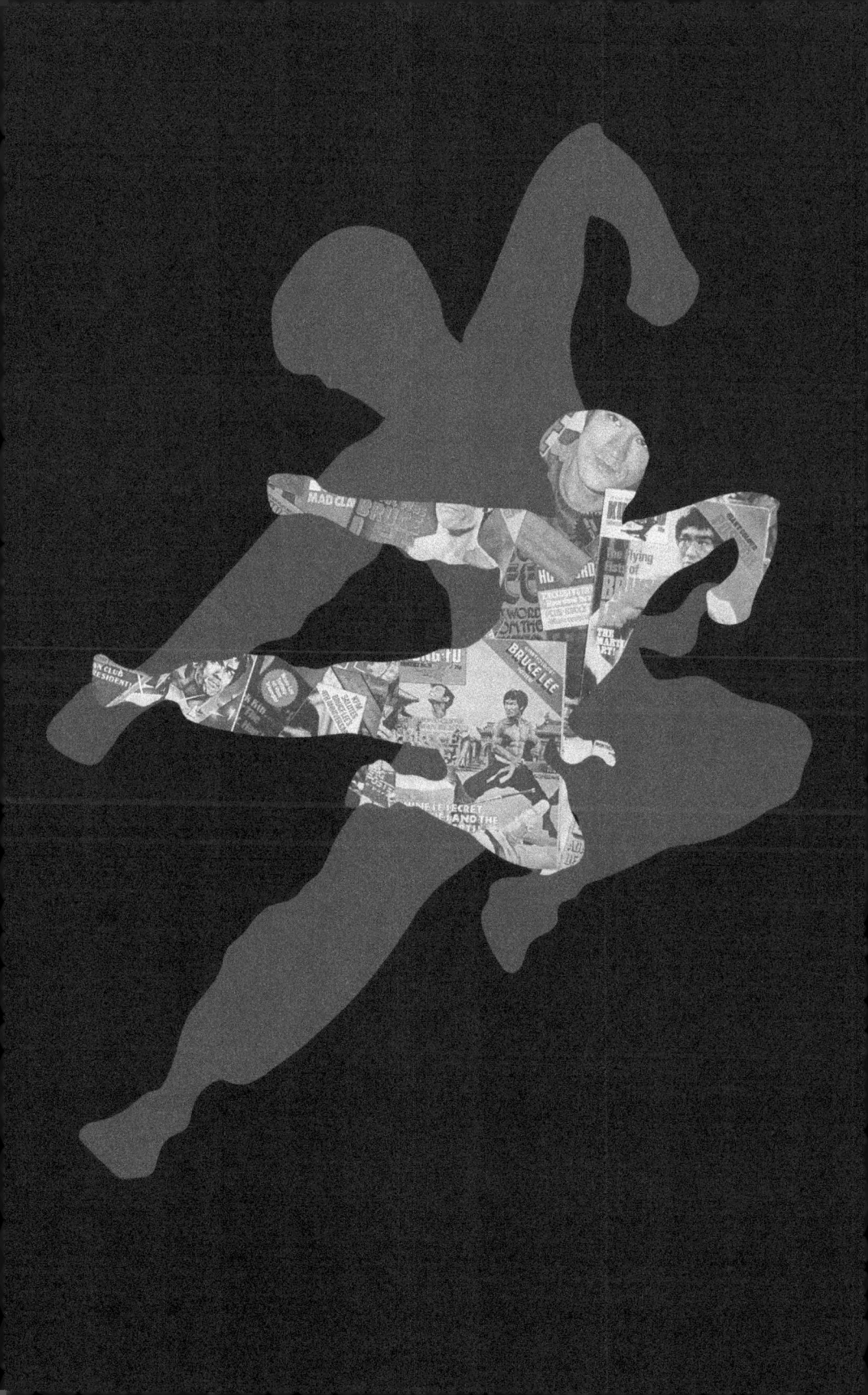

www.ingramcontent.com/pod-product-compliance
Lightning Source LLC
Chambersburg PA
CBHW042000080526
44588CB00021B/2825